DICKENS STUDIES ANNUAL

DICKENS STUDIES ANNUAL
Essays on Victorian Fiction

EDITORS

Stanley Friedman
Edward Guiliano
Anne Humpherys
Michael Timko

DICKENS
STUDIES
ANNUAL

Essays on Victorian Fiction

VOLUME
32

Edited by
Stanley Friedman, Edward Guiliano,
Anne Humpherys, and Michael Timko

AMS PRESS
NEW YORK

DICKENS STUDIES ANNUAL
ISSN 0084-9812

COPYRIGHT © 2002 by AMS Press, Inc.
Dickens Studies Annual: Essays on Victorian Fiction is published in cooperation with Queens College and the Graduate Center, CUNY.

International Standard Book Number
Series: 0-404-18520-7
Vol. 32: 0-404-18932-6

Dickens Studies Annual: Essays on Victorian Fiction welcomes essay- and monograph-length contributions on Dickens and other Victorian novelists and on the history of aesthetics of Victorian fiction. All manuscripts should be double-spaced and should follow the documentation format described in the most recent *MLA Style Manual*. The author's name should appear only on a cover-page, not elsewhere in the essay. An editorial decision can usually be reached more quickly if two copies of the article are submitted, since outside readers are asked to evaluate each submission. If a manuscript is accepted for publication, the author will be asked to provide a 100- to 200-word abstract and also a disk containing the final version of the essay. The preferred editions for citations from Dickens's works are the Clarendon and the Norton Critical when available, otherwise the Oxford Illustrated or the Penguin.

Please send submissions to The Editors, *Dickens Studies Annual*, Ph.D. Program in English. The Graduate Center, CUNY, 365 Fifth Avenue, New York, NY 10016-4309. Please send inquiries concerning subscriptions and/or the availability of earlier volumes to AMS Press, Inc., Brooklyn Navy Yard, Bldg. 292, Suite 417, 63 Flushing Ave., Brooklyn, NY 11205.

Manufactured in the United States of America

All AMS books are printed on acid-free paper that meets the guidelines for performance and durability of the Committee on Production Guidelines for Book Longevity of the Council on Library Resources.

Contents

Illustrations

Preface

Because this is an additional issue of *Dickens Studies Annual,* it includes no survey articles reviewing recent studies of Dickens and his contemporaries. This volume permits us to avoid accumulating a large backlog of accepted submissions and also enables us to reduce by one-half the periodicity lag that arose in *DSA*'s early years.

The range of essays included confirms our belief that the multiplicity of interests pursued by Dickens and other Victorian novelists attracts scholars and critics of diverse and at times conflicting persuasions.

We thank all those who have submitted manuscripts to us, and we also are grateful to a number of scholars who have generously served as outside readers. Besides helping *DSA* remain receptive to different types of scholarly approaches, the evaluations prepared by these reviewers often include detailed recommendations that enable contributors to strengthen their work.

For continued practical assistance, we thank the following administrators: President Frances Degen Horowitz, Provost William P. Kelly, Ph.D. Program in English Executive Officer Joan Richardson, and Linda Sherwin, Assistant Program Officer, Ph.D. Program in English, all of The Graduate Center, CUNY; and Interim President Russell Hotzler, Dean Tamara S. Evans, and Department of English Chair Nancy R. Comley, all of Queens College, CUNY.

We thank, too, Professor John O. Jordan, Director of The Dickens Project at the University of California, Santa Cruz, and JoAnna Rottke, Project Coordinator for The Dickens Project, for placing on the Project's website the tables of contents for volumes 1-27 of *DSA,* as well as abstracts for subsequent volumes. (These materials are included in the Project's Dickens Electronic Archive.) The Dickens Project can be reached at http: //humwww.ucsc.edu/ dickens/index.html

We greatly appreciate the encouragement and steadfast support given by Gabriel Hornstein, President of AMS Press, and we are again happy to acknowledge the cooperation and valuable assistance given by Jack Hopper, our editor at AMS Press. Finally, we thank our editorial assistant for this volume, Janine Utell, for her diligent, exemplary help with many different tasks.

—The Editors

Notes on Contributors

MARIA K. BACHMAN is Assistant Professor of English at Coastal Carolina University. She has published articles on Richardson, Disraeli, and Dickens. She is coeditor of two forthcoming volumes: *Reality's Dark Light: The Sensational Wilkie Collins* and an edition of Collins's final novel, *Blind Love*.

SUSAN LYNNE BECKWITH, a doctoral candidate at Wayne State University, is currently writing her dissertation on illness and narrative in primarily Victorian and Gothic literature, as well as completing a lengthy work of fiction.

GEORGE SCOTT CHRISTIAN received his doctoral and law degrees from the University of Texas at Austin. He is currently practicing law and pursuing his research interest in comic theory and the Victorian novel.

DON RICHARD COX is Professor of English and Associate Dean at the University of Tennessee. His books include *Arthur Conan Doyle* (1985), *Sexuality and Victorian Literature* (1984), and *Charles Dickens's* The Mystery of Edwin Drood: *An Annotated Bibliography* (1998). He is coeditor of two forthcoming volumes: *Reality's Dark Light: The Sensational Wilkie Collins* and an edition of Collins's final novel, *Blind Love*.

H. M. DALESKI is Professor Emeritus of English at the Hebrew University of Jerusalem. He has published books on D. H. Lawrence, Charles Dickens, Joseph Conrad, and Thomas Hardy, as well as two volumes of critical essays.

JULIE M. DUGGER is Associate Professor of Literature and Languages at Benedictine University. Her previous work includes an essay on Percy Shelley's political radicalism in *Better Living Through Poetry: The Shelley Circle's Utopia Project*. She is researching the relationship between Carlyle and the writers of the Young Ireland movement.

SIMON JOYCE is Associate Professor of English and Director of Literary and Cultural Studies at the College of William and Mary. His book, *Capital*

Offenses: Geographies of Class and Crime in Victorian London (which includes the essay on *Bleak House* in this volume) is forthcoming. He is currently at work on *The Victorians in the Rear View Mirror*, a booklength study of the Victorian self-image and current cultural (mis-)conceptions.

MARK KNIGHT is a lecturer in English Literature at Roehampton University at Surrey. He has published articles in *English Literature in Transition, Literature & Theology, Christianity & Literature*, and *Wilkie Collins Society Journal*. At present he is editing an edition of Mary Cecil Hay's *Old Myddleton's Money* and completing a book on "Chesterton and Evil."

HUGUES LEBAILLY is Senior Lecturer at Paris-1 Panthéon-Sorbonne University. He has published several papers in the journal of the French Society for Victorian and Edwardian studies, *Les Cahiers Victoriens et Edouardiens*, as well as in various collections of essays published by French university presses. He has read papers at international conferences suggesting a new approach to Lewis Carroll's artistic and cultural interests. Some of these papers have been printed in *The Carrollian*, the Lewis Carroll journal edited by the Lewis Carroll Society of Great Britain.

MIRIAM O'KANE MARA teaches at The University of New Mexico, where she is earning her Ph.D. In addition to Dickens, her fields of interest include colonial/post-colonial studies, modern British, and postmodern Irish literature.

LILLIAN NAYDER is Associate Professor of English at Bates College, where she teaches nineteenth-century British fiction. Her books include *Wilkie Collins* (1997) and *Unequal Partners: Charles Dickens, Wilkie Collins, and Victorian Authorship* (2002). She is writing a biography of Catherine Dickens.

JUDE V. NIXON is Associate Professor of English at Oakland University and Director of the Honors College. He is the author of *Gerard Manley Hopkins and His Contemporaries: Liddon, Newman, Darwin, and Pater*, and his work has appeared in *Renascence, The Hopkins Journal, The Carlyle Studies Annual, Modern Philology, Victorian Poetry*, and *Texas Studies in Literature and Language*. He is also guest editor of a recent special issue of *Religion and the Arts*. He is at work on a book tentatively called "Race and The Victorians: Representing Blackness."

JOHN R. REED is Distinguished Professor of English at Wayne State University. His most recent book was *Dickens and Thackeray: Punishment and Forgiveness* (1995). He is currently at work on a booklength study of the armed forces in nineteenth-century British literature and culture.

PAUL SCHLICKE is Senior Lecturer in English at the University of Aberdeen, Scotland. Past President of the Dickens Society, he is the author of *Dickens and Popular Entertainment* (1985) and compiler of the Dickens entry in *The Cambridge Bibliography of English Literature,* 3ʳᵈ edn. (1999). He is preparing the Clarendon edition of *Sketches by Boz.*

CLAIRE SENIOR is a doctoral candidate in the Department of English at the University of Western Ontario, Canada. She is working on her dissertation, which focuses on the construction and presentation of gender in Dickens's novels.

JEANETTE ROBERTS SHUMAKER is Professor of English at San Diego State University, Imperial Valley Campus, six blocks from Mexico's border. She publishes articles on Victorian fiction and on modern Irish women writers.

DANIEL SIEGEL is Assistant Professor of English at the University of Alabama at Birmingham. He is author of an essay on the failure of Victorian condescension forthcoming in *Victorian Literature and Culture.*

JEFFREY L. SPEAR is Associate Professor of English at New York University. He is the author of *Dreams of an English Eden: Ruskin and His Tradition in Social Criticism* (1984) and essays on Victorian literature and culture.

Embracing the New Spirit of the Age: Dickens and the Evolution of *The Old Curiosity Shop*

Paul Schlicke

As The Old Curiosity Shop *evolved out of* Master Humphrey's Clock, *Dickens engaged with a number of concerns in his life, his art, and his times. The image of an innocent child in threatening circumstances took powerful hold of his imagination. Quilp personifies that threat, but it is the pathological addiction of Nell's grandfather to gambling which undoes her, and the countryside to which they flee offers no escape. In his development of Swiveller from a Regency gent into a responsible Victorian hero Dickens found a positive way to link the imaginative responsiveness of a city-dweller with moral responsibility.*

1

On 14 July 1839 Dickens wrote to Forster outlining plans for a new work. It was an exhilarating prospect: young, energetic, and ambitious, in less than three years he had progressed from parliamentary reporting and the writing of newspaper sketches to a position in the foremost ranks of English authors. After the modest success of *Sketches by Boz*, *The Pickwick Papers* had been a publishing sensation; *Oliver Twist* displayed his talent in a different key; *Nicholas Nickleby*, now halfway through its serial run, was outselling the combined might of the previous two novels put together (Forster 109; 2: ch.

2). Although the example of Pierce Egan's faded celebrity was held up as a warning to Dickens "to make his hay while the sunshine lasts" (Collins 1971: 68–69), reviewers were already comparing him to Scott, Fielding, Hogarth, and Shakespeare. Meanwhile, he was busy wresting disadvantageous contracts from his publishers and securing more remuneration for his writing. His literary reputation and financial prospects seemed assured, and he stood ready to consolidate his fame and fortune.

Dickens's letter to Forster exudes confidence. Noting that he has been wooed by other publishers to write for a percentage of profits ("straightforward offers from responsible men"), he instructs Forster, in acting as his agent, to urge Chapman and Hall (his publishers for *Pickwick* and *Nickleby*) "to step gallantly forward" and "do something handsome" if they hope to secure his services for the new work he has in mind. The prospects of success for that work, he triumphantly proclaims, are "great, very great; indeed, almost beyond calculation" (*Letters*, 1: 562–65).

But Dickens was also circumspect. He confided to Forster a twofold concern: lest the public tire of his long serially published stories (he had been producing two serial novels simultaneously for most of the previous two and a half years), and (with the example of Scott's final years fresh in his mind—Lockhart's *Life of Scott* had been published the previous year) lest he burn himself out by overtaxing his imagination (Forster 139; 2: ch. 6). Instead of writing a new novel, Dickens proposed, he would undertake to edit a miscellany. He planned

> to introduce a little club or knot of characters and to carry their personal histories and proceedings through the work; to reintroduce Mr Pickwick and Sam Weller, the latter of whom might furnish an occasional communication with great effect; to write amusing essays on the various foibles of the day as they arise; to take advantage of all passing events; and to vary the form of the papers by throwing them into sketches, essays, tales, adventures, letters from imaginary correspondents and so forth, so as to diversify the contents as much as possible.

He proposed in addition to write a series of stories about London long ago, to contribute satirical papers ("something between *Gulliver's Travels* and *The Citizen of the World*") and, "in order to give fresh novelty," to send in correspondence from Ireland or America, where he would travel specially for the purpose (1:562–65).

The proposal had obvious attractions. Dickens's training had been that of a journalist; his first published imaginative work had taken the form of sketches; he had already acted in the capacity of editor for *Bentley's Miscellany* and was later to conduct the hugely successful miscellany *Household Words* and its successor, *All the Year Round*. Moreover, the plan followed a tested formula of other authors much admired by Dickens: in the letter to

Forster he cited *The Tatler, The Spectator,* and Goldsmith's *Bee.* These classic works offered proven evidence a periodical miscellany could prosper with the public.

They offered precedent not only for a successful serial miscellany, but also for an attractive authorial relationship with the public. Dickens's early reviewers noted with approval the establishment of the figure of "Boz," the genial and informed spokesman for the moral worth of the everyday activities of ordinary men and women. In the words of his soon-to-be father-in-law George Hogarth, Boz was "a close and acute observer of character and manners, with a strong sense of the ridiculous and a graphic faculty of placing in the most whimsical and amusing lights the follies and absurdities of human nature."[1] A common feature of magazines of the 1830s was the distinctive editorial persona of the author-observer, and in 1828 the influential *Athenaeum* had held up the editorial stance found in *The Tatler* and *The Spectator* as models worthy of emulation.[2] No wonder Dickens was sanguine over the prospects of his new work.

But for all his hopes, the plan had serious flaws. The editorial strategy, as developed in another letter to Forster a few months later (*Letters* 2: 4), depended on Master Humphrey, a lugubrious old cripple, boring in his own person and as narrator lacking the flexibility of "Boz."[3] The reintroduction of Mr. Pickwick and the Wellers undercut their novelistic identities, implying that they had lives of their own independent of *The Pickwick Papers* while denying them the context which had brought them to life in the first place. The miscellaneous format of the work eliminated the interest of a coherently developing narrative, and in the event, the opening numbers of *Master Humphrey's Clock* lacked even the variety which Dickens had promised.[4]

Above all, the plan represented a radical redirection of the perspective which had been instrumental to his success. Whereas Dickens's early reputation was based on the freshness of his humor and the excellence of his depictions of contemporary life, his new proposal was decidedly old-fashioned.[5] Although he spoke of the "novelty" of his proposal for *Master Humphrey's Clock,* in fact his explicit models had flourished in a previous century. *The Tatler* and *The Spectator* dated from the very beginning of the eighteenth century, between 1709 and 1712; *The Bee* was published in 1759, and *The Lounger,* Henry Mackenzie's journal (invoked by Dickens in the preface to *Nickleby,* written two months later, as an example of successful serial publication), dated from 1785. Sentimental writing of this sort was far from fashionable by Dickens's day: always controversial, it had been subjected to savage attack in the later years of the eighteenth century (Todd, 129–46), and the distrust of emotion found in Jane Austen's *Sense and Sensibility* (1811) epitomized longstanding conservative tradition (Butler, 182–96). Furthermore, the energies of sentimentalism had been substantially redirected by generations of writers who predated Dickens. Cultivation of sensibility as an end in itself became for Wordsworth and Coleridge a mode of introspection which made possible their revaluation of the powers of imagination. Delicacy of feeling, the preoccupation of Sterne and Mackenzie, was distilled into the sheer intensity of Gothic sensationalism in the hands of Walpole, Mrs. Radcliffe, and Monk Lewis. And in Dickens's own lifetime concern with fellow-feeling was being vigorously rechannelled into a celebration of domesticity as a locus for essential human values. Thus redirected, sensibility was alive and well in 1839, but as mere nostalgia Dickens's plan scarcely engaged with the swelling currents of the day. It lacked that openness to experience and eye for the particular and original which, for R. H. Horne, was to make Dickens the foremost representative of the new spirit of the age (Horne 1:1–6).

I have focussed on Dickens's plans for this project because they introduce what seems to me a watershed in his career. Success had come quickly to him: he wrote easily, and he had casually taken on a welter of commitments. The idea which was to become *Master Humphrey's Clock* was an attempt to consolidate his position in three principal ways: it would provide him with a new vehicle to keep his name before the public once *Nickleby* had run its course; it would give him more explicit editorial control over his work; and it would offer him the most advantageous financial terms he had secured to date. There were further considerations as well, both public and private, which made the enterprise look attractive. That it did not work out as planned was to have momentous consequences. The redirection of energies which led to *The Old Curiosity Shop* marked the end of his literary apprenticeship. For all its distinctiveness, Dickens's fiction up to 1840 clearly followed in the established traditions of English literature. With *Barnaby Rudge*, *Martin Chuzzlewit*, and the novels which followed, however, he stepped boldly forward as the great Victorian novelist, whose work owed less to the past than to his own artistic genius, in deep affinity with his age. That achievement was to emerge, in part, from the failure of *Master Humphrey's Clock*.

Dickens sought to initiate a new kind of work with Chapman and Hall to follow *Nicholas Nickleby* because he was exasperated over his long-standing obligation to write a conventional three-volume novel for Richard Bentley. Despite having resigned in January 1839 as editor of *Bentley's Miscellany*, he was still legally bound to deliver to Bentley the completed manuscript of *Barnaby Rudge* on the first day of January 1840, and the contract expressly forbade Dickens from writing anything else until it was completed (*Letters* 1: 674). Previous arrangements with regard to *Barnaby Rudge* had been several times postponed at Dickens's insistence, and his acrimonious relationship with Bentley left him with little enthusiasm for the novel. He wrote bitterly to Forster in January 1839 that "This net that has been wound about me so chafes me, so exasperates and irritates my mind, that to break it at whatever cost—*that* I should care nothing for—is my constant impulse" (*Letters* 1: 494). And when Bentley advertised in December of the same year that *Barnaby Rudge* was "preparing for publication," Dickens wrote in fury to his solicitors instructing them to inform the publisher that he would not have the manuscript ready at the contracted time (*Letters* 1: 616–18). In contrast, Dickens was eager to enter into a new commitment with Chapman and Hall, who had been generous in previous dealings with him and were accommodating to the terms of his new project. In defiance of his legal obligation to Bentley, proposals for *Master Humphrey's Clock* were agreed formally on 15th October, and the contract signed on 31 March 1840 (*Letters* 1: 681; 2: 464–71). In the end Dickens never did write the three-volume novel for Bentley: on 2 July Chapman and Hall acquired the contract for the title (*Letters* 2. 471–77),[6] and *Barnaby Rudge* was written the following year for publication within the weekly format of *Master Humphrey's Clock*.

Second, Dickens was determined to exercise independent control over any future work he edited. In November 1836 he had eagerly agreed to undertake the editorship of *Bentley's Miscellany*, but there were disputes from the outset over what he saw as Bentley's interference with his own editorial prerogatives. Bentley altered copy which Dickens had approved, added and deleted contributions, and generally made it clear that, for all that Dickens was nominally the editor, the *Miscellany* was indeed Bentley's. In his letter setting forth the plans for *Master Humphrey's Clock*, Dickens allowed that he might require assistants, but he stipulated that "this assistance is chosen solely by me, and that the contents of every number are as much under my own control, and subject to as little interference, as those of a number of *Pickwick* or *Nickleby*" (*Letters* 1: 564). He had no intention of entering into a situation of divided editorial responsibility again.

Third, it rankled with Dickens that the financial rewards from his works had not kept pace with his rising expectations as his popularity burgeoned. Contracts he had freely entered into when his marketability was unknown and the primary risk was the publisher's, seemed to him mean when additional income accrued primarily to the publisher. In fact, his publishers (including Bentley) did make adjustments in his favor when sales rose, but he fulminated to Forster about the "immense profits" which *Oliver Twist* was realizing for Bentley, in comparison to the "paltry, wretched, miserable sum it brought to me," performing "slavery and drudgery" on "journeyman-terms" (*Letters* 1: 493). With his next contract, he insisted "that I be made a proprietor in the work and a sharer in the profits" (*Letters* 1: 565). In the event, although *Master Humphrey's Clock* achieved greater sales during its serial publication than any other work published throughout his entire career, and Dickens's portion of the proceeds were accordingly higher, for a variety of reasons financial results were, as Robert Patten explains, "disappointing for everyone" (Patten 1978, 112).

Dickens was keen at this time, then, to develop his career in a new direction. In format *Master Humphrey's Clock* was conceived as a work substantially different from anything he had previously attempted, and it was contracted to secure new editorial independence and greater financial reward. Unlike his previous work, it was to appear in weekly instalments, in order, as he told Cattermole, "to baffle the imitators and make it as novel as possible" (*Letters* 2: 7). It was to be illustrated not by full-page plates but by woodcuts integrated into the text.[7] And by a significantly more advantageous agreement than any of his previous contracts, Dickens was to retain half the copyright and receive half the profits, in addition to a weekly salary of £50 (*Letters* 2: 464–71).

In content, too, the new work marked a departure from Dickens's earlier work. Desiring to tap the precedent of a particular kind of admired literary publication from the past, he sought to free himself from the pressures of intense involvement with topical concerns. There were both public and private circumstances which made such a project appealing. If ever there was a period in Dickens's career when the signs of the times were ominous, it was now: Britain was beset by events which were decidedly disturbing to contemplate. The country was at war abroad, both in Afghanistan and China, and seemed on the brink of civil war at home, as Chartist riots and Corn Law agitation rocked the country. Disillusion over Reform and suffering caused by trade depression and poor harvests were intensified by lack of confidence in the government. The Whigs had been unable to consolidate their position after the Reform Act, and in May 1839 Melbourne's ministry resigned, only to resume office three days later and limp feebly on until the end of August 1841. On the throne sat the still inexperienced young queen, who did not yet command the authority which was to give the age her name. Scandal in spring of 1839 surrounding the death of a lady-in-waiting brought denunciation of Victoria in the press and catcalls and hissing when she rode out. There were three break-ins at royal residences that year, and between 10 June 1840 and 3 July 1842 three assassination attempts.[8] Religious controversy, disquiet over the new geological theories, concern about conditions in factories and mines, and opposition to the New Poor Law were among other factors adding to the general uncertainty. A comfortable periodical, featuring old men telling old tales, must have seemed an attractive alternative to engagement with a fraught present.

In his private life, too, Dickens had ample cause to seek less taxing work than a full-length novel of contemporary life. Although he was never one to shirk hard work, and although he felt able to record in his diary on his birthday on 7 February 1839 that the previous year had been for him "most prosperous and happy" (*Letters* 1: 640), he had a number of personal worries.

He remained deeply afflicted long after the death in May 1837 of his beloved sister-in-law Mary. His wife Catherine was ''alarmingly'' ill and depressed after the birth of each of their children—there were three, and a miscarriage, between January 1837 and November 1839. His parents were a source of worry, due to his father's persistent debts. To get them out of London in March 1839 Dickens went house-hunting and found them a cottage in Alpington, near Exeter, but the move turned out to be no solution at all; John Dickens was soon forging his son's name to bills, and by March 1841 Dickens was exasperated to the extent that he advertised publicly his refusal to honor any such debts (*Letters* 2: 224–6, nn). Meanwhile in late autumn 1839, his own family having outgrown their house in Doughty Street, he went through ''the agonies of house-letting, house-taking, title proving and disproving, premium paying, fixture valuing, and other ills too numerous to mention'' (*Letters* 1: 603), and moved to Devonshire Terrace. In these circumstances his confession that he wished to avoid the strain of writing a long story seems perfectly understandable.

What happened next is well known. After initial high sales, orders for *Master Humphrey's Clock* fell off alarmingly in subsequent weeks. Dickens consulted with his publishers, and the miscellany gave way to the extended story of *The Old Curiosity Shop*. Although the transition was less precipitous than is often alleged (Patten 1970, 44–64), nevertheless Forster's judgment that Dickens wrote the story of Nell ''with less direct consciousness of design on his own part than I can remember in any other instance throughout his career,'' seems indisputable (Forster, 117; 2: ch. 7).[9] But however rapidly the novel was conceived, it rescued *Master Humphrey's Clock*: as the sole remnant of Dickens's original conception, it pushed sales over 100,000 per week. The story of Nell aroused extremes of reaction: Macready and Jeffrey wept; Landor declared that he wished to buy then sacrificially burn to the ground the house where Dickens first thought of his heroine; Poe, more circumspectly, called the work's conception ''simply and severely grand.''[10] The extravagant admiration suggests that—for whatever reasons—*The Old Curiosity Shop* struck a responsive chord with its first readers.

Later readers, notoriously, reacted differently. Henry James, Gerard Manley Hopkins, and Arnold Bennett all declared themselves unmoved by Dickens's sentiment. Swinburne called Nell ''a monster as inhuman as a baby with two heads''; Wilde quipped that one would need a heart of stone to read the death of Nell without laughing; Aldous Huxley singled out the work as a classic instance of ''vulgarity'' in literature.[11] But this distaste is as significant as the early applause, in clearly indicating that factors which moved readers in 1840 had by a later date lost their appeal.

The Old Curiosity Shop was, in short, occasioned by immediate practical concerns: adverse public response to *Master Humphrey's Clock* dictated a change of direction, and the conception of a child surrounded by ancient and grotesque objects aroused Dickens's sudden and deep interest. Enthusiastic public response, followed by adverse reaction, are further signs of the work's topicality. It is an uneven work, and its reputation has never been other than controversial (Schlicke 1988: xi-xx). But as it rapidly evolved, Dickens was once more to engage deeply with a number of pressing concerns in his life, his art and his times. What began as a soft option was to become a giant stride towards the maturity which was to make him the foremost novelist of the age.

2

The vignette called "*The Old Curiosity Shop*," which was to become the opening chapter of the extended story, recounts, through Master Humphrey's narration, the old man's night-time adventure with a little girl lost in London. As Robert Patten has suggested, in its original telling in the fourth number of *Master Humphrey's Clock* the episode is self-contained and structured on a series of contrasts (Patten 1970: 44–64). In narrative method, tone, and formal organization, that is, the story is wholly consonant with Dickens's planned procedures for his miscellany,[12] in which Master Humphrey was to be the device for introducing materials of wide diversity. But already in this chapter a crucial development can be seen. Instead of the mere juxtaposition of opposites—what Dickens had described in *Oliver Twist* as the "streaky bacon" method of organization[13]—here the contrasts are inextricably linked to one another. At the very outset of composition Dickens stressed the importance of the contrasts in his instructions to his illustrators,[14] and later, when he added three paragraphs to the chapter for the novel's first publication independent of the *Clock* framework, he was to spell out explicitly (in his narrator's words) the importance he had by then come consciously to recognize in the interconnections.

> We are so much in the habit of allowing impressions to be made upon us by external objects, which should be produced by reflection alone, but which, without such visible aids, often escape us; that I am not sure I should have been so thoroughly possessed by this one subject, but for the heaps of fantastic things I had seen huddled together in the curiosity-dealer's warehouse. These, crowding upon my mind, in connection with the child, and gathering round her, as it were, brought her condition palpably before me. I had her image, without any effort of imagination, surrounded and beset by everything that was foreign to its nature, and furthest removed from the sympathies of her sex and age. If these helps to my fancy had all been wanting, and I had been forced to imagine her in a common chamber, with nothing unusual or uncouth in its appearance, it is very probable that I should have been less impressed with her

strange and solitary state. As she was, she seemed to exist in a kind of allegory; and, having these shapes about her, claimed my interest so strongly, that (as I have already remarked) I could not dismiss her from my recollection, do what I would.[15]

The significance of the development recorded in this paragraph is considerable. Instead of the merely random diversity which had been the plan for *Master Humphrey's Clock*, Dickens's conception here depends on a Coleridgean fusion of disparate parts. Master Humphrey (and Dickens) would have been "less impressed with her strange and solitary state" but for the context of ancient things. Nell and the grotesque objects are linked, that is, in a single, coherent imaginative vision, in which the differing parts exist in necessary relation to each other. Moreover, that vision is not simply observation of external detail, but a plumbing to the essential meanings of the dynamic interrelation of the whole. As Master Humphrey is made to say, picking up a notion which Thomas Hood was to observe well before the story was complete (Hood 887–88), Nell "seem[s] to exist in a kind of allegory": the personages and settings are conceived not only on the level of story, but as vehicles for imaginative insight into general and abstract truths.

Such organization differs fundamentally from that of a miscellany, and indeed, from the largely episodic organization of Dickens's previous extended narratives. *The Pickwick Papers* and *Nicholas Nickleby* follow the eighteenth-century precedent of Defoe, Fielding, and Smollett, achieving such coherence as they have by leading their heroes through a random series of adventures. *Oliver Twist* is somewhat different, dramatizing spiritual forces of good and evil in a clash which Graham Greene has called "Manichaean" (Greene 79–86), but *The Parish Boy's Progress* (as the novel is subtitled) defuses the polarity by killing off Sikes and Fagin, the primary embodiments of evil, and allowing Oliver, the "principle of good" to triumph unopposed. Nell's "progress," in contrast, dramatizes the opposing forces as irreducible and mutually destructive. As Dickens follows through the logic of his conception, neither Nell, young, beautiful, and good,[16] nor Quilp, the extreme embodiment of all the grotesque things, can compromise with the values of the other, and neither can exist without the other. In the imaginative world of the novel only a different sort of character, independent of the polarities—what Gabriel Pearson has called the "third force" of the novel (Pearson 77–90)—can survive, combining elements of goodness from the one and vitality from the other, in the imaginative synthesis that was to become Dick Swiveller. There are rough edges to *The Old Curiosity Shop*, to be sure, and the moral valences are as extreme as those of *Oliver Twist*; nevertheless, in this novel Dickens achieves artistic coherence far more complex and satisfying than anything in his previous work, and liberating for the novels yet to come.[17]

From the opening pages of *The Old Curiosity Shop* complexities arise not so much out of the mixed nature of individual personages as from the combination of distinct embodiments of abstract qualities, presented in a clash of opposing forces. In his book *The Melodramatic Imagination* Peter Brooks argues that such art is historically and culturally conditioned, coming into being as a mode of clarification in times of confusion and uncertainty, and that it is necessarily metaphoric, extrapolating signs of essential reality from the surface which it documents (Brooks 1–23). These insights seem to me highly illuminating for proper appreciation of *The Old Curiosity Shop*. The very nature of Dickens's idea moves beyond random observation to a search for essential meaning, conceived to reside within the surface reality. Attention to detail is vital, because the observed surface is charged with significance. That meaning is necessarily ethical, because it depends on moral opposition. Once he had thought of "the child in the midst of a crowd of uncongenial and ancient things," in short, there was no possibility of Dickens proceeding with a miscellany; if the idea was to be developed, coherent engagement with the meanings of his materials was an inevitable consequence.

The role of Master Humphrey was an almost immediate casualty of this engagement. Not only did the old man lack the vibrant flexibility of the persona of Boz, but as a character within the story he was poorly placed to deal with its tendency towards abstraction. The narrative of *The Pilgrim's Progress* is effective because it is a dream vision in which all the characters are allegorical figures. Lacking the Puritan vision which views everything in the visible world typologically, Master Humphrey is less capable than Bunyan's narrator of finding significance in the personages he describes—to say nothing of the practical difficulty of fitting the old man into all of the story's action as scenes proliferated. Recognizing the problem, Dickens gave Master Humphrey a discreet exit at the end of chapter 3, replacing him with an omniscient narrator. In the first of his novels to be published under his own name, the authoritative voice of "Charles Dickens" was ideal for presenting the story of Nell, surrounded by grotesque objects.

Why did this image take so strong a hold on Dickens? Three reasons seem to me of particular importance: one a cultural inheritance, another an intimately personal trauma, and the third a recent public development. Each concerns the figure of an individual young person in a disturbing context, and each called forth the bridging power of imagination to make sense of the disjunction.

First, as is well known, Dickens was one of the foremost inheritors of the tradition of celebrating childhood as a special state.[18] This tradition was fed by two main streams, Romanticism and Evangelicalism, further assisted by Dickens's mythologizing of his own childhood. Inheriting from Rousseau, through Wordsworth, the conception of innocence as the natural state of childhood, Dickens thought of the child as a being endowed with special capabilities of sensitivity, wonder, and imagination. In *Oliver Twist* Dickens had written the first major novel to place a child at its center, and the appearance of Tiny Tim, Paul Dombey, Poor Jo, and Johnny Harmon in later works shows the recurring importance of the child-figure for Dickens.

According to Sir David Wilkie, reporting on remarks Dickens made at the dinner party celebrating the completion of *Nickleby* at the Albion Hotel on 5 October 1839, Dickens considered Wordsworth's poem ''We Are Seven'' ''one of the most striking examples'' of the poet's genius (A. S. 197–98). Presumably one aspect of its appeal was the juxtaposition on which the poem is structured. As in another of Wordsworth's poems, ''Anecdote for Fathers,'' the wise insight of a child is highlighted by contrast with the obtuse literal-mindedness of an adult. Although unthreatened, the child must defy a figure of authority in steadfastly upholding its innocent vision in the face of uncomprehending objections. An uncongenial situation is the context which gives value to the child's wisdom.

The Romantic idea of the child as a figure of special powers unrecognized and stultified by adults was one of great resonance for Dickens personally, as is patent in the outburst of bitter self-pity in his autobiographical fragment, where he contemplates his days in the blacking warehouse and shudders at the possibility that he might not have escaped his lot there: ''I never afterwards forgot, I never shall forget, I never can forget, that my mother was warm for my being sent back'' (Forster 35; 1: ch. 2). The intensity of feeling, underlined by the repetition, belies his gloss that ''I do not write resentfully or angrily.'' His sense of his own childhood experience as one of lonely innocence, beset by crushing oppression, fits neatly into the pattern of disjunction between the sensitive child and hostile surroundings.

Disjunction even more radical lay at the heart of Evangelical appropriation of childhood as a vehicle of consolation and elevation in the face of human mortality. Tracts of the time are full of the uplifting moral to be found in the deaths of pious youngsters: *The Young Cottager* (1818); *Pious Harriet* (1819), *A Child's Memorial, or a new token for children, containing an account of the early piety and happy death of Miss Dinah Doudney of Portsea, aged nine years, delivered to a congregation of children in Orange-Street Chapel on New Year's day, 1805* (7th edition), are random examples.[19] In 1840, the year of *The Old Curiosity Shop*, the Evangelical Reverend Baptist Noel published an entire book of lives of children who died young, entitled *Infant Piety: A Book for Little Children*. Among those celebrated are Louisa Mortlock (born 10 July 1810, died 8 May 1820, who fell ill and began to fret, but was sorry to sin so, and by reading the Bible regularly, died happy. Annie T. (born 14 November 1831, died 5 March 1835) loved to have the Bible read to her, pitied the one-eyed boy and died without fretting. Little Nanette, who died in 1819, preferred to pray than to play, and loved God who made trees and flowers. Little Elizabeth (1814–23), grieved to hear of anyone breaking the Sabbath and worried about the Faquirs in India, who (she was sure) wouldn't do their terrible practices if they knew the Gospel. David Brown, who died aged 4 in 1834, was very good and everyone loved him; he often thought of God and was sorry after being naughty. There are many more edifying examples in *Infant Piety*, and a closing moral to children, urging them to love God, trust Jesus, read the Bible daily, learn hymns, ask parents what big words mean, love parents, play nicely, be tidy, read lives of good children, and not to lie. In each case the sentiment depends on the collocation of hopeful infancy with the finality of death.

Dickens was, of course, far from sympathetic to what he considered the excesses of Evangelical religion, as the depiction of Little Bethel in *The Old Curiosity Shop* is alone sufficient to demonstrate. But he was certainly aware of improving literature which depicted child figures in a context of mortality, and he was not uninfluenced by it. One proximate example he is virtually certain to have known, as Robert Patten has demonstrated (Patten 1965: 188ff), is a story called *Morals of the Churchyard* by the Reverend Edward Caswall. Caswall was author of *Sketches of Young Ladies*, to which Dickens's own *Sketches of Young Gentlemen* was advertised as a companion (*Letters* 1: 355n.). Published two years before *The Old Curiosity Shop* by Dickens's publishers Chapman and Hall, and illustrated by Hablot Browne, Dickens's illustrator, *Morals of the Churchyard* is a fable for children which depicts a young girl, invariably referred to as ''the little maid,'' who regularly visits a graveyard with her aged grandfather. *Morals of the Churchyard* has no intrinsic literary merit, but the sweet goodness of the heroine, depicted in association with angels, graveyards, gardens, and sickness, prefigures Dickens's presentation of Nell, and the simplifying, allegorizing nature of Caswall's work illustrates with particular clarity a tradition of religious writing in which Dickens's work participates.

Such sentiment was not confined to tract literature. Tennyson's ''The May Queen'' (1832, 1842), for example, is the monologue of a young girl dying happily. Two relevant verses (ll. 9–12. 17–20) give the flavor:

It seem'd so hard at first, mother, to leave the blessed sun,
And now it seems as hard to stay, and yet His will be done!
But still I think it can't be long before I find release;
And that good man, the clergyman, has told me words of peace . . .

He taught me all the mercy, for he show'd me all the sin,
Now, tho' my lamp was lighted late, there's One will let me in:
Nor would I now be well, mother, again if that could be,
For my desire is but to pass to Him that died for me.

As Philip Collins has observed (Collins 1971: 100–01), a particularly reveal-ing summarizing statement of this attitude to childhood death comes from Ruskin, *Fors Clavigera*, letter 90, May 1883:

> I think the experience of most thoughtful persons will confirm me in saying that extremely good girls (good children, generally, but especially girls), usually die young. The pathos of their deaths is constantly used in poetry and novels; but the power of the fiction rests, I suppose, on the fact that most persons of affectionate temper have lost their own May Queens or little Nells in their time. For my own part of grief, I have known a little Nell die, and a queen of May, and of December, also, die;—all of them, in economists' language, as good as gold, and in Christian language, only a little lower than the angels, and crowned with glory and honour. And I could count the like among my best-loved friends, with a rosary of tears
> (Ruskin 29: 424–25).

The literary tradition had great poignancy because it reflected the stark reality of youthful mortality in the nineteenth century, as Dickens had cause to know. The most frequently offered explanation for Dickens's interest in Nell is that she served as a vehicle by which he could deal with the over-whelming emotions aroused by the sudden death of his beloved sister-in-law, Mary Hogarth. The evidence is clear: we have Dickens's own word, in letters he wrote at the time, that he was thinking of Mary when writing about Nell's death (*Letters* 2: 170–71, 181–82). Most commentators who discuss *The Old Curiosity Shop* in relation to Mary's death do so to Nell's disparagement, and Dickens's, but three factors seem to me essential to any proper valuation of this event on the novel. First, as Kathleen Tillotson and Michael Slater have both demonstrated, Nell's character bears little resemblance to Mary's distinctive personality. What contributes most to the pathos of Nell's adven-tures is not her sex but her lonely, frightened, and prematurely responsible condition, which corresponds to Dickens's private image of his own child-hood.[20] Second, as David Parker has argued, just as Dickens reconstructed his image of his own childhood when he looked back as an adult, so too it was only later, *after* Mary's death, that Dickens's emotions took on special intensity. No surviving evidence suggests adulation or infatuation when she was alive, but her death "released her from context into text": Dickens reconstructed her life and death in order to assimilate her into his art as "the object of every variety of emotion it is possible for a man to feel for a woman" (Parker 67–75). And third, as Dickens's letters from the time prove, he was in ebullient high spirits much of the time he was writing *The Old Curiosity Shop*, going on expeditions with friends to Astley's circus, to the Eel Pie House in Twickenham, by steamer to Gravesend; taking his young family on holiday to Broadstairs; walking, riding, dining, joking, theater-going; in short, expending his prodigious energy in these and countless other ways. As the editors of the Pilgrim edition of Dickens's letters observe, Dickens's remark to Forster that he had been "trying to get into" a "state" over Mary in order to write the book's final chapters provides "evidence against emotional obsession" (*Letters* 2: xii).

The biographical context, in short, will not support a claim of unhealthy erotic passion and uncontrolled wallowing in grief; rather, it contributes to proposition that Dickens was imaginatively gripped by the image of a healthy, happy young person in an antithetical context of death and sorrow, and that *The Old Curiosity Shop* provided an artistic medium in which to explore the significance of the seemingly incompatible opposites. We can not be certain at what stage in the story's composition Dickens determined that Nell should die. Forster claims that Dickens "had not thought of killing her, when, about half-way through, I asked him to consider whether it did not necessarily belong to his own conception" (Forster 151; 2: ch. 7)[21] At whatever point the decision that she should die was actually taken, the evidence we have adduced so far corroborates Forster's view that death is intrinsic to Dickens's conception of Nell. In a story conceived in contrasts, which became increasingly polarized as Dickens wrote on, death was indeed the logical opposition to her innocent youth.

In addition to cultural and biographical influences on Dickens's conception of Nell, there was a third major reason why the idea held such attraction for Dickens and his readers at the time. This was the presence of a petite young woman on the throne of England. The ascension of the Victoria in 1837, less than a month after her eighteenth birthday, came at a time when respect for the monarchy was "at a low ebb," and her youth, her sex, and her strong sense of duty provided a marked contrast with her immediate predecessors, George IV and William IV.[22] But although she was welcomed with hopefulness, a distinct sense of uncertainty colored the response of the newspaper and periodical press. The *Quarterly Review* worried over her youth and inexperience in the face of difficult times (240–73); *Bentley's Miscellany*, then edited by Dickens, printed a poem which wondered "That youth, which has not yet seen womanhood,/Should counsel for the aged and the rude!" (568–89), and *Blackwood's* printed a poem characterized by vague idealization of Victoria's innocence, royalty, virtue, truth, and courage:

> And fair is thy sweet opening youth,
> Signed with the seal of holy Truth:
> Thine is a bosom without guile;
> Faith claims thy unsuspicious smile;
> And Virtue calls that heart her own,
> Which beats beneath thy virgin zone.   (634–35).

By the time of her marriage just under three years later, the queen had given evidence of her strength of character in the bedchamber incident, when she defied Peel over the party affiliations of the Ladies of the Bedchamber ("Reflections" 190–200), but she was still not yet twenty-one, and her marriage was a reminder of her sex and youthfulness—and of the prospect of royal domesticity.

Victoria's marriage to Albert on 10 February 1840 dominated the hearts and minds of Britons in the early months of that year. Dickens's response, more or less simultaneous with his initial thought of Nell, was to turn the royal wedding into an extravagant private joke. For a fortnight he loudly lamented to friends that he was himself desperately in love with the Queen:

> Society is unhinged here [he wrote to Landor], by her majesty's marriage, and I am sorry to add that I have fallen hopelessly in love with the Queen, and wander up and down with vague and dismal thoughts of running away to some uninhabited island with a maid of honour, to be entrapped by conspiracy for the purpose.   (*Letters* 2: 23).

And to Forster he wrote that his unrequited love for the queen was driving him to thoughts of suicide, murder, or "of turning Chartist" (*Letters* 2: 24). Dickens's outlandish fantasy has a distinct air of Quilp about it in his pretence of being goaded into frenzy by a young woman of honor and virtue, and the reference to Chartism as an instance of destructiveness mirrors the juxtaposition of innocence and disorder which we find in *The Old Curiosity Shop*. Richard Stein, in his valuable book *Victoria's Year*, suggests that "The uncertainty about the new Queen in 1837 is a token of a general uncertainty about the present" (Stein 63). I want to apply that insight to Dickens's novel, and to suggest the idealized sentiment with which Nell is presented is in part a reaction against a troubling present, imaged as the inhospitable world in which Nell finds herself.

I do not for a moment wish it to be thought that I am suggesting that Queen Victoria served somehow as a model for Little Nell. What I do wish to propose is that Victoria's ascension to the throne was seen at the time to usher in a new era, fundamentally different in tone from the immediate past. In place of the lecherous old man who had ruled first as Regent then as king for twenty years before her, and his successor, who had fathered a string of illegitimate Fitz-Clarences, the new monarch was an attractive young woman, hardly more than a girl, whose marriage reminded contemporaries of the hope and promise which she represented for them in anxious times. In their responses, they idealized, familarized, and mythologized Victoria. Thus for Dickens to offer an idealized image of an innocent young girl as the heroine of his novel was singularly appropriate at this moment in English history. Like the young Queen, Nell serves as a cultural icon representing cherished values in the face of national anxieties. Anyone who lived in Britain a century and a half later is aware of the way in which industrial decline, mass unemployment, fiscal uncertainty, loss of international stature, and political divisiveness provided a cultural milieu in which another royal young woman assumed a prominent place in the national consciousness. Like the young Victoria, Princess Diana, a woman whose personal qualities were largely unknown (save for her distinctive taste in hats) was welcomed in the 1980s as an icon of hope and glory. Diana's image smiled from the cover of every other British magazine for several years, in glowing if vague reassurance that all was well. In such fashion, I am suggesting, the royal presence of Victoria functioned for her subjects in the early days of her reign. For Dickens, the ruler of a troubled country provided further reinforcement for the image of youth in uncongenial surroundings at the center of *The Old Curiosity Shop*.

3

In the story's opening chapter, the ancient and grotesque things which surround Nell contrast boldly with her youth and beauty, but she is quite oblivious to any threat they might hold. Master Humphrey is startled to find her wandering alone in the metropolis at night, but Nell is entirely fearless, and concerned only that she has lost her way home. When Master Humphrey accosts her, again she is unafraid, cheerfully responding to his questioning with confident assurance that he means her no harm. When they reach the shop, Humphrey is struck once more by incongruity: the ugly antique objects in the shop, with Nell's grandfather explicitly numbered among them, seem to him utterly inappropriate surroundings for a sweet young girl. Nell, however, is astonished that he could consider anything amiss and is entirely comfortable to call the shop her home. Whereas Master Humphrey is troubled by the whole situation and finds the idea of Nell left alone and unprotected in the shop so disturbing that despite heavy rain and his own fatigue he lingers outside "for two long hours," she finds nothing ominous in her grandfather's nocturnal departure. She and the old man live in loving intimacy and mutual devotion, and after he leaves, Nell sleeps peacefully in her bed while Master Humphrey lingers outside.

In this first chapter, then, the antitheses exist in secure equipoise, with Master Humphrey's anxiety the sole element out of key with the rest. Nell is perfectly at her ease among the old things, to the extent that she merrily refers to the only other youthful person present, "a shock-headed shambling awkward lad," as "old" Kit. (To reinforce the point, in the next chapter Nell's brother Fred, several years Kit's senior, is described as "young" Trent.) It is only when Dickens starts to extend the story beyond the initial episode that the dangers implicit in Nell's surroundings are made overt.

Discord erupts with the appearance of new characters. Fred Trent, the first to arrive, expresses affection for Nell, but he is openly antagonistic to their grandfather, defying the old man's age and authority and questioning his financial probity. Fred's companion Dick Swiveller favors the company with choice observations intended to promote "the taper of conwiviality, and the wing of friendship" (*OCS*, ch. 2), but he is quickly duped into participation in Fred's plot to entrap Nell for financial gain. It is a sign of Dickens's uncertainty in the story's early stages that the dangers represented by Fred and Dick soon proved to be false starts. Although Dickens was fascinated throughout his career by sibling rivalry, from Bob and Arabella Allen in *Pickwick* to Tom and Louisa Gradgrind in *Hard Times*, Charley and Lizzie Hexam in *Our Mutual Friend*, and Neville and Helena Landless in *The Mystery of Edwin Drood*, he quickly lost interest in the subject for the purposes of *The Old Curiosity Shop*, and Fred, after initial encounters with Nell, Dick, and Quilp, largely disappears from the story. Similarly, although mercenary marriage was another recurrent theme for Dickens, he soon found other things to do with Swiveller, whose insouciant self-dramatizing would in any case have effectively prevented him from ever becoming a real threat to Nell.

Dickens showed no hesitation regarding the function of the character who follows Fred and Dick into the shop. From the moment of his first entrance Daniel Quilp is established as the story's principal villain, threatening Nell and her grandfather in multiple ways. Terrifying in his very appearance, Quilp is the grotesque embodiment of the active malignity which surrounds Nell. In his open lust the threat is sexual; in his financial power over her grandfather it is economic and domestic; in his antagonism to her friends it is social; in his contempt for her moral integrity it is metaphysical. Quilp seems to be everywhere: he appears in her dreams at night; he pursues her into the countryside; his jaunty mockery is reembodied in the Punch showmen and in Mrs. Jarley's waxen effigies. In these ways he becomes an archetypal image, at once a brilliantly realized grotesque character and a fantastic projection of all Nell's fears. In the character of Quilp, Dickens gives contemporary anxiety mythic dimension.

Yet even Quilp is not the proximate cause of Nell's first major trail; rather, the dwarf is able to assume power only as a result of the moral failing of Nell's grandfather, who, to feed his obsession with winning riches at the gaming table, borrows money from Quilp, loses, and keeps borrowing and losing until he loses all, including his health, his sanity, his shop, and Nell's home. Grandfather justifies his action by insisting that he stakes money not from personal avarice but from a selfless hope of making Nell rich; the result, however, renders that distinction meaningless, for both he and Nell are ruined.

The thematic importance of gambling in *The Old Curiosity Shop* has attracted critical attention, but its topicality has not been properly recognized

(Dvorak 52–71).[23] During the 1830s and 1840s there was widespread concern that gambling was a national disgrace which was gaining in prevalence. Where only a few gaming houses, largely exclusive to aristocracy and royalty, were thought to have existed in London in the late eighteenth century, within a few decades the West End had come to "absolutely glow" with gambling halls, and the turf was degraded into "a mere gambling arena" ("Nimrod" 16: 22, 750). James Grant estimated that by 1837 between £7.5 and £8 million was lost annually in gaming, which he condemned as "the source of more evils to society in the metropolis, than any other vice which exists." He attributed "half" the suicides and "the great majority of robberies" to gambling; forgery, robbery, and even murder were also laid at its door (Grant 1: 159–220). But the evil was not only moral; gambling had social and national implications as well. Commentators lamented that the upper classes were setting a bad example for their social inferiors; the servants of nobility and gentry lost "upwards of £1 million" annually in gaming houses, while tradesmen had their business habits and principles corrupted by the spirit of speculation (Grant 1: 209). Moreover, the evil was considered peculiarly English: the spirit of gaming was nowhere more prevalent and had become the "reigning quality of the age" ("Nimrod" 16: 9–10, 226).

Plays, novels, journalism, and parliamentary debate of the day all inveighed against the evils of gambling, and grandfather's bankruptcy in the early chapters of *The Old Curiosity Shop* follows closely the outlines of numerous case studies offered by Dickens's contemporaries. Nell's grandfather is an otherwise honest and responsible tradesman, whose business is destroyed by gambling. With the abandonment of his self-discipline and domestic obligation, he suffers physical and mental collapse, as well as moral and financial ruin. Typically, this fate is offered as a moral exemplum of the inevitable consequence of what Quilp scorns as the "mad career" of a "mere shallow gambler" (*OCS*, ch. 9).

Dickens found the topic sufficiently congenial to his purposes to develop it as the story proceeded. As others have observed, Fred is destroyed by his association with List and Jowl, the very gamblers who lead his grandfather into crime; Dick Swiveller, betting imaginary stakes and playing with a young lady rather than for her, provides a healthy alternative.[24] Of greater interest is the artistry with which Dickens probes the later career of Nell's grandfather. At a point in their travels when they seem to have achieved greater security than any they had found since leaving the shop, Nell and the old man are forced by inclement weather to stop at the Valiant Soldier public house, where the sight of men playing at cards rivets grandfather's attention. " The child saw with astonishment and alarm that his whole appearance had undergone a complete change. His face was flushed and eager, his eyes were strained, his teeth set, his breath came short and thick, and the hand he laid upon her arm trembled so violently that she shook beneath its grasp'' (*OCS*, ch. 29). He demands money from Nell, enters the game, playing until his money runs out, at which point he pores over the cards, certain that his luck was about to change. On learning that Nell has more money, he creeps into her room, in a luridly vivid scene, and robs her.

The basis of this depiction is the contemporary view of gambling as a pathological state. Commentators at the time described the impulse to gamble as an addiction which was nearly impossible to overcome. "So terrible, indeed, is it in its tyranny, that, in many cases, the wretched victim has no refuge from its fury unless it be the madhouse or the grave'' ("Nimrod'' 16: 17)

Precedent for the course of such a compulsion is to be found in a frequently staged melodrama of the time, *The Hut of the Red Mountain; or, Thirty Years of a Gamester's Life*. Adapted from the French for production at the Royal Coburg in 1827, it had been staged in at least three English versions by 1831, and Dickens still found it compelling years later, when he saw a production in Paris in 1855.[25] In the play, a "detestable passion'' for gambling drives the protagonist to robbery, murder, and finally suicide. Early in Act 1 he explains the nature of his compulsion:

> Never in my life did I know the same colour to lose nine times running. I continue to double my stake—the tenth is lost; this threw me into a fever, and I could feel my nails eat into my flesh. Still I mastered my agitation, and, smiling like one on the point of death, I stake again; 'tis upon my word for two thousand pounds—the fatal card is turned up—scarcely dare I look upon it—my blood is stagnant with intense anxiety; but I hear it pronounced black again, and it falls like a thunderbolt upon my heart. It crushes all to powder, and leaves behind it an eternal night. (Milner 5–6).

And like Nell's grandfather, Augustus refuses to accept the advice that his losses are "a dreadful lesson . . . a warning from the voice of Heaven itself''; rather, he protests, "Had I been more attentive and staked on the opposite side, I should now be worth a million.''

Similarly, in *The Young Duke* (1831), Disraeli conceives of the passion for gambling as a kind of insanity:

> On they played, and the duke lost more. His mind was jaded. He floundered—he made despairing efforts, but plunged deeper in the slough. Feeling that, to regain his ground, each card must tell, he acted on each as if it must win, and the consequences of his insanity (for a gamester at such a crisis is really insane) were, that his losses were prodigious.

But where Nell's grandfather gambles to his doom and Nell's, Disraeli's duke is rescued from "the darkness of his meditations'' by thoughts of a virtuous young woman: in a "flash" of "celestial light" he thinks of May Dacre and his mind is filled with "everything that was pure and holy and beautiful and luminous and calm" (Disraeli 4: ch. 8).

Nell's frantic attempts to reclaim her grandfather are unavailing, and his robbery seals their fate. It is an enactment of Nell's nightmare in which the old man's blood came "creeping, creeping" under her door (*OCS* ch. 9), and it gives him a Quilp-like potency, which even Nell's goodness and fortitude cannot withstand. From that moment, her hope is gone; she weakens, collapses, and finally dies. The episode has both mercenary and sexual implications (Cordery 43–61; Dvorak 52–71), but in its primary impact, characteristic of Dickens's best art, it dramatizes an issue which troubled the age. It is a vivid psychological portrait, compelling in itself, and one tightly integrated into Dickens's vision of Nell in relation to antagonistic forces. Dickens's engagement with an anxiety of the time gives it an impact which transcends the local and exemplary.

When Nell flees from the shop with her grandfather in chapter 12, her expressed object is to escape from the power which his gambling losses have put into the hands of Quilp, and to escape to a vaguely imagined haven in the countryside. Wishing to leave behind the "dark rooms and melancholy houses" and "the heartless people by whom she had been surrounded," she proposes as an alternative to "walk through country places, and sleep in fields and under trees, and never think of money again, or anything else that can make you sad, but rest at nights, and have the sun and wind upon our faces in the day, and thank God together" (*OCS*, ch. 9). In its general outline, this movement traces a pattern which is the very reverse of topical: Dickens is drawing on the age-old contrast between city and country, between a place of restless energy, random disorder, and human indifference, and a contrasting vision of pastoral tranquillity.[26]

If the contrast can be traced back for millenia, however, it was taking on new resonance in the first half of the nineteenth century as pressures of urbanization, industrialization, and population explosion gave pastoral a particularly relevant appeal. In Wordsworth's poetry moral sustenance otherwise unavailable "'mid the din of towns and cities" was to be found in the "beauteous forms" of Nature;[27] Cobbett's *Rural Rides* (1830) was fired by a deep concern for the condition of the rural worker; the evocation of ivy-covered English villages in Washington Irving's *Sketch Book* (1819–20) was bathed in nostalgia. Each of these writers found freer and fuller possibilities for the expression of human sensibility and the cultivation of values hallowed by time, in an idealized rural setting depicted as simpler and less frenetic than anything to be found in a modern town.

Dickens had successfully tapped such attitudes in *The Pickwick Papers*, but from the very outset of his career he was admired for his evocation of the city, and modern readers have been decidedly unhappy with the depiction of the countryside in other of his early works. Certainly the chapters of *Oliver Twist* which deal with Rose and Harry Maylie in their country retreat lack the vibrancy of Dickens's depiction of Fagin's den, and the hero's purchase of his father's country home at the end of *Nicholas Nickleby* evades issues raised elsewhere in that novel. Far more vocal condemnation has been directed at the sentiment in *The Old Curiosity Shop* centered on Little Nell and her journey to death in a country village. It is undeniable that those chapters dealing with Quilp and Swiveller in London are better written than those dealing with Nell in her final resting place, but I wish to argue, nevertheless, that it was by following through the logic of his materials in *The Old Curiosity Shop* that Dickens was able to revalue his conception of the city-country contrast, in ways central to the achievement of his subsequent fiction.

For Nell and her grandfather the countryside holds promise of healthy open air, natural beauty, untroubled repose, and escape from the unfeeling, aggressive persecution which overwhelms them in the city. From the outset, however, their progress holds a double paradox, in the vagueness of their hope and the utter impossibility of its realization. Dickens signals both of these contradictions immediately. Even as they step out of the shop their destination is unknown to them: they set forth "wandering they knew not whither" (*OCS*, ch. 12). Dickens sustains the dreamlike quality of the rural setting by explicit reference to *The Pilgrim's Progress* (*OCS*, ch. 15; R. Bennett 423–34), by the patently emblematic nature of Nell's journey through Vanity Fair, over water and into fire, (*OCS*, ch. 19, 43, 44), and by the notable absence of place names.[28] The countryside through which Nell and her grandfather pass is by far the least realistic setting in all of Dickens's novels, and the technique reinforces Dickens's focus on the essential meaning of his heroine in uncongenial surroundings.

The second paradox is the inescapable presence of the dangers from which Nell seeks to run away. The peace and safety which she so ardently desires is, Dickens makes clear, unattainable. In its aimlessness, her journey causes bafflement and anxiety; it brings her into bewildering contact with a motley assemblage of extraordinary personages, a number of whom are as unfeeling and threatening as any she left behind; and in its arduousness her travelling requires more strength than she can summon even to survive. She flees from Quilp, but he follows her out of London, actually coming into her sight at one point (*OCS*, ch. 27). He haunts her dreams, and his threat is re-embodied in the self-seeking Punch showmen, in the sexual dangers at the race-meeting and on the barge, in the inhuman ugliness of the waxworks, and above all in the Quilplike invasion of her bedroom by her grandfather.

Seeking security after her grandfather's nearly mortal illness, Nell is instead brought repeatedly face to face with the ultimate danger, death. The first people she meets out of London tell her of the death of the cottager's child (*OCS*, ch. 15). In the following chapter she passes through the wicket gate (with its echo of Bunyan) into a churchyard, where she comes upon Codlin and Short seated among the graves, and Punch perched jauntily on a tombstone (*OCS*, ch. 16). The next morning she returns to the churchyard, where she meets the widow whose husband had died long ago (*OCS*, ch. 17). Running from Codlin and Short, he stops with the schoolmaster and witnesses the death of the little scholar (*OCS*, ch. 25). In the manufacturing district she receives succour from the motherless man whose only nurse was the furnace (*OCS*, ch. 44), then is refused charity by the unemployed man whose third child has just died (*OCS*, ch. 45). Shortly thereafter Nell herself collapses, and she finds her own final rest in a place of old men, ancient buildings, and a graveyard.

For all the extremity of the oppositions, in short, Nell's journey into the countryside dramatizes the inextricable fusion which, I have suggested, was implicit in Dickens's vision from the outset. And although the prevailing mood of this portion of the story is shadowy and dreamlike, two aspects of Nell's adventures in particular are charged with topical urgency. Both of these have received extensive analysis elsewhere and need only brief mention here.

Besides the marriage of Queen Victoria, the issue which most preoccupied the national consciousness in early 1840 was the Chartist unrest which was sweeping Britain. During the year before Dickens began writing *The Old Curiosity Shop*, the General Convention of the Industrious Classes met in London; Parliament rejected the first National Petition; riots erupted in Wales, Birmingham, Newport, and Sheffield, and there were widespread arrests. In January 1840 three Chartist rioters in Newport were sentenced to death; a petition for clemency with 21,000 signatures was sent to the queen, who commuted their sentence to transportation.[29]

The popular unrest and threat of revolution which gripped the country find direct expression in Dickens's novel in chapter 45, where Nell and her grandfather meet a torchlight parade of unemployed workers. Some critics have considered this scene an extraneous interpolation into the novel, but others have recognized that it is symptomatic of Dickens's method from the start: Nell's innocence is juxtaposed with grotesque figures everywhere about her.[30] Dickens's description is lurid because it is a child's vision of hell; the encounter adds poignancy to her isolation and spurs her on in her search for peace and tranquillity. As Michael Hollington puts it, "dream and fantasy are merged with the frightening realities of modern society" in a vision which forms part of the book's "central structural principle" (Hollington 79–95). Chartist unrest was a prominent manifestation of social disquiet in Britain in the 1830s and early 1840s; the terrifying mob in *The Old Curiosity Shop* is Dickens's specific evocation of this historical phenomenon. What is significant about the scene for our purposes, however, is that its power depends on

Nell's presence in it: the episode is focussed from her perspective. Chapter 45 is thus a local instance of the pathos of Nell's plight generally, in which Dickens's imaginative response to social events of the time feeds his image of a child in a frightening world.

Another topical concern which looms large in the countryside section of *The Old Curiosity Shop* is the changing state of popular entertainment. I have argued elsewhere that the presentation of the itinerant entertainers whom Nell meets is the single most timely of all Dickens's concerns in the book. The prosperity of travelling showfolk was declining sharply during the 1830s as Evangelical hostility to idleness of every sort, lifestyles altered by urban crowding and industrial work patterns, and commercial pressures favouring more sophisticated, larger-scale forms of entertainment, were eroding the means of livelihood of traditional street and fairground performers. They were dealt what was seen at the time as a symbolic body blow when, in the summer of 1840, even as Dickens was writing *The Old Curiosity Shop*, the most famous of all English venues of entertainment was officially suppressed by the London City fathers. Commentators at the time lamented the closure of Bartholomew Fair as a class issue; curtailment of such humble forms of pleasure was seen as an infringement on the contentment of working men and women. Dickens places Nell in contact with a series of showfolk in the course of her travels, and much of the pathos of the book arises out of the demonstration that a culture hostile to entertainers, whose age-old function was the nourishment of life-sustaining fancy, would be unable either to value or to support the ideals of goodness represented by Little Nell (Schlicke 1985: 87–136).

For all the vagueness of Nell's dream of escape into the countryside, then, Dickens locates pressing and specific concerns of his time in that very setting. What had been offered without real conviction in *Oliver Twist* and *Nicholas Nickleby*, and had been sought so fervently by the heroine of *The Old Curiosity Shop*, turns out to be no haven at all, but a place where real issues still threaten. Instead of an alternative to urban misery, this pastoral countryside represents a nightmarish distortion of it, and a dead-end for the values embodied in Nell. As we have already observed, Forster claimed that the death of Nell belonged "necessarily" to Dickens's own conception (Forster 157; 2: ch. 7); it is less a development of Dickens's story than a probing of its inherent meaning.[31] In following through the implications of his original image of the beautiful child surrounded by grotesque objects, Dickens clarified some of his central preoccupations as a man living and writing in Britain in 1840.

Nostalgia for a remote pastoral, he came to recognize, was no answer to the problems of the age. Just how clear that recognition was is signalled in the novel which followed immediately after *The Old Curiosity Shop* in the pages of *Master Humphrey's Clock*: in *Barnaby Rudge* Joe Willett flees from the rural peacefulness which Nell had sought. The Maypole Inn is the reverse of a congenial retreat; for him it is a place of confinement, frustration, and stultification. Health and vitality must be sought elsewhere. In the novels which followed (with the possible exception of David Copperfield's trip to the mountains after the death of Dora), pastoral was never again an easy alternative to urban problems. Dickens satirized such notions vigorously two years later in *Martin Chuzzlewit*, ridiculing Pecksniff as old Adam in his gardening costume and educating young Martin in the American dystopia called Eden. After *The Old Curiosity Shop* the country came to be presented as a variation within a complex, integrated vision, rather than as simple alternative.

But even in *The Old Curiosity Shop*, as I have been attempting to show, the alternative was far from simple. The version of the pastoral which Dickens presents is charged with destructive elements, just as the city is. Nell finds stasis and death in the countryside, but Quilp, for all his ferocious energy, fares far worse. With his greed, brutal indifference, restlessness, and frenzied activity Quilp is, as Malcolm Andrews has observed, a "microcosm" of the city.[32] But although he seems to have the measure of country values with a "choice retreat" of his own, the summer house called "The Wilderness" where he mocks Swiveller's romantic mooning (*OCS*, ch. 21) and gleefully schemes against honest Kit with Sampson and Sally Brass (*OCS*, ch. 51), his scorn for sentiment turns hollow in the end. In contrast to Nell's peaceful passing, which occurs off-stage, his death is violent and painful and described in ghastly detail; she is surrounded at last by friends who cherish the memory of her exemplary life, whereas he dies in self-imposed isolation and is buried, unmourned, at a crossroads with a stake through his heart. The oppositions remain stark, even as they are linked. The result is not, as is too often claimed, confusion but fusion, as Dickens interweaves the contrasts which form the book's structure.

4

In his exploration of the image of a child surrounded by grotesque objects, Dickens came to see more clearly than ever before the implications of a vision rooted in the city, and in so doing immeasurably strengthened his responsiveness to the new spirit of the age. One of his great achievements, as it seems to me, was his ability to ground his artistry in sources which reflected centrally the emerging cultural context. Where Wordsworth, the foremost spokesman of the previous age, had loathed the city and turned to a pastoral landscape for inspiration, Dickens found artistic sustenance in the streets of the burgeoning metropolis. As a general point, this is no more than to repeat the truism that Wordsworth was a Romantic writer and Dickens a Victorian.[33] But to watch what happened while Dickens was writing *The Old Curiosity Shop* is to chart more specifically the translation of one world-view into another. Dickens had, of course, already written about the heady pleasures of responding to the urban environment in some of his earliest sketches,[34] but only as he followed Little Nell on her journey to death did he fully realize that for him it was mere convention to seek essential human values in a pastoral countryside. And it was also while working out the mutual destructiveness of the story's polarities that he found a positive way to link the imaginative responsiveness of a city-dweller with moral responsibility. In the vacuum left by Quilp and Nell Dickens found a rôle for Dick Swiveller, which transformed that character from a vestigial survival of the Regency dandy into an utterly engaging example of a responsible Victorian.[35]

During the 1830s and 1840s, as Ellen Moers has demonstrated, a new type of figure, known derisively by his betters as the "gent," came into prominence on the lower fringes of the respectable class, among the young clerks, apprentices, and students of the day. Young, gullible, fresh, and vulgar, with dreams of falling into easy money, they admired Count D'Orsay as their patron saint, and were circumstantially satirized in the pages of *Punch*, in Thackeray's *History of Samuel Titmarsh and the Great Hoggarty Diamond* (1841), in Samuel Warren's *Ten Thousand a Year* (also 1841), and further defined a few years later by Albert Smith in *The Natural History of the Gent* (1847). Dickens himself, with his long hair and outrageous waistcoats, shared prime characteristics of the species before it had a name, and he had previously described the gent in *Sketches by Boz* (collected in two series in 1836) and *Sketches of Young Gentlemen* (1838).[36] Swiveller (whom Moers does not mention) is the very epitome of the type: "... a creature of once-a-month sprees and splurges, of false fronts and calico shirts, or phony jewellery, half-price tickets to the theatre, greasy hair and dirty ears. He was a second-hand, shop-worn imitation of the dandy" (Moers 215).[37]

Such a figure hardly seems promising material for the eventual hero of a story driven by moral imperatives, but Dickens was obviously fascinated by Swiveller from the outset. "I *mean* to make much of him," he told Forster after introducing the character in chapter 2 (*Letters* 2: 70). Like his creator, Swiveller attends scrupulously to the smartness of his dress; his knowledge of popular theater and song is extensive, his curiosity regarding the oddities of everyday life keen, and his fascination with rhetorical potentialities of language endless. Again like Dickens, Swiveller had an actor's delight rôle-playing, exaggeration, and the impression he made on others. His office as "Perpetual Grand" of the Glorious Apollers reflects Dickens's own participation, a couple of years previously, in the Cerberus Club, a convivial society exclusive to himself, Forster, and Ainsworth and dedicated to youthful silliness and high spirits.[38] Even his name, Dick Swiveller, suggests an affinity with Dickens. With such resemblances, it is no wonder that of all the splendid characters Dickens created, Swiveller is one of the most true-to-life, as well as the most delightful.

In the early chapters of *The Old Curiosity Shop* set-piece encounters between the cheerful wastrel and Fred Trent, Sophy Wackles, and Quilp provide Dickens with opportunities to work variations on Swiveller's attractiveness as "a literary gentleman of eccentric habits, and of a most prodigious talent in quotation" (*OCS* ch. 73), and the fact that he routinely cut dialogue involving Swiveller when revising his manuscript to fit the requirements of part-publication (Easson 1970: 93–128) attests to Dickens's confidence in his powers of inventiveness with a type he knew so well. When, midway through the narrative, he places Swiveller in the office of Sampson and Sally Brass (*OCS* ch. 33), there is nothing to suggest that even at that stage he had any further function in mind for this character, beyond witty remarks and self-dramatizing gestures.

But, having exploited characteristics of his gent to glorious comic effect, Dickens now probed beneath the behavior to see what might plausibly lie inside, and in so doing dramatized the single most important affirmation of his own artistic vision, what he was later to call "the romantic side of familiar things."[39] Before he discovers Sally Brass's abused maid-of-all-work, Swiveller has encountered nothing to move him beyond affectation and carelessness. But when she strongly rouses his curiosity, she also wakens a previously latent moral sense. Swiveller talks with her, plays with her, offers her drink, and gives her a name. Quite literally he can be said to have created her, and saved himself. For when, immediately afterwards, Swiveller falls desperately ill, it is the Marchioness who runs away to his bedside to nurse him back to life. To Swiveller himself, the rescue is something out of fairy tale; " 'It's an Arabian Night, that's what it is,' " he declares (*OCS* ch. 64). It is also an enactment of Keats's metaphor for the power of imagination, Adam's dream: "he awoke and found it truth" (Keats 37). Above all, it is an example of Victorian heroism in a quintessentially Dickensian manner: as he was later to show in characters such as Louisa Gradgrind and Lizzie Hexam, the person who gives full play to imagination proves to have an unshakeable core of moral responsibility. Where his early works were full of entertainers and entertainments, in *The Old Curiosity Shop* Dickens shifted his focus from things which stimulate fancy to the quality itself; it is not the songs, poems, and plays which matter so much as Swiveller's inherent responsiveness to them which effects his moral transformation.[40]

In following through the career of Dick Swiveller, then, Dickens found within a Regency cast-off a Victorian hero; the gent learns social responsibility, rescuing Kit from false imprisonment, exposing the villainy of Quilp and the Brasses, and earning domestic contentment as his reward. Within the structure of *The Old Curiosity Shop*, Swiveller is less prominent than either Nell or Quilp, and it has been argued that he lacks sufficient weight for his vitality to counterbalance their course to destruction (Marcus 129–68). But Swiveller is, it seems to me, the most important figure in Dickens's early fiction, both for his positive function within *The Old Curiosity Shop* and in terms of what was to come. He undergoes greater maturation than any previous figure and thus paves the way to *David Copperfield* and *Great Expectations*. His moral growth affirms that responsiveness to unpretentious entertainment, far from promoting idleness, can prove an essential ingredient for psychic health, a theme to which Dickens returned in *Hard Times*. His rescue of the Marchioness dramatizes the creative power of imagination, which was to become the increasingly powerful linchpin of Dickens's fiction, most notably in *Dombey and Son* and *Hard Times*. And his strength of character, essentially that of a city-dweller, is resilient despite the city's corrosive power and prefigures Dickens's later affirmations of the possibilities of urban survival in *Little Dorrit* and *Our Mutual Friend*.

The Old Curiosity Shop consolidated Dickens's position as the foremost novelist of his age; by the time of his death it was widely viewed as cause for embarrassment. This shift in reputation has been generally seen in relation to shifting attitudes to sentiment, and there is much to be said for that explanation.[41] But, as I have attempted to suggest, a further reason for its decline in reputation was its immersion in urgent issues of its time; as these changed, so too did attitudes to a work which confronted them. Near the end of the second world war Edward Sackville West, writing under the pseudonym Lionel Cranford, proposed that in its bold emotional appeal *The Old Curiosity Shop* was a work most likely to evoke favorable response in an age like his own, when benevolent aspects of human nature cannot be taken for granted (Sackville West 13–26). So far as I am aware, there is no evidence to suggest that his judgment was widely shared then, but the book's reputation is higher today than at any time since its initial reception.[42] Perhaps events of recent years have contributed to create a cultural climate once again favorable to Dickens's concerns: the worldwide breakdown of social cohesion, the revaluation of gender issues, and the prevailing concern with evil not as a theological concept but as a sense of uncontrollable, aggressive, grotesque, absurd forces let loose in the world. In 1841 Forster wrote to Dickens thanking him for a work which he believed "would do me lasting good" (*Letters* 2: 187–88n.). For our own age, as full of complexity, uncertainty, and menace for us as Dickens's and Forster's was for them, that assessment seems to me as timely as it was a century and a half ago.

NOTES

I am grateful to Michael Slater, Adam Roberts, and David Duff for advice and encouragement in the preparation of this essay. An earlier version was presented in September 1996 as "The Topicality of Little Nell" at the Conference "Dickens, Empire, and Children" in Grahamstown, South Africa. It was completed with support from an Arts and Humanities Research Board (AHRB) grant.

1. As reprinted in D[exter] 43. Recent commentators have argued that the forging of his public persona was the foremost achievement of Dickens's early career; see Grillo, Genet, Easson 1985, and Chittick 1990.
2. Stebbing 305–07. The significance of this essay for Dickens's thinking about *Master Humphrey's Clock* has been proposed by Genet 324–34, 383–92.
3. Many critics have noted Humphrey's narrative inadequacy. Thackeray found him "dull" (1.438). See in particular Chittick 1982: 156–64.
4. On the lack of variety in *Master Humphrey's Clock*, see Andrews 1971: 70–86, and Mundhenk 645–61.
5. Chittick has brilliantly demonstrated just how retrogressive Dickens's design for *Master Humphrey's Clock* was (1990: 130–51).
6. For Dickens's relations with Bentley see Johnson 1:234–53, and Patten 1978: 75–87.
7. The importance of changed method of illustration has been explored extensively. See Stevens 113–33; Harvey103–29; Steig 51–57; Cohen passim. According to Patten, it was the woodcuts which ate most heavily into the profits (1978: 111–12)
8. The queen's apparent insensitivity during the Lady Flora Hastings affair, in which a young noblewoman from a Tory family was rumored to be pregnant when actually dying of a liver condition, led to public condemnation of Victoria in the national and provincial papers and in the underground press in 1839. See Charlot 128–40. For the queen's part in the governmental crisis, the break-ins at Windsor Castle and Buckingham Palace, and the assassination attempts, see Charlot 140–46, 146–47, 221–23.
9. Elizabeth Brennan judiciously assesses Forster's rôle in the composition of *The Old Curiosity Shop* and his retrospective account of it in her introduction to the Clarendon Edition of the novel.
10. Macready 2:116; Young 2:111; Forster 145n.; 2: ch 7; Poe 248–51.
11. James 786–87; Hopkins 279; Bennett 2:104; Swinburne 20–39; Wyndham 119; Huxley 54–59.
12. Andrews demonstrates how smoothly the tone and method of the first numbers of *Master Humphrey's Clock* lead into the opening chapters of *The Old Curiosity Shop* (1971: 70–86).
13. "It is the custom on the stage: in all good, murderous melodramas: to present the tragic and the comic scenes, in as regular alternation, as the layers of red and white in a side of streaky, well-cured bacon" (*Oliver Twist*, ch.17).
14. "The object being to show the child in the midst of a crowd of uncongenial and ancient things," he wrote to Samuel Williams, illustrator of "The Child in her

Gentle Slumber'' (*Letters* 2: 49). See also his letter to the engraver Ebenezer Landells regarding the headpiece illustration (*Letters* 2: 45).

15. Dickens, *The Old Curiosity Shop*, ch. 1. Future references to the novel are to the Clarendon edition and noted parenthetically by chapter number.

16. Dickens had the words "young, beautiful, and good" carved on the gravestone of Mary Hogarth (Forster 85; 2: ch. 1).

17. This is not to deny the melodramatic vision of *Oliver Twist*; rather, I am arguing that in *The Old Curiosity Shop* Dickens develops his art with greater complexity and with greater potential for the work to follow. For a different but complementary approach to this development, see Eigner, passim.

18. Important assessments of the child and the child's vision in Dickens include Van Ghent 419–38; Coveney 111–61; Collins, "The Rights of Childhood" (1963: ch 8); Wilson 195–227; and Andrews 1994. I have written on the subject myself, in "Popular Entertainment and Childhood" (1985: ch 2).

19. For studies of Dickens's use of this tradition, see in particular Pickering 107–22 and Qualls 85–138.

20. Tillotson 1954, passim; 1960: 833; 1961: 133–37; Slater 95–96.

21. Malcolm Andrews assesses the evidence for dating Dickens's decision to have Nell die (1998: 133–35).

22. Briggs, *Age of Improvement* 454–62.

23. Dvorak is an exception. He notes topical concern about gambling, but his analysis is somewhat limited by too close an identification of gambling with avarice, which contemporary observers—including Dickens, I suggest—considered less important a motive than the addictive excitement of play. For other modern views of gambling in *The Old Curiosity Shop*, see Pearson 77–90, and Cordery 43–61.

24. Pearson 77–90 and Cordery 43–61.

25. Nicoll 4.542. Forster reports Dickens's later interest in the play (604; 7:5). Davis notes *Thirty Years of a Gambler's Life* as a possible source for *The Old Curiosity Shop* (139).

26. For more general discussion of these issues, see Schwarzbach and Williams. Marcus offers a brilliant analysis of pastoral in *The Old Curiosity Shop*. See also Lucas 73–92.

27. "Tintern Abbey," lines 23–26.

28. In a letter to Forster Dickens noted, "You will recognize a description of the road we travelled between Birmingham and Wolverhampton" (*Letters* 2.131–32), but in the story itself the location is unspecified. The only explicit indication of place after Nell leaves London is a reference to "the blue Welch mountains far away" (*OCS*, ch. 46), which has led topographers to surmise that the village where Nell dies is Tong, near Shrewsbury.

29. Briggs, *Chartist Studies* 408; "Chronicle," *Annual Register* (1840): 7–13.

30. Brantlinger 85–88; Craig 75–90; Fawkner, 120–22 and passim; Gomme, passim; House 179–81; Oddie 100–01, 106–07; Smith 75–84, 250.

31. As Eigner judiciously observes, "There is nothing progressive in Dickens's conception of Nell or of her book. . . . The intention of the expanded story is not dramatically to bring Nell into meaningful collision with this fallen world but lyrically to repeat the initial vision with variations" (32).

32. Andrews 1971: 19. See also Andrews 1973: 164–65.
33. Wordsworth drew poetic stimulus from the city, of course, as the London sections of *The Prelude* give evidence, but he found it fundamentally antipathetic, in contrast to Dickens's complex attraction.
34. In "Shops and their Tenants," for example, first published 10 October 1834, he wrote, "What inexhaustible food for speculation do the streets of London afford!" Similarly, in "Omnibuses," first published 26 September 1834, he noted that urban transport provides "an extensive field for amusement and observation."
35. Stewart argues that Sam Weller is an earlier and more successful example of a morally upright imaginative figure (chs. 1 and 4). While not denying Sam's combination of Cockney shrewdness and devoted duty to Mr Pickwick, I suggest that his moral growth is less fully presented than Swiveller's.
36. See "Making a Night of It," "Hackney Coach Stands," and "Private Theatres" in *Sketches by Boz* and "The Theatrical Young Gentleman" in *Sketches of Young Gentlemen*. In 1845 Dickens chose D'Orsay as a sponsor for his newborn son Alfred D'Orsay Tennyson Dickens.
37. Several of the examples of contemporary depictions of the gent noted in this paragraph are discussed by Moers in her chapter on Dickens (215–50).
38. A Memorandum by Dickens hilariously recording the rules of the projected club is reproduced in *Letters* 1.637n. For an account of Swiveller's club, see Schlicke 1994: 171–78.
39. Preface to *Bleak House* (1853).
40. I have discussed these issues more fully in Schlicke 1985: 131–36.
41. See Collins 1974; MacPike 33–38, 70–76; and Schlicke 1990: 189–99.
42. I base this judgment on the response of participants at conferences devoted to *The Old Curiosity Shop*, at the University of California, Santa Cruz, in August 1989, and at Birkbeck College, University of London, in March 1990, and on the tone of recent publications in scholarly journals.

WORKS CITED

Andrews, Malcolm. "The Composition and Design of *The Old Curiosity Shop*: A Study in the Working of Dickens's Imagination." Ph.D. diss. U of London, 1973.

——— (as M. Y.A.) "Elizabeth Brennan (Ed.) *The Old Curiosity Shop*." *Dickensian* 94 (1998): 133–35.

———. *Dickens and the Grown-Up Child*. Basingstoke: Macmillan, 1994.

———. "Introducing Master Humphrey." *Dickensian* 67 (1971): 70–86.

———. "Introduction." *The Old Curiosity Shop*. By Charles Dickens. Ed. Angus Easson. Harmondsworth: Penguin, 1972

Bennett, Arnold. *The Letters of Arnold Bennett*. Ed. James Hepburn. 4 vols. Oxford: Oxford UP, 1968.

Bennett, Rachel. "Punch versus Christian in *The Old Curiosity Shop*." *Review of English Studies* 22 (1971), 423–34.

Brantlinger, Patrick. *The Spirit of Reform: British Literature and Politics 1832–1867*. Cambridge, MA: Harvard UP, 1977.

Briggs, Asa. *The Age of Improvement 1783–1867*. London: Longman, 1959.

———, ed. *Chartist Studies*. London: Macmillan, 1959.

Brooks, Peter. *The Melodramatic Imagination: Balzac, Henry James, Melodrama, and the Mode of Excess*. New Haven: Yale UP, 1976.

Butler, Marilyn. *Jane Austen and the War of Ideas*. Oxford: Clarendon, 1975, 1987.

Caswall, Edward. *Morals of the Churchyard*. London: Chapman and Hall, 1838.

——— (as "Quiz"). *Sketches of Young Ladies*. London: Chapman and Hall, 1837.

Charlot, Monica. *Victoria: The Young Queen*. Oxford: Blackwell, 1991.

Chittick, Kathryn. *Dickens and the 1830s*. Cambridge: Cambridge U. P., 1990.

———. "The Idea of a Miscellany: *Master Humphrey's Clock*." *Dickensian* 78 (1982): 156–64.

Cohen, Jane R. *Charles Dickens and His Original Illustrators*. Columbus: Ohio State UP, 1980.

Collins, Philip, ed. *Dickens: The Critical Heritage*. London: Routledge and Kegan Paul, 1971.

———. *Dickens and Education*. London: Macmillan, 1963.

———. *From Manly Tear to Stiff Upper Lip*. Wellington, N. Z.: Victoria UP, 1974.

Cordery, Gareth. "The Gambling Grandfather in *The Old Curiosity Shop*." *Literature and Psychology* 33 (1987): 43–61.

Coveney, Peter. *Poor Monkey* (1957), revised as *The Image of Childhood*. Harmondsworth: Penguin, 1963.

Craig, David. "The Crowd in Dickens." In *The Changing World of Charles Dickens*. Ed. Robert Gittings. London: Vision, 1983.

Davis, Earle. *The Flint and the Flame: the Artistry of Charles Dickens*. London: Gollancz, 1964.

D[exter], W[alter]. "The Reception of Dickens's First Book." *Dickensian*, 32 (1935): p. 43.

Dickens, Charles. *Bleak House*. Ed. George M. Ford and Sylvère Monod. New York: Norton, 1977.

――――. *The Letters of Charles Dickens*. The Pilgrim Edition. Ed. Madeline House, Graham Storey, et al. 12 vols. Oxford: Clarendon, 1965–2002.

――――. *The Old Curiosity Shop*. Ed. Elizabeth M. Brennan. Oxford: Clarendon, 1997.

――――. *Oliver Twist*. Ed. Kathleen Tillotson. Oxford: Clarendon, 1966.

Disraeli, Benjamin. *The Young Duke* [1831]. Ed. Philip Guedella. London: Davies, 1926.

Dvorak, Wilfred P. "Charles Dickens's *The Old Curiosity Shop*: The Triumph of Compassion." *Papers in Language and Literature* 28 (1992): 52–71.

Easson, Angus. "*The Old Curiosity Shop*: From Manuscript to Print." *Dickens Studies Annual* 1 (1970): 93–128.

――――. "Who is Boz? Dickens and His Sketches." *Dickensian* 81 (1985): 13–22.

Eigner, Edwin. *The Metaphysical Novel in England and America: Dickens, Bulwer, Melville and Hawthorne*. Berkeley/Los Angeles: U of California P, 1978.

Fawkner, Harald William. "Animation and Reification in Dickens's Vision of the Life-Denying Society." *Acta Upsaliensis Studia Anglistica Upsaliensia* 31. Stockholm: Almquist and Wiksell, 1977.

Forster, John. *The Life of Charles Dickens* [1872–74]. Ed. J. W. T. Ley. London: Cecil Palmer, 1928.

Genet, George Malcolm. "Charles Dickens and the Magazine World: The Periodical Author in the Eighteen Thirties." Ph.D. diss. U of California, Berkeley, 1975.

Gomme, A.H. *Dickens*. London: Evans, 1971.

[Grant, James]. "The Gaming Houses." Ch 4 of *The Great Metropolis*. 2 vols. London: Saunders and Otley, 1837. 1:159–220.

Greene, Graham. "The Young Dickens" [1950]. In *Collected Essays*. London: The Bodley Head, 1969; rpt. Harmondsworth: Penguin, 1978): 79–86.

Grillo, Virgil. *Charles Dickens'* Sketches by Boz: *End in the Beginning*. Boulder: Colorado Associated UP, 1974.

Harvey, John. *Victorian Novelists and Their Illustrators*. New York: New York UP, 1971.

Hollington, Michael. "*The Old Curiosity Shop* and the New Curiosity Shop." In *Dickens and the Grotesque*. London: Croom Helm, 1984.

[Hood. Thomas.] "*Master Humphrey's Clock* by Boz." *Athenaeum*, 7 November 1840: 887–88.

Hopkins, Gerard Manley, *The Letters of Gerard Manley Hopkins to Robert Bridges.* Ed. Claude Colleer Abbott. London: Oxford UP, 1935.

Horne, Richard Hengist. *A New Spirit of the Age.* 2 vols. London: Smith, Elder, 1844.

House, Humphry. *The Dickens World.* 2nd ed. New York: Oxford UP, 1942.

Huxley, Aldous. *Vulgarity in Literature.* London: Chatto and Windus, 1930.

James, Henry. "*Our Mutual Friend.*" *The Nation* 1 (1865): 786–87.

Johnson, Edgar. *Charles Dickens: His Tragedy and Triumph.* 2 vols. Boston: Little, Brown, 1952.

Keats, John. *The Letters of John Keats.* Ed. Robert Gittings. London: Oxford UP, 1970.

Lucas, John. "*The Old Curiosity* Shop." In *The Melancholy Man: A Study of Dickens's Novels.* London: Methuen, 1970.

MacPike, Loralee. " 'The Old Cupiosity Shape': Changing Views of Little Nell." *Dickens Studies Newsletter* 12 (1981): 33–38, 70–76.

Macready, William Charles. *The Diaries of William Charles Macready.* Ed. William Toynbee. 2 vols. London: Chapman and Hall, 1912.

Marcus, Steven. "The Myth of Nell." In *Dickens: From* Pickwick *to* Dombey. London: Chatto and Windus, 1965.

Milner, H. M. *The Hut of the Red Mountain, or Thirty Years of a Gamester's Life.* Cumberland's Minor Theatre (London: Cumberland [1830])

Moers, Ellen. *The Dandy: Brummell to Beerbohm.* London: Secker and Warburg, 1960.

Mundhenk, Rosemary. "Creative Ambivalence in Dickens's *Master Humphrey's Clock.*" *Studies in English Literature* 32 (1992): 645–61.

"New Reign, The." *Quarterly Review* 49 (1837): 240–73.

Nicoll, Allardyce. *A History of English Drama 1660–1900.* 6 vols. Cambridge: Cambridge UP, 1955.

"Nimrod" [C. J. Apperley]. "The Anatomy of Gaming." *Fraser's Magazine* 16 (1837): 9–24, 368–78. 748–57; 17 (1838): 269–79, 538–45.

Noel, Baptist. *Infant Piety: A Book for Little Children.* London: Nisbet, 1840.

Oddie, William. *Dickens and Carlyle: The Question of Influence.* London: Centenary, 1972.

Parker, David. "Dickens and the Death of Mary Hogarth." *Dickens Quarterly* 13 (1996): 67–75.

Patten, Robert. *Charles Dickens and His Publishers*. Oxford: Clarendon, 1978.

———. "Plot in Charles Dickens' Early Novels," (Ph.D. diss. Princeton, 1965).

———. " 'The Story Weaver at His Loom': Dickens and the Beginning of *The Old Curiosity Shop*." In *Dickens the Craftsman: Strategies of Presentation*. Ed. Robert B. Partlow, Jr. Carbondale: Southern Illinois UP, 1970.

Pearson, Gabriel. "*The Old Curiosity Shop*." In *Dickens and the Twentieth Century*. Eds. Pearson and John Gross. London: Routledge and Kegan Paul, 1962.

Poe, Edgar Allan. *The Old Curiosity* Shop." *Graham's Magazine* 18 (May 1841): 248–51.

Pickering, Samuel, Jr. "*The Old Curiosity Shop* and Legh Richmond's Tracts. In *The Moral Tradition in English Fiction, 1785–1885*. (Hanover, NH: UP of New England, 1976.

Qualls, Barry V. "Transmutations of Dickens's Emblematic Art." In *The Secular Pilgrims of Victorian Fiction: The Novel as Book of Life*. Cambridge: Cambridge UP, 1982.

"Reflections on Punch—Morals and Manners," *Blackwood's Edinburgh Magazine* 45 (February 1839): 190–200.

Ruskin, John. *The Works of John Ruskin*. Ed. E.T. Cook and Alexander Wedderburn. 39 vols. London: George Allen, 1903–12.

Sackville-West, Edward. "Dickens and the World of Childhood." In *Inclinations*. London: Secker and Warburg, 1949; incorporating "Books in General." *New Statesman and Nation* n.s. 29 (10 February 1945): 95–96.

Schlicke, Paul. *Dickens and Popular Entertainment*. London: Allen and Unwin, 1985; with revisions, Unwin Hyman, 1988.

———. "Glorious Apollers and Ancient Buffaloes." *Dickensian* 90 (1994): 171–78.

———. "The True Pathos of *The Old Curiosity Shop*." *Dickens Quarterly* 7 (1990): 189–99.

Schlicke, Priscilla, and Paul Schlicke, *The Old Curiosity Shop: An Annotated Bibliography*. New York: Garland, 1988.

Schwarzbach, F.S. *Dickens and the City*. London: Athlone, 1979.

Slater, Michael. *Dickens and Women*. London: Dent, 1983.

Smith, Sheila M. *The Other Nation: The Poor in English Novels of the 1840s and 1850s*. Oxford: Clarendon, 1980.

Spectator 11 (31 March 1838): 304; reprinted Collins (1971).

Stebbing, Henry. "Unpublished Lectures on Periodical Literature. 2," *Athenaeum* no. 20 (1 April 1828): 305–07.

Steig, Michael. *Dickens and Phiz.* Bloomington: Indiana UP, 1978.

Stein, Richard. *Victoria's Year: English Literature and Culture, 1837–38.* Oxford: Oxford UP, 1987.

Stevens, Joan. " 'Woodcuts Dropped into the Text': The Illustrations in *The Old Curiosity Shop* and *Barnaby Rudge.*" *Studies in Bibliography: Papers of the Bibliographical Society of the University of Virginia* 20 (1967): 113–33.

Stewart, Garrett. *Dickens and the Trials of Imagination.* Cambridge, MA: Harvard UP, 1974.

S[uzannet], A[lain de]. "Dickens's Love for Wordsworth." *Dickensian* 29 (1933): 197–98.

Swinburne, Algernon Charles. "Charles Dickens." *Quarterly Review* 196 (1902): 20–39.

Thackeray, William Makepeace. *Letters and Private Papers.* Ed. Gordon N. Ray. 4 vols. London: Oxford UP, 1945.

Tillotson, Kathleen. "A Letter from Mary Hogarth." *T.L.S.* (23 December 1960): 833; and *Dickensian* 57 (1961): 133–37.

————. *Novels of the 1840s.* Oxford: Clarendon, 1954.

Todd, Janet. *Sensibility: An Introduction.* London: Methuen, 1986.

"To Her Royal Highness the Princess Victoria," *Blackwood's Edinburgh Magazine* 41 (June 1837): 634–45.

V., W. R. "Ode to the Queen." *Bentley's Miscellany* 2 (1837): 568–89.

Van Ghent, Dorothy. "The Dickens World: a View from Todgers'." *Sewanee Review* 58 (1950): 419–38.

Williams, Raymond. *The Country and the City.* London: Chatto and Windus, 1973.

Wilson, Angus. "Dickens on Children and Childhood," *Dickens 1970.* Ed. Michael Slater. London: Chapman and Hall, 1970.

Wyndham, Violet. *The Sphinx and Her Circle: A Biographical Sketch of Ada Leverson, 1862–1933.* London: Andre Deutsch, 1963.

Young, Charles Young. *A Memoir of Charles Mayne Young.* 2 vols. London: Oxford UP, 1871.

Narrating History in Scott and Dickens

H. M. Daleski

This essay sets out to compare how Scott and Dickens, writing as novelists, approach historic material that is an essential part of their narratives. A common ground for the comparison is provided by their descriptions of historic riots that involve the storming of prisons, that of the Tolbooth during the Porteous Riots in The Heart of Midlothian, *and of Newgate during the Gordon Riots in* Barnaby Rudge. *The critical criterion for the comparison, following a dictum of Joseph Conrad, is the degree to which the novelists succeed in making us visualize the events they describe. The analysis suggests that Scott works much more like an historian than does Dickens. Scott sticks close to his sources and is careful not to deviate from them. Dickens vouches for the authenticity of his descriptions of the riots, but gives his imagination free rein in his evocation of them and in the way he integrates this material in the narrative as a whole.*

In "The Art of Fiction," Henry James roundly declared that there is very little difference between the work of a novelist and that of an historian:

> To represent and illustrate the past, the actions of men, is the task of [both the novelist and the historian], and the only difference that I can see is, in proportion as he succeeds, to the honour of the novelist, consisting as it does in his having more difficulty in collecting his evidence. (6)

Certainly, some novelists have presented themselves to their readers as historians in the very titles of their novels: we have only to think of *The History*

Dickens Studies Annual, Volume 32, Copyright © 2002 by AMS Press, Inc. All rights reserved.

of Tom Jones and *The History of Henry Esmond.* In *Middlemarch* George Eliot, modestly distinguishing between herself and Fielding, whom she calls that "great historian," refers to herself as a "belated historian." The question that arises is how novelists set about their work when their narratives actually engage historic material. I propose to compare Scott and Dickens in this respect. The common denominator will be the historical basis of an attack by a rioting mob on a prison. I wish to start with Scott's account of the Porteous Riots and the breaking into the Tolbooth in *The Heart of Midlothian,* and place that beside Dickens's description of the Gordon Riots and the storming of Newgate in *Barnaby Rudge.*

The problem in attempting such a comparison is to find a basis that will enable us to determine whether novelists imagine such events in the same kind of way. A criterion that suggests itself may be derived from the pronouncement of a major novelist on the essential nature of his art. In the preface to *The Nigger of the "Narcissus,"* Conrad defined his task in the following terms:

> My task which I am trying to achieve is, by the power of the written word to make you hear, to make you feel—it is, before all, to make you *see.* That—and no more, and it is everything. If I succeed, you shall find there according to your deserts . . . —all you demand—and perhaps, also that glimpse of truth for which you have forgotten to ask.   (x)

Conrad's emphasis, it is clear, is on making the reader respond with his senses, above all, on making him see. To achieve this the novelist has to particularize so that we can visualize. But such intensified description is but a means to an end, for the visualization is what yields the "glimpse of truth." It is the object itself, in other words, that is made to manifest the truth it contains, such a truth being analogous to James Joyce's *"quidditas,"* when, in the moment of epiphany, the "soul" or "whatness" of an object "leaps to us from the vestment of its appearance" (213). The aim, then, will be to see how the given descriptions of the two novelists measure up to such a standard.

* * *

Scott is one of those novelists who likes to present himself as a historian. In his first novel, *Waverley* (1814), he refers on a number of occasions to his narrative as "[his] history" (6, 30), calling it also "this memorable history" (28), and himself an "unworthy historian" (51). A few years later, in *Old Mortality* (1816), his fictional editor complains that his publisher "[does] not approve of novels (as he injuriously [calls] these real histories)" (II, 303);

and for good measure a crucial incident in the narrative is footnoted as follows: "This incident, and Burley's exclamation, are taken from the records"
(II, 140). In *The Heart of Midlothian* (1818), the novel that provides us with
our prison scene, once again the narrator appears as an "historian," who has
a "due regard to veracity" (84); and the novel comes replete with notes, a
glossary, and an index, as if in an expository work. The following note, for
instance, bolsters the depiction in the text of measures taken to punish the
city of Edinburgh after the riots. It recounts an amusing scene in the proceedings and we would not be without it, but it nonetheless epitomizes an imperi-
ous drive to historicity:

> The Magistrates were closely interrogated before the House of Peers, concern-
> ing the particulars of the Mob, and the *patois* in which these functionaries made
> their answers sounded strange in the ears of the Southern nobles. The Duke of
> Newcastle having demanded to know with what kind of shot the guard which
> Porteous commanded had loaded their muskets, was answered naively, "Ow,
> just sic an ane shoots *dukes and fools* with." This reply was considered as a
> contempt of the House of Lords, and the Provost would have suffered accord-
> ingly, but that the Duke of Argyle explained that the expression, properly
> rendered into English, means *ducks and waterfowl.*   (554)[1]

In *The Heart of Midlothian*, however, Scott is equivocal about his standing.
Despite the historical paraphernalia, the narrative opens with an elaborate
series of frames that demand recognition of its fictionality. The outer frame
is provided by Jedediah Cleishbotham, the fictional editor of the manuscript,
who writes what he calls a "prolegomenon" to the narrative that follows, in
which he attacks the maligners who have "impeached [his] veracity and the
authenticity of [his] historical narratives" (xvi). Chapter I of the novel proper
proffers a second frame, in which Peter Pattieson, Cleishbotham's assistant
and the actual writer of the manuscript, describes his encounter, in a lively
first-person narrative, with two lawyers and Dunover, a debtor who has been
imprisoned in the Tolbooth, the jail of Edinburgh known as the Heart of
Midlothian. This narrative is presented as occurring in the present time of
writing or publication. In it Dunover is said to tell tales of the Tolbooth that
provide Pattieson with the narrative that then follows. In Chapter II there is
an abrupt shift both in time—the narrative switches to the year 1736, the year
of the Porteous Riots—and in narrative method, for though Pattieson is still
the narrator, his presence now is almost erased in the generally impersonal
narrative that ensues. This procedure effectively establishes a difference between the present and past times of the narrative, but by the time we have
passed through Cleishbotham to Pattieson, and then to Dunover and back to
Pattieson, all immediacy is forfeited. The frames may vouch for the historian's
detachment from his material, but they keep it at a distance, leaving it in an
initial inertness.

Chapters II-VII, some fifty pages, are devoted to the events that lead up to the Porteous Riots and to their culmination in the storming of the Tolbooth. What is particularly notable in this section of the novel is the way in which the narrator veers between the roles of historian and novelist. One of the distinguishing features of the novelist's art is the prerogative of omniscience, unless of course he has chosen to adopt a restricted point of view. He knows exactly why his characters behave as they do, and will usually tell us so. The historian, on the other hand, knows only what is revealed to him by his sources, and so is driven to assume what is not directly revealed. As the narrator begins his account of the doings of Captain Porteous, his narrative is regularly peppered with words such as "seem" and "as if," with which the conscientious historian registers grey areas in his portrayal. To quote but a few examples: "[T]he honour of his command and of his corps seems to have been a matter of high interest and importance" to Porteous (26). Porteous "seems . . . to have been disqualified [to command] by a hot and surly temper . . . " (27). "On the present occasion . . . it seemed to those who saw [Porteous] as if he were agitated by some evil demon" (27–28). "One part of his conduct was truly diabolical, if indeed it has not been exaggerated by the general prejudice entertained against his memory" (28).

When Porteous is reprieved, the crowd that has assembled to witness his hanging disperses, and we are told that it is only by hearing what they say that "a stranger could estimate the state of their minds." At this point the narrator declares, "We will give the reader this advantage, by associating ourselves with one of the numerous groups who were painfully ascending the steep declivity of the West Bow." The authorial intrusion marks the novelist's release into fiction, and there follows a lively exchange between some fictional characters that is more vivid then the tempered historical account that has preceded it:

> "An unco thing this, Mrs. Howden," said old Peter Plumdamas to . . . [a] saleswoman, as he offered her his arm to assist her in the toilsome ascent, "to see the grit folk at Lunnon set their face against law and gospel, and let loose sic a reprobate as Porteous upon a peaceable town!"
> "And to think o' the weary walk they has gien us," answered Mrs. Howden, with a groan; "and sic a comfortable window as I had gotten, too, just within a pennystane cast of the scaffold—I could hae heard every word the minister said—and to pay twal pennies for my stand, and a' for naething!"   (37)

The interlude between the dispersal of the crowd and the outburst of the rioting is filled with a continued account of the doings of fictional characters. A further change of role by the narrator is once again marked by a telltale intrusion: "The guard-house," we are told, "was a long, low, ugly building (removed in 1787), which to a fanciful imagination might have suggested the

idea of a long black snail crawling up the middle of the High Street . . .''
(54–55). The imagination of the novelist gives us the striking image of the
snail; the zealous mind of the historian cannot resist giving us the date of the
destruction of the guard-house, sacrificing immediacy in the pedantic middle
distance of a time between that of the narration and of the historic event of
the riots. Such a bifurcation, the contest between the freely imaginable and
the historically verifiable, marks the description of the attack on the prison.

The assault on the Tolbooth takes two main forms. The first is an attempt
to batter down its door:

> [A] select body of the rioters thundered at the door of the jail, and demanded
> instant admission. No one answered, for the outer keeper had prudently made
> his escape with the keys at the commencement of the riot, and was nowhere
> to be found. The door was instantly assailed with sledge-hammers, iron crows,
> and the coulters of ploughs . . . with which they prized, heaved, and battered
> for some time with little effect; for, being of double oak planks, clenched, both
> end-long and athwart, with broad-headed nails, the door was so hung and se-
> cured as to yield to no means of forcing, without the expenditure of much time.
> The rioters, however, appeared determined to gain admittance. Gang after gang
> relieved each other at the exercise, for, of course, only a few could work at a
> time; but gang after gang retired, exhausted with their violent exertions, without
> making much progress in forcing the prison door.   (57–58)

It is extraordinary what Scott, with a desiderated Conradian vividness, makes
us see—and what he refuses to see. The implements that the rioters use in
their assault on the door, the sledge-hammers and iron bars and parts of
ploughs, are detailed with sharp particularity. And the door, which is the
focus of the rioters' attention, the door ''of double oak planks, clenched, both
end-long and athwart, with broad-headed nails,'' is appropriately the most
strongly visualized object in the scene. But such immediacy of detail is glar-
ingly lacking in the description of the rioters. It is a ''select body'' of rioters
who demand admission, but who they are, what they look like, why they are
''select,'' in what terms and in what tones they demand to be let in—all this
is elided. They are merely a ''gang,'' and it is ''gang after gang'' that takes
its turn at trying to break down the door. As they persist in their efforts, one
would think it could be safely assumed what their purpose is, but historical
nicety will only go so far as to intimate that they ''[appear] determined to
gain admittance.''

The second mode of attack of the rioters is to burn their way into the prison.
Much the same sort of alternating particularity and vagueness appertains to
the description of the break-in to the prison. It is ''a voice,'' floating in the
air, as it were, unattached, even, to a body, that turns the tide when it calls
out, ''Try it with fire.'' But the fire itself is clearly visualized, even if those
it illuminates fade into generality: ''A huge red glaring bonfire speedily arose

close to the door of the prison, sending up a tall column of smoke and flame against its antique turrets and strongly-grated windows, and illuminating the ferocious and wild gestures of the rioters who surrounded the place, as well as the pale and anxious groups of those who, from windows in the vicinage, watched the progress of this alarming scene." The fire continues to "roar and crackle" until the door catches fire and the rioters rush into the prison over its "yet smouldering remains" (59).

The account of the attack, then, may be said to yield a negative epiphany—what is not seen. Scott sees riot but not the rioters. Why this should be so is suggested in one of the notes appended to the text:

> In chapters ii-vii, the circumstances of that extraordinary riot and conspiracy, called the Porteous Mob, are given with as much accuracy as the Author was able to collect them. . . .
> Although the fact was performed by torch-light, and in presence of a great multitude, to some of whom, at least, the individual actors must have been known, yet no discovery was ever made concerning any of the perpetrators of the slaughter.   (549)

It is the historian, solicitous of fact, who does not personalize the rioters because no one knows who exactly they were, and he remains faithful to his sources. But at the same time he is a novelist, and so the fiction that follows (though it too is in part based on fact) is propelled, as it were, from the riot, and the unnamed leader of the rioters and the young woman in the prison who refuses to flee become major players in the ensuing drama.

*　*　*

Unlike Scott, Dickens does not claim to be a historian. On the contrary, though he vouches for the authenticity of the historical events he describes in *Barnaby Rudge*, he makes it clear he is working as a novelist. "No account of the Gordon Riots," he says in the author's preface, "[has]been to my knowledge introduced into any Work of Fiction, and the subject presenting very extraordinary and remarkable features, I was led to project this Tale" (xxiv).

Dickens also differs from Scott—at least in respect of *The Heart of Midlothian*, for this does not apply to all Scott's narratives—in the way he introduces his historic material. Scott, as noted, starts with his depiction of the Porteous Riots; Dickens gives us some 250 pages devoted entirely to fictional events before he reaches the Gordon Riots. And his mode of fiction, in contrast to that of Scott, is proleptic, an art of prefiguring. Looking ahead to his central historic material, he prepares the way for it by making us slowly intimate with the lives of those who will be among the leaders of the riots when he eventually reaches them in his narrative. The historic material in *Barnaby Rudge* thus issues from the fictional, and not vice versa as in Scott. But Dickens also turns the section of the narrative that precedes the riots into a thematic springboard. In his presentation of the four characters who will be at the head of much of the rioting, he provides us with two motifs or master tropes that will in due course inform the depiction of the riots themselves.[2]

The first motif is introduced early on in the opening description of Barnaby:

> His hair, of which he had a great profusion, was red, and hanging in disorder about his face and shoulders, gave to his restless looks an expression quite unearthly—enhanced by the paleness of his complexion, and the glassy lustre of his large protruding eyes. . . .
> The fluttered and confused disposition of all the motley scraps that formed his dress, bespoke, in a scarcely less degree than his eager and unsettled manner, the disorder of his mind, and by a grotesque contrast set off and heightened the more impressive wildness of his face. (28)

This motif appears once more in the initial presentation of Hugh:

> [He was] a young man, of a hale athletic figure, and a giant's strength, whose sunburnt face and swarthy throat, overgrown with jet black hair, might have served a painter for a model. Loosely attired, in the coarsest and roughest garb . . . , he had fallen asleep in a posture as careless as his dress. The negligence and disorder of the whole man, with something fierce and sullen in his features, gave him a picturesque appearance . . . (85–86)

What links these two future rioters is the common notion of disorder, and this points ahead in several directions. It points, first, in a straight line to the civil disorder epitomized by the riots. At the same time it points to the paralysis of government, to a functional disorder in the body politic, that permits the rioters initially to gather momentum: "Fifty resolute men might have turned them at any moment; a single company of soldiers could have scattered them like dust, but no man interposed, no authority restrained them . . ." and "every man went about his pleasure or business as if the city were in perfect order" (401–02). The breakdown of order, moreover, is manifest even in the House of Commons: "In short, the disorder and violence which reigned triumphant out of doors, penetrated into the senate, and there, as elsewhere, terror and alarm prevailed, and ordinary forms were for the time forgotten" (559).

Barnaby's disorder, in the passage quoted, relates primarily to his mind, though it is first referred to his hair. In the former sense the idea of disorder leads to one of the central images of the narrative:

> [S]ober workmen, going home from their day's labour, were seen to cast down their baskets of tools and become rioters in an instant; mere boys on errands

did the like. In a word, a moral plague ran through the city. . . . The contagion spread like a dread fever: an infectious madness, as yet not near its height, seized on new victims every hour, and society began to tremble at their ravings.

(403)

The notion of illness and contagion, whether literal or metaphorical, fascinated Dickens, and he was later to make memorable use of it in both *Bleak House* and *Little Dorrit*. In *Barnaby Rudge*, the "infectious madness" that transforms the normally law-abiding into raging rioters thereafter typifies the behavior of the mob that is let loose on London.[3] Again and again, reference is made to the madness of the rioters, but one example must now suffice: "Covered with soot, and dirt, and dust, and lime; their garments torn to rags; their hair hanging wildly about them; their hands and faces jagged and bleeding with the wounds of rusty nails; Barnaby, Hugh, and Dennis hurried on before them all, like hideous madmen" (385).

The second motif adverted to in the section of the narrative preceding the riots appears first in the description of Mr. Simon Tappertit:

> [I]n the small body of Mr. Tappertit there was locked up an ambitious and aspiring soul. As certain liquors, confined in casks too cramped in their dimensions, will ferment, and fret, and chafe in their imprisonment, so the spiritual essence or soul of Mr. Tappertit would sometimes fume within that precious cask, his body, until, with great foam and froth and splutter, it would force a vent, and carry all before it.   (34)

The motif recurs when John Willet says of Hugh that he is a "chap" whose "faculties" are "bottled up and corked down" (86); and then again when the "great veins" in Dennis's neck are said to be "swoln and starting, as though with gulping down strong passions, malice, and ill-will" (282). These three future leaders of the rioters, we see, are primed for violent eruption; and the signs of such an outburst are later writ large all over London. It is a mark of the striking imaginative coherence of the narrative that both motifs come together in the presentation of Lord George Gordon. His Great Protestant Association is supposed by many to be "the mere creature of his disordered brain"; and he is looked upon as "a cracked-brained member of the lower house" (278). When he speaks, "the rapidity of his utterance" and the "violence of his tone and gesture" suggest that, "struggling through his Puritan demeanour," there is "something wild and ungovernable which [breaks] through all restraint" (270).

Erupting, then, in civil disorder, the rioters strike their main blow against established law and security when they storm Newgate. They "[work] in gangs," we are told, when they batter at the main gate of the prison (491). Scott too referred to his rioters as "a gang," but they, we recall, are individually indistinguishable. Dickens's rioters, in strong contrast, are sharply individualized. It is not only that, with Hugh and Dennis and Sim in the forefront of things—Hugh and Dennis, indeed, are the first to actually break into the prison—that Dickens's mob is given a face; the focus is constantly on individuals comprising it. In the mob there are, for instance, those who have a private purpose in attacking the prison. To be seen are "more than one woman . . . disguised in man's attire," who are out to rescue imprisoned members of their families; there are "the two sons" of a man sentenced to death; and also "a great party of boys whose fellow-pickpockets [are] in the prison" (480–81). In like manner, the weapons of the rioters are particularized in minute detail, far greater than analogously by Scott:

> Old swords, and pistols without ball or powder; sledge-hammers, knives, axes, saws, and weapons pillaged from the butchers' shops; a forest of iron bars and wooden clubs; long ladders for scaling the walls, each carried on the shoulders of a dozen men; lighted torches; tow smeared with pitch, and tar, and brimstone; staves roughly plucked from fence and paving; and even crutches taken from crippled beggars in the streets; composed their arms.   (481)

In this account of riot, then, we are constantly being made to see what is happening. But Dickens also gives us that additional "glimpse of truth" that emerges from the seeing. This would seem to be related, at least in part, to his own feelings about Newgate. In "Criminal Courts," one of the sketches that later comprised *Sketches by Boz*, he recalled his childhood response to the prison:

> We shall never forget the mingled feelings of awe and respect with which we used to gaze on the exterior of Newgate in our schoolboy days. How dreadful its rough heavy walls, and low massive doors, appeared to us—the latter looking as if they were made for the express purpose of letting people in, and never letting them out. . . . The days of [childhood] have passed away . . . but we still retain so much of our original feeling, that to this hour we never pass the building without something like a shudder.   (196)

For Dickens, Newgate would seem to have been so dreadful because of its apparently massive impregnability, its impermeability to those on whom its gates had closed. In breaching the prison, the rioters destroy not only the main gate but quotidian reality, all sense of the stable, normal order of things—and for Dickens this becomes the crucial experience of riot.

In the storming of Newgate, it is not a terrible beauty that is born but the undermining of the very foundations of life in unsettling transformations. When the rioters decide to burn their way into Newgate, they "sprinkle" the woodwork round the doors of the prison with turpentine in an act that is seen as an "infernal christening" (491). Nothing is any longer what it habitually is. As the fire begins to take, "the flames [roar] high and fiercely, blackening the prison-wall, and twining up its lofty front like burning serpents" (492).

Those burning serpents not only continue the infernal imagery but endow the
flames with a vividness and energy that make Scott's description of fire pale
by contrast: at the Tolbooth, we recall, "a huge red glaring bonfire speedily
arose close to the door of [the prison], sending up a tall column of smoke
and flame against its antique turrets . . . . " What follows in Dickens is an
astonishing twenty-five line single sentence that describes the progress of
the fire:

> At first [the rioters] crowded round the blaze, and vented their exultation only
> in their looks: but when it grew hotter and fiercer—when it crackled, leaped,
> and roared, like a great furnace—when it shone upon the opposite houses, and
> lighted up not only the pale and wondering faces at the windows, but the inmost
> corners of each habitation—when through the deep red heat and glow, the fire
> was seen sporting and toying with the door, now clinging to its obdurate surface,
> now gliding off with fierce inconstancy and soaring high into the sky, anon
> returning to fold it in its burning grasp and lure it to its ruin—when it shone
> and gleamed so brightly that the church clock of St. Sepulchre's so often
> pointing to the hour of death, was legible as in broad day, and the vane upon
> its steeple-top glittered in the unwonted light like something richly jewel-
> led—when the blackened stone and sombre brick grew ruddy in the deep reflec-
> tion, and windows shone like burnished gold, dotting the longest distance in
> the fiery vista with their specks of brightness—when wall and tower, and roof
> and chimney-stack, seemed drunk, and in the flickering glare appeared to reel
> and stagger—when scores of objects, never seen before, burst out upon the
> view, and things the most familiar put on some new aspect—then the mob
> began to join the whirl, and with loud yells, and shouts, and clamour, such as
> happily is seldom heard, bestirred themselves to feed the fire, and keep it at its
> height.   (492)

The fire here is demonic in its transformations. At first it is a rioter, leaping
and roaring as it crackles; then it is a reveller, sporting and toying with the
great door. Then the riotous fire turns amazingly into a lover, at one point
clinging to the door, then gliding away with "fierce inconstancy," only to
come back and "fold it in its burning grasp" prior to "[luring] it to its ruin."
All around is transformed too. The church clock, no longer in the dark, can
be read "as in broad day." The black stone of the walls grows ruddy, and
windows, as if touched by alchemy, shine "like burnished gold." Finally,
the very prison itself "[seems] drunk," as it appears "to reel and stagger."
It hardly needs the final comment of the narrator to inform us that "things
the most familiar put on some new aspect." Indeed, the remarkable long
sentence itself in which all this is conveyed epitomizes, in its refusal to break
itself into customary divisions of shorter linked sentences, the abrogation of
the habitual. Dickens has not only made us see riot but experience it.

    This analysis would suggest that Scott and Dickens, in narrating historic
events, write in different modes and that their approach to historic material

is radically different. Scott, in respect of the historic constituents of his fiction, is closer in approach to an historian than is Dickens. Dickens seems to strike an ideal balance, in the presentation of his historic material, between verifiable authenticity and imaginative freedom, vividly illustrating Paul Fussell's insistence in *The Great War* on "the necessity of fiction in any memorable testimony about fact." *Barnaby Rudge* is not a favorite, to say the least, among readers of Dickens, but his depiction of the riots should be seen as a major achievement.

NOTES

1. James Kerr remarks that "the lengthy discursive footnotes which appear in the Waverley novels might seem to indicate a deep anxiety on Scott's part about the perceived historicity of his work" (21).
2. John Butt and Kathleen Tillotson view the integration of the two parts of the narrative more narrowly: "By reserving the history till later [Dickens] conveys the irony of the common assumption that private lives are immune from public events" (87).
3. Jerome H. Buckley confines the idea of madness to the exploitation of Barnaby by such as Hugh and Dennis: "Barnaby serves in his 'silliness' as counterpart or analogue to a madness far deeper than his own, the militant unreason that enlists his innocent and witless support" (33).

WORKS CITED

Buckley, Jerome H. " 'Quoth the Raven': The Role of Grip in *Barnaby Rudge.*" In *Dickens Studies Annual: Essays on Victorian Fiction*, 21 (1992).

Butt, John and Kathleen Tillotson. *Dickens at Work*. London: Methuen, 1957; rpt 1968.

Conrad, Joseph. *The Nigger of the "Narcissus."* London: Dent, 1950; rpt 1964.

Dickens, Charles. *Barnaby Rudge*. London: Oxford UP, 1954; rpt. 1961.

———. "Criminal Courts." In *Sketches by Boz*. London: Oxford UP, 1957; rpt. 1966.

Fussell, Paul. *The Great War and Modern Memory*. New York and London: Oxford UP, 1975.

James, Henry. "The Art of Fiction." In *The Future of the Novel: Essays on the Art of Fiction*. Ed. Leon Edel. New York: Vintage, 1956.

Joyce, James. *Stephen Hero.* Ed. Theodore Spencer. New York: New Directions, 1944.

Kerr, James. *Fiction against History: Scott as Storyteller.* Cambridge: Cambridge University Press, 1989.

Scott, Walter. *The Heart of Midlothian.* London and Edinburgh: Adam and Charles Black, 1893.

———. *Old Mortality.* Boston: Dana Estes, 1893.

———. *Waverley: Or 'Tis Sixty Years Since.* New York: Heritage, 1961.

"They lost the whole": Telling Historical (Un)Truth in *Barnaby Rudge*

George Scott Christian

Critics have long struggled over the status of Barnaby Rudge, *both in the Dickens canon and as historical fiction. The novel, however, defies easy categorization, partly because* Barnaby Rudge *is a comic expression of history's essential unnarratability. In the novel Dickens rejects the possibility of either a complete apprehension of the historical field or a comprehensive knowledge of it. This rejection is expressed in the voice of Grip, who proves either unwilling or unable to narrate the "tale" of the Gordon Riots. Grip's narrative demonstrates that prescriptive narratives, such as "history," cannot transcend epistemological limitations on individual perception and understanding; instead, in order to teach us anything at all, it must be limited to a sympathetic exchange between individuals. Dickens imagines "truth-telling" as a comic process of breaking down the illusory coherence of all historical narratives—particularly those of the novel's master manipulators, who seek to commandeer history to serve their personal desires. In short, Grip's tale teaches us to "lose the whole" in order to gain it, to avoid being co-opted and controlled by narratives that promise social and moral improvement, but deliver only recurrent private and public violence and oppression.*

As Steven Marcus has observed, *Barnaby Rudge* has been read as divided between its fascination with the Gordon Riots of 1780 and a byzantine plot involving a murder, two pairs of star-crossed lovers, an "idiot," and a raven.

Dickens Studies Annual, Volume 32, Copyright © 2002 by AMS Press, Inc. All rights reserved.

Dickens's divided attention in the novel contributes to Marcus's conclusion that *Barnaby Rudge* deserves lesser status as the work of an "apprentice."[1] at the same time, however, Marcus is among the first critics to accord the novel any significant standing in the Dickens canon.[2] Similarly, while Avrom Fleishman gives the novel a prominent place in his analysis of the historical novel, he concludes that *Barnaby Rudge* reveals an uncertain Dickens, torn between his fear of irremediable social breakdown and his sense that the past is always with us, giving society continuity even in the midst of apparently cataclysmic change.[3] *Barnaby Rudge* thus recognizes—and even dwells upon—the anarchic tendencies inherent in modern culture, while holding out the possibility, however meager, for progress beyond the ignorance and bigotry of the past.

Like Marcus, Fleishman tends to subordinate *Barnaby Rudge* to Dickens's far more popular historical narrative, *A Tale of Two Cities*. Fleishman contends that the later novel "raises history to myth and discovers a redemptive pattern in the holocaust that allows for transcendence within history, if not beyond it" (114). Presumably, what makes *A Tale* a greater work is its visualization of history as a continual process of renewal, symbolized ultimately by Sidney Carton's act of self-sacrifice. But I would argue that *Barnaby Rudge* gives away very little to its progeny, either in terms of its vision of the historical process or its formal attributes.[4] Rather than attempting, as Marcus and Fleishman respectively do, to reclaim the novel as an important phase in Dickens's development as a novelist or as an historical narrative worthy of comparison with those of Scott and Carlyle, I read *Barnaby Rudge* as a comic expression of history's essential unnarratability. In the novel Dickens rejects the possibility of either a complete apprehension of the historical field or a comprehensive knowledge of it. This rejection is expressed in the voice of Grip, upon whom the narrative centers the authority of historical knowledge. Despite this authority, however, Grip proves either unwilling or unable to narrate the "tale" of the Gordon Riots. History, it seems, cannot transcend epistemological limitations on individual perception and understanding; instead, in order to teach us anything at all, it must be limited to a sympathetic exchange between individuals. In reducing perception and narration of historical events to the level of individual human relationships, Dickens imagines "truth-telling" as a comic process of breaking down the illusory coherence of all historical narratives—particularly those of the novel's master manipulators, who seek to commandeer history to serve their personal desires.[5]

My use of the term "comic" to describe Dickens's narrative requires further amplification. Unquestionably, Dickens is a master of comic voices and devices, even for a novelist in his "apprenticeship." *Barnaby Rudge* is replete with uses of satire, irony, and the grotesque. The novel is peopled with characters suffering from excessive "humors": John Willet's exaggerated self-importance, Sim Tappertit's ludicrous vanity, or Mrs. Varden's single-minded devotion to the Protestant Manual, for example. The novel's marriage plot is itself a conventional mode of comic emplotment. At various points in the narrative, Grip provides a comic release of tension, a kind of burlesque show in the midst of the novel's mayhem. All of these "comic" elements can be understood as falling squarely within the eighteenth-century English tradition of Fielding and Sterne, as described by romantic critics such as Hazlitt and Hunt and later by Thackeray. However, in my view Dickens's understanding and use of the comic go far beyond these narrative effects and humorous characterizations. They rather go directly to the novel's moral function, as Dr. Johnson succinctly stated: "to please (through surprise) and instruct the reader" (20).

In other words, Dickens seeks to obey the Addisonian imperative that comic literature must civilize society by modeling individual acts of sympathy, as opposed to fostering the socially corrosive effects of Hobbesian exultation in one's own superiority, as savage wit and satire do.[6] But to do so, Dickens must persuade the reader *not to believe* in the seductive but false coherence of historical narrative, which tends to reinforce old Hobbesian habits, while at the same time making that argument in familiar narrative terms. Narrating the unnarratable thus creates an inexorable tension in *Barnaby Rudge*, a tension that contributes to the text's extreme ranges of tone, subject matter, and emotion. Considered in this context, Grip becomes the only possible teller of this tale. Otherwise, the omniscient, detached narrator would be as guilty of prescribing history as are the text's Hobbesian "tyrants"[7]—Gordon, Chester, John Willet, Mrs. Varden—who seek mastery, both in familial and personal contexts and in wider social and political ones. It is left to Grip to silence the tyrants without setting up others in their places. His narrative solution, as we will see, is comic silence, an intersubjective, sympathetic space in the text that is relatively free of external prescriptive narratives.

Since its publication, critics and readers of *Barnaby Rudge* have puzzled over the role and function of Grip, the title character's pet raven. In an important sense, the narrative is mediated by the irrational yet strangely prophetic words of this apparently immortal bird. The preface opens with a frame narrative worthy of Scott, complete with an obscure reference to a seemingly irrelevant subject: "The late Mr. Waterton having, some time ago, expressed his opinion that ravens are gradually becoming extinct in England, I offered the few following words about my experience of these birds" (39). The narrator goes on to explain that the "raven in this story is a compound of two great originals," an account of whose lives and deaths is then given. At this point, the narrative abruptly shifts to the Gordon Riots, foreshadowing the sudden shift in the novel between the private and public plots: "No account of the Gordon Riots having been to my knowledge introduced into any Work of Fiction, and the subject presenting very extraordinary and remarkable features, I was led to project this Tale" (40). The narrator thus appears to announce that this "Tale" is about two things: ravens and the Gordon Riots of 1780. More specifically, Charles Waterton, a naturalist whose essay on the absence of ravens ostensibly triggers the narrator's account of his personal experience with the talking, acquisitive birds, and the absence of a fictional account of the Gordon Riots are explicitly connected. At the beginning of the novel, then, we are confronted with a "ravenless" narrator whose lack of a narrative of the riots inspires a novel that will give us both—that is, both a raven and a narrative of the Gordon Riots. *Barnaby Rudge* is first concerned with filling a lack or an absence, with giving voice to a silence.

This being said, the question becomes: whose voice fills that narrative void? In chapter 6, the redoubtable locksmith Gabriel Varden is closeted with Edward Chester, who is recovering from an attack by the mysterious stranger first encountered at the Maypole Inn in chapter 1. Varden himself had already seen the stranger on the road in chapter 2 and again in chapter 5 at Mary Rudge's door.

> "It is as I feared. The very man was here to-night," thought the locksmith, changing colour. "What dark history is this!"
>
> "Halloa?" cried a hoarse voice in his ear. "Halloa, halloa, halloa! Bow wow wow. What's the matter here! Hal-loa!"
>
> The speaker—who made the locksmith start as if he had been some supernatural agent—was a large raven, who had perched upon the top of the easy-chair, unseen by him and Edward, and listened with a polite attention and a most extraordinary appearance of comprehending every word, to all they had said up to this point; turning his head from one to the other, as if his office were to judge between them, and it were of the very last importance that he should not lose a word. (98–99)

The comic effect of this moment lies, of course, in its incongruity. Varden has divined a "dark history" involving the stranger and the locksmith's former love interest. The dramatic tension of this realization is suddenly punctuated by the "hoarse" voice of Grip, whose barking query both verbalizes the question in the reader's mind ("What's the matter here?") and distracts attention from it. The narrator's commentary on the apparent "supernatural" prescience of the bird is likewise comically incongruous, releasing the tension of the dramatic moment and diverting narrative energy from the mysterious and potentially malevolent stranger/Mary Rudge relationship to the whimsical and strangely disquieting Grip/Barnaby one. In this narrative displacement we see not only a Kantian dissipation of pent-up expectation into nothing, but a disruption or "rekeying" (to use a metaphor more closely suited to the novel) of the "dark history" Varden (as well as Dickens) attempts to narrate.

It is important to note that Varden's rhetorical mode is not necessarily interrogative, but exclamatory. Instead of asking what might explain and connect the series of events he has witnessed, Varden merely comments upon the obscure nature of those events, as though altogether surrendering the possibility of explanation or causation. Grip breaks in upon this observation, then exclaims further: "Halloa, halloa, halloa! What's the matter here! Keep up your spirits. Never say die. Bow wow wow. I'm a devil, I'm a devil, I'm a devil. Hurrah!" (99). Varden's response is to validate, at least provisionally, Grip's narrative: "I more than half believe he speaks the truth. . . . Do you see how he looks at me, as if he knew what I was saying?" (99). The "truth" here may be that Grip is a devil, that Grip understands what Varden and Edward have been saying, or more generally that Grip somehow "knows" the obscure history suggested by the events linking Chigwell and London. Perhaps Grip cannot only narrate what the matter is—the facts that constitute the field of historical inquiry—but the causal connection between the facts, the story that contextualizes historical matter and inspires belief in the truth of the historical narrative. Varden more than "half believes" in the truth spoken by Grip, further investing the raven with a narrative authority that the supposedly omniscient narrator reinforces time and again throughout the novel.[8]

Barnaby, moreover, is already a true believer in Grip's truth-telling ability:

"But who can make him come! He calls me, and makes me go where he will. He goes on before, and I follow. He's the master, and I'm the man. Is that the truth, Grip?"

The raven gave a short, comfortable, confidential kind of croak;—a most expressive croak, which seemed to say, "You needn't let these fellows into our secrets. We understand each other. It's all right."   (99–100)

In a novel replete with "master-man" relationships, Barnaby's characterization of his relationship with Grip is both of thematic and epistemological importance.[9] *Barnaby Rudge* is "about" many things: the consequences of religious intolerance, motivations for mob violence, the clash of middle-class values and working-class aspirations, the basis for authority in private and public relationships, the virtues of the criminal justice system, the psychology of murder. But it is also about, as Barnaby puts it, the power to "call" and make someone follow, the creation and maintenance of a *persuasive* authority. This imperative to persuade compels the narrative itself. We have already seen that Dickens felt compelled to supply a lack of narrative about the Gordon Riots. While he tells us that part of his purpose is "to teach a good lesson'' (40), Dickens conveys a real sense that the Gordon Riots cannot exist as ''reality'' in the absence of a ''Work of Fiction'':

> That what we falsely call a religious cry is easily raised by men who have no religion, and who in their daily practice set at nought the commonest principles of right and wrong; that it is begotten of intolerance and persecution; that is senseless, besotted, inveterate and unmerciful; all History teaches us. But perhaps we do not know it in our hearts too well, to profit by even so humble an example as the ''No Popery'' riots of Seventeen Hundred and Eighty.   (40)

To frame ''History'' within a fictional narrative is to inscribe that history ''in our hearts.'' In other words, until history is given voice by the novelist, it is a silence, a ''dark history'' of events and occurrences as mysterious as those Gabriel Varden meets with on the road between Chigwell and London. The novelist thus becomes the caller, the truth-teller who summons the reader to belief in the ''truth'' of a consciously fictionalized history over a simple account of historical events. Just as Grip gains mastery over Barnaby, and even Varden, by the persuasive power of his prophetic, all-knowing speech, Dickens attempts to master the reader by providing an account of the Gordon Riots that is more ''true'' than that contained in history books. In reading and internalizing that truth, the reader is to be converted to a renewed vision of community, one that rejects mob violence and practices the ''commonest principles of right and wrong.''

While this vision may appear pietistic and pander to bourgeois moral standards, it is never that simple with Dickens. Returning to Grip's entrance into the novel, Dickens raises the epistemological question of ''truth'' at the very point of comic disruption of the novel's ''dark history.'' By shifting, or at least suggesting a shift, of the situs of truth from Varden, whom the narrator has introduced as an archetypal English ''yeoman'' (''bluff, hale hearty, and in a green old age: at peace with himself, and evidently disposed to be so with all the world'') and the novel's primary representative of bourgeois morality (63), to Grip, whom we first see ''exulting in his infernal character'' (99), Dickens complicates both the possibility of narrating ''truth'' *and* the ''truth'' of conventional, middle-class morality. While much has been said of Grip's association with evil and prophecy, I would contend that the real significance of the raven is as a mediator and projector of Dickens's comic perception of history in *Barnaby Rudge*. Through the raven's voice, Dickens rejects representation of history as either a description of objects within a given historical field or as a strictly moral lesson.[10]

This rejection is exemplified in the ''dialogue'' between Grip and Barnaby in chapter 57, as Barnaby stands guard in the stable while Hugh, Dennis, and the rioters sack the Maypole Inn and fire The Warren:

This call (to dinner), the bird obeyed with great alacrity; crying, as he sidled up to his master, ''I'm a devil, I'm a Polly, I'm a kettle, I'm a Protestant, No Popery!'' Having learnt this latter sentiment from the gentry among whom he had lived of late, he delivered it with uncommon emphasis.
''Well said, Grip!'' cried his master, as he fed him with the daintiest bits. ''Well said, old boy!''
''Never say die, bow wow wow, keep up your spirits, Grip Grip Grip, Holloa! We'll all have tea, I'm a Protestant kettle, No Popery!'' cried the raven.
''Gordon for ever, Grip!'' cried Barnaby.
The raven, placing his head upon the ground, looked at his master sideways, as though he would have said, ''Say that again!'' Perfectly understanding his desire, Barnaby repeated the phrase a great many times. The bird listened with profound attention; sometimes repeating the popular cry in a low voice, as if to compare the two, and try if it would at all help him to this new accomplishment; sometimes flapping his wings, or barking; and sometimes in a kind of desperation drawing a multitude of corks, with extraordinary viciousness.   (518–19)

Here Grip bursts into a dizzying revelation of his multiple identities, as if Dickens himself were shouting, ''I'm John Willett! I'm Gabriel Varden! I'm John Chester! I'm Miggs! I'm a talking raven! No History!'' Grip's ability to mimic identity is of course akin to the novelist's, whose pervasive mimicry is the voicing of history as a work of fiction. As the exchange progresses, Grip elaborates and recombines these identities in bizarre ways, becoming a Protestant kettle, a tea-drinking dog, a rioting parrot. But when Barnaby attempts to persuade Grip to repeat ''Gordon for ever,'' the raven balks and the narrative prevaricates. We are told that Grip repeats the ''popular cry . . . as if to compare the two, and try if it would at all help him to this new accomplishment,'' and then he flaps, barks, and draws corks. Even though Gordon ironically appears at this moment in the narrative, Grip never utters his name, and it is unclear whether he ever achieves that ''new accomplishment'' at all. Moreover, Grip's physical reaction to Gordon's name is described as ''vicious,'' further suggesting both an insuperable barrier to naming Lord George and a rejection of mimicking Gordon's particular identity. Indeed, if we accept that Grip holds a certain narrative authority in the novel, Grip's paralysis at Gordon's name represents a peculiar compound silence in the text, a text whose ostensible design is to provide a fictional narrative of the Gordon Riots for individual and collective moral gain. In other words, Dickens uses Grip's voice to elide the very namesake of the riots that are the novel's stated cause and motivation, as if to say that history, or even a fictional narrative of history, can have neither cause nor motivation. What the narrator gives, Grip takes away.

This passage also seems to invert the master-man relationship between Grip and Barnaby, which is established at Grip's initial appearance in the text. In contrast, it is the *narrator* who describes Barnaby as the master, not

Barnaby himself, as he does in chapter 5. This may not appear that significant, but it is an example of the way Dickens again compromises the authority of his own narrative voice by devolving it onto other characters. We already know that Barnaby follows Grip's call, and that in this instance it is the servant Barnaby's role to feed his master, much as Lazarillo obtains food for his various destitute masters in the picaresque novel, *Lazarillo de Tormes*. In fact, the Grip/Barnaby relationship bears many picaresque characteristics, from the episodic nature of their wanderings to the hand-to-mouth quality of their economic status. We also see something of the picaresque's inversion of master and servant, as the lower appears both to sustain, control, and manipulate the higher, who is generally either corrupt or incompetent. In this context, for example, we see Grip providing food for Barnaby and his mother by performing along the London road in chapter 47, and again betraying Hugh and Dennis by uncovering their stash of stolen goods in chapter 57. These picaresque features serve to fragment narrative coherence, as authorial voices are continually compromised and undermined.

This dissolution of narrative coherence through inversion of authorial voices is likewise mirrored in one of the novel's major thematic movements, manipulation of both Gordon and the rioters by Gashford, whom (not coincidentally) Dennis the Hangman calls "Muster." Of course, Gashford is nominally Gordon's servant, just as Grip is Barnaby's, Tappertit is Varden's, and Miggs is Mrs. Varden's. This pattern of nominal authority is consistent with the father-son relations in the novel, in which the sons, Joe Willett and Edward Chester, imitate the rioters' rejection of patriarchal authority in their rebellion against their "masters."[11] In a novel crossed with power struggles of such immense intensity, the reader is faced with the daunting task of finding a "muster" whose voice is uncompromised by the fear and intimidation that marks the novel's patriarchal, master-servant relationships. Of course, authorial manipulation involves, in one sense, a tacit agreement between the novelist and the reader. The reader expects to follow the novelist's call, to cede authority to teller of the tale. But what happens when the teller's authority is manipulated or subverted? What happens when the nominal author, the ostensible master, becomes the servant of another, a more powerful subversive force? In a picaresque novel the ostensible master is usually beaten to within an inch of his life or stolen blind, or both. In *Barnaby Rudge*, however, the stakes are even higher. For Dickens, the answer to the question is clear. When the teller of the tale, the history-writer, is unable or unwilling to command authority, the result is a riot. By ignoring Gordon's pleas for order and nonviolence, the rioters "rewrite" Gordon's history to validate Gashford's and their own personal motives, which largely involve looting and drinking. By ignoring the novelist-historian's plea for tolerance and adherence to "the commonest principles of right and wrong," as demonstrated by the "lesson" of the Gordon riots, Chartists, trade unionists, and other oppressed groups will likewise rewrite that history—and, so it would appear, succumb to the same selfish, Hobbesian motivations as their current masters do. Both Gordon and the historians of "his" riots ultimately fail to command belief in their respective narratives, leading to continued, recurrent personal and public violence.[12] Now Dickens, the creator of a "Work of Fiction," supplying the lack that Gordon and the historians could not fill, is faced with the same dilemma.

Critics of *Barnaby Rudge* detect this devolution of narrative control, or perhaps more accurately, the dilemma of controlling the uncontrollable.[13] Readers frequently admire the account of the riots, while dismissing the novel's melodramatic elements as flat and contrived. To such readers the novel has two distinct pieces, the five-year hiatus between chapters 32 and 33 dividing them as cleanly as if the text had been sliced in half. More contemporary readings of the novel emphasize the complexity of the plot, the thematic connections between the two halves of the novel, and the carefully worked out design of the "apprentice" novelist. But these readings do not fully account for Dickens's dividedness over the narrative's authoritative voice. In my view Dickens in part devolves such authority to dramatize in the narrative the very implications of authorial irresponsibility he warns against in the novel's preface. This dramatization is effected through Grip's ironic mastery of the text, a mastery characterized by Grip's inability or unwillingness to narrate the events over which he is "master." If Grip does know all, as Varden more than half believes, he remains silent. As we have seen, Grip cannot even utter Gordon's name, denying the historicity of both the man and the events attached to his name. The riots are thus plucked out of history, decontextualized, presented as a miasma of erroneously motivated human desires for personal dominance. History is imagined not as a coherent narrative of causes and effects, but as an uncontrollable "'mad'" riot, which takes a "'child's doll'" for "'the image of some unholy saint'" and roasts canaries alive until they scream "'like infants'" (600). Dickens's history of a parodic, inverted, "'devilish'" Inquisition is Grip's tale, a narrative of "'brimstone birth'" in which the truth-teller is struck dumb by the awfulness of that truth.

The intensity of the language used to describe the riots conceals the unnarratability of the "'dreadful spectacle'" the narrator has unleashed (606). The narrative loses focus, as we see when the mob is assailing the vintner's house in chapter 67:

> As he spoke, and drew Mr. Haredale back, they had both a glimpse of the street. It was but a glimpse, but it showed them the crowd, gathering and
> ᐧ clustering around the house: some of the armed men pressing to the front to break down the doors and windows, some bringing brands from the nearest
> ᐧ fire, some with lifted faces following their course upon the roof and pointing

them out to their companions: all raging and roaring like the flames they lighted up. They saw some men thirsting for the treasures of strong liquor which they knew was stored within; they saw others, who had been wounded, sinking down into the opposite doorways and dying, solitary wretches, in the midst of all that vast assemblage; here a frightened woman trying to escape; and there a lost child; and there a drunken ruffian, unconscious of the death-wound on his head, raving and fighting to the last. All these things, and even such trivial incidents as a man with his hat off, or turning around, or stooping down, or shaking hands with another, they marked distinctly; yet in a glance so brief, that, in the act of stepping back, they lost the whole, and saw but the pale faces of each other, and the red sky above them.   (609)

Here the historical event is seen in a single, momentary glimpse as a collision of unconnected perceptions and "trivial incidents." But just as quickly as it comes into focus, the coherence of the vision is lost, leaving only Haredale and the vintner to look into the "pale face" of the other. The "vast assemblage" of rioters disappears into the limited mode of individual perception, which ultimately can truly apprehend and internalize only one other face. If Dickens indeed fails to offer a coherent narrative of historical events, it is because individual experience cannot truly see the whole, cannot interpret and project an historical event in narrative. All individual experience can do is make a single connection with a single individual in a single moment of time.[14] Hence the novel's closing gesture towards marriage and reproduction is at once a conventional "comic" culmination of the melodramatic love plot and a rejection of the novel's status as "history." To attempt to master history, to impose it upon individual consciousness as an ordered whole, results in the same old round that Dickens sees in the Gordon Riots, the Chartist unrest, and the troubled and often violent individual and collective relations to private and public authority in general. It is to "lose the whole," with catastrophic individual and social effects.[15]

By reducing the field of perception to the creation and maintenance of a single intersubjective relationship, Dickens reimagines history as a comic process of socialization through sympathetic self-projection and its attendant internalization of individual differences. Consequently, the only value in a narrative of the Gordon Riots is to demonstrate their essential irrelevance to genuine social improvement. In other words, it is not the tale of the Gordon Riots that instructs the reader, but the novel's true "surprise": real history is made in fleeting moments of intersubjectivity, when the mind focuses on and exchanges sympathy with another. Dickens emphatically underscores this "moral" at the end of the novel, when Grip is rendered "profoundly silent" for a year. The raven's silence creates a space for the narrator to insert his fictional attempt to re-establish a productive, pastoral society around a restored and improved Maypole Inn. But at "the expiration of that term . . . the bird himself advanced with fantastic steps to the very door of the bar, and there cried, 'I'm a devil, I'm a devil, I'm a devil!' with extraordinary rapture'' (738). The effect of the ending is thus ironized and collapsed by the eruption of the raven's infernal incantation. When the raven's silence is broken, so is the illusion of narrative—and historical—coherence that the conclusion is designed to sustain. Rather than imagining a conventional, comic restoration of an ordered society, Dickens sees comedy as essential to destroying the coercive relationships upon which individual and social structures are based, to demystifying the tyrannical myth of the patriarchal master-servant hierarchy wherever it is found.[16]

When Miggs is finally rejected and turned out into the street, Gabriel stifles Mrs. Varden's compassion by saying, "It's a thing to laugh at, Martha, not to care for" (722). Miggs, who despite her vanity holds the "key" to many of the novel's major characters, seems to end up as an object of Hobbesian derision. But Gabriel then adds, "What does it matter? You had seen your fault before." Here Gabriel means that Hobbesian laughter is out of place because Mrs. Varden has already recognized her "fault" in allowing Miggs to manipulate her and no longer requires the corrective of laughter. Miggs is not laughable in the Hobbesian sense because she is no longer "inferior"; Mrs. Varden's awareness of her own unwitting complicity in Miggs's schemes, the consequence of her overweening pride, chastens her and, in an important sense, saves Miggs. Miggs's fate, in fact, is mild compared to that of the novel's other master manipulators, who are silenced by more violent, Hobbesian means. Indeed, it is arguable that the most brutal punishment is reserved for Sim Tappertit, who is left lying legless in the street, "exposed to the derision of those urchins who delight in mischief" (734). The utterly objectified Tappertit is the sole remaining artifact of the novel's central historical event, the cause *and* effect of the very riots that the conventional ending of the novel tries so hard to forget. The laughter of the street urchins is a savage form of retribution, crueler perhaps than the death penalties exacted against Chester, Gashford, Hugh, and Rudge. Such retribution redeems nothing, leaves no space for the renewal and regeneration of personal and social bonds. Miggs's treatment, while hardly compassionate (she finds a place as a turnkey in a women's prison, comically regaining mastery as a chastener of false vanity) salvages something in that it does not make her solely a grotesque object. In the world of *Barnaby Rudge*, this is an affirmation that, however limited, should not be gainsaid.

This contrast between Miggs's and Tappertit's respective fates helps illuminate Dickens's resolution of the narrative tension in *Barnaby Rudge*. It would be easy to say (as many critics have) that Dickens ultimately accepts, in Hayden White's terms, an ironic mode of historical representation. According to White, irony expresses "the irreducible relativism of all knowledge" (38), the inability to narrate any objective truth beyond the perceptions and impressions of a single subjective mind. Grip's refusal to cry "Gordon for ever" could be read as embracing such an inability, and Tappertit's humiliation, as well as that of the novel's other would-be tyrants, shows us that irony itself can easily become a violent Hobbesian game of self-aggrandizement at the expense of others—especially if we are always at the mercy of a more powerful aggressor's narrative. But Dickens is true to his vision of the false coherence of such narrative to the last. As we have seen, Grip's year-long silence, broken finally by the unnerving repetition of "I'm a devil," provides the antidote to an ironic narrative of history. Grip, who bedevils the text's every suggestion of coherence, ends by exploding even ironic historiography. "For ever" is indeed a false coherence, but truth-telling does not have to be. Such truth lies somewhere within the intensely personal exchange of sympathy between "pale faces," which lose the whole in order to gain it.

Grip's tale indeed "teaches a good lesson," one of which Addison himself might have been proud. In the wake of the Gordon Riots, corrosive Hobbesian comedy is no longer the prescription for individual and social improvement.[17] Only when the tyrants of history end their ceaseless, repetitive attempts to order history in a way that dehumanizes Miggs and Tappertit, Joe Willett and Edward Chester, Hugh and Barnaby, will public and personal violence be brought under the sway of "the commonest principles of right and wrong." In *Barnaby Rudge*, that end is at least provisionally achieved by the raven's comic silence. Comic silence clears a space for intersubjective relations, however imperfect they may be, and allows for the possibility of self and social redemption. But Grip reminds us also that the devil is never far away. It lies just beneath the surface of every ego, waiting to seize an opportunity to revert to Hobbesian savagery. Comic silence, like sanity itself, is fragile in *Barnaby Rudge*, always vulnerable to predation and subversion. Even so, it is the apprentice's achievement that we might profit by even so humble a history as this.

NOTES

1. Marcus uses the term "apprenticeship" to describe the production of a novel that problematizes the function and social efficacy of the master-apprentice relationship. If Dickens is an apprentice, who is the master? And if masters, as Dickens suggests in *Barnaby Rudge*, have questionable authority, or even abuse authority, over their apprentices, what does this say about the status of the novel and the "apprentice" who wrote it? See also Rice, who views the novel as the "end of Dickens's apprenticeship as a novelist" (173).

2. *Barnaby Rudge* has received increasing attention from critics in recent years. For example, John Reed reads the novel as imagining a society fixated on "retribution

and revenge'' at the expense of Christian "love and forgiveness" (132). Others have argued that *Barnaby Rudge* is a reaction to the tradition of the historical novel as developed by Scott. For a negative comparison of *Barnaby Rudge* with Scott's historical novels, see Newman. On Dickens's anxiety over Scott's influence, see Michasiw. For a reading of *Barnaby Rudge* as a revision of *The Heart of Midlothian*, in which Dickens rejects Scott's conventions for historical fiction, see Case.

3. Fleishman writes: "The dominant emotion with which the novel leaves us is neither the hopeful sense of an open future, in line with Victorian ideas of progress, nor a nostalgic resistance to change (which is here regarded as inevitable and constant), but a sense of the great weight to be moved in any transcendence of the past. If the novel is an expression of Dickens's deep-set fears of the end of social order, it also bears his sense of the sheer persistence of the past, even amid change, which makes for social permanence." (113)

4. . For a compelling argument in favor of the novel's structural unity, see Rice.

5. Similarly, Case argues that Dickens rejects Scott's attempts to impose coherent narrative patterns on historical events, which are essentially uncontrollable and subject to social and economic upheaval. Instead of positing a developing historical consciousness, as Scott does, Dickens attempts to replace it with an "ahistorical family" and a "moral code which is supposed to transcend historically conditioned, class- or culture-bound values" (144). Ultimately, Dickens figures Scott himself as the madman Lord Gordon, "undoubtedly well-meaning, but dangerously deluded, and all too persuasive" (145).

6. Tave and Paulson have fully developed the argument that Addison, Steele, and others developed a theory of "amiable humor," which encourages sympathy, as a direct response to the perceived savagery of Hobbes's rule that comedy arises from a vicious feeling of superiority over the weak and deformed. According to Tave, "By the middle of the nineteenth century, it was a commonplace that the best comic works present amiable originals, often models of good nature, whose little peculiarities are not satirically instructive, but objects of delight and love" (iii).

7. Kincaid uses the term "tyranny" to describe the novel's preoccupation with oppression, both private and public. I borrow it here to describe the tendency of Dickens's manipulators to seek control over the "history" of the Gordon Riots.

8. The issue of narrative authority is discussed by McGowan, who argues that "the narrative in *Barnaby Rudge* evidences a drive toward completion, a need to connect disparate fragments, to dispel ignorance. The narrative of this historical novel reveals an 'historical bias' in its reliance on history's ability to explain the present. . . . However, in the temporal schema such as we have here, appearances, while they do not contain the whole truth, are all we have, are all that is present. Appearances are synecdochic over time; they are only part of the whole, but the only part which exists in the present moment. All the pieces of information necessary to determine a thing or an event's meaning do not exist in the present; the search for meaning is always an historical investigation, with success dependent on uncovering those elements of the past, now absent, which have constituted the present. And since those elements no longer exist, they must be reconstructed

in terms of evidence offered by the present'' (38). This analysis, solid as it is, overlooks the silence at the center of the text. The mystery of history cannot be reconstructed, much less told, if the narrator chooses not to tell it. This is the case with Grip.

9. Juliet McMaster construes Grip as "the canny extension of Barnaby's simple mind" (2). She thus accords Grip an important role, as she argues that Barnaby's "vision," his ability to see beyond the mere perception of the actual, is the privileged narrative mode in the novel. "Recurrently we are shown that his visions are previews, his shadows foreshadowings of actual events. He is not merely an idiot, but the Holy Fool endowed with a path to truth more direct and immediate than that available to educated minds" (2). For McMaster, Barnaby's narrative of visions and, by analogy, his "extension" of Grip's menacing prophecies represent the power of the unconscious to project and shape reality in the conscious world. Even the riots become "a dreamlike emanation from the unconscious" (10). This relation of the unconscious and the conscious likewise accounts for the novel's supernatural elements. See also Magnet, who treats Grip as "a satirical commentary on Barnaby, who with his defect of soul is a man who is not quite human" (79), just as Grip is not quite animal.

10. Buckley likewise takes a positive view of Grip's role in the novel, although he doesn't accord Grip much more than a choric presence in the narrative. See Buckley also on the representation of ravens in English literature as associated with omen and symbol.

11. On the relationship of the riots to patriarchal oppression of women in the novel, particularly Dolly, Mrs. Varden, and Miggs, see Flynn.

12. This sense of the endless repetition of violence and tyranny has led some critics to conclude that Dickens sees no possibility for community within history. Kincaid expresses the majority view when he states: "The root causes of the sickness are indicated, but not only is there no programme developed to deal with them, there is even a slight sense that the illness is finally incurable, the nation really already lost" (107).

13. See, for example, Dransfield, who argues that Dickens sees social violence as a result of an individual's "loss of self-possessed reason" and the "consequent loosing of dangerous 'passions' " (69). Dransfield situates the novel within a larger nineteenth-century discourse of social reform, particularly criminal law and prison reform and improvements in the treatment of the mentally ill. Dickens's novel, criticized for failing to resolve the problems it identifies, in fact implies such resolution in the humane regulation of "society's pathologies" (70).

14. Rice argues that Dickens employs a "spectatorial" narrative mode in the novel. This mode implies that the individual observer of history is the "creator of his world," much as the novel's "narrator-god" both controls and judges the characters' actions (183–84). In my reading, the "unity" of Dickens's narrative depends on its abjuration of unity beyond the shared perception of two observers observing each other within a fleeting moment of history. But in that fleeting moment, a comic connection—a community—can be created, if not quite sustained.

15. Indeed, Kincaid contends that the novel's rhetorical structure enacts its thematic content by first presenting private comic themes and then violently reconstructing

them as public disasters. "By laughing at John Willet we have been supporting tyranny; by laughing at Sim Tappertit we have been at the same time dismissing its significance. We have, in other words, created with our laughter an assumed world of safety and comfort which is blown apart as violently as Newgate itself. England here becomes the reader and the awful warning becomes sharply personalized as Dickens seeks to make the hidden tendency of our laughter literal: the custard pie *did* contain sulphuric acid, and we are not only responsible for, but richly deserve, the retaliation which follows" (108). Dickens turns our own Hobbesian laughter against us, revealing it as both cause and effect of arbitrary patterns of historical consciousness.

16. In a similar vein, Palmer argues that Dickens rejects Scott's romantic model of historical representation in favor of a "counter text of Social Realism that cuts sharply against the grain of the historical illusions of order, reform, and institutional benevolence that the Victorian age (and its Utilitarian historians) was constantly nurturing and proselytizing. . . . In Dickens's view, the real history of the Victorian age was one veering precariously toward an escalating confusion that would culminate in a thoroughly historical chaos" (15). This New Historicist approach elides the force of Grip's comic silence and the power of aesthetic structures to shape Dickens's accounts of "historical" reality.

17. Indeed, as Magnet concludes in an extended analysis of the novel, "If society does not undertake to fulfill its duty of civilizing and humanizing its citizens, then whole classes of them will remain brutes" (171). This is the Hobbesian condition, but, as we have seen, Dickens's cure involves the humanizing influence of Addisonian sympathy, not socially prescribed remedies.

WORKS CITED

Buckley, Jerome H. " 'Quoth the Raven': The Role of Grip in *Barnaby Rudge*." *Dickens Studies Annual* 21 (1992): 27–35.

Case, Alison. "Against Scott: The Antihistory of *Barnaby Rudge*." *CLIO* 19 (1990): 127–45.

Dickens, Charles. *Barnaby Rudge*. Ed. Gordon Spence. New York: Penguin, 1973.

Dransfield, Scott. "Reading the Gordon Riots in 1841: Social Violence and Moral Management in *Barnaby Rudge*." *Dickens Studies Annual* 27 (1998): 69–95.

Fleishman, Avrom. *The English Historical Novel: Walter Scott to Virginia Woolf.* Baltimore: Johns Hopkins UP, 1971.

Flynn, Judith. "The Sexual Politics of *Barnaby Rudge*." *English Studies in Canada* 16 (1990): 56–73.

Friedberg, Joan B. "Alienation and Integration in *Barnaby Rudge.*" *Dickens Studies Newsletter* 11 (1980): 11–15.

Johnson, Samuel. "Of the Novel." *The Rambler.* Vol. 1. Ed. Donald D. Eddy. New York: Garland, 1978. 19–24.

Kincaid, James R. *Dickens and the Rhetoric of Laughter.* Oxford: Clarendon, 1971.

Magnet, Myron. *Dickens and the Social Order.* Philadelphia: U of Pennsylvania P, 1985.

Marcus, Steven. *Dickens: From Pickwick to Dombey.* New York: Basic, 1965.

McGowan, John P. "Mystery and History in *Barnaby Rudge.*" *Dickens Studies Annual* 9 (1981): 33–52.

McMaster, Juliet. " 'Better to be Silly': From Vision to Reality in *Barnaby Rudge.*" *Dickens Studies Annual* 13 (1984): 1–17.

Michasiw, Kim Ian. "*Barnaby Rudge*: The Sins of the Fathers." *ELH* 56 (1987): 571–92.

Newman, S. J. "*Barnaby Rudge*: Dickens and Scott. *Literature of the Romantic Period 1750–1850.* Eds. R. T. Davies and B. G. Beatty. Liverpool: Liverpool UP, 1976. 171–88.

Palmer, William J. *Dickens and New Historicism.* New York: St. Martin's, 1997.

Paulson, Ronald. *Don Quixote in England: The Aesthetics of Laughter.* Baltimore: Johns Hopkins UP, 1998.

Reed, John R. *Dickens and Thackeray.* Athens: Ohio UP, 1995.

Rice, Thomas Jackson. "The End of Dickens's Apprenticeship: Variable Focus in *Barnaby Rudge.*" *Nineteenth-Century Fiction* 30 (1975): 172–84.

Tave, Stuart M. *The Amiable Humourist: A Study in the Comic Theory and Criticism of the Eighteenth and Early Nineteenth Centuries.* Chicago: U of Chicago P, 1960.

White, Hayden. *Metahistory: The Historical Imagination in Nineteenth-Century Europe.* Baltimore and London: Johns Hopkins UP, 1973.

Of Jews and Ships and Mob Attacks, Of Catholics and Kings: The Curious Career of Lord George Gordon

Jeffrey L. Spear

Though it was the largest civil disturbance since Monmouth's Rebellion, the Gordon Riots constitute a neglected chapter of English history, one most often invoked as background to Barnaby Rudge. *This essay looks around Dickens's novel and the tradition it helped establish to the riots themselves and the circumstances around Gordon's conversion to Judaism. It then returns to the novel to suggest that the discrepancy between the political issues of Gordon's time and those ascribed to him and the rioters in historical fiction adumbrates a radical political novel that Dickens had neither the will nor what Pierre Bourdieu calls the cultural "space possibilities" to write.*

As my title suggests, I am addressing many things concerning Lord George Gordon and the Gordon Riots, the eighteenth-century backdrop for Charles Dickens's *Barnaby Rudge*. The Gordon or "No Popery" riots of 1780 were the greatest civil disturbance in England since Momouth's Rebellion was put down in 1688. The gates of London prisons were forced and their cells emptied for the first time since the days of Wat Tyler and Jack Straw in the fourteenth century. When after six days the riots were finally suppressed on the 8th of June, at least 285 of the rioters had been killed outright, or fatally wounded, and 173 injured. Langdale's distillery and 21 adjoining houses had been destroyed by arson in a blaze so spectacular that onlookers feared another great fire of London. There were 450 people arrested, 160 tried, 62

Dickens Studies Annual, Volume 32, Copyright © 2002 by AMS Press, Inc. All rights reserved.

condemned to death, 25 actually hanged. The government paid out £7000 in damages to individuals and £30,000 to cover damage to public buildings without fully covering their losses (Rudé 275–76).

It might be going too far to call the riots one of the great repressed events of English history, but with few and mostly recent exceptions historians have referred to the events of 1780 more than they have studied them and so repeated the received story of bigotry and madness. Most historical references to Lord George himself might as well have been written more than a century ago. By contrast, the Wilkes riots of the previous decade have an extensive and various bibliography. Whatever "Wilkes and Liberty" may have meant, it is obviously a more attractive slogan than "No Popery," and historians of popular politics, resistance, and repression, may well prefer to concentrate on clashes between the populace and authority less tainted by religious bigotry. But the crowds that gathered in St. George's Fields 1769 on behalf of Wilkes's aborted election and the Protestants gathered there in 1780 had a similar class make-up and some overlapping interests—liberty being one of them.

The great event that stood between the Victorians and the events of 1780 and shaped their perception of them was, of course, the French Revolution and its aftermath. In a few short years the perceived threat from the Continent was transformed from a fear of Jacobites to fear of Jacobins, from fear of the Pope to fear of Napoleon. While anti-Catholic feelings persisted, they were thereafter divorced from fear of foreign invasion. The political radicalism of late eighteenth-century dissenters was all but forgotten having been overshadowed by more immediate memories of radical, anti-clerical French rationalism and the subsequent emergence of Chartism and then socialism.

When the riots of 1780 were invoked in the nineteenth century, it was almost invariably as a dire portent of anarchic, revolutionary, mob violence as in this nearly hysterical evocation by Southey in 1829:

> . . . ask yourself what security there is that the same blind fury which broke out in your childhood against the Roman Catholics may not be excited against the government, in one of those opportunities which accident is perpetually offering . . . were your Catilines to succeed in exciting as general an insurrection as that which was raised by one madman in your childhood! Imagine the infatuated and infuriated wretches, whom not Spitalfields, St. Giles and Pimlico alone, but all the lanes and alleys and cellars of the metropolis would pour out—a frightful population, whose multitudes . . . might exceed beliefs! The streets of London would appear to team with them like the land of Egypt with its plagues of frogs: and the lava floods of a volcano would be less destructive than the hordes whom your great cities and manufacturing districts would vomit forth.[1]

By Dickens's generation the broader political culture to which Lord George belonged had been eclipsed, and he had to be thought either bad or mad, if not both.

The events that briefly brought mobs and "No Popery" together again, and very likely gave Dickens's long-postponed novel about the "riots of '80" its occasion, was the opportunistic alliance between the two extremes of British politics in 1840, the physical force wing of the Chartists and anti-Catholic Ultra Tories—the Tories, that is, who rejected Sir Robert Peel's new Conservatism. This unlikely and short-lived alliance came together after twenty-four Chartists demonstrating for the release of jailed colleagues were killed during the Newport Rising of 1839. Certainly the contrast Dickens draws between the dreamy passivity of Lord George Gordon in *Barnaby Rudge,* who is essentially a tool of his fictional familiar Gashford, and the demonic activity of Sir John Chester, the backstairs Tory begetter of both Hugh and mayhem, is more suggestive of the politics of 1840, when the radical extremes of left and right united against the Whig ministry of Lord Melbourne, than the politics of 1780.[2]

My purpose here, however, is not to elaborate the circumstances of the 1840s, nor am I concerned with the question of what specific sources Dickens had and what use he made of them. I am not going to look back through Dickens's novel to the events of 1780, but rather try to look around the tradition Dickens did so much to fix to examine Gordon's career itself, with an eye to what has been repressed or denied in the traditional accounts, before concluding with a brief look at the novel against this history.

Lord George Gordon was born on Boxing Day, the 26th of December 1751 and baptized in January with King George II himself standing as godfather. He was the sixth and last child of Cosmo George, the duke of Gordon, who died nine months later. In 1856 his 38-year-old mother married a junior Army officer, Staates Long Morris, who was then 25. In the standard history of these events, the lively but largely unannotated *King Mob,* Christopher Hibbert cuts four years off Morris's age and refers to him as an "adventurer," neglecting to note that he was heir to the immense estate of Morrisania in New York (17). Had there been no Revolutionary War, this marriage would most likely be recalled as a grand, transatlantic alliance. After the war Morris sold the estate to his younger brother Gouveneur, who represented New York at the Constitutional Convention and is remembered for proposing language there that would have outlawed the "nefarious institution" of slavery (Peters 149). In 1858 the three boys, the duke Alexander, William, and George, who was then only seven, were sent to Elton. The family influence was used to gain William an army commission. George was switched over to the navy and destined to become a midshipman immediately upon graduation.

The eighteenth-century British navy was a brutal and brutalizing institution. For every sailor killed in action during the Seven Years' War, for example, nearly a hundred died of disease or noncombat injuries, and this was after the efficacy of limes against scurvy had been discovered (Pope 131). "No man will be a sailor who has contrivance enough to get himself into jail," said Dr. Johnson, "for being in a ship is being in jail, with a chance of being drowned," and indeed if you were grabbed by a press gang ashore or snatched off a merchant ship your service was involuntary (Boswell 211). The 14-inch width allowed for slinging a hammock was more confining than a jail cell at night, and discipline short of capital punishment was enforced by beatings and whippings that could be taken to near fatal extremes. Serving as an impressed seaman in the British navy was as close as a white man was likely to get to the conditions of plantation slavery. In fact many British sailors were actually of African descent.[3] Ship's biscuit, that staple of the seaman's diet, was commonly infested with weevils that the sailors had to pick out and dispose of before sailing. Gordon set the tone for his naval career in his first assignment by complaining to his captain on behalf of the common sailors about the infested food and a corrupt system of supply.

Fortuitously, Gordon's first extended tour of duty in 1768–69, which sent him to the Atlantic Coast of North America and the Caribbean, coincided with the posting of his stepfather's regiment to the colonies. Most likely through family influence, Lord George was able to obtain an extended shore leave to tour the American colonies and meet his colonial relatives. In a parliamentary speech he recalled how warmly he had been received as "a young nobleman, a little midshipman." He was shown every possible kindness and regard as "a youth of rank from England, who might one day be sent out to them as one of their governors," received in their houses and sent in a coach and four all the way from New York to Boston (*Parliamentary Register* XVII: 296, hereafter PR). He became from that point on a supporter of the rights of the colonists and, like Gouveneur Morris, an enemy of slavery—a position that was underscored by six months stationed in Jamaica where he was appalled by the overt brutality he witnessed and by the breaking up of slave families.

As Gordon's colleague and apologist, Dr. Robert Watson notes in his 1795 *Life,* Lord George became known in the Navy as "*the sailor's friend,*" and that "produced a contrary effect at the *Admiralty*" (6) He passed his lieutenant's exam in March of 1872, but no command came his way, which is hardly surprising given the prevailing view of naval discipline, a politicized assignment process, and his outspoken admiration for the increasingly restive North American colonists. After a year or more of waiting, he requested an audience with the first lord of the Admiralty, the earl of Sandwich. Told that he would have to wait his turn for a ship, but suspecting that he was being put off indefinitely, Gordon returned his commission and decided to attempt a parliamentary career.

Lord George has been on leave in the Hebrides the previous summer, and eager there as he had been in the New World to converse about local conditions, he learned to speak Gaelic. He now put that knowledge to extraordinary use by declaring himself candidate for Parliament from the shire of Inverness in the Highlands. With the exception of a few so-called ''scot and lot'' boroughs, places that by historical accident enfranchised all local taxpayers, an eighteenth-century election was generally arranged or purchased, not democratically contested. Gordon, however, campaigned like a modern politician, using his knowledge of Gaelic to speak to everyone, voter or not. He wore the tartan and philabeg where that was the custom, though they were still forbidden at that time. He danced reels, played the bagpipe and the violin and, as a climax to his campaign, gave a great ball going so far as to bring fifteen young ladies of the traditionally well-favored Maclead family to Inverness by ship from the Isle of Skye. This flamboyant campaign was doubtless a strain on his resources, which were only £500 per year as opposed to his oldest brother's £20,000, but it was a great success.

Foreseeing defeat, General Fraser, the incumbent since 1761, turned to his father Lord Lovat, who in turn contacted Lord George's brother, the duke of Gordon, who, as head of the family, agreed that General Fraser should purchase another seat for his rival in order to keep his own. So it happened that at the age of twenty-two Lord George Gordon entered Parliament from the pocket borough of Luggershall in Wiltshire, a seat purchased from George Augustus Selwyn, without ever setting foot there. It was eighteenth-century politics as usual, leaving the young man at this point with neither a genuine constituency nor a cause.

By all accounts Lord George in his twenties was a witty, polite, well-spoken gentleman, and many who knew him were baffled by his later role as the apparent instigator of riot and inclined to attribute it to some alienation of the mind. Descriptions of him in Parliament note the lank hair that was said to give him the mien of a Puritan, which is to say that he neither wore a wig nor curled and powdered his hair, as was the fashion. There were subsequent attempts to make him out to be a libertine. While Hibbert and others repeat rumors, nothing so specific attaches to his name as to that of the duke, who after having seven children by his wife fathered four more with his mistress, or that of his older brother William. William had to drop out of society for a time after accompanying the lovely Lady Sarah Bunbury when she bolted from Sir Charles. Neither did William marry Lady Sarah after her eventual divorce, but rather a Chancery ward seventeen years his junior, Francis Ingram. She was a pious woman whose special cause was, ironically enough in light of Lord George's later history, the conversion of the Jews.

Lord George made no particular mark in his first years in Parliament, and never became as accomplished a parliamentary speaker as he was a campaigner. Though capable of witty remarks in the course of debate, he had more taste for invective and particularly for documentation and historical argument than his contemporaries thought germane. In April of 1780, for example, after crediting him with a good double pun on the name of Mr. Eden, the *Parliamentary Register* notes that ''in his usual and very singular way of speaking, his lordship brought in a number of strange allusions to recent matters, tying and connecting what had occurred many years since, with what had occurred lately, in a most extraordinary manner'' (XVII: 220). His support of the colonies lead him at first to side with Burke and the Rockingham Whigs, but as time went on he came to think of himself as a direct agent of the people rather than of any party, to the exasperation of both sides. When the opposition challenged the King's Civil List, for example, Lord George rose to oppose meddling with the list, or ordering the king's table to be served by contract, until the opposition clear themselves of suspicion by resigning sinecure positions in the Exchequer. It was said by friend and enemy alike that there were three parties in the House: Whig, Tory, and Lord George Gordon.

We are at this point in the midst of what the English now refer to as the American War, but what George III called ''a Presbyterian War'' sometimes referring to the rebels themselves as ''Oliverians.'' That may seem a strange way to look at the American Revolution, but it was understood by Burke who saw New England's ''communion of the spirit of liberty'' as directly descended from the most extreme of the seventeenth century's Protestants, the very ''dissidence of dissent; and the protestantism of the Protestant religion'' (Burke, ''Conciliation'' 134). This religious frame may be the only point of agreement between the king, Burke and Lord George, who denounced ''the unhappy civil war'' against the Protestants in America (Watson 10). Some modern historians have revived this viewpoint, seeing our revolution as the last in a series of religious wars; as, indeed, a civil war across religious fault lines present on both sides of the Atlantic.

For our purpose it is enough to consider the implications of the Quebec Act of 1774. That act did two things to prepare the ground for rebellion: first, it recognized the established Catholic Church in what had been French Canada and, second, it blocked westward expansion of the seaboard colonies by retaining the Ohio Valley in that entity. This was territory that Virginia, Connecticut, and Massachusetts each assumed would come to them in compensation for their loyal service in the Seven Years' War. Recognizing Catholics while stopping westward movement made for a combustible combination of religious and territorial interests that became specific charges against George III in the *Declaration of Independence* where he is accused of ''abolishing the free System of English Laws in a neighboring Province, establishing therein an Arbitrary government, and enlarging its boundaries so as to render it at once an example and fit instrument for introducing the same absolute rule into these colonies.'' (Phillips 92–93).

On the whole, anti-Catholic sentiment in England had been waning as the efforts at Stuart restoration grew more feeble and the hierarchy of the English Church more open to toleration, but that was not true in America. The Oxford historian J.C.D. Clark has gone so far as to declare that ''the virulence and power of popular American anti-Catholicism is the suppressed theme of colonial history'' (272). Those French and Indians we Americans fought on our front of the Seven Years's War were to our forbears more specifically *Catholic* French and Indians. To many a New England Congregationalist or Presbyterian it seemed obvious that a government that would reestablish popery in the new world would not scruple to install Anglican bishops, a move that both the king and the hierarchy of the Church of England were known to favor.

Dissenters on both sides of the Atlantic saw in George III's attempts to restore royal prerogatives while officially tolerating Catholics dangerous gestures in the direction of Stuart absolutism and possible violations of his coronation oath. A delegate of Huguenot descent, John Jay, who was to be with Madison and Hamilton one of the authors of the Federalist Papers, addressed the people of Great Britain on behalf of the Continental Congress predicting that the Quebec Act would lead to a wave of Catholic immigration that would ''reduce the ancient free Protestant colonies to a state of slavery.'' He expressed ''astonishment that a British Parliament should ever consent to establish a religion that has deluged your island in blood and spread impiety, bigotry, persecution, murder and rebellion throughout every part of the world'' (cited in Ketchum 15).

While there was no thought of establishing Roman Catholicism in the home islands, the stage for the Gordon Riots was set, nevertheless, by the passage of a Catholic Relief Act in 1778. It was a bill that seemed mild enough to those who accepted any toleration at all. It removed the threat of life imprisonment from priests who celebrated mass, and from clergy and lay Catholics who kept or taught in schools. It also removed restrictions on the buying, holding, and inheriting of real property conditional upon swearing a specific oath of allegiance. The Act was privately cleared with English Catholic leaders, and with the support of both the government and leaders of the opposition it was introduced by Sir George Savile and quietly passed at the end of the 1778 session. But it only applied to England proper. In the next session an extension to Scotland was proposed, but by that time a side effect of the loyalty oath had became obvious: it permitted Catholics to serve in the armed forces. More specifically, it enabled the government to recruit impoverished Catholic Highlanders to fight American Protestants. Opposition in Scotland was immediate and violent, with riots in major cities. Catholic houses, chapels, and shops were attacked. In Edinburgh a new chapel was burned, and Roman Catholic leaders had to seek sanctuary in Edinburgh Castle. The English act had been passed so quietly that only one newspaper had published the actual text in Scotland, so that its extent was easy to exaggerate, and the secret negotiations that had proceeded it were darkened into a conspiracy.

The popular fear of Catholic violence and Protestant martyrdom in the absence of overt acts is hard to understand unless one recalls that Foxe's *Book of Martyrs* was on the shelf of nearly every Protestant household in Britain that had any books at all, and that it was regularly revised and reprinted with updated illustrating into the nineteenth century.[4] It "provided the central components for a subsequent vision of the nation as an identity of church and kingdom: a myth of origins; a scenario for the working out of Providence; a record of persecution; a promise of deliverance; a world mission" (Clark 48; fig. 1). Moreover, as Linda Colley has pointed out, the Act of Union only dated from 1707 and in so far as there was a British as opposed to English, Scottish, and Welsh identity, it was a Protestant identity with Catholics as its primary, defining other. Bonnie Prince Charlie and the "45," the last of the three serious attempts to restore the Stuarts in the century, was well within living memory. There had been, in addition, four invasion false alarms and, of course, Britain's major wars in the eighteenth century were with Catholic powers. British identity as well as English liberty were inseparable from Protestanism in the minds of the majority of the population. Only in the Victorian period did the empire supplant Protestant identity in this unifying function.

In the face of Scottish unrest the Government withdrew its bill in 1779, and John Wilkes, who knew a thing or two about riots, predicted trouble in London. The next step was the formation of Protestant associations in England to petition for repeal of the 1778 bill. Their model was probably Christopher Wyvill's County Associations, which organized gentlemen to lobby Parliament for perform. Gordon supported the petitions in parliamentary speeches reprinted in the Scottish press that raised issues of both religion and defense, particularly the vulnerability of the Scottish coast to attack. These were the days of John Paul Jones's daring raids, and French warships threatening invasion had actually appeared in the English Channel off Portsmouth in 1779, if only to engage in a dance of mutual ineptitude with a British fleet.

On November 12, 1779, James Fisher of the London Association asked Lord George Gordon to be president of the United Protestant Association of Scotland and England. In his letter of acceptance Gordon states quite baldly the central political tenant of Anglo-Saxon, Protestant political ideology dating back to the days of Elizabeth, a truth so self-evident that, in his words,

Fig. 1. *The Times* according to the Protestant Association, featuring reminders of Catholic tyranny and Protestant martyrdom. The way of the Catholics is blocked at the right by Scots in Scots: "The Deel a ane of that Popish crew shall come this way."

the Roman Catholics must know as well as we do, that "Popery when encouraged by Government, has always been dangerous to the liberties of the people" (Watson, 16).

The Protestant petitions from various constituencies were being routinely tabled in the House of Commons, so the Protestant Association collected signatures for a single, mammoth petition. On January 4, Gordon met with Lord North, who refused either to support the petition or any bill repealing the 1778 relief act. A leading Catholic, Lord Petre, arranged to call upon Lord George who recounts being asked to withdraw from the Protestant Association on the basis that they, unlike his lordship, were "a mean set of people" who would then "soon dwindle away" (Watson 18) Barring withdrawal, Lord Petre proposed postponing the repeal movement to see whether or not Catholics in fact abused toleration or grew in numbers. Lord George of course declined, arguing that were he to step down, some Wat Tyler might arise who would refuse to negotiate with the government and possibly foment a civil war. He also expressed puzzlement as to how any true Catholic could swear allegiance to the house of Hanover "as long as there was an hereditary Popish Prince, of the antient and royal family of Stuart (my own near, dear and lawful relation)" (Watson 17–18). Whether or not Burke sponsored this visit by Lord Petre, Lord George reported its failure to him directly and from that time forward Burke refused all contact from Gordon who had been friendly and an ally, at least in support of the colonists (Gordon, *Innocence* 10).

Using the privilege of his rank, Lord George requested and received four audiences with the king between January and the 19th of May when Gordon had the audacity, in effect, to cross-examine George III on his contention that he could be both a Protestant and a friend to toleration, reminding him that the only reason the electors of Hanover were kings of England rather than the hereditary house of Stuart was to defend the Protestant interest, thus implying that the king had violated his coronation oath. When the king stated that the Repeal was a Parliamentary action in which he had no part, Lord George pointed out that it only became law through his assent. He then cited Locke and John Wesley to the effect that "no government, not Roman Catholic, ought to tolerate Popery." (Gordon, *Innocence* 16). This was, needless to say, Lord George Gordon's last royal audience. After the riots when the government decided to try him for treason, there was certainly no objection from the palace.

Having exhausted every other form of pressure, Lord George determined to go ahead with a mass meeting of the petitioners from all over the United Kingdom. Over the objection of more moderate members, he insisted upon a mass march on Parliament bearing the petition. The petitioners, an estimated 17,000 of them, formed four divisions to maintain good order—London,

Westminster, Southwark, and Scots (with whom Lord George marched)—and the appropriate magistrates were requested to attend to control "any riotous or evil minded persons who may wish to disturb the peaceful and legal deportment of His Majesty's Protestant Subjects." Said magistrates, however, had made no plans whatsoever regarding public safety during this publicly planned and well-publicized event. Singing hymns, waving blue banners and wearing the blue cockade that was their emblem, the marchers crossed the Thames bridges and converged in and around the Palace Yard and into the very lobby of Parliament, their number now mixed with the tumultuous London crowd that was traditionally party to public demonstrations. Members were harassed on their way into Parliament. Lords in particular were subject to abuse—their carriages destroyed; their wigs snatched, the premier himself, Lord North, had his coach stopped and had his hat cut up and the fragments put up for sale before he was rescued by the Horse Guards. The bishop of Lincoln had the wheels taken off his carriage and was choked. Sir George Savile, proposer of the Relief Bill, had his coach demolished. Lord Mansfield the chief justice had to escape on the river—all this to cries of "No Popery" (de Castro 28–41).

While some people may indeed have been in fear of their lives, this kind of treatment was not unheard of in London politics of the eighteenth century. Just a few months earlier, the very leader of the opposition Charles James Fox together with Lord Derby and the duke of Ancaster, all, it was said, drunk, actually joined the rioters celebrating Admiral Keppel's court marshal acquittal, helping to break the windows of Lord George Germain and of Lord North in Downing street before breaking through the gates of the Admiralty and forcing the earl of Sandwich to flee into the night to the Horse Guards with his mistress Miss Ray in tow. In 1771 the so-called Printers Mob actually assaulted Lord North and several other MPs who suffered more injury than any person of quality endured during the Gordon Riots. (Gilmour 334–35).

While what was called "without doors" pressure was a standard tactic in eighteenth-century urban politics (and the precedent for such events of our colonial history as the Boston Tea Party), it had not been practiced on so large a scale, nor with a crowd rather than a few delegates in the lobby of the House. Needless to say, most members of Parliament did not appreciate being asked to legislate under this kind of duress. Colonel Holroyd threatened to run Lord George through on the spot should any rioters attempt to force their way into the House itself, and Henry Herbert dogged his steps to make good the threat if necessary (de Castro 40). Gordon periodically addressed the crowd from the head of the gallery stairs reporting the progress of the debate, whether to incite them, as was later charged, or to attempt to keep them in order as he claimed. Such of his words as were recorded can be read both ways. He hoped for a peaceful outcome in contrast to Scotland, where relief had only come after chapels were destroyed. He urged patience, assuring the crowd that "the King is a gracious monarch" who would ultimately instruct his ministers to honor their just demands, while reporting that he nonetheless mistrusted delay and that the cause was making no progress in the House. When he informed those within reach of his voice that there would be no action taken until Tuesday, four days later, he urged the crowd to leave and beware of any who would incite them to mischief. Guards were called in to free the House and, and they moved through the crowd, they enabled the beleaguered Lords and Members of Parliament to depart. Gordon was home in bed around 10:30. The petitioners had melted away (PR XVII: 359–60; de Castro 39–41).

Meanwhile, disregarding Lord George's words, or reading encouragement between the lines, or unaware of them given the extent of the crowd, or simply seizing the moment, gangs moved that night to attack the Sardinian and Bavarian chapels where diplomats from Catholic countries worshiped. A relative handful of the original marchers would have been enough to initiate the attacks since each action drew a local crowd of onlookers and participants. Everything that could burn was passed out of the chapels and set alight in the street. The house of the Bavarian ambassador behind the chapel was ransacked. The Sardinian chapel caught fire, and while the mob permitted the fire brigade to protect surrounding houses, it would not permit the chapel to be saved. About 100 Foot Guards arrived and arrested 13 people, but most of them proved to be spectators and none ring leaders of the group.

Saturday morning a large crowd watched the 13 arrested brought to Bow Street under strong escort without taking action. The House of Lords convened without incident to debate the policing of the city, particularly the advisability of a police force modeled on that of Paris, and even repeal Catholic Relief and the Quebec acts. Chief Justice Loughborough calls attention to this lull in his charge to the Grand Jury indicting rioters on July 10th, though for obvious prosecutorial motives.

> Upon the 3rd of June there was a seeming quiet, *a very memorable circumstance!* For sudden tumults when they subside are over. To revive a tumult evinces something of a settled influence, and something so like design, that it is impossible for the most candid mind not to conceive that there lies at the bottom a preconcerted, settled plan of operation. Sunday, the next day, a day set apart by the laws of God and man as a day of rest, and not as a day to be violated even by the labours of honest industry; in broad sun-shine, buildings and private houses in Moorfields were attacked and entered, and the furniture deliberated brought out and consumed by bonfires. *And all this was done in the view of the patient magistrates!*   (AR XVIII: 280)

Quite possibly a concerted show of force on Saturday would have prevented further outbreaks. Almost all the attacks on property were to be confined to a relatively small area, only four parishes in central London and two across the river in Southwark and Bermondsey. Back on April 6th, the ministry had called upon the Guard to be prepared to deal with a mob expected to accompany Fox to a meeting in Westminster Hall, so anticipatory orders were not unheard of. The failure of the North government to act decisively is inexplicable, though consistent with its general tendency to dither. The relative passivity of the city magistrates, however, may have had a political side to it. While the Lord Mayor and others later expressed fear for their own houses, no retaliatory attacks against the authorities had taken place as yet. The London area was a center of radical politics both antiwar and hostile to George III and his ministry. London commercial interests were hurt by the war, and it is no accident that Gordon's chief supporter in the Commons, Alderman Frederick Bull, was a tea merchant representing the City. While Gordon's only stated aim was repeal of Catholic Relief, he and City interests likely hoped to precipitate the collapse of the weak North government and possibly an end to the war, which was going badly. At least one bill had been introduced in 1780 requiring negotiations with the rebel colonies.

In any event, when the violence resumed on Sunday, the authorities were not prepared to meet it. The Lord Mayor later said he found his constables unwilling to attack the mob and complained that Lord Stormont only offered him seventy-three men from the Tower in small detachments. Some of the civil side did refuse orders. There were returning servicemen in the crowds, particularly sailors, whose presence may have given authorities some reason to doubt their troops. Nevertheless, despite rumors that it would violate their oath to fire upon Protestants in conflict with Catholics, when the riot act was read and orders duly issued, military discipline usually prevailed. The authorities, however, were generally two steps behind the rioters, and without proper orders constables and guardsmen would not intervene as houses were pulled down—which was not the work of a moment.

Lord George and the Protestant Association issued a circular pleading for orderly conduct on Sunday, but to no avail. These were no longer the people gathered by the Association. While some overlap between the petitioners and the mob is possible, even probable, it is a striking fact that not one of the 44,000 signers of the great petition was among those arrested for rioting. Over the next two days, representatives of the government tried to get Lord George to call off his mob. Lord George avowed, quite sincerely, that he had no contact with any rioters, only his own respectable associates, all the while insisting, in his monomaniacal way, that the means to distinguish the law abiding from the rioters was to repeal the offending legislation and so take away their excuse for disorder. Lord George informed the government of reports that that his own house had been threatened by Catholics and sent all of his household to safety with the exception of his manservant. The government then suggested he might want to leave London and perhaps go to Holland for a while for is own good, but took no action against him.

When the House reconvened on Tuesday, rather than vote on the Protestant petition it passed a resolution denouncing the rioting, recommended compensation for the destruction committed on chapels and houses of Foreign States and his majesty's subjects, and promised to take up the several petitions of Protestant subjects after the tumults subsided. It then adjourned until the 8th, whereupon all hell broke loose. By five o'clock Justice William Hyde had read the riot act and ordered the Horse to disperse the mob. One James Jackson, the prototype of Hugh in *Barnaby Rudge,* a huge man on a carthorse who later that night led the attack on Newgate, cried out "to Hyde's House Ahoy" and a contingent poured out into St. Martin's Street to attack the justice's town house, emptying it of enough furnishings to supply six bonfires (Hibbert, 102; fig. 2).

Lord George's place amid the mayhem can be symbolized by an incident that night. As members of Parliament passed through the line of Guards, Sir Philip Jennings Clerke found himself near Lord George, whom he did not know personally, and so pressed by the crowd that he appealed to him for protection. Ever the gentleman, Lord George agreed and borrowed a chariot from someone he knew at the Horn Tavern. Sir Philip asked to be dropped at Whitehall, but the crowd surrounded the chariot, took the horses off and regardless of the occupants' wishes pulled it through Temple Bar and the City stopping at the Mansion House to cheer the Lord Mayor and then on to Alderman Bull's residence. Gordon, Clerke testified, pleaded with his escort that they "for God's sake go home. While you behave in this unpeaceable way nothing in your petition can be complied with; the House will never consent to it." The crowd, of course, paid their hero no heed and Lord George appeared to those who noted his progress through the street that night to be the very lord of misrule (*Trial,* 24–26, fig. 3). On Wednesday he attempted to see the king to offer his services in controlling the riots but was turned away. He did help disperse a crowd threatening the house of Alderman Pugh, but when he tried that night to join those defending the Bank of England, Lord Rodney turned him away in disbelief.

The Gordon riots can be thought of as a three-tiered event. The top level was political: the petition movement, the march, the official calls for repeal of Catholic Relief and the Quebec Act. It is striking, for example, that the London Common Council actually debated and passed a resolution calling for repeal of Savile's Act right in the middle of the rioting. On June 23, after the riots were put down, Savile addressed one of the central concerns of the opponents of emancipation by offering a bill "to restrain Roman Catholics from educating the children of Protestants" (PR XVII: 377). This was the level at which Lord George sought to function, but lobbying had little effect after Parliament's first refusal to consider the petition. Lord George neither anticipated, nor it seems to me, desired so complete a breakdown of civil

Fig. 2. An immediate response to the mob attacks on public institutions on June 8th. "No Pope, No K[ing] No Ministry Dam[n] my Eyes."

Fig. 3. The trampling of the Protestant petition and toppling headgear suggests that the English Crown is as much Gordon's target as popery. The collar around the neck of the ass begins the French saying *honi soit qui mal y pense;* evil to him who thinks evil.

authority as occurred. The threat of violence might have advanced his cause, but violent acts were fatal to it and in the end actually strengthened North's government.

The second tier might be thought of as a version of Protestant, nationalistic populism. The late eighteenth century was a period of religious revival spearheaded by Methodists and evangelical preachers who were often militantly anti-Catholic, while the Catholic Church itself under Bishop Challoner was developing new institutions, new schools, and a proselytizing ministry directed at the same class of tradesmen and servants that the evangelicals appealed to. If religion can be said to have an infrastructure, that, rather than Catholic people, was the target of the Gordon rioters: Catholic places of worship, schools, and property—public houses, businesses, and homes that Catholics would not have, in the view of militant Protestants, had the laws being repealed by Savile's act actually been enforced.

The attack on Catholic property had a ritualistic quality. Particularly in the case of private houses, the leaders of the gangs, sometimes announced by bells, were careful to gather testimony and evidence as to the affiliation of the household, generally statements of neighbors and the examination of books, whether confirmatory Catholic publications, or an exculpatory *Book of Common Prayer,* before pulling down the house. Pulling down rarely meant total destruction, but a removal and burning of property and what structural damage could be effected by crowbars and the like. For the most part, moveable property was burned in the street, though some looting took place as one would expect with thieves and street people of all sorts mingling in the mobs. In these attacks the rioters were careful to let the fire brigade protect houses and avoid a general conflagration. When all was said and done, sixty Catholics houses had been destroyed or damaged, only a few of them in predominantly Catholic neighborhoods, primarily Moorfields. "They attacked the homes of gentlemen and tradesmen who were likely to give financial support to the foundation of new chapels and schools, the principal objection of Protestant associators to the Relief Act" (Rogers, 166).

The one spectacular exception to this generally measured destruction took place at Langdale's distillery in Holborn. As a Catholic business said to contain a chapel, the distillery was long rumored to be a target, and a large crowd gathered there on Black Wednesday. Undefended while troops concentrated on protecting the Bank of England, Langdale tried to bribe the crowd with cash and free gin, but as the sun went down, the distillery went up, igniting an estimated 120,000 gallons of raw gin. Most of the accounts of wild drunkenness—of people lapping up liquor from the gutter, falling from widows and dying on the street—refer to this event. The mob let the fire brigade through, but it was said that the pumps were actually sucking up raw gin and feeding the flames that eventually destroyed 21 surrounding Protestant houses.

As Dickens vividly conveys, people certainly felt threatened by the "No Popery" mobs, particularly in Moorfields where there were many Irish, but there were no wholesale attacks on Catholic people. While the official statistics may not cover everything, the rioters do not seem to have killed or maimed anyone, and one reason we have so many partial eyewitness accounts is that while some may have left town, many people of quality felt secure enough to go out and watch what was happening—rather like the spectators at Waterloo in Thackeray's *Vanity Fair*.

The third tier of the riots involves attacks upon secular institutions and the property of government officials. It is at this level that Protestant dissent joins with proto-revolutionary radicalism. These attacks began as retaliation against specific authorities like Justice Hyde, but in the last two days of the riots they became an assault upon institutions particularly hateful to working people and tradesmen on London's economic margin: the toll booths on the Blackfriars bridge, for example, that had been kept in place after the bridge was paid off in 1770, and crimping houses, where citizens impressed for military service were held for assignment. To understand the depth of feeling about these houses, consider the case of Mary Adey, one of the two murderers freed form Newgate. She had quarreled with a neighbor who sent to Bow Street for a constable. The constable's idea of how to settle the dispute was to attempt to take Mrs. Adey's husband for impressment into the armed forces, whereupon she assaulted the constable and somehow killed him (Linebaugh 338). Sponging houses, where those arrested for debt were held while they tried to raise bail to avoid prison, were also destroyed. But the places most feared and despised were the prisons, especially Newgate.

The attack on Newgate is the event most often depicted in graphic representations of the riots. It was the shock of seeing Newgate in flames and people who had committed crimes against property set free that broke the tacit political alliance between disenfranchised rate payers and the class below them on the social scale. It was that cross-class alliance with the threat of civil disorder that had provided the social space for libertarian politics in the eighteenth century (Rudé 293ff; Rogers). But even more than political influence, the middle class, even middle-class radicals, wanted what was locked up, whether people or property, to stay that way (fig. 4). After the riots, people with property turned away from "without doors" pressure and began agitation for direct participation in national politics through an extended franchise.[5]

As the country grew more prosperous, there were more and more things to lock up and more and more thieves taking advantage of the weakness of traditional locks to get at them. Peter Linebaugh in *The London Hanged* points out the fetishistic power of keys—something that Dickens certainly understood as evidenced by the original title of *Barnaby Rudge*, "Gabriel

Fig. 4. Religion as a cover for arson and theft.

Vardon, the Locksmith of London,'' and Esther's jingling keys in *Bleak House*. The original subtitle of the novel may have been a reminder to Dickens's readers that in 1781, in the wake of the riots, Joseph Bramah revolutionized lock making by introducing moveable wards for the purpose of saving household effects from burglars without and from rum-dubbing, that is lockpicking, servants within—a "dub" being a key.

The power to open and close associates keys with magic and divination. After the house of Newgate's gatekeeper Mr. Akerman was set ablaze and he escaped with his family over the rooftops, the gates of the prison came under attack. Francis Mockford, a coffee house waiter, emerged from Akerman's blazing house with the keys to Newgate. Linebaugh suggests that "the *sight* of them caused the turnkey to open the gate," which, indeed may have been his signal to do so under normal conditions (345, fig. 5) The Newgate keys seemed to have something uncanny about them, and Mockford, after showing them around his lodging house, grew increasingly uneasy and dropped them into the Thames off Westminister Bridge while the burning prison was being vacated—remarkably without asphyxiating any of the inmates, many of whom specialized in breaking or picking locks.

With Newgate ablaze, a segment of the mob broke into the house of William Murray, earl of Mansfield, lord chief justice of the King's Bench, the mightiest jurist in the English-speaking world and, as far as the rioters were concerned, the most hated. As the chief justice and his family fled out the back door, rioters burned his magnificent collection of books, manuscripts, and paintings as well as some 200 of the justice's own notebooks. All histories of the riots quite rightly lament this destruction, but few ask why Mansfield should have been so hated that the mob not only wrecked his Bloomsbury Square establishment, but traveled all the way out to Kenwood near Hampstead Heath to attack his country house when, were they true revolutionaries, they might have been trying to hold London.

Mansfield was the key figure in adapting English common law to the needs of merchants and business men, in effect making laws, as Linebaugh says, "for the buying and selling of commodities, affreightment of ships, marine insurance, bills of exchange and promissory notes"—the very stuff of emerging capitalism. An admirer of Roman and Continental law, he adapted an essentially feudal system of common law that preserved liberty in terms of rights and relationships into a system that gave priority to the rights of property. Blackstone, for example, originally stated that a slave coming to England was free on arrival; Mansfield modified Blackstone to say the master probably or possibly (depending on the edition) retained a right to unpaid service. (Linebaugh 357–69).[6] It is no accident that the American colonists cited his elder colleague Blackstone in opposition to Mansfield in justifying their actions (Clark 125–40; Lorimer 65–67).

Fig. 5. Composed after the event, this print published by Mitchell and Fielding shows the class, gender, and racial makeup of the mob and their activities on the 7th of June in almost Hogarthian detail. The Newgate keys are raised aloft on the tine of a pitchfork at the center rear.

England was in the process of changing labor relations from a system of mutual obligation on a feudal or household model, a system of journeyman and apprentice or master and servant, a system in which low wages were in some measure compensated for with rights to gifts in kind (on Boxing Day for instance) into a system of free labor in which, as Carlyle was famously to lament in *Past and Present,* no one was connected to anyone except by a cash nexus. While Mansfield favored property rights over traditions of mutual obligation, the more immediate source of the mob's anger was his advocacy of toleration in religion combined with his ferocious application of the bloody code when he was on the bench. The spikes on the wall of King's Bench Prison were known as "Lord Mansfield's teeth." In seven court sessions over eleven years he had 29 people branded, 448 transported and 102 hanged. It had been 12 years since Mansfield presided at the Old Bailey, but friends and family of some he had condemned might well have been in Bloomsbury Square at midnight on the 6th of June (Linebaugh, 360).

In the eighteenth century "many capital statutes were passed without debate or division; until 1772, indeed, a bill or a clause creating a new capital offense did not even have to be scrutinised by a committee of the whole house," and this at a time when attempted murder was in most circumstances a misdemeanor (Gilmour 148). The fate of a few of the rioters is a reminder of what could get a person hanged or transported in the eighteenth century. John Gray was convicted of having a bottle of his Lordship's liquor, sentence: death. Letitia Holland, "an handsome young woman about 18," for possessing two petticoats belonging to Lady Mansfield; sentence: death (*Annual Register* 1780:275). Then there was the case of William Brown who extorted a shilling. Brown had been a sailor on the *Serapis* when it was surrendered to John Paul Jones. He had made his way back from captivity in France on his own, but had no livelihood. He told the court: "I was wounded in the engagement with Paul Jones, and lose my sense when I have drank a little. I have done a great deal of good to the nation, my lord, and I hope you will save my life and let me serve his majesty again." Guilty. Death (Linebaugh 343–44).

The first fatal shots fired during the riots were in defense of Mansfield's House by troops commanded, coincidentally, by someone Lord George had dined with on the previous weekend, his brother-in-law Col. John Woodford. Six or even rioters were killed and the mob dispersed only to reform after the troops left, determined now not simply to pull down the house, but to burn it down. Troops from around the country were being called into London and were setting up camp in Hyde Park. The king and his privy council were not going to wait on the North government or local authorities any longer. They obtained a ruling from Justice Mansfield that circumvented the Riot Act by asserting that soldiers in a riot situation can act to defend property as if they were ordinary citizens defending their homes, and do so by any means including deadly force. "Then so let it be done," said the king. By Wednesday night troops with the freedom to fire at will supplemented by the militia and a volunteer *posse comitatis* were patrolling the city.

Political radicals who had been split over the repeal issue rallied to the government. The bridges were secured with many deaths at Blackfriars, which was packed with rioters. The final target of the riots was the very symbol of the financial systems, the Bank of England, now protected by armed men and roped off with naval hawsers. Three attempts were made to march on the Bank. The first at sundown was turned away with 20 dead. A second attack, led by a mounted brewery drayman riding on a carthorse festooned with chains and manacles from Newgate, was met the same way with many more killed. Little strategy was involved on either side. Under the command of the gentleman who had threatened Lord George in Parliament, Colonel Holroyd, troops and volunteers simply fired into the massed ranks of rioters, for which the colonel was rewarded by being created Lord Sheffield. The final attempt on the Bank was made at four in the morning. For the first and only time some of the rioters had firearms to supplement the clubs, marlin spikes, and cutlasses that had been their weapons, but they were no match for the guards.

On Thursday there were some clashes south of the river and a bloody battle on Fleet Street in which horse guards were attacked at such close quarters that they had to use their bayonets leaving 20 dead and many wounded. London was now patrolled by 10,000 troops as well as militias and civil authorities. The riots were over. On the ninth of June Lord George Gordon was arrested on a charge of high treason and conducted to the Tower. According to the *Public Advertiser* "the Guards that attended him were by far the greatest in number ever remembered to guard a state prisoner" (de Castro 180).

Probably the most detailed single eyewitness account of the climax of the riots was published some thirty-five years later by Sir Nathaniel Wraxall in his *Historical Memoirs of My Own Time*. With three other gentlemen he set out on the 7th of June in effect to tour the riots witnessing the burning of Lord Mansfield's possessions, the Langdale fire, the burning of the Fleet and King's Bench Prisons. He also recounts what was reported to him about the slaughter on the Blackfriars Bridge and at the Bank, suggesting that if the French had acted so forcibly in 1789 the French Revolution might have been suppressed at its birth and Europe spared Napoleon. He then actually gives voice to the thought that lies half-repressed under most traditional accounts of the Gordon riots.

If the populace had been conducted by leaders of system or ability, London must have been fundamentally overturned on that night. The Bank, the India

House, and the shops of the great bankers, would in that case have been early attacked; instead of throwing away their rage, as they did, on popish chapels, private homes, and prisons. When they began, after their first fury had exhausted itself, to direct their blows more systematically and skillfully, the time for action was passed. Government, which was accused with reason of having appeared supine in the first days of June, awoke early enough to preserve the metropolis and public credit, from sustaining the shock of popular violence.   (140)

To some lower down on the social scale, however, these events remained the great liberty riot of 1780. Whatever his degree of participation, the young William Blake was definitely in the crowd before Newgate when the gates were opened. The engraving that Victorian commentators renamed "Glad Day" was his commemoration of the riot, which was certainly one source for Blake's imagery of repression and freedom with its making and breaking of chains and shackles. In 1976 he added a caption to his print, probably alluding to Burke's reference to "the death dance of democratic revolution" in his *Letters to a Noble Lord.* "Albion rose from where he labour'd at the Mill with Slaves/Giving himself for the Nations, he danc'd the dance of Eternal Death" (1792): Albion at once dancing and cruciform, liberator and sacrifice (Erdman 7–10).

While Lord George waited in the tower, the rioters were tried. Despite the almost universal belief that the riots had been a conspiracy of the French, or the rebel Americans, or paid agents of the opposition, or other shadowy figures associated with the better-dressed people spotted in the crowds, only one political figure other than Lord George was tried, Henry Maskall, a radical pro-American apothecary who was acquitted. The government took the unusual step of allowing paid informers to testify. Usually their information was only used to identify a suspect whose guilt had to be established by other, untainted witnesses. Consequently, many of the accused were persons of better character and reputation than those making the charges, which may account for the fact that almost two-thirds of those arrested were dismissed without trial. Of those who stood trial, leaving aside Maskall and Edward Dennis the public executioner, who was convicted but reprieved, 22 were small employers, shopkeepers, peddlers or craftsmen, 4 were soldiers, 6 were sailors, 36 were journeymen or apprentices, 13 waiters or servants, 11 laborers leaving 50 whose occupations were unstated. Twenty were women. (Rudé 283). Burke's plea to show mercy to those guilty of lesser crimes against property were brushed aside, but his prudent warning against a parade to Tyburn that might irritate rather than humble the lower and middling people was heeded and the twenty-one hangings were disbursed to 13 locations in the parishes in which the crimes were committed and carried out without publicity (Linebaugh 364).

Meanwhile the prisoner in the Tower remained president of the Protestant Association, and was visited by well-wishers including John Wesley, who noted that "he seemed to be well acquainted with the Bible and had abundance of other books enough to furnish a study" (Hibbert 180). A subscription was raised for his defense enabling him to hire two outstanding lawyers, Lord Kenyan and his own cousin Thomas Erskine. Certainly he needed a good defense because the presiding judge was none other than Lord Mansfield himself, whose house and property had been destroyed and whose view of the riots as "a systematic plan to usurp the government of the country" was well known. He used the charge of high treason in his speech before the House of the Lords on June 19th to argue for the legal right for the government to take extreme actions against civil disturbances without a reading of the Riot Act, the failure to disperse after the reading becoming an additional offense (excerpted in de Castro 204–07).

Mansfield's charge to the jury extended the notion of high treason to encompass not only the person but the majesty of the king, and went so far as potentially to make any attempt to lobby the legislature that degenerated into a civil disturbance treasonous. "Somehow or another," Horace Walpole remarked, "the Constitution will be brought in guilty for Lord Mansfield is the judge" (510). Erskine's brilliant summation is generally credited for Gordon's acquittal, but the jury, noting the government's concession that Lord George had not personally concurred in any act of violence, may have felt that to encourage, incite, or promote civil disturbance, while making him guilty of something, did not add up to high treason regardless of their instruction from the bench.

Doubtless the government, and most likely his family, hoped that Lord George was through with public life, but in the summer of 1781 he agreed to stand for the City of London seat left open by the death of Alderman Hayley. After a number of opponents infiltrated a meeting, broke windows and the next day spread rumors of more Gordon riots, however, he wisely withdrew his name. He kept up a voluminous correspondence with any and everyone associated with what he saw as the cause of liberty. In 1783 he took up the cause of the Athol Highlanders who had mutinied at Portsmouth. Instead of being discharged after their term of service, which only ran until the end of the American War, their contract had been sold to the East India Company for service in India against Hyder Ali. As their ballad notes:

> When the news to London went
> Lord George Gordon down was sent
> To look upon the men's complaint,
> How they were used that morning . . .
> Lord George Gordon should not be forgot,
> Who is a true and trusty Scot,
> But may damnation be their lot
> Who approves of Murray's roguery[7]

In that same year Gordon orchestrated a public campaign against a Shop Tax proposed by Pitt's government that forced them to withdraw the bill. The last straw for the government came in late 1784 when Gordon took up the cause of discharged soldiers and sailors who wanted to fight for the Dutch in their war against the Catholic Austrian Empire. He seems actually to have arranged the offer of a frigate for that purpose, an interference with foreign policy no government could tolerate—at least without conniving in it. When disgruntled sailors were heard to shout "Gordon and Liberty," the government doubtless began watching for a way to be rid of him. In 1786 Lord George gave them their chance. He was put on trial for libel.

In 1782 he had visited France and predictably had been disgusted by the contrast between the ostentation of the court, particularly the queen, and the misery of the people. When that great imposter who styled himself the count de Cagliostro was sent into exile with his property forfeit, despite being acquitted of involvement in the notorious swindle known as the Case of the Diamond Necklace, Gordon gave him refuge and took up his cause. He was not alone in supporting the "Count." Cagliostro was a Mason who "merged the teachings of Falk and Swedenborg into the flamboyant Egyptian Rite" (Suchard 118). Dr. Falk, a London Jewish alchemist, had instructed Cagliostro's patron the duke of Orleans, Marie Antoinette's archenemy, in cabalistic magic. The Prince of Wales and his brothers, particularly the Duke of York and the king's alienated brother the Duke of Cumberland, were active in various irregular Masonic orders with Continental connections. Perhaps because Gordon knew Cagliostro and, most likely, Dr. Falk, the Prince asked Lord George to entertain Orleans's mistress, Madame de Glenis, when the duke visited the Prince of Wales in 1785.

The Scottish Rite Masons had been active supporters of American independence, but even without that connection it was likely enough for Gordon that Cagliostro had been a friend of the people and an enemy of the Catholic queen. He defended Cagliostro in a public letter and in doing so called the honesty of Marie Antoinette into question. The queen's honesty had been questioned more vulgarly by her own countrymen, but the French government made a formal complaint. The Pitt government did nothing until it could add another cause—trying an Englishman for libeling the French not being a sure winner.

The transportation of criminals had been suspended since the loss of the American colonies. When the government proposed to renew the practice with Botany Bay in Australia as the destination, Lord George composed a pamphlet in the voice of a Newgate prisoner laced with the language of the Bible and the pulpit contrasting the harshness of the Bloody Code and its many capital offenses with Mosaic law. "The just punishment ordained by God for our trespass of thievery is profanely altered by men, like ourselves, that his adequate judgment of our offenses, mingled with mercy, is not executed upon us in righteousness, that the everlasting law of his statues Is changed, and perverted to our destruction . . . falsified and erased by the lawyers and judges who sit with their backs to the word of the living God, and the fear of man before their faces, till the streets of our city have run down with a stream of blood, instead of righteousness." This is language the court found libelous, but Blake would have understood it. Indeed, some Blake scholars have suggested that Gordon influenced him directly and is represented in his work.[8]

Putting aside the prophetic language, Gordon's point was that crimes against property rather than persons do not merit capital punishment nor cutting people off from their society. Dickens's Magwitch may have got there and back again, but roughly twenty-five percent of the people who were transported to Australia died on the voyage out, and sailors compared the condition on prison ships to those on slave vessels. With no subscription for lawyers this time, and his cousin already in the employ of the government, Gordon defended himself to no avail. However clever it may have been to assert that the character of the queen of France was such that she could not be libeled, it was not a good courtroom tactic; nor was his lengthy history of English criminal law studded with quotations from Blackstone. As for capital punishment, Mr. Erskine defended English practice in these rather chilling terms. "The reason why executions in England are very frequent, is from the lenity of our laws; for we have no racks or tortures here. God forbid! But if there were, executions would be very rare indeed."[9]

Having alternately bored and alarmed the jury, Lord George was found guilty, but the court was adjourned before sentencing without a demand for bail. This oversight, if oversight it was, enabled him to flee to Holland. He was quickly expelled because of objections by the French government, and he returned secretly to Birmingham, his public career at an end. After seven months he was denounced and MacManus, a Bow Street runner, traveled north to convey him to London. There on Dudley Street in the poor neighborhood known as the Froggery, he was introduced to a bearded man in a broad brimmed Polish hat who gave his name as Israel bar Abraham George Gordon. Lord George Gordon had become a Jew.

Jewish rights had been one of Gordon's causes in the 1780s, and one of his anti-war schemes involved an appeal to Jewish bankers to stop financing them, but conversion was no mere strategy. Very likely he applied to Rabbi Tevele Schiff of the Duke's Place Synagogue for conversion before his trial in 1786, but was refused. Jews do not take converts casually. Moreover, one of the conditions under which Cromwell allowed Jews to reside officially in England had been that they not proselytize. Public outcry over the so-called "Jew Bill" of 1753 allowing Jews to be naturalized without taking a sacrament, a bill that was repealed under public pressure, was well remembered in the Jewish community and had uncomfortable parallels to the controversial bill for Catholic Relief (Solomons 241–42).

Gordon was well versed in the history of the English Revolution, and he became a student of religion, most likely during his time in the Tower. Protestant literalism has always focussed on the Old Testament and the life of Jesus as history, and English Protestants since the days the Fifth Monarchists of Cromwell's time had been fascinated by the prophecy of a Jewish return to Jerusalem as a prelude to the End of Days. Douglas Hay suggests that Gordon was directly influenced by James Murray, the head of the Protestant Association in Newcastle, an anti-war, anti-Catholic, egalitarian Presbyterian in the Leveller tradition, who argued that the laws of man should conform to those of God. His disciple Thomas Spence issued seven commemorative medals of Lord George after Gordon's death portraying him in his Jewish attire (Hay 83–85; for a sample medal see Rubens 45). There was an active Restorationist movement in the 1780s led by dissenting Protestants and such Unitarians as the scientist Joseph Priestley, who published his *Letters to the Jews* between 1786 and 1794. Priestley denied the preexistent divinity of Jesus and foresaw a millennial reconciliation between Christianity and Judaism that fused Christian and Jewish eschatology. "Enlightened Jew would coexist with purified Christian in peace and harmony, ruling with Christ from the New Jerusalem and having natural pre-eminence as 'the older branch of the family.' " This "unitarianism . . . would end the appalling 'idolatrous worship of Jesus Christ' and those who had persecuted God's special people would be made to pay." (cited in McCalman, "New Jerusalems" 316). Iain McCalman notes that Priestley's respondent, the autodidact translator and spokesman for Jewish orthodoxy David Levi, was one of Gordon's instructors in Judaism along with the scholar Meyer Joseph.

Writing under the pseudonym Solomon de A.R., George Horne argued that it was more logical for someone of Priestley's beliefs to become a Jew than for a Jew to give up his religion for Unitarianism, which is neither Jewish nor properly Christian: "openly profess the religion of which you think such great things and no longer let your name be numbered among the uncircumcised. . . . Submit to the operation."[10] Gordon seems to have earnestly followed the logic of Horne's satiric *reductio ad absurdum* response to Priestley. Like Priestley, Gordon had come to believe that the laws of Moses had not been supplanted and applied, moreover, to all Christians. That belief was implicit in his protest against the Bloody Code. He might well have known about the Traskites, who held that belief in Cromwell's time, and who were persecuted for their Judiazing. Though not a convert, Traske was condemned to have a "J" branded on his forehead, and some of his followers were rumored to have actually become Jews after fleeing to Amsterdam.

Gordon was attempting, as some Protestants have periodically, to recover the form of religion closest to that practiced by Jesus, who did, after all, live and die a Jew. Whether he was aware of it or not, the position he adopted in effect revived the heresy of the first-century Ebionites, who called themselves Christians, yet denied the divinity of Jesus and believed Christians were subject to Mosaic law. He underwent circumcision and was initiated into the covenant of Abraham by Rabbi Jacob of Birmingham. Gordon still signed himself President of the Protestant Association, but saw no contradiction in that. In 1789 he explained to the Rev. Peard Dickinson, an associate of John Wesley, that "as our Lord was born in Judea, and conformed to Jewish customs, opinions, and manners, so we are bound to imitate his example in these things. . . . I think it right to conform to his example in appearing as a *Jew* and in maintaining an external conformity to his life and manners" (cited in Hay 91).

Of course, Gordon's reemergence as a Jew gave the makers of satiric prints a field day. Depicting Gordon as *The Birmingham Moses* bearing Mosaic Laws, W. Dickie may allude both to his anti-transportation tract and Gordon's comparison of his audiences with George III in 1780 to those of Moses' with Pharaoh (fig. 6). Even the *Times* began referring to Gordon as Lord Crop, and in September of 1785, the scurrilous *Rambler Magazine* printed a satiric dialogue complete with a copper plate titled "The Loss of the Prepuce; or, Lord George Riot suffering a clipping in order to become a Jew."

. . . *Mordicai* to daughter Susannah: Ids Gentleman wants to be made fit for de Synagogue. Ave you got one pair of de scissors to perform de operation?
Susannah. Yes, Dat I Av, and day are sharp come UN razor.
Lord G. Will the operation be attended with much pain?
Susannah. Point de tout. Child would not cry out for such an operation. Unbutton, my lord, sail vows plait. Me no stand for de ceremony.
Ceremony and business be two very different things. If your lordhip vent vidout *breeches,* as dey do in Scotland, you would not ave de trouble to unbutton.
(fig. 7)

Back in London, Lord George was condemned to five years of imprisonment for the libels, a considerable sentence. By contrast, his Newgate fellow, Thomas Townly Macan, only got three for attempting to blow up King's Bench Prison. Lord George was also required to find £10,000 for security for his good behavior for 14 years and two sureties for £2,500 each. The severity of his sentence suggests not only a reaction to his political meddling, but a warning by the government to well-born illuminati with French connections. It is worth noting that in addition to political radicals, the Duke of York and the Duke of Cumberland were among Lord George's visitors in Newgate.

Lord George served his entire sentence, but was not released because, in what may have been a bit of political theater, he presented as his sureties

Fig. 6. *The Birmingham Moses.* "And wonder not he stole to misbelievers,/ Since they of stolen things are oft receivers."

Fig. 7. *Lord George Riot made a Jew*

two impoverished Polish Jews. Lord George's family remained on speaking terms with him and could certainly have afforded to buy his freedom. In all likelihood, he would not promise them or anyone the fourteen years of good behavior. In any event, he continued to live on the more comfortable state side of the prison as a Jew. He was attended during the days by one Jewish maidservant (Polly Levi) and one Christian. He wore phylacteries and a taillit, and on shabbat a minion of poor Polish Jews joined him for prayers. He kept up his correspondence from prison, cheering the liberation of French Jews after the Revolution and chiding the solicitors of relief for the new government of Poland for not doing likewise for the Jews of their country. He concluded his letter to the fundraisers with well wishes since "the present King of Poland is my own cousin, and I have many more relations there"[11] He held a place of honor among the political prisoners, and conversed with inmates form Germany, France, and Italy in their own languages (fig. 8). He played the violin and bagpipes and was at times accompanied by the Duke of York's orchestra.

One account in the duke's papers of an attempt to visit Lord George records an amusing encounter between His Highness and Gordon's Jewish maid on the prison's narrow stairs and ends with a telling insight into how much being a duke's brother mattered even if you had become a Jew in Newgate. "All the Keepers of the Prison have behaved with the most becoming propriety towards his Lordship ever since his Commitment; refusing money from several who wished mainly to satisfy their curiosity in seeing his Lordship, without coming upon Business, nor having any acquaintance with him, or a proper introduction" (Add.mss 27,777.f21). The inevitable, typhoid fever, finally caught up with Lord George in 1793 when he died, it was said, with his favorite song, *Ça Ira,* the Cry of Freedom, on his lips.

His last and most enduring representation came in 1790 in the *Reflections on the Revolution in France* of his onetime ally Edmund Burke.

We have Lord George Gordon fast in Newgate; and neither his being a public proselyte to Judaism, nor his having, in his zeal against Catholic priests raised a mob (excuse the term, it is still in use here) which pulled down all our prisons, have preserved him a liberty of which he did not render himself worthy.... We have prisons almost as strong as the Bastille, for those who dare to libel the queens of France. In this spiritual retreat, let the noble libeller remain. Let him there meditate upon his Talmud, until he learns a conduct more becoming his birth and parts ... or until some persons from your side of the water, to please your new Hebrew brethren, shall ransom him. He may then be able to purchase, with the old boards of the Synagogue, and a very small poundage, on the long compound interest of the thirty pieces of silver ... the lands ... usurped by the Gallician church. Send us your popish archbishop of Paris, and we will send you our Protestant rabbin.   (95–96)

Burke then seizes upon the fact that Dr. Richard Price, the pro-revolutionary

Fig. 8. Newton's *Promenade in the State Side of Newgate.* Lord George is the center figure with the broad-brimmed hat and clay pioe.

minister, preached the sermon on "Love of our Country" that Burke so deplored from the Old Jewry. As Michael Ragussis points out, Burke reiterates "the society of the Old Jewry," "the Old Jewry doctrine," and like phrases again and again. The revolutionaries themselves are like Jews, with a "stock jobbing constitution." French nobility will be so corrupted as to resemble usurers and Jews. To betray one's English identity by being converted to revolutionary doctrines becomes rhetorically equated with Lord George Gordon's apostasy. The result, fifty years before Marx walks into the British Museum is an equation between Jews and the threat of revolution. "In Burke's emotional rhetoric," to quote Ragussis, "it is dimly hinted that revolution is the site where parricide, regicide and deicide—the traditional Christian charges against the Jews—become one" (124, fig.9).

In defense of what he admits to be Burke's "intellectually and ethically dubious" linking of Gordon, Dr. Price, and Marie Antoinette, Iain McCalman endorses his depiction of Gordon as "a distinctive, subversive and modern revolutionary figure" (1996:366). Gordon may have seemed a modern subversive in the 1780s, but by Dickens's time millenialism and a critique of English secular law and institutions that assumed the Law of Moses to be both binding and more merciful had become an anachronism. Executions for property crimes were already falling in the 1790s, and it was Jewish law that nineteenth-century reformers portrayed as inconsistent with either Christian mercy or Utilitarian reason (see Hay 108–11). Dickens's unhistorical execution in *Barnaby Rudge* of Edward Dennis the public hangman, and his sympathetic recital in his 1868 preface of the case of Mary Jones, who was rendered destitute after her husband was impressed and hanged in 1777 for stealing a bolt of linen to clothe her children, reflect the changed attitude toward capital punishment for crimes against property.

Dickens's sympathy with Gordon regarding the Bloody Code calls attention to the repression, deflection, and diffusion in *Barnaby Rudge* of other issues current in 1780. Dickens reduces the American War to an historical backdrop, so the riots are largely cut off from issues of law and public policy. Dickens even mistakes the purpose of the Protestant Petition as the prevention of a law for Catholic relief rather than its repeal (*Rudge,* 269). Mr. Hardale's complaint to Sir John Chester that he can only hold his estate by subterfuge, like his assertion that Catholics should surely have the right to educate their own children when "thousands of us enter your service every year, and to preserve the freedom of which, we die in bloody battles abroad, in heaps" were all issues remedied by the 1778 law (*Rudge,* 327, 330). Indeed the fear that Catholics, now able to enter the armed forces legally, might be recruited for war against American Protestants was one of the triggers for the petition drive and the riots.

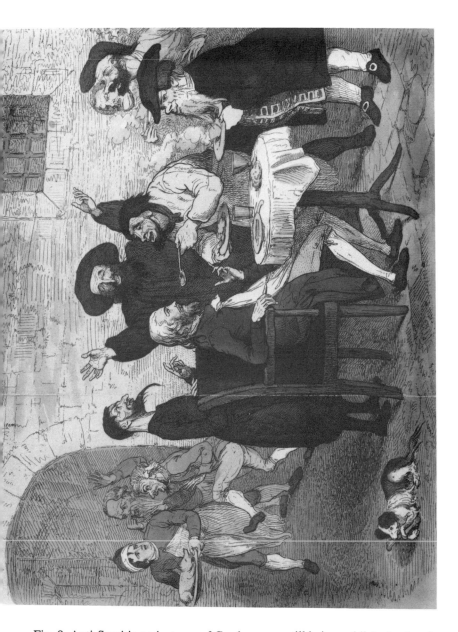

Fig. 9. Anti-Semitic caricatures of Gordon were still being published a decade after his death. *Moses Chusing His Cook* under the aegis of a Fagin-like Jew dates from 1803.

Having given short shrift to the politics of 1780, Dickens is free to treat the riots in a Carlylean vein as a matter of public and private hysteria unleashed primarily by the failure of paternal authority both public and private. In the public sphere that failure is reflected by the dithering of the London authorities and the perfidy of titled villains; in the private sphere by John Willit's abuse of his son that drove Joe from his proper place as heir to the Maypole Inn.[13] The mob is cynically whipped up by the fictional Gashford, while a quixotic Lord George, the aristocratic double of the simpleminded Barnably, alternately mouths Gashford's words and dreams of turning Jew. Protestant enthusiasm is essentially relegated to the realm of petty treason, with the servant Miggs and Mrs. Varden subverting the rule of her husband, the good master.

Likewise, the real issue behind Sim Tappertit's demand for the restoration of "ancient rights and holidays," the dislocations caused by transition from a household model of master and servant or apprentice and journeyman with mutual obligations to a free labor system, is degraded into a right to "break heads" by its hypocritical spokesman and his clownish "Prentice Knights." In so far as they participated in the riots, apprentice and journeyman were not pitted against each other; rather the arrest records show apprentice and journeyman together. The rural Maypole Inn, its society disrupted by a bad father, burned in riot, then rebuilt and rehabilitated, has generally been treated as an anachronism, a nostalgic symbol of old English values given a sentimental restoration through the marriage of Joe and Dolly. But given the changes taking place in the nature of employment and the place of the worker in a free labor system, the urban Vardon household can be viewed in the same light.

In *Rudge* Dickens upgrades the profession of the gin distiller Langdale to "honest vintner," and he and Phiz render the firing of the distillery and the ensuing mayhem in graphic detail. In contrast, the attacks on those public institutions against which the London populace had genuine grievances are merely mentioned. The name "the Warren" is transferred from an actual target of the rioters, the Woolich Arsenal, to the private home of Mr. Hardale. The injustices suffered by the likes of Mary Jones in Newgate are ignored in favor of rescuing Dolly from Hugh's threat of rape by the timely return of her beloved from the American War.

Dickens took some vicarious pleasure in imagining the riots: "I have let all the prisoners out of Newgate, burnt down Lord Mansfield's and played the very devil . . . . I feel quite smoky when I am at work" (Forster, 1:219). But Dickens had neither the wish nor the will to write a revolutionary novel. It was not within what Pierre Bourdieu terms "the space of possibilities" for him to do so (64). Dickens was no lover of Newgate, and the Barnaby story expresses Dickens's sympathy for the downtrodden. But his plotting prevents linkage of those aspects of the riots that expressed popular grievances against repressive institutions. Rather, he offers his readers a happy ending and distributive justice, the hangman hung and the lovers one, while in fact the hangman was pardoned.

Nowhere is the repression of social grievance more evident than in Dickens's choice of a hero. As Butt and Tillotson note, Dickens found a reference to a "one armed man" among the rioters in *Fanaticism and Treason,* an anonymous contemporary account of the riots. He would, most likely, have been a military man returned from the war, and so, in a sense, the love plot that culminates with Dolly's rescue is an elaborate back story proving that the maimed man was not taking treasonous action against his government, but was really Joe Willit "disguised as one of them" (520).

Reversing the figure and ground of the plot, another story takes shape if we ask what a one-armed infantryman with a grudge against patriarchs might actually have had to look forward to upon returning to England in 1780 after fighting people very like himself in America (fig. 10). Might not another man have caught Dolly's eye, perhaps someone who found it more expedient to sell red coats to the army at home than to wear one overseas? Joe's words at the end of chapter 78 would take on a different meaning then: "What have I done, what have I done to meet with this reward?" (602). Might not such a Joe, the shadow hero of this repressed history, with neither a bride with her dowry nor property to inherit, like other impoverished ex-soldiers and sailors in those surging crowds want to burn down the house? Might not such a Joe standing with Blake before Newgate in flames, having made common cause with the journeymen and apprentices, carters and small shopkeepers, debtors and returned servicemen down on their luck, turn, raise his cudgel, point towards Threadneedle Street and shout: "To the Bank of England, Ho!"?

NOTES

An earlier version of this article was presented as a lecture at the 1999 Dickens Universe at UC Santa Cruz, which was devoted to *Barnaby Rudge*. Illustrations 1,3,4,5,8 and 10 are reproduced with the permission of the British Museum; illustrations 2, 6 and 9 by permission of the Library of the Jewish Theological Seminary; illustration 7 by permission of the British Library.

1. *Sir Thomas Moore: or Colloquies on the Progress and Prospects of Society,* 1829. Cited in Conner (216). Catiline's plot to assassinate Roman consuls was foiled by Cicero.
2. See Thomas J. Rice, "The Politics of Barnaby Rudge," in Giddings.
3. See Pope, chs. 15 and 17; chs. 7 and 8.
4. Editions edited by Paul Wright after 1780 contained a print depicting the Protestant Association's march to the House of Commons as an orderly procession.

Fig. 10. The miserable state of crippled, demobilized servicemen, in this case
sailors, is the basis of Rowlandson's criticism of the appointment of Sir Hugh
Palliser as the governor of Greenwich Hospital in 1780. "To what a condition
alas! am I brought/Who so many Battles so bravely have fought."

5. The relationship between the middle-class reaction to the riots and subsequent extension of the franchise would be more evident were it not for the intervening period of reactionary government in England occasioned by the Napoleonic Wars.

6. In the Somerset Case, however, Mansfield ruled that a master could not compel an escaped slave to leave England. Although abolitionists argued that this ruling outlawed slavery in England, it did nothing to prevent the reenslavement of people who left. See Lorimer 65ff.

7. Bulloch, *"Mutiny"* (19). According to Bulloch it was not General Murray, the founder of the regiment, who sold their contract as the men believed.

8. See, for example, Mee and Schuchard.

9. Gordon and Erksine are quoted from *The whole proceedings on the trials of two informations . . . against . . . Lord George Gordon . . .* taken in shorthand by J. Gurney. London 1787. There is a copy of the entire 1787 *Prisoners Petition to the Right Honourable Lord George Gordon, to preserve their Lives and Liberties, and prevent their Banishment to Botany Bay* printed by Thomas Wilkens, who was tried and convicted for its publication, in the Public Record Office. For an extended extract collated with biblical passages and contextualized in contemporary political and religious discourse see Hay.

10. *The Reply of the Jews to the Letters Addressed to Them by Doctor Joseph Priestley* (Oxford, 1787) cited in Ruderman, 174. For more on David Levi's importance as a translator of Jewish materials into English see Ruderman and Popkin.

11. *To W. Smith, Esq., M.P. . . .* a letter signed G. Gordon from Felon-side Newgate Prison, 2nd Aug. 1792. London 1792. Stanislas Poniatowski, the last king of Poland was the great-grandson of Lady Catherine Gordon, see Bulloch 1908, ch. 4.

12. For an extended discussion of the theme of paternity in the novel and the England of *Barnaby Rudge* see Stigant and Widdowson.

WORKS CITED

The Annual Register . . . for the Year 1780. London: J. Dodsley, 1788.

Anon. "Lord George Riot Made a Jew. *The Rambler Magazine* (Sept. 1785), 342–43.

Bourdieu, Pierre. *The Field of Cultural Production.* Ed. Randal Johnson. New York: Columbia UP, 1993.

Bulloch, John Malcolm. *The Gay Gordons.* London: Chapman & Hall, 1908.

———. *The "Mutiny" of the Atholl Highlanders & an Account of the Sheelagreen Gordons.* Privately Printed. Blackie, 1911.

Burke, Edmund, "Speech on Moving Resolutions for Conciliation with the Colonies." 1775. In *Selected Writings and Speeches on America.* Ed. Thomas H. D. Mahoney. New York: Bobbs-Merrill, 1964.

――――. *Reflections on the Revolution in France*. 1790. Ed. Thomas H. D. Mahoney. New York: Bobbs-Merrill, 1955.

Butt, John and Kathleen Tillotson, *Dickens at Work*. London: Methuen, 1957.

Clark, J. C. D. *The Language of Liberty 1660–1832: Political Discourse and Social Dynamics in the Anglo-American World*. Cambridge: Cambridge UP, 1994.

Colley, Linda. *Britons: Forging the Nation 1707–1837*. New Haven: Yale UP, 1992.

Conner, Steven, "Space, Place and Body of Riot," in *Charles Dickens*. Ed. Steven Conner. London: Longman's, 1996.

de Castro, J. Paul. *The Gordon Riots*. London: Oxford UP, 1926.

Dickens, Charles. *Barnaby Rudge*. Oxford Illustrated Dickens. Oxford: Oxford UP, 1987.

Erdman, David. *Blake: Prophets Against Empire*. Princeton: Princeton, UP, 1954.

Forster, John. *The Life of Charles Dickens*. 2 vols. London: Chapman and Hall, 1872.

Gilmour, Ian. *Riot, Risings and Revolution: Governance and Violence in Eighteenth-Century England*. London: Hutchinson, 1992.

Gordon, Lord George. *Innocence Vindicated: Intrigues of Popery and its Abettors Displayed*. London: R. Denham, 1783.

――――. *To W. Smith, Esq., M.P. . . .* London, 1792.

Hay, Douglas, "The Laws of God and the Laws of Man: Lord George Gordon and the Death Penalty," in *Protest and Survival: Essays for E. P. Thompson.*, Eds. John Rule and Robert Malcolmson. London: Merlin Press, 1993.

Hibbert, Christopher. *King Mob: The Story of Lord George Gordon and the London Riots of 1780*. Cleveland: World Publishing, 1958.

Kemp, Peter. *The British Sailor: A Social History of the Lower Deck*. London: Dent, 1970.

Ketchum, Richard. *Saratoga: Turning Point of America's Revolutionary War*. New York: Holt, 1997.

Linebaugh, Peter. *The London Hanged: Crime and Civil Society in the Eighteenth Century*. Cambridge: Cambridge UP, 1992.

Lorimer, Douglas. "Black Resistance to Slavery and Racism in Eighteenth-Century England," in *Essays on the History of Blacks in Britain*. Eds. Jagdish Gundara and Ian Duffield. Aldershot: Avebury, 1992.

McCalman, Iain. "Mad Lord George and Madame La Motte: Riot and Sexuality in the Genesis of Burke's *Reflections on the Revolution in France.*" *Journal of British Studies* 35 (1996): 343–67.

————. "New Jerusalems: Prophecy, Dissent and Radical Culture in England, 1786–1830," in *Enlightenment and Religion: Rational Dissent in Eighteenth-Century Britain*. Ed. Knud Haakonssen. Cambridge: Cambridge UP, 1996.

Mee, Jon, " 'The Doom of Tyrants': William Blake, Richard 'Citizen' Lee, and the Millenarian Public Sphere," in *Blake, Politics, and History*. Eds. Jackie DiSalvo, G. A. Rosso, and Christopher Z. Hobson. New York: Garland, 1998.

Peters, William. *A More Perfect Union*. New York: Crown, 1987.

The Parliamentary Register; or, History of the Proceedings and Debates of the House of Commons during the Fourth Sessions of the Fourteenth Parliament. 17 vols. London: John Stockdale, 1802.

Phillips, Kevin. *The Cousins' War: Religion, Politics, and the Triumph of Anglo-America*. New York: Basic Books, 1999.

Pope, Dudley. *Life in Nelson's Navy*. London: Allen & Unwin, 1981.

Popkin, Richard H. "David Levi, Anglo-Jewish Theologian," *The Jewish Quarterly Review 77* (1996): 77–101.

Ragussis, Michael, *Figures of Conversion: "The Jewish Question" & English National Identity*. Durham: Duke UP, 1995.

Rice, Thomas J. "The Politics of *Barnaby Rudge*," in *The Changing World of Charles Dickens*. Ed. Robert Giddings. London: Vision Press, 1983.

Rogers, Nicholas. *Crowds, Culture and Politics in Georgian Britain*. Oxford: Clarendon Press, 1998.

Rubens, Alfred. "Portrait of Anglo-Jewry 1556–1836." *The Jewish Historical Society of England Transactions*. 1955–9): 13–52.

Ruderman, David B. *Jewish Enlightenment in an English Key: Anglo-Jewry's Construction Of Modern Jewish Thought*. Princeton: Princeton UP, 2000.

Rudé, George. *Paris and London in the 18th Century: Studies in Popular Protest*. London: Collins, 1970.

Schuchard, Marsha Keith. "Blake's *Tiriel* and the Regency Crisis: Lifting the Veil on a Royal Masonic Scandal," in *Blake, Politics, and History*. Eds. Jackie DiSalvo, G. A. Rosso, and Christopher Z. Hobson. New York: Garland, 1998.

Solomons, Israel. "Lord George Gordon's Conversion to Judaism." *The Jewish Historical Society of England Transactions 7* (1911–14) Rpt. London: Wm. Dawson & Sons, 1971, 222–71.

Stigant, Paul and Peter Widdowson, "*Barnaby Rudge—A Historical Novel?*" *Literature and History* 2 (1975): 2–44.

The Trial of George Gordon, Esquire, Commonly Called Lord George Gordon for High Treason. Taken in shorthand by Joseph Gurney. London, 1781.

Walpole, Horace. *The Letters of Horace Walpole.* Ed. Peter Cunningham, Vol. 7. London: Richard Bentley, 1891.

Watson, Robert. *The Life of Lord George Gordon.* London: H. D. Symonds. 1795.

The Whole Proceedings of the Trials of Two Informations . . . Against Lord George Gordon . . . One for a Libel on the Queen of France . . . the Other for a Libel on the Judges. Taken in short hand by Joseph Gurney. London, 1787.

Wraxall, Sir Nathanial, Bart. *Historical Memoirs of My Own Time.* 1815. London: Kegan, Paul, Trench, 1904.

"What the Waves Were Always Saying": Submerging Masculinity in *Dombey and Son*

Claire Senior

It is surely fair to say that Dombey and Son*'s almost constant references to water gradually "submerge" the masculine realm represented by the novel's title character. Dickens's construction and subsequent deconstruction of femininity, however, is far more problematic. While Florence's female sentimentality is continually viewed as dangerous by her father, it is she who extends the life of her beloved brother, and she who is able to attain emotional fulfilment through the community of the Wooden Midshipman and, ultimately, marriage to Walter Gay. Dombey's second marriage to Edith Granger, a woman who is unable to express this sort of feminine feeling, brings him no such happiness, but the idealized domesticity of the Midshipman is portrayed in a decidedly uneven fashion, a microcosm of Dickens's apparent inability to decide whether to praise or condemn the aquatic dissolution of the male. In the end, while Dickens provides the expected ending, there is no real resolution of these issues.*

I

Numerous critics of Charles Dickens's *Dombey and Son* have addressed the question of gender representation in a novel that seems, at least on the surface,

Dickens Studies Annual, Volume 32, Copyright © 2002 by AMS Press, Inc. All rights reserved.

to divide the masculine and the feminine into two distinct camps. That masculinity is undercut in *Dombey and Son* is hardly a revolutionary statement—the argument was made most famous by Julian Moynahan, and has more recently been picked up by Robert Clark, Andrew Elfenbein, Helene Moglen, and Mary Montaut, among others. However, while there seems to be fairly universal agreement on this point, there is far less consensus about the role that femininity plays within this novel. Is it unequivocally celebrated, or does Dickens's use of the oft-commented water imagery that dominates the novel problematize both genders? Drawing upon the critics named above as well as a number of others, the present essay seeks to demonstrate that as the masculine world gradually sinks beneath the waves, the feminine world emerges as both an ideal realm of the kind proposed by Gaston Bachelard and a sickly fantasy every bit as damaging to human development as Dombey's uncompromising masculinity. Dombey's fear of all things feminine is clearly unnatural, and Dickens does his best to make that point as often as he can, but at the end of the novel, when redemption seems to become surrender, we are left in the uncomfortable position of questioning whether the novel's sentimental ending actually represents a step forward, or a step back.

Dombey and Son opens upon a scene that seems, at least initially, to define much of the novel—the division of the world into two distinctly gendered spheres. Mrs. Dombey, who has just given birth, is little more than an incidental player in an environment where the male predominates. As such, while Mr. Dombey contemplates his newborn son, his neglected daughter seeks comfort in the arms of her equally forgotten mother, and "[t]hus, clinging fast to that slight spar within her arms, the mother drifted out upon the dark and unknown sea that rolls around the world" (60). This image, as Gaston Bachelard notes in *Water and Dreams*, is "a maternal image . . . illustrat[ing] an unforgettable love"[1] (115–17), a love that Dombey cannot share in:

> The last time he had seen his slighted child, there had been that in the sad embrace between her and her dying mother which was at once a revelation and a reproach to him. Let him be absorbed as he would in the Son on whom he built such high hopes, he could not forget that closing scene. He could not forget that he had had no part in it. That, at the bottom of its clear depths of tenderness and truth, lay these two figures clasped in each other's arms, while he stood on the bank above them, looking down a mere spectator—not a sharer with them—quite shut out.   (83)

Water, within this novel, seems to represent the "eternal voice of the Oceanic mother" (Clark 73); a shared community of feminine feeling (though not limited in its expression to the female gender) which excludes Dombey. But while he is indeed shut out of this tableau, the fact remains, as Moynahan was probably the first to point out, that the female figures below him who have unashamedly shared their love are represented as having been drowned. This is not surprising, given that Dombey seems to believe that the sharing of love demands the erasure of his masculine self. He is on his own on the bank, but he is safe—a position that he does his best to occupy for most of the novel.

The question thus becomes whether Dombey is a representative of normative Victorian masculinity. He does not conform to any of James Eli Adams's models of masculine identity; indeed, Adams's discussion of Dickens leaves out Dombey entirely, focusing instead on Sydney Carton and Eugene Wrayburn, aristocratic idlers whose resistance to masculine discipline serves to define them. Nor can he be linked in any meaningful way to Carlyle's representation of the hero, for the essential selfhood of that model demands a disregard for public pressures which cannot be assigned to Dombey, who, though isolated, is extremely conscious of his own place within the world: "What the world thinks of him, how it looks at him, and what it says—this is the haunting demon of his mind" (809). What *is* clear is that Dombey defines himself entirely in terms of his work, which he views as an exclusively male sphere, and thus he sees no place for femininity—particularly the femininity represented by his daughter—in his life. There is certainly a pronounced division between the male world of work and the female world of the home, mirroring the culture/nature divide that is perhaps best epitomized in the images of the railroad and the water, but Dombey seems to be more self-consciously masculine than anyone else in the novel, as he blocks out the feminine at any cost. When his sister suggests (in tears) that Miss Tox might be a suitable choice to act as little Paul's godmother, his refusal is swift: "'Paul and myself will be able, when the time comes, to hold our own—the House, in other words, will be able to hold its own, and maintain its own, and hand down its own of itself, and without any such commonplace aids" (102–03). Paul will have no mother; indeed, the image that Dombey presents here is one of the male line perpetuating itself ad infinitum with no female intervention whatsoever—a sealed-off, wholly masculine world of industry that excludes the very notion of motherhood.

This is a vision that Dombey appears to take quite seriously, given his repeated attempts throughout Paul's short life to deprive him of what he considers the damaging influence of the maternal sphere. Dombey has "[a]n indescribable distrust of anybody stepping in between himself and his son; a haughty dread of having any rival or partner in the boy's respect or deference" (103), and though Miss Tox is eventually admitted to the coveted post "in virtue of her insignificance" (103), it is clear that Dombey will not share the duties that he seems utterly incapable of performing himself. His feelings for his son are not based on filial fondness, but on future positioning within the industrial world. Paul is little more than a commodity to him, one that he expects will eventually pay dividends. Occupying such a position, Paul would advance the masculine line, safe from the debilitating feminine love represented by Florence.[2]

Nevertheless, in spite of her father's efforts, Florence acts as a maternal figure, a part that she aches to play. "Oh, pray, pray, let me lie by my brother to-night, for I believe he's fond of me!" (106) serves as a near-hysterical reminder of her constant desire to give and receive love, providing guidance to others as they enter, for want of a better description, the ocean of feeling. Indeed, it is telling that Florence's normal means of displaying emotion is to produce tears—she cries on eighty-four separate occasions (Zwinger 434). Her main preoccupation, however, is her younger brother. Paul, in describing his tiredness to his father, tells him that "I lie down in Florence's lap, and she sings to me. At night I dream about such cu-ri-ous things!" (154). Dombey is not long in conferring with his son's aunt and godmother on that very subject. As a logical man of business, the equation of Florence's constant caresses with Paul's tiredness cannot have failed to present itself. If A causes B, then A must be removed. It is not the action of a normal father figure, but Dombey, paranoid about femininity, is not a normal father. Though it is clearly impossible to defend such a decision in human terms, it makes perfect sense as a business proposition.

Significantly, the doctor recommends sea-air, and this gives Dombey pause: " 'Sea-air,' repeated Mr. Dombey, looking at his sister. 'There is nothing to be made uneasy by, in that,' said Mrs. Chick" (158). Dombey *is* uneasy, though he is consoled by the description of Mrs. Pipchin,[3] a decidedly unmaternal dragon. Paul and Florence are thus sent to her establishment, where Paul's chief delight is to sit by the sea with his sister and watch the waves rolling in from the horizon. He believes that they are trying to say something to him, and "[v]ery often afterwards, in the midst of their talk, he would break off to try to understand what it was that the waves were always saying" (171). When Dombey deposits his son at Dr. Blimber's, telling him that "You are almost a man already" (208), his son replies "Almost" (209), for it is a mantle that he is not ready to assume:

> "Shall we make a man of him?" repeated the Doctor.
> "I had rather be a child," replied Paul.
> "Indeed!" said the Doctor. "Why?"
> The child sat on the table looking at him, with a curious expression of suppressed emotion in his face, and beating one hand proudly on his knee as if he had the rising tears beneath it, and crushed them. But his other hand strayed a little way the while, a little farther—farther from him yet—until it lighted on the neck of Florence. "This is why," it seemed to say, and then the steady look was broken up and gone; the working lip was loosened; and the tears came streaming forth. (210)

Masculinity as it is performed by his father holds no appeal for Paul. He cannot restrain his feminine tears when confronted by what he must become. In spite of his father's attempts to separate him from the feminine world—from his mother, from his wet-nurse and finally, from Florence—he defines himself in relation *to* them, rather than *against* them, as his father wishes him to do. His identity, then, is invalidated because he cannot perform his gender, or as Moglen puts it, "[n]ecessarily overwhelmed . . . by the great expectations of his projected manhood, he escapes into an "old-fashioned" time, associated by Dickens with the timeless sea. . . . This time . . . belongs exclusively to women, for it is, like them, identified with nature: outside of history, beyond the reach of society, part of an Edenic past. Paul can claim it finally only through the rejection of his gender identity in death" (162).

Paul's inevitable death comes in chapter 16, aptly titled "What the Waves were always saying." The movement of the water quite literally carries the action, flowing from Paul's fear of death into acceptance: "His only trouble was the swift and rapid river . . . and when he saw it coming on, resistless, he cried out! But a word from Florence, who was always at his side, restored him to himself, and leaning his poor head upon her breast, he told Floy of his dream, and smiled" (293). The emphasis placed on the breast within this context of rushing water, which occurs again and again throughout the narrative, recalls Bachelard's view that "all water is a kind of milk" (117), and reinforces the idea of Florence as a sort of water-nymph, a guide to the common pool of human emotion.[4] From this maternal image the narrative flows from Paul's metaphorical mother to his biological one, and Paul thinks that "she must have loved sweet Florence better than his father did, to have held her in her arms when she felt that she was dying—for even he, her brother, who had such dear love for her, could have no greater wish than that" (295). The close embrace, when one surrenders everything, does not frighten Paul as it does his father. Indeed, he longs for it, and with his mother awaiting him, Paul clasps the hands that are around his sister's neck in the attitude of prayer, and dies as the "golden ripple" (297) returns to the wall of the nursery. The old world, with its eternally flowing cycle of life and death, has triumphed over the new world of bourgeois capitalism. Dickens assumes his most sentimental guise here, proclaiming that all who see the "golden ripple" should thank God "for that older fashion yet, of Immortality! And look upon us, angels of young children, with regards not quite estranged, when the swift river bears us to the ocean!" (297–98).

Dombey, of course, does not see the angels. For him, there can be no such consolation, and he can only push his grief aside by burying himself once again in the male world of work. Florence, on the other hand, weeps, prays, and makes affectionate little trinkets for her unresponsive father: "Thus she gained heart to look upon the work with which her fingers had been busy by

his side on the sea-shore; and thus it was not very long before she took to it
again—with something of a human love for it, as if it had been sentient and
known him; and, sitting in a window, near her mother's picture, in the unused
room so long deserted, wore away the thoughtful hours'' (318). Such an
image is touching, but emphasizes the gulf between masculine and feminine.
Florence's offerings are constantly rebuffed by her father, who stubbornly
isolates himself from the domestic realm. To Dombey, her lovingly-made
trinkets represent weakness, and he will not accept them. Andrew Elfenbein
identifies Florence as James Carker's counterpart, noting that ''[h]er brand
of management consists entirely of her ability to form personal relations
through the strength of her affections, the ability that Carker utterly lacks.
Yet the Angel in the House . . . disrupts the absolute supremacy of Victorian
patriarchy'' (366).[5] Florence may be a manager, but ''her dedication to Paul
cannot save him . . . The novel's abstract morality unswervingly valorizes the
feminine values associated with Florence over the masculine ones associated
with Dombey, but the action of the plot suggests, equally unswervingly, that
Florence's virtue causes catastrophe for those she loves in a world run by
Dombey's patriarchal values'' (375). And this is exactly what Dombey fears.
As far as he is concerned, Florence's all-encompassing love serves to weaken
not only male authority, but male identity.

II

If Florence represents weakness, Dombey is determined to choose as a second
wife a domestic manager who shares his disdain for his daughter's overflow-
ing emotions. Edith Granger's frosty manner contrasts sharply with Florence's, and Dombey is ''pleased to see his handsome wife immovable and
proud and cold'' (584). She represents not only a female version of himself,
but also a masculinized presence to fortify his own position. Dombey ''might
have read'' (584) any number of conflicting emotions in his wife's performance of his construction of idealized femininity (a performance that Louise
Yelin suggests is Edith's initial strategy for survival),[6] but he chooses not to.
Consequently, when Edith begins to exhibit unmasked feeling, he does not
know what to do. He sees her affection for Florence as a threat to himself,
and brings in Carker as a sort of male managerial replacement for her—a
plan that fails spectacularly.[7] He resolves to conquer, but cannot defeat, one
who epitomizes such an uneasy synthesis of gender. Edith, however, realizes
the precariousness of her position. When Florence, whose name is forever
echoing in Edith's head and ''speaking to her in the beating of her heart''
(652), seeks out her ''Mama'' before the latter's mad flight to Dijon, Edith
is terrified: '' 'Don't call me by that name! Don't speak to me! Don't look

at me!—Florence!' shrinking back, as Florence moved a step towards her, 'don't touch me!' '' (754). If Florence acquiesces in the notion that women can be defined in terms of their role within the domestic (or "female") sphere, Edith rebels against it. Characterized as "Mama" by Florence, she is ultimately unable to fulfil that role. She has been raised by a mother who has subverted her own femininity by treating her daughter as a commodity to be bartered and exchanged. As such, Edith can act the part of Woman, but, apart from hearing Florence's name whispered in her ear like the waves breaking upon the shore, she cannot live it. "She cannot define an authentic identity because the only concepts she possesses, the only language she can use, are projections of the male world by which she has been formed" (Moglen 167). Edith, like Dombey, is completely isolated from the ocean of common feeling: " 'I am a woman,' she said, confronting him steadfastly, 'who from her childhood has been shamed and steeled. I have been offered and rejected, put up and appraised, until my very soul has sickened. I have not had an accomplishment or grace that might have been a resource to me, but it has been paraded and vended to enhance my value' '' (856). In the end, as Mary Montaut suggests, Edith goes back to being alone, free not only from the suffocating demands of the ocean of love, but from "the ordinary cares and 'woman's work' which Florence so happily embraces as the novel closes" (150).

Bachelard's equation of water with maternal milk is echoed, as previously noted, in Dickens's frequent references to the female breast.[8] Frank McCombie suggests that Dombey is, in fact, sexually repressed, and that this repression is echoed through his lack of response to the very feminine (in terms of appearance) Edith, whom he configures in purely financial terms. Indeed, this lack of response is emphasized through Carker's reaction to her. The business manager clearly feels a very strong sexual pull towards Edith, and, as McCombie notes, Carker "gazes on more than one occasion directly at Edith's bosom" (29). Edith, in this case, represents not maternity but sexuality—a sexuality that Dombey finds extraordinarily threatening because he equates it with emasculation.[9] And he may not be entirely off the mark. Dickens does appear to have been rather uneasy with Edith as a strongly sexualized character, and wastes little time in exiling her from the novel, concentrating instead on the non-sexual Florence, who becomes responsible for the breast/bosom imagery.[10] It is this image that Dombey attempts to destroy, as he strikes his daughter on the breast and leaves a lasting mark, a blow that McCombie suggests is directed "with great deliberation against that part which has symbolized female sexuality throughout the novel . . . Florence takes literally upon her bosom the savage revenge of the man who was determined not to accept the sexuality of his wife, her femaleness, her femininity, and has never been able to bear it in his daughter" (36). By striking his daughter in this manner, Dombey makes a desperate attempt to reassert his masculine dominance. He could not be all to his son—little Paul was determined to have a mother—and his attempts to control his wife have proven to be futile, as another, seemingly more "masculine" man has swept her away. However, as usually turns out to be the case when he attempts to assert his masculinity, Dombey finds himself alone, at least until Florence rescues him and he can lay his face (or, more exactly, have it placed by his daughter) "[u]pon the breast that he had bruised, against the heart that he had nearly broken" (939).

III

If the problematization of gender through water imagery were limited to the Dombey household, this study might end here, but the trope encompasses a significant percentage of the novel's characters. At the Wooden Midshipman, the mythology of the sea clearly predominates. Indeed, if Dombey displays no understanding of the ebb and flow of the tides, Sol Gills's stock comprises "chronometers, barometers, telescopes, compasses, charts, maps, sextants, quadrants, and specimens of every kind of instrument used in the working of a ship's course, or the keeping of a ship's reckoning, or the prosecuting of a ship's discoveries" (88). These are not instruments with which to control the sea, but for measuring and observing it, indicating a sophisticated degree of understanding. However, Sol Gills's skills seem limited to observing the flow of "the human tide" (90) and to predicting changes in time and weather—abstract skills which have little application in mercenary London. The little Midshipman, "absorbed in scientific pursuits, had no interest with worldly concerns" (330), and Gills is well aware of his limitations: "I am an old-fashioned man in an old-fashioned shop . . . I have fallen behind the time, and am too old to catch it again. Even the noise it makes a long way ahead, confuses me" (94). Consequently, Gills urges his young nephew to follow the path laid out for him by Dombey, to "[b]e diligent, try to like it, my dear boy, work for a steady independence, and be happy! . . . As to the sea . . . - that's well enough in fiction, Wally, but it won't do in fact; it won't do at all" (94). Nevertheless, having imparted this advice, the old man begins to talk of the sea "with an air of stealthy enjoyment" (95). It is an apparently irresistible compulsion, and one that suggests that his attempt to integrate himself (even vicariously) into Dombey's world will be absolutely futile. There is, significantly, a great deal of emphasis placed on the domestic realm in the descriptions of Sol Gills and Captain Cuttle.[11] At various points they are seen cooking, cleaning, and comforting the charges that fate brings to their door, and Auerbach argues that, in the end, "Gills and Cuttle exchange loss of power for female selfhood'' (121). Gills may be able to perform masculinity through the guise of the Wooden Midshipman, but his is clearly a failed commercial enterprise.[12] When he hangs up Walter's silver mug and tells him that ''We must begin to drink out of glasses to-day, Walter. We are men of business. We belong to the City. We started life this morning'' (91), it is obvious that Gills could never survive in the city as Dickens represents it. By chapter 9, he hovers on the brink of utter financial ruin, and Captain Cuttle's only solution is to appeal to Dombey for help in a scene perhaps best remembered for reinforcing the point that ''Girls . . . have nothing to do with Dombey and Son'' (197). While the appeal is successful, Walter emerges from the agreement ''humbled and cast down'' (199) by his own lack of masculine power.

Barbara Lecker notes that ''[t]he nautical instrument-maker's shop is a living testimony to the powers of the imagination, existing in defiance of all the cold realities which surround it. There are no customers, no commercial dealings; the abode of the Wooden Midshipman deals finally in the products of Romance'' (25). Cuttle believes that he understands the business world, but ''unlike as [Florence and Cuttle] were externally . . . in simple innocence of the world's ways and the world's perplexities and dangers, they were nearly on a level. No child could have surpassed Captain Cuttle in inexperience of everything but wind and weather; in simplicity, credulity, and generous trustfulness'' (776). These qualities ultimately serve to hasten Walter's departure, and when Walter attempts to explain the reason for his journey to the sea-captain, Cuttle can only reply in the language of the sea:

> ''Keep her off a point or so!'' observed the Captain, in a contemplative voice.
> ''What did you say, Captain Cuttle?'' inquired Walter.
> ''Stand by!'' returned the Captain, thoughtfully.
> Walter paused to ascertain if the Captain had any particular information to add to this, but as he said no more, went on. (280)

This bizarre exchange merely emphasizes Cuttle's lack of useful function within the masculine sphere. Though he later stretches out his hand to Walter's and pledges eternal friendship, it is hard to forget his ineffectual words. Indeed, ''he soon got off into the deepest of water, and could find no bottom to his penetration'' (285). Cuttle, the man of the sea, cannot move beyond it. He decides that Walter's interpretation of the situation—that he has been cast off in part because Dombey dislikes him—must be mistaken, and he wastes no time in making his way to Dombey's offices. It is, of course, an exercise that is doomed to fail, for the sincerely naive Cuttle does not stand a chance against the poisonous Carker. It never occurs to the Captain that Carker's professed feeling could be false.

Ultimately, there is something rather ridiculous about ''the old ship's company'' (636). Once Walter disappears somewhere near the West Indies, Sol

Gills goes after him, and it seems clear that his absence from the novel has to do with both thematic and stylistic considerations, because Gills and Cuttle are fundamentally the same character: "The hapless Toots confounds the two nautical characters, referring alternately to Captain Gills and Sol Cuttle, and the two are, in fact, insufficiently distinguished from each other to allow for any dramatic play. Both are indefatigable dreamers, characterized by their boundless optimism and expressing themselves in colourful nautical language" (Lecker 27). Individuality is erased in the water. Gills and Cuttle may anticipate the domesticated figure of Joe in *Great Expectations*, as Paul Schact suggests, but the homosocial continuum that inhabits the Wooden Midshipman is still problematic. Toots,[13] a later addition, who "when he began to have whiskers . . . left off having brains . . . possessed of the gruffest of voices and the shrillest of minds" (206), ambles through the book as a kind of cherubic imbecile, while "The Toot's Joy," a six-oared cutter that frequently finds itself floating past the riverbank where Florence often sits, is as ridiculous a carrier as Toots is a character. The society associated with the Midshipman presents an alternative to the masculine world of hard reality, but do its members ever really accomplish anything? Gills and Cuttle do eventually transform themselves from "old-fashioned men" dealing in archaic nautical instruments into men who can assume a comfortable place within the capitalist society at the end of the novel. Of course, it is Dombey's money that allows Gills to climb out of debt, and we later learn that some obscure investments have magically come to maturity. At the end of the novel, Cuttle delights in his name on the door of the Wooden Midshipman, rejoicing in the *fiction* of a prosperous business—but nothing has really changed. "Not another stroke of business does the Midshipman achieve beyond his usual easy trade" (971).

This opposition between the masculine world of ruthless practicality and the feminine world of sentimentality is given an additional twist through a number of other characters. Dombey's formidable sister, Louisa Chick, constantly performs femininity through effusive displays of emotion (real or imagined), and appears to recognize its inherent weakness: "I know it's very weak and silly of me . . . to be so trembly and shaky from head to foot, and to allow my feelings to completely get the better of me, but I cannot help it" (55) she tells her brother.[14] For Mrs. Chick, however, emotion can also be used as a means of asserting dominance and control, particularly in the matrimonial sphere. If she cries, Mr. Chick is quick to accede to her demands, and her turning on the passive Lucretia Tox later in the novel is made all the more effective through her claim that her trusting and pure love for her former friend has been violated. Mrs. Chick is only redeemed when she is at last able to abandon false tears in favor of actual joy, and once she has done this, she quietly disappears from the narrative. "Good" Mrs. Brown, herself a disturbing caricature of normative motherhood, is nevertheless able to articulate feminine feeling. Though she seizes Florence's clothes, she is unable to bring herself to cut the child's hair, telling her that "If I hadn't once had a gal of my own—beyond seas now—that was proud of her hair . . . I'd have had every lock of it. She's far away, she's far away! Oho! Oho!" (131). This is a cry of genuine grief, in spite of the way in which she has perverted the title of "mother." It is a cry that "thrills to the heart of Florence" (131), perhaps because it is a sentiment that she understands even though it comes from, as Marsh describes her, a "quasi-masculine, pipe-smoking creature [who] would still pimp for her own daughter" (409). Rob the Grinder, who is a part of the soft Toodles family at the beginning of the novel, also works for a brief time for Captain Cuttle. However, he is clearly out of place in the "sacred" (636) parlour of the Wooden Midshipman, and his eventual defection comes as no real surprise. He *displays* feeling as he departs, but it is clear which side he is inclined towards: "Rob, snivelling and sobbing, and grievously wounded in his feelings, took up the pieces one by one, with a sob and a snivel for each" (635). He is, of course, quickly schooled in the ways of male capitalism by his new patron, and when he is seized by "Good Mrs Brown" and her daughter, he can only repeat the lesson that "blabbing, if it's only about the number of buttons on my master's coat, won't do. I tell you it won't do with him. A cove had better drown himself. He says so" (729). The notion that "a cove had better drown himself" is frequently repeated, as Rob, who cannot mould himself into Carker's model either, seems to long for such a release. Confronted by the pair again later in the novel, he can only blubber: "What, young woman! . . . are you against me too? Call yourselves females too! . . . I'm surprised at you! Where's your feminine tenderness?" (826). The Misses Brown do not represent the models of femininity epitomized by Florence and by Rob's own mother, and his only response is to dissolve into feminine weakness—it is hardly surprising, then, that he finds himself back in the feminine world at the end of the novel.

IV

It should be quite evident by this point that one of the most obvious problems with Dickens's use of the water trope is his apparent inability to decide whether to privilege the masculine or the feminine. Walter Gay, for example, was not originally meant to enjoy the happy connubial union with Florence that he is blessed with after his triumphant return at the end of the novel. Instead, Dickens had planned to trace the descent of the high-spirited youth into "negligence, idleness, dissipation, dishonesty, and ruin,"[15] but his change of heart allowed for

a realization of the Dick Whittington myth and with it a vanquishing of the
world of fact by fancy in narrative terms. . . . The fairy-tale aspirations of the
nautical characters are first seen as part of the elaborate fiction which characterizes their existence, and even the dreamy-eyed Walter recognises their implausi-
bility; but Dickens chose to give authority to the sphere of Solomon Gills, and
the Wooden Midshipman and the values which it represents are finally affirmed.
(Lecker 21–22)

This is one of several apparent contradictions in Dickens's text; it is on a par
with Captain Cuttle's restoration of Florence to herself. He "fairly overflowed
with compassion and gentleness," but as she attempts to bless him for his
actions, "he divined her purpose, and held her up like a true man" (762).
Furthermore, "[i]t would seem as if there never was a book written, or a
story told, expressly with the object of keeping boys on shore, which did not
lure and charm them to the ocean, as a matter of course" (96). If boys are
drawn to the sea in much the same manner as girls are, then Dombey is
fundamentally wrong. He is an extreme model of masculinity, but Cuttle and
Gills are the novel's "real men." But how then to explain the characterization
of these two individuals? As Cuttle says, surveying the nautical instruments
that surround him, "it's a fine thing to understand 'em. And yet it's a fine
thing not to understand 'em. I hardly know which is best" (98). Apparently,
Dickens had the same problem, since neither Dombey nor the crew of the
Wooden Midshipman are presented as viable alternatives.

The ocean-as-love trope presents other difficulties as well. As Perera notes,
when Dickens rails against hypocrisy, he suggests that, if moral pestilence
were made visible, "[t]hen should we see how the same poisoned fountains
that flow into our hospitals and lazar-houses, inundate the jails, and make the
convict ships swim deep, and roll across the seas, and over-run vast continents
with crime" (738). In addition to this contradictory image, it is worth noting
that the journey that most of the book's characters undertake does not necessarily result in redemption. The transported convict Alice Marwood is still
"ruined" when she returns, and Edith's journey across the sea leads only to
her "grave." Moreover, if the domestic realm excludes masculinity, and the
mercantile world only permits a self-destructive, isolating model of masculinity to succeed, is there really any possibility for success? One area of overlap
that might permit a normative, healthy masculinity is in the sea itself—that
is, employment as a sailor. But there are no successful sailors in this work.
Those that depart with Walter are drowned, and the novel's ex-sailor, Captain
Cuttle, clearly falls on the side of feminine softness, as do Gills and his
nephew both before and after their return. It is hardly a glowing appraisal of
the possibilities for masculinity.

The return of Walter further complicates things, as Florence "had no
thought of him but as a brother, a brother rescued from the grave; a ship-
wrecked brother saved and at her side; and rushed into his arms. In all the

world, he seemed to be her hope, her comfort, refuge, natural protector''
(784). The notion that Florence requires a protector—and that the protector
is Walter—would appear to infuse him with masculine power. However, he
is not a husband or lover, but a brother; the same sort of watery being
(one who required rescue, no less) as Florence. It is, in a certain sense, an
emasculating gesture on the author's part, and one that is not enhanced by
Walter's description of his career to Florence: ''I am but a wanderer . . . making voyages to live, across the sea. That is my calling now'' (805). Is Walter
really a participant in the masculine world? It is a bit difficult to accept,
particularly given his somewhat miraculous incorporation into that world at
the end of the novel. The ''deep, exhaustless, mighty well of love, in which
so much was sunk'' (884) may provide sweet water, but it is stagnant all the
same. When Walter's ship again departs, it is not the sailors who are placed
in the foreground: ''Upon the deck, image to the roughest man on board of
something that is graceful, beautiful, and harmless—something that it is good
and pleasant to have there, and that should make the voyage prosperous—is
Florence'' (907), and of course, the waves that continue their seemingly
endless whispering ''of love, eternal and illimitable, not bounded by the
confines of this world, or by the end of time, but ranging still, beyond the
sea, beyond the sky, to the invisible country far away!'' (908).

V

If Dickens seems to problematize both masculinity and femininity throughout
the novel, he nevertheless dismantles only one—masculinity—at story's end.
Following Carker's death, we are told that ''[t]he sea has ebbed and flowed
through a whole year [. . . and] the tides of human chance and change have
been set in their allotted courses'' (908). The ship named *Dombey and Son*
has fallen victim to the storm after a ''fight for life, against cross accidents,
doubtful rumours, unsuccessful ventures, unpropitious times, and most of all,
against the infatuation of its head, who would not contract its enterprises by
a hair's breadth, and would not listen to a word of warning that the ship he
strained so hard against the storm was weak, and could not bear it'' (908).
William J. Palmer, in his study of ''Dickens and Shipwreck'' (49–100), suggests that Dickens, inspired by Carlyle, sought a metaphor to represent the
mid-nineteenth century and found it in the shipwreck, ''one of the most
commonplace events of English social history . . . the recurring event that
exerted continual influence on Industrial Revolution economics'' (49).[16] Indeed, it is the sinking of the *Son and Heir* that signals the beginning of the
end for the Dombey firm, and the wreck of the firm itself is the final trigger
that begins Dombey's nearly fatal descent into remorse and self-loathing.

Alone in a house that even the rats are deserting, he finally allows himself to weep over "the stain of his domestic shame" (935). Finally, he stabs himself and watches his blood flow across the floor (938–39) until, in one of the happiest instances of lucky timing ever seen in Dickens, Florence arrives to save him. Her child has been born at sea, but "[t]he moment I could land, I came back to you" (940). Dombey, already at the water's edge, is now ready to enter it, and does. As Zwinger suggests,

> [u]ntil Dombey loses the last vestige of his patriarchal, socially constructed power, he need not treat his daughter (who is all women) or any other women (who are all daughters) with anything other than a lordly contempt, a contempt that masks the fear generated by any oppressed domestic population. . . . So, having brought *Dombey and Son* to the verge of a radical truth, Dickens brings Dombey himself to the extremity of need in order to effect a proper restoration of the domestic order, and in doing so consigns his story to the proper order of domestic fiction.   (436–37)

Florence's mission has apparently been fulfilled.[17] But is this a touching conclusion or a disturbing one? Florence's begging her father for forgiveness is certainly problematic: "Papa! Dearest Papa! Pardon me, forgive me! I have come back to ask forgiveness on my knees. I never can be happy more without it! . . . Papa, dear, I am changed. I am penitent. I know my fault. I know my duty better now. Papa, don't cast me off, or I shall die!" (939). Even Dombey seems to recognize how patently ridiculous it is to have his injured daughter abasing herself before him. He also recognizes, as the reader should, that she is "[u]nchanged still. Of all the world, unchanged" (939). There has been no growth or development on Florence's part, she still professes complete dependence on her heretofore defiantly independent father, and even her child seems to have been born on the same vapid sea of sentimentality upon which her marriage was made. Andrew McDonald agrees that "[d]espite neglect, suffering, and danger, despite numerous changes of role and status, she remains the innocent and pure votary of selfless love" (17), which is linked to Mary Armstrong's assertion that "[t]he mechanism for this dynamic of collapse and resurrection is the novel's construction of sentimental feminine flawlessness, specifically in the figure of Florence Dombey . . . the perfect (always subordinate, passive, and structurally heterosexual) female subject of ideology" (281). Conversely, Lyn Pykett suggests that "the central "movement" of this novel might rather be said to be one of constancy to a childlike state, as exemplified by Paul and Florence (among others), or a regression, a return to or rediscovery of the lost innocence of childhood, as exemplified by Dombey" (17).[18] There is clearly a common theme here—the idea that, in spite of her weakness as both character and ideological force, Florence's sentimental love, implausibly, utterly defeats her father's mercantile masculinity. Having begged forgiveness, Dombey prepares himself for departure, "with a docile submission to her entreaty" (940–41), and makes his feeble way outside. All that remain in the house are the tearful Miss Tox and Polly, and a depressed Rob the Grinder, whose failed foray into the capitalist world is punished by a reentry into the domestic. Having briefly made his own way in life, he is now counselled to remember that "I hope you will never forget that you have, and have always had, a good mother, and that you will endeavour so to conduct yourself as to be a comfort to her" (941).

After arguing that "daughters have no value at all" in the commercial world, Patricia Marks suggests that "[b]y the end of the novel . . . the commercial principle has been replaced with a powerful new precept—motherhood. . . . Dombey, who fails as businessman, husband, and father, and whose dependents are like the protected and starving labourer, must learn to be a mother, after all" (14). Motherhood has many faces[19] in the text, and Dickens's valorization of motherhood in *Dombey and Son* may, Marks suggests, be part of a trend towards domestic culture and "woman worship."[20] Zwinger, however, points out the main problem with Florence as heroine: the fact that "[w]hat is objectionable in Dombey's surrender to a power sentimentality represented as greater than his is that everyone "knows" that domestic influence is not stronger than capitalist power, that sentimental hierarchies are not superior to patriarchal ones, and, from the standpoint of that knowledge, Dombey's end looks not only like capitulation but an unnecessary and rather frightening one" (440). Ultimately, the sentimental reunion resembles a metaphorical emasculation, and no matter how much we might long for father and daughter to be reconciled, no matter how we might wish for Florence's value as Woman to be recognized at last, this is highly problematic.

The novel ends on an Edenic seashore, with Walter having miraculously integrated himself into the business world and the reconstituted Dombey family watching the waves—the waves that a reformed Mr. Dombey is at last able to hear: "The voices in the waves speak low to him of Florence, day and night . . . They speak to him of Florence and his altered heart; of Florence and their ceaseless murmuring beyond the sea, beyond the sky, to the invisible country far away" (975–76). The male world of trade is nowhere to be seen, though it is perhaps implied in Walter's absence from the tableau.[21] Dombey's identity as a man has been nearly erased, and he appears to spend all of his time dwelling on his past sins and lovingly stalking his granddaughter. After the waves have finished their whispering, Dickens adds one final exhortation to the reader, as if to remind us of the imagery that has tied the exercise together: "Never from the mighty sea may voices rise too late, to come between us and the unseen region on the other shore! Better, far better, that they whispered of that region in our childish ears, and the swift river hurried us away!''[22] The dominant term has become female, excluding (indeed, submerging) the male with little apparent resistance, and one cannot help but wonder whether this is truly a happy ending. Florence's brother, who could not become the "man" that his father wanted, is dead. Carker, whose "feminine" traits served only to poison, dies in front of the ultimate representative of the masculine industrial age, the locomotive.[23] Edith, who can perform femininity but represents masculine hardness, has been "left . . . in the grave" (969), Alice Marwood literally suffers the same fate, and Dombey is not so much redeemed as he is carried unyielding into the sea.

Robert Newsom points out, as Moynahan does, that the novel can be viewed as a struggle between "firmness" and "wetness." As he puts it, "Dombey is the head of a "firm," and he and it embody firmness, he in the literal firmness of his rigid, inflexible face and body. Opposed to him are Florence, forever dissolving into tears, and the sea. . . . The significance of wetness is real, but what also needs to be stressed is the loss of wholeness entailed in dissolving or melting" (199–200). This is a compelling echo of Moynahan's more gendered argument: "Before his collapse Dombey inhabits a . . . tensely masculine world, a society of heads without hearts. Florence's sphere of influence is a slackly feminine one, consisting in a society of hearts without heads. Dickens's attempted solution of this cultural impasse merely perpetuates it. Dombey moves from hardness through debility to a maundering, guilt-ridden submission to feminine softness" (130). Dickens could hardly be characterized as a feminist—much of his writing, not to mention his own life, suggests that he really had very little understanding of women in general. But *Dombey and Son* supports the notion that he was not unwilling to question traditionally masculine virtues, the virtues of "hardness, calculating and unyielding rationality, independence, aggressiveness, and acquisitiveness" which, as Schact notes, "were naturalized and sanctified by nineteenth-century political economy" (96). The problem is that although Florence and her water-babies seem to offer an alternative, it is not necessarily a viable one, for the idealization of the hyper-feminine has a nasty tendency to efface identity altogether. This is undoubtedly one of the reasons why it is so difficult to see Florence as an individual. As Armstrong puts it, she represents "the perfect Victorian female; beautiful to the point of otherwordliness, selfless to the point of invisibility" (282). There are certainly very few individuals remaining at the end of the novel, as personality appears to have been subordinated to feeling, and ultimately, one has to question whether Cuttle's claim that "[w]e're all shipmets here"[24] (879) implies a rudderless voyage through life.

NOTES

With thanks to Suzanne Bailey, Mary Wilson Carpenter, and D. M. R. Bentley.

1. Gerhard Joseph reads the waves slightly differently, arguing that they are meant to represent "the mystery of cosmic repetition," as in "Dover Beach" (180). J. Hillis Miller suggests that the waves should not be recognized as a feminine trope, but rather, "an authentic religious motif . . . the apprehension of a transcendent spirit, present in nature and reached through death, but apparently unattainable in this world" (148). I would quibble with this reading of "the sea of death" not only because it is too simplistic, but because a sort of oneness with the sea without dying clearly *can* be attained, as Florence, Walter, Cuttle et al. demonstrate. As Miller concedes, there is "an immediate, immanent form of this fluidity: human feeling, an undifferentiated current of sympathy, potentially existing in anyone's heart as the same presence, and flowing out through the prisons of language and inalterable peculiarities to bathe all those around in a warm glow of love" (149).

2. Dickens's decision to name his sentimental heroine Florence, or "Flo[w]" is surely no coincidence, just as the names "Gills," "Cuttle," and "Wa[l]ter" all have nautical connotations.

3. McCombie suggests that the name is meant to be a play upon "pipkin"—a small earthenware pot without a spout—emphasizing her uselessness "as a supplier of nutriment to Paul" (27).

4. Julian Moynahan phrases it slightly more eloquently (though cynically): "Within the circle of Florence's influence even the sea of death is transformed into a vast welter of eternal love which reaches from the barren shores of this life to the shores of heaven. To claim this is to claim that Florence is more angel than woman, and that is exactly what she is called with damnable iteration; she is a sentimental heroine upon whom angelic powers and attributes have been arbitrarily grafted" (127).

5. Elfenbein does not, however, share Moynahan's view that Florence is one of the novel's most powerful beings:

   Dickens carefully preserves gender hierarchies even as he valorizes the feminine emotion associated with Florence. As a result, the novel's conclusion, often interpreted as an idyllic and regressive portrayal of domestic bliss, reveals the strain in Dickens's conception of Florence as an adequate response to the dangers that the manager poses. When, after the destruction of Carker and of Dombey's business, the plot leaves behind the analogy between home and office, the previously masked contradictions in Florence's position emerge in a strikingly awkward and fragmented conclusion. She becomes an ideal domestic manager who is almost never shown inside her home, while her husband Walter Gay becomes an ideal business manager who is never shown on the job. (366–67)

Such a reading supposes that the analogy between home and office dominates the novel, which I am not sure that it does, particularly given the paradoxical position of the Wooden Midshipman, which functions as both. Moreover, Walter's final role seems to me to be more of a concession to the necessity of maintaining some semblance of male trade, while gesturing towards the falsity of such a conclusion.

6. See Yelin, "Strategies for Survival: Florence and Edith in 'Dombey and Son,' " *Victorian Studies* 22 (1979), 297–319.

7. Elfenbein suggests that Dombey's "chief weapon in combating the relationship between Florence and Edith is the relationship between himself and Carker"—which might have set up a very interesting battle between the sexes were it not for the instinctive bond between Carker and Edith, who both "sense their mutually subversive relationship to the same authority" (377).

8. Mrs. Pipchin is not described in such terms, which emphasizes the possibility that she may be read as a female version of Dombey (as she seems to have been represented in Hablot K. Browne's illustrations for the book [cf. McCombie 27]). Dombey likes her—he does not like the constant female presence of Polly, whose breasts nourish his son.

9. A number of critics have noted that Phiz's drawings seem to support Dombey's fears. In addition to the tableau of Diana and Actaeon in "Mr. Dombey and his 'Confidential Agent,' " the ironically titled "Mr. Carker in his Hour of Triumph" includes a picture "of Judith drawing the sword with which she is to decapitate Holofernes: there is enough similarity in the dress of Judith and Edith to make the symbolic identification unmistakable" (McCombie 31). See also Jane R. Cohen, *Dickens and His Original Illustrators*, 99.

10. Edith only appears in nine of the novel's twenty numbers, while Florence appears in all but one.

11. It is worth noting that Cuttle is never given a first name, only a nautical title—an interesting contrast to the "Mr." by which the elder Paul Dombey is almost invariably addressed.

12. Failed capitalism is not limited to the domestic society centered on the Wooden Midshipman. While visiting the Skettles's home, Florence comes upon "a very poor man, who seemed to have no regular employment, but now went roaming about the banks of the river when the tide was low, looking out for bits and scraps in the mud; and now worked at the unpromising little patch of garden-ground before his cottage; and now tinkered up a miserable old boat that belonged to him" (424). The emphasis is placed upon the love that the man bears for his sickly daughter, but there are a number of references to his useless work in and around the river. Florence, thrilling to the notion of such an uncompromising love, nevertheless feels compelled to leave the man some money, knowing that his labors are insufficient. It is a point that is given further emphasis through the reading of Sol Gills's will, for Gills has a great deal of love to give, but apparently little else, as he bequeaths to Walter, if he is still alive, "what little there may be" (640).

13. Toots's masculine identity is nearly non-existent, so subsumed is he in the rhythm of the waves, and his fumbling courtship of Florence is configured in ridiculous terms. He "is so enslaved that he has not a scrap of free-will left" (669).

14. Mrs Chick's frequent performances of this sort are more often accompanied by the pseudo-apologetic "It's very foolish of me."
15. See Forster 473. Forster was adamantly opposed to his friend's original plan for Walter Gay.
16. Shipwrecks occurred on a disturbingly frequent basis (much to the morbid fascination of the public), claiming a large number of lives and resulting in often crippling financial losses. Drawing on a wide variety of shipping statistics and studies, Palmer proves quite convincingly that ships were frequently dangerous, due to inadequacy, neglect, and sometimes even criminal intent (whereupon rotten ships known amongst the sailors as "coffin-ships" were overloaded, over-insured, and expected to sink), while captains were often inept, sailors untrained or inexperienced, and the ships themselves lacked basic navigational equipment—presumably of the sort sold in Gills's shop.
17. All of the other characters within Florence's sphere of influence flourish as well, and, at the end of the novel, Captain Cuttle prepares to sing a round of "Lovely Peg," a sea-shanty (975), to celebrate their lives.
18. The idea that the novel's conclusion is fated from the very beginning is one of the cornerstones of Pykett's argument: "[I]n *Dombey and Son*, history is redeemed by a different, more providential and certainly more optimistic version of destiny, a destiny which is, of course, manufactured and controlled by the author, but which appears to derive from the wise passivity of the romance hero and heroine. Progressively throughout the novel, and especially in the symbolism of the sea, it is suggested that something is taking its course, that there is a destiny to be fulfilled" (26–27).
19. Marks includes Miss Tox, Gills, Cuttle, Toots, Harriet Carker, and Polly Toodles in her analysis.
20. As Judith Schneid Lewis notes, motherhood signified above all else "rational and moral virtues" (71).
21. Elfenbein suggests that the Wooden Midshipman becomes the novel's ideal business, and Walter the ideal mercantile manager, though the latter, tellingly, is never represented in that capacity. Thus, the world of business cannot appear because "[o]nly once the family and the business, the private and the public worlds, have been entirely divorced can they function as they should" (381). The same might be said for the male and the female. As Walter moves closer towards Dombey's old role, he moves into the city and away from the beach (which is located, significantly, outside of London).
22. As Kathleen Tillotson has shown, *Dombey and Son* represents Dickens's first conscious attempt to concentrate his novel around a single unifying theme—that of pride—rather than simply providing an excess of characters and scenes to move the story along (cf. Tillotson 157–201).
23. Because of the length of this essay and the complexity of his character, I have not said much about Carker. Readers who wish to pursue studies in this area are advised to begin with Andrew Elfenbein's "Managing the House in *Dombey and Son*," Anne Humphrey's "Carker the Manager," or Lewis Horne's "The Way of Resentment in *Dombey and Son*."

24. This statement could certainly be read as implying that the world of the Midship-man is in fact a sort of homosexual continuum. Indeed, Dr. Mary Wilson Carpen-ter, in reading over an earlier draft of this paper, suggested that the narrative perceives a threat not only in the femininity of the waves, but the effeminate world of male homosexuality. Such a reading certainly helps to explain why the domestic world of Gills and company is also a world of capitalist failure.

WORKS CITED

Adams, James Eli. *Dandies and Desert Saints: Styles of Victorian Masculinity*. Ithaca.: Cornell UP, 1995.

Armstrong, Mary. "Pursuing Perfection: *Dombey and Son*, Female Homoerotic De-sire, and the Sentimental Heroine." *Studies in the Novel* 28:3 (1996): 281–302.

Auerbach, Nina. *Romantic Imprisonment: Women and Other Glorified Outcasts*. New York: Columbia UP, 1986.

Bachelard, Gaston. *Water and Dreams: An Essay on the Imagination of Matter*. Ed. Joanne H. Stroud and Robert S. Dupree. Trans. Edith R. Farrell. Dallas: Pega-sus, 1983.

Carlyle, Thomas. *On Heroes, Hero-Worship and the Heroic in History*. Lincoln: U of Nebraska P, 1966.

Clark, Robert. "Riddling the Family Firm: The Sexual Economy in *Dombey and Son*." *ELH* 51 (1984): 69–84.

Cohen, Jane R. *Charles Dickens and His Original Illustrators*. Columbus: Ohio State UP, 1980.

Dickens, Charles. *Dealings with the Firm of Dombey & Son: Wholesale, Retail and for Exportation*. 1848. Harmondsworth, Eng.: Penguin, 1970.

Elfenbein, Andrew. "Managing the House in *Dombey and Son*: Dickens and the Uses of Analogy." *Studies in Philology* 92 (1995): 361–82.

Forster, John. *The Life of Charles Dickens*. Ed. J. W. T. Ley. London: Cecil Palmer, 1928.

Joseph, Gerhard. "Change and the Changeling in *Dombey and Son*." *Dickens Studies Annual* 18 (1989): 179–95.

Lecker, Barbara. "Walter Gay and the Theme of Fancy in *Dombey and Son*." *Dicken-sian* 67 (1971): 21–30.

Lewis, Judith Schneid. *In the Family Way: Childbearing in the British Aristocracy, 1760–1860*. New Brunswick: Rutgers UP, 1986.

Marks, Patricia. "Paul Dombey and the Milk of Human Kindness." *Dickens Quarterly* 11:1 (1994): 14–25.

Marsh, Joss Lutz. "Good Mrs. Brown's Connections: Sexuality and Story-Telling in *Dealings with the Firm of Dombey and Son.*" *ELH* 58 (1991): 405–26.

McCombie, Frank. "Sexual Repression in *Dombey and Son.*" *Dickensian* 88 (1992): 25–38.

McDonald, Andrew. "The Preservation of Innocence in *Dombey and Son*: Florence's Identity and the Role of Walter Gay." *Texas Studies in Literature and Language* 18 (1976): 1–19.

Miller, J. Hillis. *Charles Dickens: The World of His Novels.* Cambridge: Harvard UP, 1959.

Moglen, Helene. "Theorizing Fiction/Fictionalizing Theory: The Case of *Dombey and Son.*" *Victorian Studies* 35 (1992): 159–84.

Montaut, Mary. "The Second Mrs. Dombey." *Dickens Quarterly* 4:3 (1987): 141–53.

Moynahan, Julian. "Dealings with the Firm of Dombey and Son: Firmness *versus* Wetness." *Dickens and the Twentieth Century.* Ed. John Gross and Gabriel Pearson. Toronto: U of Toronto P, 1962. 121–31.

Newsom, Robert. "Embodying *Dombey*: Whole and in Part." *Dickens Studies Annual* 18 (1976): 197– 219.

Palmer, William J. *Dickens and New Historicism.* New York: St. Martin's, 1997.

Perera, Suvendrini. "Wholesale, Retail and for Exportation: Empire and the Family Business in *Dombey and Son.*" *Victorian Studies* 33 (1990): 603–20.

Pykett, Lyn. "*Dombey and Son*: A Sentimental Family Romance." *Studies in the Novel* 19 (1987): 16–30.

Schact, Paul. "Dickens and the Uses of Nature." *Victorian Studies* 34 (1990): 77–102.

Tillotson, Kathleen. *Novels of the Eighteen-Forties.* Oxford: Oxford UP, 1954.

Yelin, Louise. "Strategies for Survival: Florence and Edith in 'Dombey and Son.' " *Victorian Studies* 22 (1979): 297–319.

Zwinger, Lynda. "The Fear of the Father: Dombey and Daughter." *Nineteenth-Century Literature* 39 (1985): 420–40.

Inspector Bucket versus Tom-all-Alone's: *Bleak House*, Literary Theory, and the Condition-of-England in the 1850s

Simon Joyce

It has recently seemed something of a litmus test for new schools of literary theory to demonstrate themselves through a close reading of Bleak House. *Taking up the challenge to examine the novel through the lens of cultural studies, this essay seeks first to locate the novel in its historical context. Written less than a decade after the appearance of a small unit of London detectives, the text reflects early anxieties about the efficiency and impartiality of these public servants, although Dickens's own journalistic writings tended to exaggerate the abilities of officers like the real-life Inspector Field. Where New Historicist criticism in particular has tended to take such claims at face value, early readers of* Bleak House *were confused by Inspector Bucket, and identified instead with the crossing sweeper, Jo. Read in relation to the "condition-of-England" novels by Gaskell and others, and Dickens's own interest in welfare and sanitary reform, Jo shows the weakness of contemporary projects of social amelioration, including those that operated through the agency of the new police. In that sense, Bucket's insistence that Jo simply "move on" from place to place illustrates a larger political failure to develop reform strategies for the urban poor.*

Since the ability to provide a compelling interpretation of *Bleak House* has become something of a litmus test among Victorianists in recent years, it is

Dickens Studies Annual, Volume 32, Copyright © 2002 by AMS Press, Inc. All rights reserved.

perhaps advisable to ask at the outset whether we need another reading of Dickens's novel. My answer, it should be clear, is "maybe one more." In many ways, what still draws me to this text is its capacity to be read by just about every critical school of the last twenty years, and to exhaust each of them while still remaining strangely resistant to all of our attempts to corral it. It is perhaps best seen as the Victorianists' white whale, the one text that we are all destined to take a shot at. Consider some recent history. When British literary critics decided that the perniciousness of fictional realism rested on its production of an omniscient subject position which could actively manage or transcend different points of view, Catherine Belsey identified the dual narratives of *Bleak House* as offering just such a perspective to the reader: "By thus smoothing over the contradictions it has so powerfully dramatized in the interests of a singly, unified, coherent 'truth,' " she concluded, "*Bleak House*, however critical of the world it describes, offers the reader a position, an attitude which is given as non-contradictory, fixed in 'knowing' subjectivity" (79–81).[1] When Marxism took on board Althusser's concerns about the possible disjunction between content and form, Terry Eagleton regarded the same text as exemplifying a productive tension between the two, so that Dickens was forced "to use as aesthetically unifying images the very social institutions (the Chancery Court of *Bleak House*, the Circumlocution Office of *Little Dorrit*) which are the object of his criticism. It is, ironically, these very systems of conflict, division and contradiction which provide Dickens with a principle of symbolic coherence" (129).

Eagleton's point was not, I think, that these formal images moderate or smooth over social tension, but rather that they enable its expression. Another wave of criticism would, however, see such a gesture as itself suspect. D. A. Miller, for instance, considered such a recovery as wishful thinking, and as complementary to a deconstructive reading by which the novel's—indeed, any novel's—unifying impulses are always already subject to critique. By the 1980s, *Bleak House* became one of the paradigm texts for a New Historicist thesis, according to which Eagleton's positing of a critical function for art and deconstruction's tendency to disseminate an epistemological undecidabilty across Western culture were both equally naïve: " 'Against' Marxism," Miller wrote in 1983, "we stress the positivity of contradiction, which, far from always marking the fissure of a social formation, may rather be one of the joints where such a formation is articulated. Contradiction may function not to expose, but to construct the ideology that had foreseen and contained it. And 'against' deconstruction, we should urge . . . that undecidability must always be the undecidability of *something in particular*" (99). Drawn to the argument of Foucault's *Discipline and Punish* that the nineteenth century saw the generalization of insidious schemes of Panoptic surveillance throughout the social fabric, Miller found its perfect confirmation in *Bleak*

House, a novel which "is profoundly concerned to train us . . . in the sensibility for inhabiting the new bureaucratic, administrative structures" (89). Since it plots a continuum linking the police investigation undertaken by Inspector Bucket with a series of micro-investigations on behalf of "amateur detectives" like the lawyer Tulkinghorn or Mrs. Snagsby, Dickens's text can be read as dissolving the division between "public" and "private" matters, thus confirming the Foucauldian thesis; indeed, it seems to do this so ingeniously and thoroughly that—had it not already existed—Miller might have had to write it himself.

As the literary-critical tide began to turn against the New Historicism, *Bleak House* was put to service again: in a Bakhtinian response from Dominick LaCapra, for instance, in which the bureaucracy which triumphs in Miller's account is instead subjected to a "powerfully carnivalized criticism" (127); or Judith Newton's feminist riposte which seeks to emphasize "the chaotic threat of women's autonomous desires" where Miller's reading "phases out broad-based relations of domination and subordination and elides what feminists see as the text's representation of, and investment in, and anxiety over gender difference and women's agency" (458). With hindsight, it is perhaps less surprising that such critiques of a landmark New Historicist project like Miller's began to appear than that they would advance themselves through a required alternative interpretation of a Dickens novel, as if close reading was the final arbiter of the relative merits among different theoretical positions. I am mindful, then, of what it means to offer one more reading of *Bleak House*, even as I am drawn to ask here what that text might look like from the perspective of the new dominant critical paradigm, cultural studies—and indeed, it may be that it can't lay a serious claim to critical hegemony until it has produced such a reading. What follows is a preliminary attempt to take up that challenge.

There have been a number of essays that have tried to map the relationship between cultural studies and the New Historicism, two schools of theory which seem in many ways to be close relations.[2] Most often, the basic distinction being made is that cultural studies holds out a hope for forms of resistance, either collective or subjective, which would seem to have been ruled out in advance by New Historicists like Miller, who emphasize instead the ability of power systems to contain opposition. While this is a crucial difference, and one which will return when I come to offer my own reading of *Bleak House*, it can obscure the real affinities between the two critical schools: both deny literature, art, or culture a transcendent or autonomous status, for example, and see them instead as the products of social and political processes; both would question even that basic distinction between something called "culture" and something called "society," and would want equally to challenge any suggestion that the former is merely a reflection of the latter; both would insist on the agencies—especially political ones—which are articulated by texts and the interests they serve, and would tend to see those interests and agencies in broadly structural terms rather than the simple possessions of individuals (like authors or characters); both aim to set texts in their historical contexts, and to read them in light of contingent discourses and relevant social debates as well as present concerns and agendas; and so on. Where they divide is perhaps more a question of emphasis, or even attitude. If New Historicists are generally pessimistic about the possibilities of a progressive and transformative agency, both in the past and (by extension) the present, that is because it would inevitably have been contaminated by, contained within, and even produced by the dominant power; by contrast, practitioners of cultural studies tend to be more optimistic in part because they focus more on the present or future moment, and not on a past which has its sins already on record.

We can begin to see why questions of *policing* (both as a literal activity and a metaphor for more general forms of social control) can be crucial here, and furthermore, why *Bleak House* seems so germane to these debates. Following Foucault, Miller sees in the mid-nineteenth century a post-Enlightenment generalization of more insidious and dispersed forms of power, which no longer operate with reference to a sovereign ruler but work instead through discourses, institutions, and apparatuses, among which the law and the police are two obvious examples. One corollary of this change is that culture is no longer available as an immediate vehicle of political protest, as Foucault himself insists it was earlier in the century—and it's surely relevant that the examples he uses are of crime texts: the speeches of condemned men, especially as they were sold at public executions, or criminal memoirs which allowed for a subjective identification on the part of their readers.[3] All of this supposedly gets supplanted by detective fiction, in which the reader is allowed to identify only with the force of the law, just as surely as public executions are replaced by the penitentiary system which sought to reform the individual from the inside; thus, if policing becomes a privileged metaphor for Foucauldian criticism, then detective fiction is also a privileged literary genre which functions equally well as an emblem of the work of art in the age of Panopticism.

Bleak House (1852–53) more or less fits the temporal framework of the argument—for, although there is no official dating of the Panoptic era, most of Foucault's examples come from the late 1830s and '40s—and certainly satisfies its thematic obsessions. The novel features, after all, one of the first appearances of a detective in British fiction, and I hope not to anticipate too much of my later argument by here acknowledging Inspector Bucket's sheer novelty among the novel's first reviewers: "Here comes a man whom it is even exciting to watch," declared the *Illustrated London News*; "it is the celebrated detective officer, Buckett [sic]. Mark him well. He can find out anything. See him in the streets, in the day time. Follow him at night. Notice how he behaves to various characters. Now, he is in operation—he will infallibly reach what he is seeking. What is it? Again, it is nothing—or nothing which greatly influences what has thereafter to be unfolded.''[4] Bucket is a novelty, entirely fascinating but also (and perhaps as a result) confusing—and I'll return later to exactly what he does and what he's looking for, questions which in each case yield answers which are significantly different from Miller's. For now, though, I want to follow up on the suggestion that one key context for an historically-informed reading of *Bleak House* is the novelty of the detective police, which had in fact only been introduced as recently as 1842.[5]

This marks one clear difference from France, which had not only had a police force for much longer but also took it for granted that their work was essentially political, and supplemented where necessary by spies and paid informants—hence Foucault's obsession with mechanisms of *surveillance*, a term which is inadequately conveyed by the term "discipline" in English translations. As early as 1763, Sir William Mildmay's *The Police of France* had warned of the potential intrusion of such a force into the lives of "freeborn Englishmen," describing how the Parisian police "go under the name of military establishments, and consequently cannot be initiated by our administration, under a free and civil constitution of government"; in contrast to France, he argued, England was "a land of liberty, where the injured and oppressed are to seek for no other protection, but that which the law ought to afford, without plying for aid to a military power; a remedy dangerous, and perhaps worse than the disease" (quoted in Emsley 21). These same concerns were addressed to successive Parliamentary inquiries between 1789 and 1829. In 1822, for example, Sir Robert Peel commissioned a Select Committee to investigate the policing of London, which reported back that "[i]t is difficult to reconcile an effective system of police with that perfect freedom of action and exemption from interference which are the great privileges and blessing of society in this country," concluding that the "forfeiture or curtailment of such advantages would be too great a sacrifice for improvement in police, or facilities in detection of crime, however desirable in themselves" (quoted in Radzinowicz 4:163). This emphasis on civil liberties had a decisive impact on the form of Peel's new Metropolitan police force of 1829, which worked on the principle of crime prevention, rather than detection, through a system of beat patrols.

In his summary of these developments, Leon Radzinowicz has concluded that their defining characteristic was that "the need to absolve the police from any suspicion of spying took precedence over the general needs of detection and prevention" (4:188–89). Spying was not outlawed as such, however, but merely driven underground, as it were. Just four years into the life of the new police, and the same year that a jury verdict of "justifiable homicide" was returned on a man charged with killing a constable during a rally of the National Union of the Working Classes at Cold Bath Fields, charges were brought against a policeman named Sergeant Popay, that he had infiltrated the National Political Union, amended their resolutions to reflect a more inflammatory rhetoric, suggested that they practice with firearms and broad-swords, and had then reported back to police authorities. The investigating Parliamentary committee considered that Popay had overstepped the bounds of his duties by acting as an *agent provocateur*, and reproved him for "car-rying concealment into the intercourse of private life."[6] Taken together, these incidents suggest an unstable political climate which would only become worse with the beginnings of the Chartist movement, and they also reveal that techniques traditionally associated with French policing were quietly being imported into Britain despite widespread public opposition. In 1842, after a series of unsolved murders, a small detective unit consisting of two inspectors and six sergeants was finally introduced, yet more than twenty-five years later it had only grown to a total of sixteen men. A new version of the Popay scandal erupted in 1845 when undercover police were again accused of acting as spies, and from then until 1862 such tactics were used only in cases of "urgent necessity" and required special orders from police superintendents (Radzinowicz, 4:188–89).

Dickens was one of the first and most vocal supporters of these London detectives, publishing a series of admiring essays in *Household Words* which sometimes read like awestruck fan mail. The most famous of these, "On Duty with Inspector Field," describes a night spent on patrol with one of the inspectors (who has often been taken as the model for Bucket)[7] and attributes a remarkable degree of investigative efficiency to the new detective police; indeed, Dickens would have us believe that the contrast between old and new systems—as illustrated by the compelling authority of Field—was so great that this squad of eight might be able to subjugate London's entire criminal underworld. As if to prove the point, they bring the author to a cellar in Rat's Castle, at the center of the rookery of St. Giles. Dickens duly notes that the population there "is strong enough to murder us all, and willing enough to do it; but let Inspector Field have a mind to pick out one thief here, and take him; let him produce that ghastly truncheon from his pocket, and say, with his business-like air, 'My lad, I want you!' and all Rat's Castle shall be stricken with paralysis, and not a finger raised against him, as he fits the handcuffs on!'' (516).

What seems odd is that such a scene never actually occurs, as the essay anticipates Bucket's own questionable effectiveness in *Bleak House*. Indeed, Field behaves less like the feared and omniscient detective of mystery fiction than the modern-day community policeman: at one point on the tour, for example, he leads Dickens into an outhouse which is home to "ten, twenty, thirty–who can count them" Irish, takes pains to find the landlord, and gives him money to buy them all coffee in the morning (517–18). He seems moreover well-known and respected by the criminals they encounter, as "pickpockets defer to him; the gentle sex (not very gentle here) smile upon him. Half-drunken hags check themselves in the midst of pots of beer, or pints of gin, to drink to Mr. Field. . . . One beldame in rusty black has such admiration for him, that she runs a whole street's length to shake his hand," and so on (518–19). There is one sense in which detection takes precedence over crime prevention here, although not the sense intended by the detectives' supporters, as two parallel scenes illustrate. In the first, the party visits a crowded room in a poor lodging-house where, as a precaution against theft, the sheets have been inscribed with the warning "STOP THIEF!" (520) Later, in another lodging-house owned by a belligerent landlord, Bark, they again examine the bedding: here, however, the message reads "STOLEN FROM BARK'S!" (525) Where the first is presumably designed to prevent theft by rendering the sheets useless for resale, the second would seem to offer an alternative—and probably more likely—assessment of its inevitability: resigned to the fact of theft, Bark would prefer to maximize the chances of getting his property back in the event that the thief is ever arrested. Such an outcome would seem to be a remote possibility at best: a squad of eight Metropolitan detectives were, after all, facing what amounted to a critical mass of criminality, concentrated in labyrinthine rookeries like Rat's Castle, and engaged in a wide array of illegal activities.

Given the odds, Dickens's faith in Field seems misplaced, or maybe a willful exaggeration aimed at inculcating a much-needed public confidence in the new detective force. Immediately following the first of these scenes, for example, he imagines himself in the position of a thief wrapped up in these same imprinted sheets, the inscription of which must function as "my first-foot on New Year's day, my Valentine, my Birthday salute, my Christmas greeting, my parting with the old year. STOP THIEF!" Dickens continues to imagine the thief's life:

> And to know that I *must* be stopped, come what will. To know that I am no match for this individual energy and keenness, or this organized and steady system! Come across the street here, and . . . examine these intricate passages and doors, contrived for escape, flapping and counter-flapping, like the lids of conjuror's boxes. But what avail they? Who gets in by a nod, and shows their secret working to us? Inspector Field.   (520; emphasis in original)

That italicized "must" is presumably intended to denote the inevitability of capture. Given the context of this passage, however, a second possibility presents itself—that it signifies instead an urgent *necessity* and thus a tone closer to ideological prescription than to realist description.

Dickens is clearly invested in promoting an image of police efficiency here, just as D. A. Miller is when he writes about Field's fictional counterpart. In a key scene which introduces us to the rookery of Tom-all-Alone's, the closest the novel comes to a Rat's Castle or St. Giles, Mr. Snagsby accompanies Inspector Bucket in search of the crossing sweeper Jo, about whom I will be saying much more in a moment. Their failure to find him causes a telling problem for Miller, who wants to offer it as testimony to the ways in which the detective police have "saturated" the criminal underworld. The problem that he faces is that the considerable knowledge of crime amassed in this way does not readily translate into any arrests: offenders may well be "known" to the police, but that does not appear to deter them from committing crimes, as contemporary theories of preventive policing suggested it should. This dilemma can only be averted by reinterpreting the scene through a perverse logic, according to which the underworld is only an effect of the operation of an all-pervasive power, which produces, maintains, and contains such sites specifically in order to police them more efficiently: thus, according to Miller,

> [i]f the saturation does not appear to have much curtailed delinquency, or even, strangely, to have prevented Tom-all-Alone's from continuing to serve as a refuge for those wanted by the police, these perhaps were never the ends of police penetration. What such penetration apparently does secure is a containment of crime and power together, which both become visible mainly in a peripheral place "avoided by all decent people." The raison d'etre of Tom-all-Alone's is that it *be* all alone.   (76–77; emphasis in original)

This reading may be ingenious, but it is ultimately disingenuous, I think. As many critiques of Foucault have argued by now, if such failures can in fact be adduced as evidence of surreptitious success, and criminals contained simply by being left alone, then there really is no imaginable outside or reverse side of power: such a theoretical model, as Fredric Jameson noted a long time ago, "would seem slowly and inexorably to eliminate any possibility of the *negative* as such, and to reintegrate the place of an oppositional or merely "critical" practice and resistance back into the system as the latter's mere inversion" (91; emphasis in original).

I don't think that this critique necessarily requires us to endorse a romantic idealization of criminality, although that impulse has sometimes been present within contemporary cultural studies; only that we see the image of the detective in Dickens's work (or Poe's for that matter) as an ideological fiction which promoted or exaggerated the abilities of a force that was severely limited in its operations. Bucket's failures might even play into such a strategy, if we read them as making a case for an expansion of police powers, one which was repeatedly made during the 1850s as opposition began to fade with the lessening of political tensions. As Robert Reiner has noted, it became increasingly clear to opponents of the new police as early as the 1840s that "reformers were using rising crime statistics to justify the extension of a preventive police, the efficacy of which was called into question by those very figures" (37). The dilemma these advocates faced was that any public celebration of the police's knowledge and efficiency inevitably led to questions about their apparent restraint: as *Fraser's Magazine* editorialized in 1857, "The public is aware that most, if not every one of the ticket-of-leave men who have spread the reign of terror in the well-lighted and crowded metropolis, are in the black list of the police and *wants to know* why they are not taken up" (quoted in McGowen, 46; emphasis in original). This journalistic rhetoric is working to make two opposing points simultaneously: crucially, it aimed to justify the current methods and powers of the police to a public which might still harbor suspicions, and also to minimize the dangers posed by criminal elements; while at the same time, it highlighted the opposite case by calling for increased manpower, tougher sentencing, and greater surveillance, which were presumably required because the Victorian "war on crime" was in fact being lost.

Considered in this light, Inspector Bucket—as well as the response he elicited—can be read anew. Another of his "failures," for instance, comes during a passage that famously highlights how he personifies those characteristics of disinterested omniscience and super-vision which we generally associate with a master-detective like Sherlock Holmes. Setting off in search of Lady Dedlock, Bucket "mounts a high tower in his mind, and looks out far and wide. Many solitary figures he perceives, creeping through the streets; many solitary figures out on the heaths, and roads, and lying under haystacks. But the figure he seeks is not among them" (824). By the time Bucket manages to find Lady Dedlock she is already dead, on the steps of the cemetery containing the body of Captain Hawdon, her former lover. It is surely significant that this heroic act of willful self-abstraction fails to produce the desired results, while at the same time offering a key image of his Panoptic power. (Indeed, I am reminded that, whatever its suitability as a metaphor, no Panopticon was actually built in Britain on the basis of Bentham's designs, having been judged too costly. The closest approximation, London's Millbank penitentiary of 1816, was dogged by financial difficulties, incompetent employees, and prisoner riots).[8]

If Inspector Bucket's celebrated abilities seem to have been oversold, the same also might be said for the professed impartiality which grounds his performance. He boasts of an apparent blindness to social distinctions, with an intimate acquaintance with the crimes committed in the homes of "genteel families" like the Dedlocks as well as those of Tom-all-Alone's, but

such a claim is thrown into question by the fact that he is also *working for*
Sir Leicester Dedlock, who instructs him before the start of his search that
"If I have not . . . in the most emphatic manner, adjured you, officer, to
exercise your utmost skill in this atrocious case, I particularly desire to take
the present opportunity of rectifying any omission I may have made. Let no
expense be a consideration. I am prepared to defray all charges. You can
incur none, in pursuit of the object you have undertaken, that I shall hesitate
for a moment to bear" (773). Bucket's motives thus seem suspect when he
declares, on wrongly arresting George for the murder of Tulkinghorn, that
"I tell you plainly there's a reward out, of a hundred guineas, offered by Sir
Leicester Dedlock, Baronet. You and me have always been pleasant together;
but I have got a duty to discharge; and if that hundred guineas is to be made,
it may as well be made by me as any other man" (735). The detective's
knowledge of the aristocracy, it seems, arises less from any direct professional
investigation of them than from time spent in their pay.

   Bucket's evident partiality flies in the face of claims that Dickens made
elsewhere for the superior performance of the new police, especially when
compared to their fondly remembered predecessors. An 1850 *Household
Words* essay on "The Detective Police," for instance, opens with the declaration that "[w]e are not by any means devout believers in the old Bow Street
Police. To say the truth, we think there was a vast amount of humbug about
those worthies. Apart from many of them being men of very indifferent
character, and far too much in the habit of consorting with thieves and the
like, they never lost a public occasion of jobbing and trading in mystery
and making the most of themselves." The blame for this false reputation,
interestingly, is said to lie with Dickens's old enemy the magistracy, along
with "penny-a-liners" who collaborated to exaggerate the professional ethics
and efficiency of the early detectives, although we have already seen that he
performed much the same role for Field and the other detectives (485). In
many ways, I think we're still blinded by the protomodernity of Bucket, a
figure whose very novelty, I would suggest, predictably means that he ends
up embodying so many contradictory attitudes and beliefs about the new
police. To really understand *Bleak House*, we need to retrace our steps back
into Tom-all-Alone's and follow instead Bucket's hopelessly overmatched
adversary, the pathetic crossing-sweeper Jo.

   If we think about the publication date of the novel, which began appearing
in 1852, another likely context emerges: the so-called "condition-of-England" debates which consumed cultural as well as political commentators
in the 1840s and '50s. Nominally inspired by Carlyle's 1839 essay on Chartism, which posed essentially the same questions in terms of the nation, the
poor ("Is the condition of the English working people wrong"), and of
humanity in general ("What are the rights of men?"), these debates especially

occupied the novelists of the period: Disraeli's *Sibyl; or the Two Nations* (1845), with its provocative subtitle, is generally thought to initiate the minor genre of British fiction termed the "industrial" or "condition-of-England" novels, which developed in turn through texts like Gaskell's *Mary Barton* (1848) and *North and South* (1854–55) and Kingsley's *Alton Locke: Tailor and Poet* (1848). Scholars like Catherine Gallagher and Joseph Childers have paid these texts a great deal of attention in recent years, but it is surprising that this interest has not overlapped with the critical popularity of *Bleak House* during the same period, perhaps because its successor *Hard Times* has seemed a better fit for the "industrial novel" rubric.

Nonetheless, *Bleak House* fits squarely into the typology of the "condition-of-England" novels, most obviously because it investigates the possible connections and disconnections among different strands and social classes which seemed to be pulling apart from one another. If we think of "the two nations" or even "north and south" as master-tropes for such an investigation, and these novels as seeking to bridge those apparent dichotomies through mutual understanding and conflict resolution, then we should immediately recognize what is at stake in Dickens's central rhetorical question:

> What connexion can there be, between the place in Lincolnshire, the house in town, the Mercury in powder, and the whereabout of Jo the outlaw with the broom, who had that distant ray of light upon him when he swept the churchyard-step? What connexion can there have been between many people in the innumerable histories of this world, who from opposite sides of great gulfs, have, nevertheless, been very curiously brought together!'' (272).

The novel provides literal answers to this question (that Jo acts as a conduit enabling Lady Dedlock to find the grave of her lover Captain Hawdon), which are also partially metaphorical ones (since he also passes along a case of smallpox to the product of that union, Esther Summerson). These in turn relate to larger questions raised in the "condition-of-England" debates about the environmental and hygienic problems of the London slums, and their link to wider forms of social unrest (including crime), about who is ultimately responsible for such problems, and whether—in its most abstract application—it is even possible to talk about a common humanity, especially in terms of rights and responsibilities.

There is a highly developed thematics of creeping contagion in *Bleak House*, which consistently threatens to reduce the privileged to an equal status with the underclass inhabiting the ground zero of Tom-all-Alone's. The second paragraph of the novel signals this equality, in the face of biological and environmental forces, with its invocation of a "[f]og everywhere. Fog up the river, where it flows among green airs and meadows; fog down the river; where it rolls defiled among the tiers of shipping, and the waterside pollutions of a great (and dirty) city. . . . Fog in the eyes and throats of ancient Greenwich pensioners, . . . in the stem and bowl of the afternoon pipe of the wrathful skipper, . . . cruelly pinching the toes and fingers of his shivering 'prentice boy on deck'' (49). Just as the fog marks no social distinction between the ship's captain and a lowly apprentice, so news of Lady Dedlock's illegitimate child proceeds via the conduit of rumor at the end of the novel through jewelers, stables, Parliament, and lending libraries, while smallpox travels just as inexorably from Jo through a servant, Charley, to her mistress, Esther. In perhaps the most apocalyptic passage of the novel, which spells out these patterns of infectious contagion and their potential for social leveling, Dickens prophesies that ''[t]here is not a drop of Tom[-all-Alone]'s corrupted blood but propagates infection and contagion somewhere. It shall pollute, this very night, the choice stream (in which chemists on analysis would find the genuine nobility) of a Norman house, and his Grace shall not be able to say Nay to the infamous alliance. There is not an atom of Tom's slime . . . but shall work its retribution, through every order of society, up to the proudest of the proud, the highest of the high'' (683).

If we recall that a cholera epidemic had recently swept through East London, we can read in this a timely reminder that disease respects neither the social distinctions of class nor the artificial boundaries by which the East End is imaginatively cordoned off from the commercial center or the fashionable residence of the West End. Six months before he began work on this novel, Dickens delivered a speech to the Metropolitan Sanitary Association, declaring that ''no man can estimate the amount of mischief grown in dirt,—and that no man can stay the evil stops here or stops there, either in its moral or physical effects, or can deny that it begins in the cradle and is not at rest in the miserable grave'': the effects of poor sanitation were as certain ''as it is that the air from Gin Lane will be carried by an easterly wind into Mayfair, or that the furious pestilence raging in St. Giles's no mortal list of lady patronesses can keep out of Almack's,'' a fashionable Pall Mall assembly room for gambling and dancing.[9] The geographical arrangement of London, as well as its architectural and social history, depends upon a prevailing wind blowing West to East, which would carry the ill effects of industry out towards the Essex marshes; consequently, the East Wind which John Jarndyce consistently predicts in *Bleak House* would bring that filth back to the center from which it emanated, again in either literal environmental terms or through the metonymies of crime and social unrest which also festered in the East End.

If we keep this context in mind, we begin to see why it was ''poor Jo'' who most interested the novel's first readers, as a metonymic representation of the problem of London's underclass. In a text which focuses so centrally on the failures of the legal system—the seemingly unending ''progress'' of Jarndyce v. Jarndyce towards its inevitable inconclusion, or the equally pointless litigation undertaken by characters like Miss Flite or Mr. Gridley—we can see Jo as Inspector Bucket's crowning failure. A figure who is almost physically constituted out of the London mud from which he makes a meager living,[10] Jo is told repeatedly to "Move on" or "hook it" throughout the novel, in a manner which confirms the police's own inability to clean up the streets (except by passing the problem on to another beat or district) and the larger inadequacies of mid-Victorian discourses of social reform. Evangelicals like Mr. Chadband, for instance, have less impact in the slums of London than on the imperial outposts of Africa and India, as Jo confirms on his death-bed: "Different times," he notes, "there was other genlmen come down to Tom-all-Alone's a-prayin, but they all mostly sed as t'other wuns prayed wrong, and all mostly sounded to be a-talking to theirselves, or a-passing blame on the t'others, and not a-talkin to us. We never knowd nothink. I never knowd what it was all about" (704, emphasis in original). Even more importantly, this philanthropic sectarianism is shown as leading to Parliamentary procrastination: "Much mighty speaking there has been," the anonymous narrator notes,

> both in and out of Parliament, concerning Tom, and much wrathful disputation how Tom shall be got right. Whether he shall be put into the main road by constables, by beadles, or by bell-ringing, or by force of figures, or by correct principles of taste, or by high church, or by low church, or by no church. . . . In the midst of which dust and noise, there is but one thing perfectly clear, to wit, that Tom only may and can, or shall and will, be reclaimed according to somebody's theory but nobody's practice. And in the meantime, Tom goes to perdition head foremost in his old determined spirit.   (683)

In passages like this, Dickens extends his initial attacks on the procrastination of Chancery to cover a wider range of governmental institutions. In doing so, however, his efforts run counter to his otherwise enthusiastic endorsement of Victorian methods of policing, which often operated accordingly a similarly single-minded application of abstract principles. After all, the blind eyes being turned by politicians and priests alike seems consistent with Bucket's own "Move on" strategy, at least in terms of their respective effects on people like Jo. The latter dies, for instance, while still possessed of an appropriately exaggerated fear of Bucket, who "in his ignorance, he believes . . . to be everywhere, and cognizant of everything" (694). The scene's considerable pathos stems from Jo's "confession" to Mr. Snagsby, in which he asks that "when I was moved on as fur as ever I could go and cou'dn't be moved no furder, whether you might be so good p'raps, as to write out, wery large so that any one could see it anywheres, as that I was wery truly hearty sorry that I done it and that I never went fur to do it" (702); the irony is that Jo never really knows why he was "moved on" by the police in the first place, even as he now prepares to "move on" one last time.

Jo's internalized sense of guilt is almost a perfect illustration of Bentham's Panopticon, in which the prisoner should feel him or herself under surveillance even when in reality he or she is not. If, however, John Bender is correct in seeing that mechanism as dependent upon a more developed identification with the institutions of power, with the goal that the offender can be reformed from within, it is precisely this capacity which Jo is shown to lack—which is why he is incapable of acting upon his guilt, except by dying. In a long meditation on the extent of his distance from the social and representational norms which elsewhere guide the novel, the narrator comments that "It must be a strange state to be like Jo! To shuffle through the streets, unfamiliar with the shapes and in utter darkness as to the meaning, of those mysterious symbols, so abundant over the shops, and on the corner of streets, and on the doors, and in the windows!" Far from being (in Louis Althusser's famous phrase) "interpellated as a subject" by the narrative form and structures of *Bleak House*, Jo remains unassimilable even to strategies of realistic representation, as mysterious as the symbols which he himself is unable to read. As the passage progresses, Jo's alienation from such systems of linguistic representation is increasingly associated with a parallel alienation from forms of political and legal representation:

> It must be very puzzling to see the good company going to the churches on Sundays, with their books in hand and to think (for perhaps Jo *does* think, at odd times) what does it all mean, and if it means anything to anybody, how comes it that it means nothing to me? To be hustled, and jostled, and moved on; and really to feel that it would appear to be perfectly true that I have no business here, or there, or anywhere; and yet to be perplexed by the consideration that I *am* here somehow, too, and everybody overlooked me until I became the creature that I am! It must be a strange state, not merely to be told that I am scarcely human (as in the case of offering myself for a witness), but to feel it of my own knowledge all my life! . . . . Jo's ideas of a Criminal Trial, or a Judge, or a Bishop, or a Government, or that inestimable jewel to him (if he only knew it) the Constitution, should be strange! His whole material and immaterial life is wonderfully strange; his death, the strangest of all.
> (274; emphasis in original)

Dickens refers here to a very real alienation from a constitutional framework of English law which continued to deny electoral rights to the poor, but in the process he also highlights the practical limitations of the abstract idea of equality under the law. Jo's ignorance, combined with his lack of the kinds of financial resources at the disposal of Sir Leicester Dedlock, reveals this to be at best an ideological fiction enabling the continuation of business as usual, as most of the litigants in *Bleak House* eventually discover. Inspector Bucket's cheering promise to Mr. Gridley on his deathbed, that "You'll lose your temper with the whole round of 'em, again and again; and I shall take you on a score of warrants yet'' (407), contains a sinister echo of ''Move on,'' in effect a ceaseless harassment which is to be repeated until the point of death with decreasing odds of victory or escape.

Here, as elsewhere, Dickens is much better at diagnosing problems and critiquing faulty solutions than he is at providing answers. If there is a hope, it has to lie in the hands-on approach favored by Esther Summerson, which sets itself strictly limited goals: ''I thought it best,'' she concludes, ''to be as useful as I could, and to render what services I could, to those immediately about me; and to try to let that circle of duty gradually and naturally expand itself'' (154–58). Here, we see the outlines of a classically liberal Victorian reformism, couched in terms that read like a preemptive critique of the impersonal bureaucracy of the welfare state. Esther's remark occurs after she accompanies Mrs. Pardiggle on a visit to a brickmaker's family, in which her companion acted ''as if she were an inexorable moral Policeman carrying them all off to a station-house.'' Once again, Jo seems to shadow this scene, as a comparable figure who is also ''not one of Mrs. Pardiggle's Tockahoopo Indians'' nor ''a genuine foreign-grown savage,'' and thus incapable of being ''softened by distance and unfamiliarity '' (696). In this way, he exposes the inadequacies of ''telescopic philanthrophy'' while seeming to make the case for Esther's alternative ''hand-on'' approach, but this too is called into question when their encounter leads to Esther's own disfigurement from smallpox. Bruce Robbins has compared this with the ''irresponsibility'' of Harold Skimpole, noting that ''[a]t some risk to herself, Esther takes the sick Jo into her house; fearful for himself, Skimpole accepts a bribe from Bucket and helps turn Jo out of the house. But Skimpole is in effect placing the burden on the public, where Dickens would agree it ultimately belongs; and Esther, taking the burden upon herself, falls ill, nearly dies, and is scarred for life'' (222). In a sense, his point is unarguable: that the exertions of any one person—whether Esther Summerson or Inspector Bucket—can be no match for long-standing and wide-ranging social problems. Unfortunately, the phrase by which he summarizes Skimpole's position, with its promotion of the panacea of ''placing the burden on the public,'' is one that *Bleak House* seeks to expose as also inadequate for what Jo represents. Far from endorsing such a prescription for ''public'' action, it seems more likely that Dickens would recognize its depersonalization of political responsibility as another kind of telescopic philanthropy, seeking by its generality to keep the problem at arm's length or simply to move it on to someone else's attention. The novel ends in a kind of stalemate, then, as Jo remains radically incomprehensible and unreformable in spite of the best efforts of Esther, Bucket, Mrs. Pardiggle, and the British Parliament.

I suggested earlier that cultural studies has acted as a corrective to the excessive pessimism of the New Historicism, in part by focusing more on a contemporary frame of analysis but also by reenergizing a language of resistance, agency, and ideological contestation. While there is precious little of that to be found in *Bleak House*, its very absence can also pose a challenge to the New Historicist containment thesis offered by D. A. Miller, since Jo's inability to resist the forces which are driving him into an early grave is the simple obverse of their inability to comprehend the problems he represents. Since no governmental, philanthropic, or judicial solutions prove effective, those problems (of poverty, ignorance, disease, social alienation) were bound to recur, as Victorian Britain discovered in the 1870s and '80s. It is to Dickens's considerable credit that he was able to recognize this fact in the early '50s, when the Chartist threat had recently subsided and "condition-of-England" novelists like Kingsley and Gaskell were offering parables of social reconciliation in the form of fantasized cross-class marriages and alliances undertaken in the name of Christian Socialism or Unitarianism.

To shift our attention from Bucket to Jo—or, more accurately, to the Bucket-Jo relationship—changes our entire perception of the novel, which emerges as a devastating critique of the pretensions of Panoptic power instead of a testimonial to its ruthless efficiency. Such a reading helps to bring *Bleak House* into step with newer critical paradigms, but it is also a return of sorts to the novel's original reception. I have already noted the relative unreadability of Bucket, a figure who now seems so familiar only because of the literary type which he anticipated. In his place, Dickens's first reviewers invested heavily in Jo, in a manner that might seem shocking now, given the character's melodramatic sentimentality. *The Westminster Review* rather prematurely declared that Jo "will be remembered always as one of the choice things that do honor to our literature," while "The gem of *Bleak House*" for the *Eclectic Review* was "'poor Jo,' the crossing-sweeper, hapless representative of a class whose very existence from generation to generation cries shame on the land in which they dwell." Similarly, *Putnam's Magazine* noted with some irony that "Poor Joe [sic], down in Tom-all-alone's, has already become a proverb. We read the deaths of a good many eminent men without emotion . . . but we cannot withhold a tear when we read the death of poor Joe, and when he is 'moved on' for the last time we too are moved. Yet we know all the time that poor Joe is an unreal phantom—a mere shadowy outline, raised by a few strokes of a pen; yet we weep over him and give him the sympathies which we would withhold from the real Joes we encounter in our daily walks."[11] That split response, combining sympathy for a fictional character with a nonchalant contempt for his real-life counterparts, is itself a form of "telescopic philanthropy," and may well indicate the strength of a desire for fantasies of reconciliation in the aftermath of Chartism: "sympathy" is, for example, the key-note of Gaskell's *Mary Barton*, which argues both for its difficulty given the prevailing social structures of the period and also its absolute necessity in order to close the gaps and divisions which had been highlighted throughout the 1840s.

Jo has not survived among either the popular or critical canons of Dickensian characters, and has failed to attain the status of such comparable suffering children as Oliver Twist (who is reformed, but then was never really "wrong" to begin with) or Tiny Tim (who miraculously "did *not* die").[12] He was at the center, however, of a whole series of theatrical adaptations of *Bleak House*—a text that doesn't easily lend itself to adaptation—from the 1850s through the 1880s. H. Philip Bolton has usefully analyzed nearly 50 of these plays, and notes the remarkable popularity of Jo. It may be understandable that the earliest versions, two of which were licensed for performance while the novel was still being serialized, should focus on his death, which is perhaps the most dramatic scene up to that point. Two of the earliest versions, from May-June of 1853, end on this note, and appear to have excited a controversy for the Lord Chamberlain's office about the recitation of the Lord's Prayer which accompanies Jo's final move; indeed, the whole scene is so overdetermined by the pathos of popular melodrama that modern readers may be tempted to recall Oscar Wilde on the death of Little Nell. The history of the novel's adaptation resumes in the 1870s with American versions entitled *Chesney Wold*, which ran for 18 years, and *Jo; or Bleak House*, which crossed over to the London stage, and was performed from 1875 to 1896, including tours in Australia, South Africa, India, and China; then we have titles like *Jo, the Waif of the Streets*, *The Life and Death of Jo*, *Dickens' Jo; or the Dedlock Disgrace*, *Jo v Jo*, and *Poor Little Jo*, by which point in the late-70s the sentimental note had to compete with theatrical burlesques which simultaneously satirized "Jo-mania." One 1882 program copy reproduced by Bolton inadvertently picks up on the character's inability to read the signs around him by advertising his name in $2\frac{1}{2}$ inch lettering, so large that even he might have a chance of deciphering it.[13]

The theatrical popularity of the character clearly survived the publication of the rest of the novel, which in May 1853 still had about a quarter left to appear, including the arrest of Madame Hortense, the death of Lady Dedlock and many others, the resolution of Esther's parentage, and her marriage to Allan Woodcourt. Of course, the success of those earliest versions may have dictated the format of later ones, which still build up to Jo's death and elevate him even more centrally in their titles. One version by George Lander, performed in London between 1876 and 1890, includes a telling revision of the death scene, which occurs in George's shooting gallery in the original novel.[14] Lander stages it to coincide with Lady Dedlock's own death, discovered by Esther and Bucket at the gates of the cemetery where Hawdon is buried. Before his recitation of the Lord's Prayer, Jo offers an uncharacteristically cogent and articulate denunciation of the political system which has hounded him, declaring,

Oh! they have moved me on. "You ain't a goin' to stop here and breed fevers," says one. "You're poisonin' our place," says another. "You're a hidle rogue, and a wagabone," says another. When I goes to the workhouse, they say—they says, "we're full; go somewhere else." Yes, the workhouse chucks me out and the bobbies won't run me in—they only moves me on. And so I wanders about like a dog—like a dog.

This last line serves as a reminder of one of Dickens's own metaphors, which compares Jo unfavorably to a sheepdog, "an educated, improved, developed dog" that thereby shows his superiority to the crossing sweeper: however, the text goes on to caution, "[t]urn that dog's descendants wild, like Jo, and in a few years they will so degenerate that they will lose even their bark—but not their bite" (275). This potential for violent retribution clearly lurks beneath the surface of Jo, even if he is incapable of exacting it, and Lander's play indicates its prime targets: symbols of authority like the magistracy and Poor Law commissioners, social health reformers, and the police. This version even allows Inspector Bucket to hear the speech and witness the results of his "Move on" strategy. As Snagsby and Jo begin their recital of The Lord's Prayer, the detective mutters "I can't bear this" and turns away, in what appears to be an admission of responsibility which Dickens's novel can never quite make clear. It is an alternative conclusion that we should bear in mind, I think, as a corrective to modern desires to lionize Bucket as the emblem of a Panoptic power which is beyond challenge or resistance.

NOTES

Many thanks to Stanley Friedman for his incisive comments on an earlier draft of this essay.

1. For other analyses of the alignments between the novel's twin narratives and its thematics of duty, secrecy, and personal knowledge, see Jaffe, 128–49. Peter Garrett also addresses the issue of narrative in this text, in chapters 1 and 2 of *The Victorian Multiplot Novel*.
2. See among others, *M/MLA (Journal of the Midwest Modern Language Association)* 24:1 (Spring 1991), a special issue on "Cultural Studies and the New Historicism"; Brantlinger; and Joyce.
3. See especially *Discipline and Punish*, 68–69 and *I, Pierre Riviere*, 40.
4. *Illustrated London News* (1853); this and other contemporary reviews are reprinted in Dyson, 49–91. Steig shares the confusion expressed in this review, arguing that Bucket is progressively "whitewashed" through the course of the novel, in a way that "undercuts [its] vision of lawyers, courts, government, and organized authority in general as parasites on the body politic, at best indifferent

to the fates of the mass of humanity, and at worst actively destructive of human happiness and life'' (578). Such a message, he suggests, is supported by our first encounters with the detective, but is weakened as he emerges later as a hero of sorts.

5. See Reith, 158–59.

6. For more on the Popay scandal, see Winter, 50–52, and Ousby, 63–64.

7. Humphry House, for example, notes Dickens's "most fanatical devotion to the Metropolitan Police," and hypothesizes that it might arise from the novelist's rejection of more individualistic schemes for self-improvement, against which he reacted (like others of the period) by favoring instead a "highly concentrated central power" as the cure for social problems (201). An alternative account of his relationship with the London detectives, which stresses that any exaggeration of their abilities proceeded from Field rather than Dickens, is offered by Long.

8. See Ignatieff, 171–73 and 193–94, including the assessment of a prison inspector in the 1840s that "Millbank represented a botched attempt to put Bentham's Panopticon inspection principle into practice" (194).

9. Cited in Butt and Tillotson, 191. The theme of contagion is discussed at some length in Arac, chapter 6, and Nord, 96–111.

10. His job was to clear a passage through the filth for wealthy pedestrians. As such, it is not surprising that "[h]omely filth begrimes him, homely parasites devour him, homely sores are in him, homely rags are on him: native ignorance, the growth of English soil and climate, sinks his immortal nature lower than the beasts that perish'' (696).

11. These reviews are reprinted in Dyson, 70, 82, and 79 respectively. One dissonant note was struck by *Blackwood's*, whose reviewer highlighted the contrast between Jo's apparent centrality in the emotional responses of Victorian readers, and his relative irrelevance to the novel's formal plot and structure, and concluded that "The poor boy Joe is a very effective picture, though we fail to discover a sufficient reason for his introduction'' (88).

12. For a very different discussion of Jo and Tiny Tim in relation to sentimentality, suffering, and the sublime, see Loesberg.

13. I am indebted to Bolton for the discussion of play versions of the novel in this paragraph.

14. The script for Lander's play appears in a 1965 microform series of "English and American Drama of the Nineteenth Century," which reprints manuscripts of plays originally submitted to the lord chamberlain between 1839 and 1855.

WORKS CITED

Althusser, Louis. "Ideology and Ideological State Apparatuses (Noted Towards an Investigation)." Trans. Ben Brewster. *Lenin and Philosophy and Other Essays.* New York: Monthly Review P, 1971. 127–86.

Arac, Jonathan. *Commissioned Spirits: The Shaping of Social Motion in Dickens, Carlyle, Melville, and Hawthorne.* New Brunswick: Rutgers UP, 1976.

Belsey, Catherine. *Critical Practice.* London: Methuen, 1980.

Bender, John. *Imagining the Penitentiary: Fiction and the Architecture of Mind in Eighteenth-Century England.* Chicago: U of Chicago P, 1979.

Bolton, H. Philip. "*Bleak House* and the Playhouse," *Dickens Studies Annual* 12 (1983): 81–116.

Brantlinger, Patrick. "Cultural Studies versus the New Historicism." *English Studies/ Culture Studies: Institutionalizing Dissent.* Ed. Isaiah Smithson and Nancy Ruff. Urbana: Illinois UP, 1994. 43–58.

Butt, John and Tillotson, Kathleen. *Dickens at Work.* London: Methuen, 1957.

Carlyle, Thomas. "Chartism." *Selected Works.* Ed. Alan Shelstone. Harmondsworth: Penguin, 1971. 149–232.

Childers, Joseph. *Novel Possibilities: Fiction and the Formation of Early Victorian Culture.* Philadelphia: U of Pennsylvania P, 1995.

Dickens, Charles. *Bleak House.* Harmondsworth: Penguin, 1971.

———. "On Duty with Inspector Field." *The Uncommercial Traveller and Reprinted Pieces.* Oxford: Oxford UP, 1958. 513–26.

———. "The Detective Police." *The Uncommercial Traveller and Reprinted Pieces.* 485–503.

Dyson, A. E. ed. *Bleak House: A Casebook.* London: MacMillan, 1969.

Eagleton, Terry. *Criticism and Ideology.* London: Verso, 1978.

Emsley, Clive. *Policing and its Context, 1750–1850.* New York: Schocken, 1983.

Foucault, Michel. *I, Pierre Rivière, having slaughtered my mother, my sister, and my brother . . .* Harmondsworth: Penguin, 1978.

———. *Discipline and Punish.* Trans. Alan Sheridan. New York: Random House, 1979.

Gallagher, Catherine. *The Industrial Reformation of English Fiction, 1832–1867.* Chicago: U of Chicago P, 1985.

Garrett, Peter. *The Victorian Multiplot Novel: Studies in Dialogical Form.* New Haven: Yale UP, 1980.

House, Humphry. *The Dickens World.* Oxford: Oxford UP, 1960.

Ignatieff, Michael. *A Just Measure of Pain: The Penitentiary in the Industrial Revolution, 1750–1850.* Harmondsworth: Penguin, 1978.

Jaffe, Audrey. *Vanishing Points: Dickens, Narrative and the Subject of Omniscience.* Berkeley: U of California P, 1991.

Jameson, Fredric. *The Political Unconscious: Narrative as a Socially Symbolic Act.* Ithaca: Cornell UP, 1981.

Joyce, Simon. "Resisting Arrest/Arresting Resistance: Crime Fiction, Cultural Studies, and the 'Turn to History'." *Criticism* 37:2 (Spring 1995): 309–35.

LaCapra, Dominick. "Ideology and Critique in Dickens' *Bleak House.*" *Representations* 6 (Spring 1984): 116–123.

Lander, George. *Bleak House; or Poor Jo.* (Orig. 1876). Ed. Allardyce Nicholl and George Freedley, *English and American Drama of the Nineteenth Century* (New York: Readex Microprint, 1965–71).

Loesberg, Jonathan. "Dickensian Deformed Children and the Hegelian Sublime." *Victorian Studies:* 40:4 (Summer 1997). 625–54.

Long, William. "The 'Singler Stories' of Inspector Field." *The Dickensian* 83: 3 (1987). 149–162.

McGowen, Randall. "Getting to Know the Criminal Class in Nineteenth-Century England." *Nineteenth-Century Contexts* 14.1 (1990). 33–54.

Miller, D. A. *The Novel and the Police.* Berkeley: U of California P, 1988.

Newton, Judith. "Historicisms New and Old: 'Charles Dickens' Meets Marxism, Feminism, and West Coast Foucault." *Feminist Studies* 16:3 (Fall 1990): 449–70.

Nord, Deborah Epstein. *Walking the Victorian Streets: Women, Representation, and the City.* Ithaca: Cornell UP, 1995.

Ousby, Ian. *Bloodhounds of Heaven: The Detective in English Fiction from Godwin to Doyle.* Cambridge: Harvard UP, 1976.

Radzinowicz, Leon. *A History of English Criminal Law*, volume 4. London: Stevens and Stevens, 1968.

Reiner, Robert. *The Politics of the Police.* Brighton: Wheatsheaf Books, 1985.

Reith, Charles. *British Police and the Democratic Ideal.* London: Oxford UP, 1943.

Robbins, Bruce. "Telescopic Philanthropy: Professionalism and Responsibility in *Bleak House.*" Ed. Homi Bhabha, *Nation and Narration.* London: Routledge, 1990. 213–30.

Steig, Michael. "The Whitewashing of Inspector Bucket: Origins and Parallels." *Papers of the Michigan Academy of Science, Arts, and Letters* 50 (1965): 575–84.

Winter, James. *London's Teeming Streets, 1830–1914.* London: Routledge, 1993.

Editorial Interventions: *Hard Times*'s Industrial Imperative

Julie M. Dugger

Critics have often noted that Charles Dickens's Hard Times *fails to suggest specific solutions to the social problems it describes. This refusal, however, should be interpreted not as a failure, but rather as a reflection of the changes wrought by industrialism in the world of London publishing, and particularly the new roles emerging for editors as a result of those changes. This essay locates* Hard Times *in the contexts of Stephen Blackpool's resemblance to Thomas Carlyle's "Editor" in* Past and Present *and of recent criticism on Dickens's work as an editor and as an author in other genres, claiming that the manufacturing world portrayed in* Hard Times *was modeled on the publishing world which produced that novel, and correspondingly that both Stephen and the novel itself pursue a figuratively "editorial" model of activism within those worlds. That is, their actions invoke a concept of reform in which the agents of social transformation pursue their ends as participants in a collaboratively- and institutionally-structured community, rather than as autonomously-inspired individuals. Focusing on the figure of the editor underlying* Hard Times *thus allows us to seek out in the literary field the same kinds of collaborative endeavors which critics have admired in reform movements in the industrial field, as well as to reexamine our expectations about how literature itself should participate in such reform movements.*

As an industrial novel occupying a sometimes uneasy role between entertainment and social commentary, Charles Dickens's *Hard Times* has been susceptible since its publication to criticism that it has its facts wrong.[1] One of the most frequently identified inaccuracies in *Hard Times* is its negative portrayal of the worker's union which ostracizes Stephen Blackpool. Critics began condemning *Hard Times*'s presentation of the union as early as 1912, when George Bernard Shaw, in an otherwise commendatory essay on the novel, cited its characterization of Slackbridge, the union organizer, as its "one real failure" (132). Shaw's comment is one inaugurating instance of a socialist tradition in criticism of *Hard Times* which continues to be influential today.[2] Yet perhaps the most troubling character in *Hard Times,* according to later criticism in this tradition, is not Slackbridge—who can be dismissed with relative ease as a caricature—but rather Stephen, the saintly worker who, in refusing either to join the union or to propose an alternative to unionized reform, seems most strongly to represent everything that is retrograde or passive about *Hard Times*'s approach to industrial-era social change.

This critical frustration with Stephen, however, overlooks the extent to which he in his very refusals plays not a helpless but a Carlylean role in the novel, and therefore the extent to which those refusals themselves may constitute a social intervention. Stephen's resemblance to Thomas Carlyle deserves further consideration not only because *Hard Times* was dedicated to Carlyle. More importantly, Stephen's refusals recall Carlyle in a very specific persona: that of the metaphorical "Editor" of *Past and Present*, who, like Stephen, abdicates responsibility for solving problems himself when others are more suited to the task. What has been called passive in Stephen, then, could instead be called editorial. That is, in refusing to join or endorse the worker's union, Stephen is not encouraging a pre-industrial retreat from collaborative reform movements. Instead, he is invoking a different, editorial model of collaboration in which the agents of social transformation pursue their ends not independently, but rather as participants in an institutionally structured community. In Stephen's case, for example, the negative act of identifying the flaws in a current social situation becomes the counterpart and complement to the positive act (to be completed by others) of finding new means to improve that situation. Thus, insofar as Stephen has become a representative figure for all that seems lacking in the way *Hard Times* approaches social reform, it is important that we reconsider his refusals as editorial interventions, not as anachronistic passivity; for if we do so we may also reconsider our expectations about what *Hard Times* can and should accomplish as a reform-oriented industrial novel.

What is more, if we understand both Stephen and *Hard Times* to be playing an editorial role in social reform, we can also begin to rethink the socialist tradition's critique of *Hard Times* by placing that critique in the context of more recent critical work on the role of editors in the Victorian publishing industry, as well as on Dickens's own involvements as both author and editor in that industry. As the literary canon has expanded, scholars have increasingly turned their attention to Dickens's work not only as a novelist, but also as a writer in other genres and as an editor himself. Our understanding of how *Hard Times* establishes its reforming role can be assisted by these new scholarly developments in two ways. First, we can ask how *Hard Times* the novel approaches the problems of industrial England by framing our question from within the context of how Dickens approached those problems in his journalism, some of which was published in the same magazine (*Household Words*) in which *Hard Times* first made its appearance. Looking at Dickens's journalism—especially when it addresses issues similar to those addressed in *Hard Times*—allows us to see some of the directions in which he could have taken his novel but did not. We can thus gain a sense of what kind of reform work Dickens expected to accomplish in his novels, and how it differs from the kinds of reform he attempted in other varieties of writing.

Secondly, recent work on Dickens and on Victorian publishing allows us to consider how changes in the publishing world might have affected Dickens's efforts as an editor. Dickens's editorial work is significant for *Hard Times* not only because he was in a sense the novel's editor as well as its author, since he edited *Household Words*. It is also significant given the larger figurative resonance of the editorial role as it informs the project of *Hard Times*. The figure of the collaborative editor, as I will discuss, becomes not only the underlying metaphor linking Carlyle's and Stephen's styles of reform, but also a metonym for the many other kinds of collaborative action by which social transformation was pursued in an institutionally-structured industrial England. This essay therefore examines Dickens's own work as an editor, using scholarship on his editing of serial novels as a window into the concept of the editor as it underlies one of those novels, *Hard Times*.

What we find when we examine Dickens's industrial novel from these perspectives is that *Hard Times* approaches the condition-of-England question using a logic imported from a world which Dickens knew well: a Victorian publishing world as transformed by industrialization as was the manufacturing world of Coketown. In using the logic of the literary field to analyze the problems of the manufacturing field, *Hard Times* is able to defy critical expectations by modeling its social role as a novel not after the role of the heroic, individualistic, and originating author, but rather after the emerging role of the collaboratively demanding editor.

The Carlylean Editor: Stephen Blackpool and the Socialist Critique of *Hard Times*

We can classify George Bernard Shaw's remarks as part of a socialist tradition in criticism of *Hard Times* for two reasons: because the Fabian Shaw's negative evaluation of the union scenes in the novel was powerfully echoed by the Marxist critic Raymond Williams in his 1958 study *Culture and Society*,[3] and also because their joint objections continue to resonate in criticism of the novel to this day.[4] Williams does not cite Shaw directly in his comments on *Hard Times*,[5] and the differences in the two critics' assessments of the novel should not be overlooked. Nonetheless, it can be instructive to examine their critiques together as early instances of an ongoing critical perspective, and not only because those critiques have been so influential. For, perhaps more importantly, in both critiques the faults that Shaw and Williams find with *Hard Times*'s union scenes exemplify the faults they find with *Hard Times* as a whole. The two critics cite both the union scenes and the novel as a whole for failing in the cause of social reform amid the particular conditions of England's industrial revolution—whether because *Hard Times* cannot transcend a Victorian middle-class narrative perspective, or because it passively neglects to offer acceptable solutions for the problems it describes. We can therefore better understand the socialist critics' positions on *Hard Times* in particular, as well as on the industrial novel more generally, by examining their positions on the union scenes; and in turn we can better understand their criticism of the union scenes by examining a focal point for that criticism, the figure of Stephen Blackpool.

Neither Shaw nor Williams condemned *Hard Times* outright. On the one hand, they cite the novel as a breakthrough work for Dickens (and possibly for nineteenth-century thought in general) because it moves away from the criticism of particular individuals or social institutions and toward a more comprehensive critique of society. As Shaw writes, *Hard Times* marks Dickens's shift from condemning "individual delinquencies, local plague-spots, [and] negligent authorities" to condemning the fundamental inadequacies of society as a whole: "rising up against civilization itself as against a disease, and declaring that it is not our disorder but our order that is horrible . . ." (127–28). And as Williams claims, compared to other novels of its period, *Hard Times* provides "a thorough-going and creative examination of the dominant philosophy of industrialism," and thus a "more comprehensive understanding" of its times (93). Shaw and Williams admire *Hard Times* for its abstractions: for providing a broader, more theoretical analysis of social ills than did earlier industrial novels or the earlier works of Dickens himself.

The two critics, however, do not always view *Hard Times*'s tendency toward abstract theoretical analysis with admiration. As Williams argues, this strength in the novel is also its weakness. What *Hard Times* gains in theoretical comprehension, it loses "in terms of human understanding of the industrial working people" (93). Williams laments the loss of the "human" particulars that are left behind by "the rigors of generalization and abstraction" (93), a loss which he notes most acutely in his reading of *Hard Times*'s "unsatisfactory" portrayal of the working classes and their trade unions (which, as he argues, Dickens dismisses "by a stock Victorian reaction" [96]). Shaw, too, objects that Dickens erred in the particulars of working-class life and politics when writing *Hard Times.* To Shaw, Slackbridge the union organizer is "a mere figment of the middle-class imagination" (132), and Dickens knew no more "of the segregated factory populations of our purely industrial towns . . . than an observant professional man can pick up on a flying visit to Manchester" (133).

It might seem at first that both Shaw and Williams become dissatisfied with *Hard Times*'s analytical move from particularities to generalities mainly when the abstractions the novel offers cease to resemble socialist or Marxist abstractions and instead begin to resemble "stock Victorian" abstractions. At another level, however, the two critics' arguments are neither quite that simple nor quite that ideologically self-interested. If Shaw and Williams criticize Dickens's "middle-class" failure to understand the day-to-day realities of working-class life and politics, they do so not merely because they distrust a middle-class perspective. They are pointing out as well that the inaccurate portrayal of the unions in *Hard Times* is inconsistent because it represents a retreat from the theoretical social analysis displayed so visibly (and so admirably) elsewhere in the novel. Both critics argue that when *Hard Times* represents the unions, it ceases to provide an analysis of industrial society and instead lapses into something else. In Shaw's case, this something else is the "idealized Toryism" which leads Stephen Blackpool to expect leadership from industrial capitalists like Josiah Bounderby: the novel, in Shaw's reading, retreats from an analysis of the industrial social system into an anachronistic nostalgia for the earlier feudal relationships between master and worker. For Williams, the something else which replaces the novel's consideration of industrialism is an emphasis on "individual persons against the system" (94–95). Rather than accepting industrialism as the condition of the times and searching for systemic industrial solutions to systemic industrial problems, Williams argues, *Hard Times* instead suggests individualism as an escapist alternative to the reformation of industrial society.

Nowhere are Shaw and Williams more pronounced in their criticism of *Hard Times* than in their objections to the figure of Stephen, the martyred worker who refuses to unionize, thereby earning ostracism from his companions but an apparent endorsement from the novel's sympathetic narrator.[6] For Williams, Stephen's passivity in the face of injustice is particularly egregious in the larger context of *Hard Times*, "as set against the attempts of the [unionized] working people to better their conditions" (96). The novel's admiration of Stephen, as Williams sees it, leaves *Hard Times* presenting the working classes at their best as an honest but helpless people incapable of solving their own problems—victims defeated by the system, rather than active and organized reformers engaged in its repair. For Shaw, Stephen's surrender of responsibility for reforming industrialism to "they as is put ower me" is the paradigmatic example of that tendency to Toryism which plagues *Hard Times*'s otherwise successful analytic efforts (133–34).

It would be a mistake to deny that Dickens's portrayal of the workers' union and its treatment of Stephen is both unflattering to and condemning of the union, particularly in its presentation of the workers themselves as a helpless group with no better wisdom than to trust in their poor leadership. Slackbridge, the union organizer, is "not so honest . . . not so manly . . . [and] not so good-humoured" as the workers he leads: "he substituted cunning for their simplicity, and passion for their safe solid sense" (105). "Safe solid sense" notwithstanding, the workers seem naively willing to follow Slackbridge's lead. And as if this were not evidence enough of their organizational incapacities, the narrator, in an aside, states explicitly that the workers' belief in improving their lot through unionization was "unhappily wrong" (105).

At the same time, however, given the amount of attention that has been devoted to criticism of the union scenes in *Hard Times*, it is surprising that more has not been said about the frequent loopholes and exceptions that Dickens inserts into this portrayal of working-class incompetence. F. R. Leavis, in an effort to "be fair" to Dickens, does point out the irony in Mrs. Sparsit's declaration that the factory owners, "Being united themselves, ought one and all to set their faces against employing any man who is united with any other man" (Leavis 357). The irony in Sparsit's declaration may serve less to endorse the workers' unions than to chide the owners for their own collective bargaining; and indeed when *Hard Times* does admire the workers, it tends to admire them more as individuals than as organized collaborators. Nonetheless that admiration is evident in moments throughout the novel which find a great deal more to praise in the members of the working classes than those sheeplike virtues of honest naivety which leave them so susceptible to Slackbridge's leadership. Stephen may deny his own capacity to propose solutions to the "muddle" that is industrial England, but when he abdicates responsibility for reform to "them as is put ower me, and ower aw the rest of us," he is not limiting his hopes to the Bounderbys and Gradgrinds of the world—the owners and parliamentarians. Although he reiterates his personal inabilities in declaring that he "canna, wi' my little learning an' my common way, tell the genelman what will better aw this," Stephen does point out that "some working men o' this town could, above my powers" (114). The superiors to whom he relegates all social and political planning thus include some of his fellow workers: his assertion of a hierarchy in which some are fittingly "ower" and "above" others is not necessarily a class-based assertion. What is more, Stephen's acknowledgment of workers "above my powers" seconds the narrator's own judgment. On introducing Stephen, the narrator observes that

Old Stephen might have passed for a particularly intelligent man in his condition. Yet he was not. He took no place among those remarkable "Hands," who, piecing together their broken intervals of leisure through many years, had mastered difficult sciences, and acquired a knowledge of most unlikely things. He held no station among the Hands who could make speeches and carry on debates. Thousands of his compeers could talk much better than he, at any time. He was a good power-loom weaver, and a man of perfect integrity. (52)

In light of this description, Stephen's refusal to prescribe the remedies for society's ills indicates merely a wise comprehension of his own limits and abilities. In pointing out all the things that "Old Stephen" was not, however, the narrator also underscores an impressive variety of working-class achievements under difficult circumstances ("piecing together their broken intervals of leisure through many years"), as well as the capacity of self-educated workers for successful political involvement and intervention (for "mak[ing] speeches and carry[ing] on debates").

There is more still to be said against the argument that Stephen's refusal to provide Bounderby with solutions represents a confession of working-class incompetence. As Nicholas Coles has pointed out, Stephen's earlier interactions with Bounderby, in which Bounderby fails spectacularly to help him with the marital problems for which he seeks advice, have already debunked the assumption that "idealized Toryism," with its conviction that workers should rely on their masters for help and leadership, can have any place amid the worker-owner relationships that characterize *Hard Times* (159). It is Bounderby who summons Stephen after the latter is ostracized by the workers' union, not Stephen who looks to Bounderby, for Stephen has little reason to believe that he can rely on his employer to solve his problems. Furthermore, Stephen's refusal to propose solutions to industrialism's problems should not necessarily be taken as a moment of passivity. In the first place, this refusal itself defies Bounderby's implicit and self-serving suggestion that employees who dare to identify problems should be prepared to solve them on their own. In the second place, Stephen, "speaking with the quiet confidence of absolute certainty," minces no words in his condemnation of Bounderby's current and proposed practices for managing his employees. If he cannot say "what will better aw this," he does insist upon saying "what I know will never do't" (114). Stephen is anything but passive in his encounter with his employer, and in fact by taking his master to task he angers Bounderby to the extent that he loses his job.

In addition, it is in his speech to Bounderby—not only in its overall philosophies, but even in its refusal to suggest solutions to the problems it cites—that Stephen most closely resembles Thomas Carlyle, the social commentator to whom *Hard Times* was dedicated. Much attention has already been given to the influence of Carlyle's thinking in *Hard Times*,[7] but it should be further noted that a great deal of that thinking is given to Stephen to articulate. Stephen's speech listing methods that will not remedy the problems of industrial England (the same speech which is introduced by his protest that "I canna . . . tell the genelman what will better aw this—though some working men o' this town could") is a virtual catalogue of Carlylean commentary. Like Carlyle, who had argued that violent responses to civil insurrection "should be avoided as the very pestilence" (*Past and Present* 22), Stephen declares that "[t]he strong hand will never do't" (114). Like Carlyle, who deplored the passivity of laissez-faire governing ("Laissez-faire and much else being once well dead, how many 'impossibles' will become possible!" [*PP* 185]), Stephen correspondingly argues that "lettin alone will never do't" (114). Like Carlyle, who bewailed the class separations which cut off one segment of humanity from another,[8] Stephen points out that "Not drawin nigh to folk . . . will never do 't till th' Sun turns t' ice" (114). And finally, when Stephen concludes that "Most of aw, rating 'em as so much Power, and reg'latin 'em as if they was figures in a soom, or machines . . . this will never do't, Sir, till God's work is onmade" (114–15), he echoes Carlyle's denunciation of his own period as an "Age of Machinery" in *Signs of the Times* (64). The only character in *Hard Times*—if character he can be called—who is given more of Carlyle's lines than Stephen Blackpool is the novel's narrator, and then only because the narrator's voice is more frequently heard in the novel.

In view of his remarkable philosophical similarities to Carlyle, Stephen's reluctance to provide Bounderby with practicable social solutions appears in a different light, for in this respect too the working-class outcast resembles the Victorian sage. Carlyle disparaged those who sought simple answers to the unhappy condition of England as a "disconsolate, discerning Public, hoping to have got off by some Morrison's Pill, some Saint-John's corrosive mixture, and perhaps a little blistery friction on the back!" (*PP* 41). Rather than a simple cure-all, he argues, much more comprehensive and less easily-administered efforts to restore the nation to health are in order: a "total change of regimen, change of constitution and existence from the very centre of it" (*PP* 41). What is more, Carlyle emphatically denies his own responsibility to prescribe the specifics of the total transformations he demands. Like Stephen, he assigns this responsibility to others:

let not any Parliament, Aristocracy, Millocracy, or Member of the Governing Class . . . ask again, with the least anger, of this Editor, What is to be done, How that alarming problem of the Working Classes is to be managed? Editors are not here, foremost of all, to say How. A certain Editor thanks the gods that nobody pays him three hundred thousand pounds a year, two hundred thousand, twenty thousand, or any similar sum of cash for saying How; —that his wages are very different, his work somewhat fitter for him. An Editor's stipulated work is to apprise *thee* that it must be done. The 'way to do it,' is to try it, knowing that thou shalt die if it not be done.   (*PP* 266)

Like Stephen, who knows himself to be "a good power loom weaver, and a man of perfect integrity," but also knows himself to have neither the aptitude nor the ambition for a political career, Carlyle leaves it to those who are "put ower" him—be they "Parliament, Aristocracy, Millocracy" or more general "Member of the Governing Class"—to devise the solutions for the problems he identifies. Also like Stephen, however, Carlyle reserves the right to identify those problems and to demand that his leaders address them, claiming as his own position of authority the role of the "Editor" whose "stipulated work is to apprise *thee* that it must be done." Thus once we begin to interpret Stephen, in his speech to Bounderby, to be claiming one kind of authority even as he relinquishes another, we find that this interpretation is underscored by Stephen's similarities to Carlyle, who makes much the same move in reproaching and exhorting his own audience. Working-class Stephen is no more passive in his refusals than the philosopher to whom Dickens dedicated the novel in which Stephen appears.

The Victorian Editor and the Publishing Field

Carlyle's identity as the "Editor" of *Past and Present* is largely metaphorical. He resembles an editor in that he positions himself and his work as mediators between the medieval *Chronicle* of Jocelin of Brakelond and the nineteenth-century audience that he hopes the *Chronicle* will reach, drawing as much significance as possible from that text for that audience. Even in the second book of *Past and Present*, however—the book which relies most heavily on Jocelin's account—the medieval author's voice is predominantly buried in Carlyle's. Jocelin's actual editor, as Carlyle gratefully acknowledges, is the "Mr. Rokewood" who has made the *Chronicle* available to Carlyle himself, and not the writer of *Past and Present*, a separate work altogether. Nonetheless the metaphor by which Carlyle compares himself to the Rokewoods of the literary world is a useful one. Carlyle may literally be *Past and Present*'s author, but by identifying himself instead as its "Editor," he emphasizes the roles that others have played in its production. *Past and Present* is not merely the autonomous work of Thomas Carlyle, but owes its existence as well to the labor of others—most notably Jocelin. Thus the editor metaphor in Carlyle's work suggests a model of collaborative production which provides an alternative to the models sought by the socialist critics. That is, the fact that *Hard Times* does not endorse the kinds of collaborative organization for reform exemplified by the union movement need not imply that the novel is in anachronistic retreat toward individualism or Toryism, and away from the collaborative and institutionalizing tendencies of its age. Instead, *Hard Times*'s adoption of a metaphorically editorial role for Stephen Blackpool may suggest another way to conceptualize collaborative reform.

This "editorial" concept of reform needs additional clarification here, however, because the critical history of *Hard Times* would seem to indicate that it is all too easy to confuse an editorial activism with passivity. Stephen's commonalties with Carlyle may underscore the assertiveness of his words to Bounderby, but they do not necessarily fit him into the role of constructive social reformer. Carlyle himself seems on the defensive in establishing his editorial territory—warding off anticipated objections (not dissimilar to those leveled against Stephen by Bounderby) that his analysis of the condition of England features all problems and no solutions. And Williams, for one, has presented Carlyle's influence as an obstacle rather than an aid to *Hard Times*'s role as an instrument of reform, arguing that in the novel Dickens's "identification with Carlyle is really negative. There are no social alternatives to Bounderby and Gradgrind . . . nowhere, in fact, any active Hero" (96). We must therefore explore the role of the metaphorical editor to understand what it offers us that the presence of an "active Hero" in *Hard Times* would not.

Finally, the editorial role as adapted for Stephen in *Hard Times* must be evaluated in light of the fact that Dickens himself played an editorial as well as an authorial role in the novel's creation. Thus the figurative resonance of Stephen's editorial presence in the novel may well be as informed by actual Dickensian editorial practice as by metaphorical Carlylean practice. In order to establish some of the implications of Stephen Blackpool's editorial position in Dickens's *Hard Times*, then, I will first consider the function of the editor as Carlyle develops it in *Past and Present*, and then examine the function of editors in the larger context of the Victorian publishing industry in general and of Dickens's participation as a serial novel editor for that industry in particular.

The "Editor's" role in *Past and Present*—that of the go-between linking Jocelin's papers from a "remote Century" to Carlyle's nineteenth-century readership—is necessarily an incomplete one. At one end of his reform effort—that of *Past and Present*'s creation—the editor is dependent on Jocelin's previously existing work for much of what he himself can write. When the *Chronicle* omits a description of King John, for example, Carlyle is left helpless: try as he might to fill in Jocelin's account with "our own eyes and appliances" (50), in his role as editor he cannot invent a firsthand account where one does not exist. Correspondingly, at the other end of Carlyle's effort—that of *Past and Present*'s influence—the editor is dependent on the response of his reading audience. Just as Carlyle cannot make Jocelin speak where the chronicler is silent, neither can he describe the acts of the still-undiscovered nineteenth-century heroes whom he hopes *Past and Present* will inspire. The editor's function is to hold up the unfamiliar past as a model for present actions, rather than to perform or even envision such actions himself.

And yet, despite Carlyle's belief in the anticipated heroic individuals who will do what he cannot—a belief which echoes persistently in *Past and Present*'s concluding call for a new "Duke of Weimar among our English Dukes"—his investment in his editorial role suggests that he also envisions reform as a potentially collaborative enterprise. The heroes whom Carlyle awaits do not propel themselves to action independently. They are motivated by the past and by those who can interpret it, including the "Editor" who, by contrasting past and present, underscores the need for present reforms even as he refuses to "say How" those reforms should be enacted. *Past and Present*'s self-justification is its ability to make connections between different parties for the purpose of reform: that is, its establishment of a chain of influence in which Jocelin provides a chronicle, which is then taken up by a mediating "Editor," who then makes of it an inspiring model for present heroic action.

If the editorial role in *Past and Present* presupposes one kind of collaborative potential, however—in which past heroes and their editors might play a role in generating present heroic action—it points to the lack of another kind: editors are necessary because the readers of the present have lost contact with the heroes of the past who should motivate them. This loss of contact is particularly important to our understanding of the editorial role because it underlies not only Carlyle's responsibility as a metaphorical editor for representing the past to a forgetful present, but also the growing importance of actual editors in the actual publishing world at approximately the time that *Past and Present* was written. It is Carlyle's task in *Past and Present* to bring the readers of the present "face to face" with the inhabitants of a "remote," unfamiliar past (45). In a similar fashion, as Gaye Tuchman has described, actual editors in the mid-nineteenth-century publishing world bridged an increasingly remote relationship between authors and audiences who had lost the opportunity for face-to-face contact. Tuchman dates the industrialization of Britain's publishing industry and its centralization in London from the 1840s (107). She describes the increasing elaboration of the editorial function in publishing at this time to include not only the interventions of the editors themselves, but also the recommendations of publishers' readers who evaluated manuscripts for them:[9]

> the readers are another layer mediating between authors and their audience. As [Jurgen] Habermas (["The Public Sphere"] 1964) might have put it, the increasingly complex structure of publishing transforms a public in the eighteenth-century sense of educated people who know one another and personally discuss ideas and policies into a "market," a category of people whose tastes

are presupposed by industrial forces and who do not necessarily know one another or get to make a choice about what will be published. The readers embody the growing rationalization—and hence the increasing internal structuring—of nineteenth-century publishing firms.   (67)

The shift Tuchman describes—a shift from a publishing business perceived to be organized around personal interactions toward a more institutionalized publishing business organized around markets—offers another instance of the shift from personal to institutional relationships which the socialist critics point to as a defining characteristic of the industrial age. Tuchman's publishing world, like the socialists' unions, responds to its times by transforming itself on an institutional rather than individual level. The results of that transformation would seem to underscore some of the very tendencies in nineteenth-century life which Carlyle found most disturbing, as cash-motivated market negotiations between authors, editors, and audiences replace authors' direct recognition of their audiences' needs. Paradoxically, however, the structure of the system in which editors and their consultants mediate between authors and readers who are strangers to one another duplicates the structure in which Carlyle as "Editor" mediates between Jocelin and nineteenth-century society, also strangers to one another.

The editorial activity in *Past and Present* is indeed closer to the institutionalized editorial activity found elsewhere in mid-nineteenth-century publishing than to the autonomous, authorial activities of Carlyle's imagined Hero as Man of Letters, described in his 1840 lectures *On Heroes, Hero Worship, and the Heroic in History.* Carlyle describes the Man of Letters "with his copy-rights and copy-wrongs, in his squalid garret, in his rusty coat; ruling (for this is what he does), from his grave, after death, whole nations and generations who would, or would not, give him bread while living" (202–03). This authorial Hero in his garret retreat, "uttering-forth . . . the inspired soul of him" (204), seems indifferent to the whims of the markets which "would, or would not" support him. The efforts of actual editors and of Carlyle the Editor to make authors accessible to audiences are not part of the heroic authorial endeavor as idealized in *On Heroes.*[10] Carlyle thus plays a collaboratively editorial rather than an independently authorial role in *Past and Present,* not only because his project requires him to revisit the work of a previous author—Jocelin—but also because his sensitivity to how that author will be perceived by present-day readers finds a parallel in the preoccupations of actual Victorian-era editors.

This effort to negotiate the disjunction between authorial production and readerly capacities or expectations is evident as well in the editorial work of Dickens himself. Ellen Casey has described how Dickens, as an editor for the serial novels which appeared in his publications, would select and revise the works of his authors in order to adapt them to the demands of the serial market as he understood it (and as, presumably, his authors did not).[11] Dickens intervened at all stages in the development of the novels he selected for publication, from setting exact specifications for the length of as-yet-unwritten works to rewriting or renumbering completed ones (95, 97). As Casey notes, Dickens "distinguished between literary merit and adaptability to serialization" (95): "there must be a special design," as he wrote to one would-be contributor, "to overcome that specially trying mode of [serial] publication" (quoted in Casey, 94). The task for a serial editor as Dickens saw it was thus not only to judge the quality of available novels, but also—and perhaps even more essentially—to judge the fitness of a particular novel to meet the needs of a particular market for a particular reading audience, and if necessary to rework a novel himself to make it fit.

Dickens's work as an editorial mediator between authors and audiences is important in the context of *Hard Times* because his own involvement in the industrial transformations of the publishing world affects the way he evaluates the manufacturing world of Coketown. The flaws *Hard Times* identifies in the manufacturing field reflect in part Coketown's failure to replicate successfully the structure of the Victorian publishing field. I use the term "field" as Pierre Bourdieu has defined it: as "a particular social universe endowed with particular institutions and obeying specific laws" (163).[12] Victorian publishing's increasing reliance upon editors marked a change in publishing's social universe: a transformation of the institutions and laws by which literary works were produced. The earlier understanding of the literary field as a two-part authorial structure dominated by relationships between authors and readers was now transformed to an understanding of the field as a three-part editorial structure with roles not only for author and reader, but for the editor organizing the interactions between them.

It is this same transformation from authorial to editorial structure which *Hard Times* seeks in the manufacturing field, and which it finds missing. The capitalist manufacturers of *Hard Times* insist upon a heroic authorial role in which they are the sole originators in their worlds of production, rather than accepting a collaborative editorial role in which they share credit for their productivity with others. Among the "fictions of Coketown" is the fiction of capitalist self-authorship. The factory owners credit their business successes exclusively to their own individual initiative: "Any capitalist there who had made sixty-thousand pounds out of sixpence, always professed to wonder why the sixty thousand nearest Hands didn't each make sixty thousand pounds out of sixpence" (90). The epitome of the capitalists' tendency toward fictitious self-authorship is of course Bounderby, who invents the story of his own self-invention: "I pulled through it, though nobody threw me out a rope. Vagabond, errand-boy, vagabond, labourer, porter, clerk, chief manager, small partner, Josiah Bounderby of Coketown'' (18). When Bounderby's self-invention is revealed as a lie, the revelation thus explodes the myth of capitalist self-authorship more generally. Bounderby owes his success not to a series of his own heroic individual efforts, but to the accumulated efforts of many: his parents, educators, and "kind master" (193). Similarly, the manufacturing world as represented in *Hard Times* is not one in which capitalists, like Carlyle's authorial Hero as Man of Letters, pull inspiration through individual effort from the heavens, but rather one in which masters and workers should labor collaboratively toward their mutual productive goals.

Coketown's capitalists thus falsely envision themselves as participating in an authorial model of production with direct relationships between authors and readers. According to this model, the capitalist factory owners themselves (in a productive role analogous to authorship) are directly responsible for their successful relationship with the consumer market (analogous to their readership). The workers, labeled as "hands," are merely the machine that carries out the authorial will of the owners. As individual agents with their own wills, they would only be an impediment to production, not an asset to it. By contrast, an editorial model of production would shift the capitalist owners from the role of author to that of editor. In such a model, the capitalist would cede a significant amount of credit for production to the workers, and accept instead credit for the role of editorial mediator: the essential go-between who identifies the needs of the market and channels the efforts of the workers toward them.

The editorial model emphasizes collaboration and individuality at the same time. On the one hand, it points out that the Bounderbys of the world can claim exclusive responsibility neither for the wealth they create nor for the social positions to which it entitles them. Instead, both of these are at least in part collaboratively produced. On the other hand, it acknowledges the work which enables this collaborative production as the effort of individuals. Factory labor, even amid the unnecessarily harsh conditions of Coketown, can be a source of individual identity. Concluding the list of the many things Stephen Blackpool is not, for example, are the two things which he is: "a good power-loom weaver, and a man of perfect integrity" (52). Stephen's laboring identity as a factory worker is presented alongside his moral identity as a man of integrity as if to indicate that the two are of equal importance. And it is his role as a laborer that Stephen clings to above all when his other social roles are endangered by his disagreement with the workers' union: "I mak' no complaints o' bein turned to the wa', o' being outcasten and overlooken fro this time forrard, but I hope I shall be let to work. If there is any right for me at aw, my friends, I think 'tis that" (108). No doubt Stephen's desire to work stems in large part from his desire to have a livelihood, but the elevation of his rights as a worker over all other social rights (including even the right to associate with Rachael, which he begins to deny himself after his ostracism by the other workers [110]) speaks powerfully to the additional importance of his labor as a defining aspect of his selfhood.

Bounderby denies Stephen and the other workers this selfhood when he claims for himself full credit for the labor that takes place in his factories, and it is this denial which forces the other workers into unions and Stephen into an editorial role. If Bounderby were willing to credit his workers for their labor—to acknowledge their contribution to his factories' productivity—then Stephen would be positioned as author rather than editor. That is, by looking at workers as active agents in the manufacturing world, we can place them in the role of the author in an editorial model of production, and shift the owners (who are after all not in a concrete sense the actual creators of material goods) to the role of editor. The process of manufacturing goods thus becomes characterized as a collaborative endeavor shared by workers and owners rather than as the self-initiated and self-sustained endeavor of the owners alone. The dilemma of *Hard Times*'s manufacturing community, however, is that the owners are unwilling to accept for themselves the role of editor and yield authorship to their workers, acknowledging the rights and the place of the workers as authoritative contributors in the field of manufacturing.

From the perspective of the publishing field, then—with its growing role for editors—the manufacturers of Coketown lag behind the times. One reason that Carlyle's metaphorical use of the term "Editor" in *Past and Present* can be so effective is that it draws upon the metonymical relationship of actual editors to industrial society more generally. That is, the role of the editor in the industrial publishing world—a role made necessary as relationships become institutional rather than individual—constitutes one part of the fuller institutionalization of industrial England, including the institutionalization of relationships between workers and capitalists through the union movement. Unfortunately for Coketown, however, *Hard Times*'s capitalists refuse to accept this social transformation. The closest Bounderby comes to acknowledging the new institutional collectivity of his age is when he writes a will attempting to establish his individual self as an institutional collectivity:

> a vain-glorious will, whereby five-and-twenty Humbugs, past five-and-fifty years of age, each taking upon himself the name, Josiah Bounderby of Coketown, should for ever dine in Bounderby Hall, for ever lodge in Bounderby Buildings, for ever attend a Bounderby chapel, for ever go to sleep under a Bounderby chaplain, for ever be supported out of a Bounderby estate, and for ever nauseate all healthy stomachs, with a vast amount of Bounderby balderdash and bluster. (217)

By diverting even a final philanthropic impulse toward community involvement into further self-replication, Bounderby demonstrates how colossally he and his fellow manufacturers have missed the point of the collaborative potential in England's newly industrial society. Thus while the publishing world was meeting the needs of its changing society by relying increasingly on the mediating work of its editors, the manufacturing world as portrayed in *Hard Times* was failing to meet those needs altogether.

If we view *Hard Times* as evaluating one field of endeavor—manufacturing—by its differences from another—publishing—then we perform a kind of literary critique which strikes a middle ground between "the tradition of internal reading, which considers works in themselves independently from the historical conditions in which they were produced, and the tradition of external explication, which one normally associates with sociology and which relates the works directly to the economic and social conditions of the moment'' (Bourdieu 163). On the one hand our analysis considers how *Hard Times* was shaped by its social context, but on the other hand it locates that context in the field with which *Hard Times* was most closely associated—the field of Victorian literary publishing. It is this middle ground between internal and external reading which escapes the notice of the socialist critics who cite *Hard Times*'s failure to find industrial-era solutions for its industrial-era problems. *Hard Times* may not favor union politics, but it does direct its readers' attention to the potential of collaborative institutional structures such as the editorial arrangements which were emerging in the field of Victorian publishing. And when we look for industrial-era solutions by examining how industrialization made its appearance in the publishing world, we take a critical perspective which looks for the transformations of the industrial age in the place where Dickens himself would have been most likely to gain firsthand knowledge of them.

The Editorial Novel

Comparing Coketown to the Victorian publishing world can help us to explain the main problem which underlies the interactions between Bounderby and Stephen and which consequently prompts Stephen's editorial speech to his employer. *Hard Times* finds fault with Bounderby for refusing to see his workers as collaborative individuals, each with individual problems and potential. Any worker who appeals to him is instead typed as a troublemaker: one among a no-good crowd of complainers who expect "to be fed on turtle soup and venison, with a gold spoon" (57, 61). Such typing is necessary for Bounderby as long as he hopes to maintain the fiction of his self-authorship, for in claiming the authorial rather than editorial role in his own success, he denies not only the contributions of all who raised and instructed him, but also of all who have labored for him. He refuses to acknowledge the potential of his workers as originating individuals, thereby creating the distance between those workers and himself which Stephen attempts to bridge. When Bounderby will not play an editorial role, Stephen must do so in his place.

In becoming the main editorial figure in Coketown, however, Stephen not only becomes the stand-in for what Bounderby refuses, but also for what *Hard Times* attempts. It is no coincidence that the same critics who find fault with Stephen's character as an industrial worker also tend to find fault with *Hard Times* as an industrial novel. The transformations which Stephen demands of Bounderby are echoed by the transformations which *Hard Times* demands of its readers; for just as Stephen urges Bounderby away from the state of denial that permits him to ignore both the plight of and the potential in his workers, so too *Hard Times* urges its society away from similar omissions and repressions. Thus, by comparing Stephen's editorial interventions in Coketown to editorialism as it was developing in the publishing world, we can see how *Hard Times* begins to suggest for itself an intervening role in its own times: how, that is, Dickens attempts to establish the industrial novel as an editorial remedy for the failures of industrial capitalism.

Examining Stephen Blackpool's place in Coketown in relation to the Victorian editor's place in the publishing field reveals both similarities and differences. In his speech to Bounderby, Stephen, like the editor, serves as a go-between connecting two parties which are unfamiliar with one another. The speech, were Bounderby truly able to hear it, would have the effect of familiarizing the master with an audience whom he no longer knows—his workers. Like the editor who, knowing the needs of the market, turns down a submission with an explanation for why it fails to fit those needs, Stephen, knowing the wrongs of his fellow workers, provides Bounderby with a list of reasons for why his current strategies as master are doomed to failure.

When compared to a literal editor, however, Stephen has two significant shortcomings—differences which help to explain why he has so often been understood as a passive figure. In the first place, he lacks the power over his employer that an editor, having the right to refuse a publication, could claim over a writer. Bounderby is under no obligation to respond constructively to Stephen's critique, and in fact his actual response (firing Stephen) only further disempowers his critic. Secondly, although Stephen's speech to Bounderby puts him in a position very like that of the metaphorical Carlyean "Editor" of *Past and Present*, he falls short of matching the more positive editorial activities of a Dickensian editor. Like the Carlylean editor, Stephen critiques the circumstances he sees and points out the necessity for their reform. But unlike Dickens—who could tell his authors what would work in a serial novel as well as what wouldn't, and who could even rewrite a novel to suit the serial market himself—Stephen's editorial proposals for Bounderby focus only on the means of reform (or perhaps more accurately the anti-reform measures) that will not work. We are back to the original criticism of Stephen, pointed out by both Bounderby and the socialist critics: Stephen can tell Bounderby how not to solve his labor problem, but he cannot suggest alternative solutions. Although Stephen, with his unflinching critique of his employer, is not in actuality a passive character, it is difficult to avoid seeing him as a negative one.

Stephen's failure to propose workable solutions for reform is all the more crucial because *Hard Times* itself has been accused of the same failure. Williams again sets the terms of the critique with his observation that in *Hard Times* "[m]any of Dickens's social attitudes cancel each other out, for he will use almost any reaction in order to undermine any normal representative position" (96). As Josephine Guy has argued, in criticizing political economics and utilitarianism, Dickens "was more confident in exhibiting the defects of those doctrines than in offering viable alternatives" (136); and as Coles has claimed, in *Hard Times* "Dickens presents a vision of society of the basis of which socially redeeming action, including his own reforming practice, is effectually impossible" (173). Coles's claim is particularly pertinent because he points out that Dickens's negativity in *Hard Times* is anomalous when placed in the context of some of his other projects, particularly his journalistic writing in *Household Words*.[13] The "methods and movements which are condemned in the novel," he writes, "are often the same ones which are urged, or at least approved, in Dickens's journalism" (149). Coles notes, for example, that Dickens's "satirical treatment of the trade union in *Hard Times*" contrasts with "his admiration, in his *Household Words* article 'On Strike,' of the conduct of the Preston Spinners' Union during their long and bitter strike of 1853–54" (162). He observes as well that even *Hard Times*'s more far-reaching critique of Utilitarianism and political economy seems incongruously unjustified given Dickens's friendships with Utilitarian reformers and his willingness to publish reform advocates such as Charles Knight and Harriet Martineau in the pages of *Household Words* (152).

Faced with *Hard Times*'s refusal to offer reform proposals, those critics who seem inclined to give this work the benefit of the doubt tend to excuse its negativity as an attribute common to fiction or the novel. R. D. Butterworth, for example, concludes his own comparison of *Hard Times* and "On Strike" with the assertion that fiction, unlike journalism, "is no place in which to make compromises, but to argue what the writer thinks is right. It is a place for vision and analysis; . . . [in *Hard Times*] Dickens looks not to the short-term but argues rather for the fundamental reform of society on the basis of principles which will, he thinks, ensure its long-term health and happiness" (101). When the union activity in *Hard Times* contradicts Dickens's observations of an actual union in "On Strike," according to Butterworth, it does so because the function of fiction is to generate enduring, big-picture theories rather than to be faithful to immediate, specific facts. From a somewhat different perspective, Leona Toker, comparing *Hard Times* as a novel this time not to journalism but to utopias, argues that plotted narratives (a category including novels such as *Hard Times*) differ from descriptive utopias in that "Narrative art tests systems of thinking about social realities, revealing their hidden flaws and potential liabilities; it is less apt to promulgate a specific vision of social good" (219). Thus narrative, according to this perspective, would be not unlike Stephen Blackpool in that it delineates problems rather than solutions. And Guy concurs that "We should . . . not look to *Hard Times* to provide a fully worked-out, practical solution to current problems in society; nor should we expect to find a particularly acute analysis of them. . . . [in *Hard Times*] Dickens is primarily interested in what we might loosely call an 'ideology' of industrialism" (126). It is task enough for the novel to explore and undermine society's "basic premises" (Guy 126); identifying specific means for altering those premises can be left to some other venue of social critique and commentary.

Yet we should consider how much these sympathetic conceptions of *Hard Times* and of fiction derive from a twentieth-century understanding of the novel as a high art form, rather than from any understanding of the novel which may have been operative when Dickens wrote *Hard Times*. As Richard Altick has pointed out, even though high art, in the nineteenth century as well as in more recent times, was expected to address the eternal or the enduring rather than the temporary and transient, nonetheless "the public taste [in novels] ran strongly toward realistic specification" (48–49). Altick has compiled lists of titles of novels which emphasize modernity, contemporaneity, or everyday fact (34–43), lists which include *Hard Times*, with its volume-edition subtitle *"For These Times."* The expectation that novels would address the everyday particulars as well as the underlying premises of their present social circumstances could only have been intensified in the case of the industrial novel, which openly addressed itself to the present and problematic condition of England. And the expectation that a novel should serve the theoretical concerns of high art may never have been entertained by an audience which originally read *Hard Times* interspersed with journalistic articles in the weekly installments of a middle-class magazine.

If we cannot excuse *Hard Times* from presenting reform proposals by conceptualizing it as a high-art novel, accountable only for long-term social generalizations and not for immediate social particulars, then we are left again with the question of what *Hard Times* should accomplish in relation to those particulars. What it doesn't accomplish, according to the critical consensus, is a specific and accurate representation of the realities of working-class life. We find this conclusion made not only by scholars of Dickens's journalism such as Coles and Butterworth, when they note the discrepancies between the facts of the Preston strike and the fictions of the portrayal of unions in

Hard Times, but also if we look again to the socialist tradition dating back to Shaw and Williams, with its claims that *Hard Times* is more faithful to middle-class stereotypes about the working classes than to any accurate depiction of their everyday realities. Sheila Smith describes this shortcoming as a failure of imagination to engage experience. The social mission of the industrial novelists, she argues, was to use

> middle-class fictions, appealing to middle-class prejudices and social attitudes, to convey the reality of the life of the poor, the Other Nation who, for the most part, did not share these prejudices and social attitudes. So, although there are occasional glimpses of the actuality of the Other Nation, the novels are inevitably what the Victorian middle class thinks and fears of the Other Nation rather than an imaginative re-creation of its life.   (258)

The industrial novels, including *Hard Times*, fall back upon the imaginative conventions of the middle-class novel rather than breaking out of those conventions for an imaginative engagement with working-class experience. As a result, an industrial novel's efforts to communicate the condition of the working classes to middle-class readers—to engage the imaginations of the latter group on behalf of the former—are likely to meet with limited success.

Significantly, however, the very effort in which *Hard Times* itself seems to fall short—the effort to gain an accurate understanding of working-class life—is the same effort to which the novel exhorts its readers at its conclusion. In the novel's final vision of the future, Louisa's projected actions demonstrate that she has acquired not only a new appreciation of fancy and the imagination, but also an interest in learning and improving the condition of the Coketown workers. She is envisioned

> trying hard to know her humbler fellow-creatures, and to beautify their lives of machinery and reality with those imaginative graces and delights, without which the heart of infancy will wither up, the sturdiest physical manhood will be morally stark death, and the plainest national prosperity figures can show, will be the Writing on the Wall, —she holding this course as part of no fantastic vow, or bond, or brotherhood, or sisterhood, or pledge, or covenant, or fancy dress, or fancy fair; but simply as a duty to be done. . . .   (219)

Louisa's future "duty" is to find a more experiential connection to the members of the working classes than that which she would gain either through divisive political mechanisms of the kind that separate factory owners from workers' unions (in an allusion to the unions, her interventions require "no fantastic vow, or bond, or brotherhood, or sisterhood, or pledge, or covenant") or through the distancing sociological facts in which she was educated ("the plainest national prosperity figures"). What is more, Louisa's future actions, once delineated, immediately become a duty passed on as well to the reader.

"Dear reader!" the novel's concluding paragraph declares, "It rests with you and me, whether, in our two fields of action, similar things shall be or not. Let them be!" (219). In calling the reader to the same obligations required of Louisa, the narrator of *Hard Times* twists the language of political economy to a new purpose, replacing a politics of inaction with one of action. The "let them be" of laissez-fair economics ("leave it alone") is transformed to the "let them be" of an interventionist social practice ("make it so").

The conclusion to *Hard Times* thus positions the novel and its narrator, like Stephen, in a metaphorically editorial role in two ways. First, by using Louisa as the model for the reader, and Louisa's efforts to gain a more experiential understanding of her "humbler fellow-creatures" as the modeled behavior, the novel at its conclusion reinvokes the moment of Stephen's editorial speech to Bounderby. Louisa's efforts to know the workers on more intimate terms will presumably be an extension of her first movement toward such knowledge: the visit to Stephen's home in which "for the first time in her life" she came into direct contact with the individual circumstances of a Coketown hand. This first visit to the working classes was inspired by Stephen's speech—of which Bounderby was, after all, not the only auditor. It is initially to Louisa that Stephen addresses himself "instinctively . . . after glancing at her face" (112), and Louisa, unlike her husband, proves receptive to that address, following Stephen home to offer assistance "in consequence of what passed just now" (119). That continuing such visits becomes an important part of the duties Louisa undertakes at the end of the novel suggests that Stephen's speech, despite its immediate ill consequences for Stephen himself, was not entirely ineffective. Furthermore, the speech was effective in the editorial sense that it pushed Louisa on to her own exploration of the lives of the poor, rather than supplying her with its preconceived conclusions. Stephen does not instruct Louisa any more than Bounderby on how to intervene in the condition of England, but he does inspire the interclass contact which will enable her to initiate her own acts of intervention.

Secondly, *Hard Times* the novel plays an editorial role in the sense that its readers, like Louisa, are ultimately left to their own devices. The novel does not itself accomplish or even specify how to accomplish the actions it demands from them. Like the "Editor" Carlyle in *Past and Present*, the novel's role is not to "say How," but rather "to apprise *thee* that it must be done." The narrator may modify Carlyle's delineation of roles to some extent by accepting some of the responsibility for the changes he demands—in place of Carlyle's "apprise *thee*," the narrator argues instead that reform "rests with you and me." But the narrator has arguably already performed his own role in that reformation process. Reader and narrator are to pursue reform "in our two fields of action," and the narrator's field of action is of course the narration of *Hard Times*, which he completes in the very act of making his concluding demand on the reader. The narrator thus requires that the reader continue where the narrative of *Hard Times* leaves off, and even pursue the kind of experiential familiarity with the working classes which the critics have found lacking in the text of *Hard Times* itself.

In editorial fashion, then, *Hard Times* positions itself in a mediating role between two groups unfamiliar with one another's ways and needs. And if it does not overcome that unfamiliarity itself—if the novel's portrayal of working-class life falls short in comprehensiveness or accuracy—it nonetheless, by encouraging its middle-class readers to know their "humbler fellow-creatures," becomes a means for such an overcoming. Williams may be correct that the one-on-one interactions modeled by Louisa's trip to Stephen's home and encouraged by the conclusion of the novel are an individualistic rather than a systemic means of reform. Louisa intervenes through personal initiative and private response, not through collaborative social action or institutional transformation. But if *Hard Times* ends by recommending individual relationships, it also institutionalizes that individualism by becoming itself a mechanism through which such relationships are inspired. As an editorial mediator, the novel need not accomplish reform itself if it can only persuade its readers of the need for such accomplishment. *Hard Times* therefore does not itself present individual experience, but rather becomes a rubric by which it is produced in others—thus in its very demand for individuality reflecting the institutionalization of its industrial times.

Conclusion

Once we have examined the emerging figure of the Victorian editor in both its literal and figurative manifestations—as it resonates in Stephen Blackpool's Carlylean speech to Bounderby, in Thomas Carlyle's narrative persona in *Past and Present*, in the imperative narrative voice at the conclusion of *Hard Times*, and in Dickens's own efforts as an editor as well as author for the publications in which his serial fiction appeared—it seems in retrospect odd that when Williams faults *Hard Times* for replicating Carlyle's negativity, he protests that the novel offers "nowhere, in fact, any active Hero." Williams is presumably working from within Carlyle's own limited inventory of possible social solutions when he looks to *Hard Times* and finds heroism lacking. In context, his statement points out that even those social solutions suggested by the pessimistic Carlyle are not presented as alternatives in the novel dedicated to him. Nonetheless, Williams's disappointment in the lack of heroic figures in *Hard Times* seems an oddly individualistic emphasis for a critic who points to that novel's investment in individualism as an escapist retreat from pressing social realities and workable systemic solutions.

Although an emphasis on individual heroism may seem out of place in the context of socialist literary criticism's desire for systemic or collaborative transformation, however, such an emphasis is not out of place in the context of literary criticism more generally. Authors have long been cast in a heroic role by literary critics. Critics, for example, have referred to Dickens's cult status as an author in order to emphasize the increasing professional prestige of the novelist in the nineteenth century.[14] But the same period which saw a rise in the importance of authors also saw a new importance in the role of editors; and until recently, criticism has underemphasized the fact that Dickens was highly active in the latter role as well as the former. Focusing on the figure of the editor allows us to seek out in the literary field the same kinds of collaborative endeavors which socialist critics have advocated for reform movements in the industrial field, and indeed to reexamine our expectations about how literature itself should participate in such reform movements. We cannot, of course, characterize the growing market-driven emphasis on the role of editors in nineteenth-century publishing as a move away from industrial capitalism and toward socialist unionization. But we can acknowledge the editor, like the unions, as one means of negotiating the new distances between groups with shared interests which resulted from the industrialization of England. Neither can we characterize *Hard Times*'s concluding demand on its readers—that they come to know one another as individuals—as any kind of direct move toward institutional social reform. But we can acknowledge this demand as issuing itself from the institutional rubric of the industrial novel, with its effort to imaginatively link the distanced groups of its middle-class readership and the working-class poor, whether by supplying a detailed and accurate portrayal of working-class experience (which *Hard Times* did not do), or by demanding that readers acquire some first-hand acquaintanceship with that experience themselves (which *Hard Times* did).

Thus, when Stephen passes responsibility for developing reform proposals to those who are over him, he is not retreating to preindustrial Tory hierarchies; and when *Hard Times* passes responsibility for improving the lot of the working classes to its readers, it is not denying itself a motivating role in such improvement. Both Stephen's and *Hard Times*'s deferrals instead demonstrate that they are acting in roles which are editorial rather than authorial. They are casting themselves as part players in a larger field of collaborative reform rather than as self-sufficient creators of complete reform plans. Their efforts address the condition of England by calling forth and drawing together the otherwise unaffiliated efforts of others. Rather than seeking to escape the social transformations of industrialism, *Hard Times* instead finds those same transformations in the literary field—the field of its own production—and imports the literary field's response to those transformations for use in improving the circumstances of the working poor. Rather than evading the problems and circumstances of their newly industrial world, then, Stephen and *Hard Times* instead bring solutions drawn from the industrialization of the literary world to bear upon them.[15]

NOTES

1. For two such early critiques, see Harriet Martineau's remarks in her 1855 essay "The Factory Legislation" and John Ruskin's comment in his 1860 note on *Hard Times*. Martineau claims that Dickens, by undertaking to educate the public through *Household Words*, accepts an obligation to convey the principles of political economy accurately, an obligation which he fails to meet most obviously in *Hard Times*. Ruskin's admiration for *Hard Times* does not prevent him from wishing that Dickens "could think it right to limit his brilliant exaggeration to works written only for public amusement" (47).
2. As I will discuss, this tradition owes its influence as much to Raymond Williams as to Shaw.
3. Their critical legacy is particularly formidable when combined with that of F. R. Leavis, whose famous 1948 citation of *Hard Times* as a "masterpiece" emphasizes the novel's strengths as a literary work rather than as social critique, but who nonetheless is in agreement with Shaw and Williams in identifying the union scenes as one of the novel's weaknesses. "[C]ertainly it doesn't need a working-class bias," he remarks, "to produce the comment that when Dickens comes to the Trade Unions his understanding of the world he offers to deal with betrays a marked limitation. . . . Dickens has no glimpse of the part to be played by Trade Unionism in bettering the conditions he deplores" (357–58).
4. For more recent criticism which questions the accuracy of the union scenes in *Hard Times* see, for example, Sheila Smith's argument that Dickens represents middle-class conceptions of the working classes rather than the workers themselves (*The Other Nation*); Catherine Gallagher, who argues that *Hard Times* equates the newly unionized working classes with children who need and lack effective paternal guidance (*The Industrial Reformation of English Fiction*); and Josephine Guy, who argues that despite his interest in exposing an "'ideology' of industrialism," Dickens does not "assess the validity of that ideology by systematically testing against the 'facts' or 'experience' (as the 'realism' of Gaskell attempted to do)" (126).
5. Williams does, however, note in his remarks on Shaw later in *Culture and Society* that the earlier writer "is always so articulate and so penetrating that he remains a classical point to which we are bound, in wisdom, to refer" (185).
6. On this count again, the critical legacy left by Shaw and Williams is bolstered by that left by Leavis, who is if anything even more sharply critical of Stephen's portrayal than are the two socialist critics: "It can be said of Stephen Blackpool, not only that he is too good and qualifies too consistently for the martyr's halo, but that he invites an adaptation of the objection brought, from the negro point

of view, against Uncle Tom, which was to the effect that he was a white man's good nigger'' (357).
7. See, for example, Michael Goldberg's *Carlyle and Dickens.*
8. A striking example is Carlyle's retelling of the story of an Irish widow dying of typhus, who—denied succor by her neighbors—''proves'' the shared humanity those neighbors refused to recognize by inadvertently infecting them with her disease, with fatal results (150–51).
9. Publishers' readers were paid by the manuscript to review books, evaluating them for qualities including their marketability and their capacity to match the publishing firm's emphases and enhance its reputation. Although readers might themselves offer authors suggestions for revision, they served primarily as advisors to editors, and were selected for their ability to judge by the standards the editor set (Tuchman 65–68). I include the publishers' readers here as part of a general ''editorial function,'' since they assisted editors in mediating between authors and audiences. The fact that the editor's role in Victorian publishing can itself be broken down into different kinds of editorial positions testifies further to the institutionalization of that role. Publication was a collaborative process: when we shift our emphasis from authorial to editorial models for intervention, we should be careful that we do not merely go looking to find individualistically heroic editors to replace individualistically heroic authors.
10. In comparing heroic authorship, Carlyle's editorship, and the nineteenth-century publishing industry, we should also remember that the reader's inability to ''make a choice about what will be published,'' as Tuchman describes it, would seem to be of little importance to Carlyle, no admirer of democracy. Certainly, the heroic Man of Letters, ''uttering-forth'' truths whether or not the present literary market is interested in them, is if anything much less sensitive to the reading preferences of the person on the street than is the editor who is ultimately accountable to the market.
11. The emphasis in Casey's study is on Dickens's editorial work for serials in *All the Year Round*, but she also includes examples of his work for *Household Words* (correspondence between Dickens and Elizabeth Gaskell, for instance).
12. I would like to thank Lawrence Rothfield for a discussion which facilitated my use of Bourdieu in this essay.
13. Although Dickens's journalism, like his serial novels, often appeared in the periodicals which he himself edited, my discussion of his journalism here focuses primarily on his work as a writer, not an editor.
14. See, for example, Tuchman, 106.
15. This essay is dedicated to Callum, the inadvertent collaborator who sped its production.

WORKS CITED

Altick, Richard D. *The Presence of the Present: Topics of the Day in the Victorian Novel.* Columbus: Ohio State UP, 1991.

Bourdieu, Pierre. "Field of Power, Literary Field and Habitus." *The Field of Cultural Production*. Ed. Randal Johnson. New York: Columbia UP, 1993.

Butterworth, R. D. "Dickens the Novelist: The Preston Strike and *Hard Times*." *The Dickensian*. 88 (Summer 1992): 91–102.

Carlyle, Thomas. *On Heroes, Hero-Worship and the Heroic in History*. London: Oxford UP, 1968.

———. *Past and Present*. Ed. Richard D. Altick. New York: New York UP, 1965.

———. *Signs of the Times*. *Selected Writings*. Ed. Alan Shelston. New York: Penguin, 1971.

Casey, Ellen. "'That Specially Trying Mode of Publication': Dickens as Editor of the Weekly Serial." *Victorian Periodicals Review* 14 (Fall 1981): 93–100.

Coles, Nicholas. "The Politics of *Hard Times*: Dickens the Novelist versus Dickens the Reformer." *Dickens Studies Annual* 15 (1986): 145–79.

Dickens, Charles. *Hard Times: An Authoritative Text, Backgrounds, Sources, and Contemporary Reactions, Criticism*. 2nd Edition. Ed. George Ford and Sylvère Monod. New York: W. W. Norton, 1990.

Gallagher, Catherine. *The Industrial Reformation of English Fiction: 1832–1867*. Chicago: Chicago UP, 1985.

Goldberg, Michael. *Carlyle and Dickens*. Athens, Georgia: Georgia UP, 1972.

Guy, Josephine M. *The Victorian Social Problem Novel: The Market, the Individual and Communal Life*. New York: St. Martin's, 1996.

Leavis, F. R. "*Hard Times*: An Analytic Note." *Hard Times: An Authoritative Text, Backgrounds, Sources, and Contemporary Reactions, Criticism*. 340–60.

Martineau, Harriet. "The Factory Legislation: A Warning Against Meddling Legislation." *Hard Times: An Authoritative Text, Backgrounds, Sources, and Contemporary Reactions, Criticism*. 299–302.

Ruskin, John. "A Note on *Hard Times*." *Hard Times: An Authoritative Text, Backgrounds, Sources, and Contemporary Reactions, Criticism*. 332.

Shaw, George Bernard. "*Hard Times*." *The Dickens Critics*. Ed. George H. Ford and Lauriat Lane, Jr. Ithaca: Cornell UP, 1961.

Smith, Sheila M. *The Other Nation: The Poor in English Novels of the 1840's and 1850's*. Oxford: Clarendon, 1980.

Toker, Leona. "*Hard Times* and a Critique of Utopia: A Typological Study." *Narrative*. 4 (October 1996): 218–34.

Tuchman, Gaye, and Nina Fortin. *Edging Women Out: Victorian Novelists, Publishers, and Social Change.* New Haven: Yale UP, 1989.

Williams, Raymond. *Culture and Society: 1780–1950.* New York: Columbia UP, 1958.

Little Dorrit and Providence

Mark Knight

Many commentators have observed that when Dickens began to write
Little Dorrit, he intended to write a story in which no one was willing
to accept responsibility for his or her actions. Although the original
title for the book, Nobody's Fault, *was subsequently abandoned, the*
initial theme remained of central importance. As a result, the reader is
encouraged to consider the issue of human responsibility in the course
of a debate between free will and determinism, a debate which, as I
argue, is located within a theological framework. The novel may include
a variety of secular parallels and alternatives to this framework, but
ultimately, it insists on exploring the issue of human responsibility via
the theological concept of providence. The second half of the article
examines three providential models that are present in Little Dorrit*:*
determinism, deism, and agent causation. While the first two models
are found wanting, the third, embodied in the character of Pancks, is
shown to provide a successful conception of providence in which an
agent, who is neither entirely determined nor completely autonomous,
is capable of asserting his individuality amid a world in which various
determinants exert a powerful influence.

Many commentators have observed that when Dickens began to write *Little
Dorrit*, he intended to write a story in which no one was willing to accept
responsibility for his or her actions. His notebook entry for January 1855
records the original idea of depicting a "people who lay all their sins, negli-
gences and ignorances on Providence" (Butt and Tillotson 223). The original
title for the book, *Nobody's Fault*, reflected this theme, but by autumn 1855

Dickens Studies Annual, Volume 32, Copyright © 2002 by AMS Press, Inc. All
rights reserved.

Dickens was having doubts about the suitability of the title. Having written the first few installments, he realized that the intended irony of the title was being lost amid a world in which various determinants exerted a powerful influence on the characters involved. In response, he altered the direction of the novel and changed both the name and the focus to *Little Dorrit*.

Despite the change in title, the initial theme remained of central importance to the novel. John Butt and Kathleen Tillotson remind us that "'Nobody's Fault' survives, and not only in the Barnacles. Its meanings are multiple. Beginning as irony, a comment on the tendency to shift responsibility, it becomes a gloomy truth pervading all parts of the novel, as a ground-tone of despair about society" (233). As a result, the reader is forced to consider the issue of human responsibility in the course of a debate between free will and determinism, a debate which, as I will argue, is located within a theological framework. Although the novel includes a variety of secular parallels and alternatives to this framework, it insists, ultimately, on exploring the issue of human responsibility via the theological concept of providence, and it is on this basis that the second half of the article will focus upon three providential models. While acknowledging that Dickens was not a religious novelist, Dennis Walder insists that he "was more aware of contemporary religious attitudes than he is often given credit for" (175). It is in this context that Walder encourages us to see the religious subtext of *Little Dorrit*: "In an important sense, religion is *itself* the central theme of *Little Dorrit*: it is the first, perhaps the only, novel of Dickens's in which plot, character, and scene are all closely involved with religion" (172).

A recognition of the pervasive influence of religion in the mid-Victorian period informs the observation with which Thomas Vargish begins his book, *The Providential Aesthetic in Victorian Fiction*: "Among the several concerns that seemed of central importance to literate Victorians the action of God's will in the world was the most transcendent . . . " (1). This concern is clear in Dickens's attitude to the novel. In a letter to Wilkie Collins (6 October 1859), written in response to Collins's criticism of the construction of *A Tale of Two Cities*, Dickens declared: "I think the business of Art is to lay all that ground carefully, but with the care that conceals itself—to show, by a backward light, what everything has been working to—but only to *suggest*, until the fulfilment comes. These are the ways of Providence—of which ways, all Art is but a little imitation" (128).

Discussions of Providence typically make a distinction between general and special providence.[1] The philosopher Richard Swinburne describes the former as "goods arising from the general structure of the world, the natural order of things; which, if there is a God, clearly he will bring about," whereas the latter is defined as follows: "God's dealings with particular individuals, however, in response to their particular needs and requests, not in accordance with any general formula, manifest God's 'special providence'. This involves his intervening in the natural order of things'' (116). In the early/mid-nineteenth century the debate between the two positions was a lively one within Evangelical communities, as Elisabeth Jay explains:

> When it came to tracing the workings of Providence in detail there was considerable disagreement among Evangelicals over the extent to which one should expect God to override natural order and interfere directly in everyday life. Many early Evangelicals seemed to have shared Wesley's view of the absolute necessity of belief in Special Providence . . . but the second generation occasionally showed an awareness of the spiritual dangers of fostering collections of these incidents. (98)[2]

Dickens's distrust of special providence is visible in *Martin Chuzzlewit* through the character of Pecksniff, a man who tries to hide his hypocrisy and corruption with the belief that "Providence, perhaps I may be permitted to say a special Providence, has blessed my endeavours'' (328). The same distrust can also be seen in Dickens's doubts about the value of intercessory prayer. Mrs. Cruncher's "flopping'' provides the opportunity for a comic interlude in *A Tale of Two Cities*, and Dickens commended the article on "Epidemics,'' written by Eliza Lynn and published in *Household Words* on 10 May 1856, which criticized the government's call for a day of fasting in response to a recent outbreak of cholera.[3] The article attacked the proposal for a day of prayer and fasting as an excuse for inactivity, and protested against the idea that "we should charge the Majesty of Heaven with the cure of our own idleness, and call that a visitation from God, which is the result of human uncleanliness and carelessness'' (398).

At the same time, the fall of the house of Mrs. Clennam in *Little Dorrit* seems to provide a counter-argument to the suggestion that Dickens favored general providence. Initially, this event, described as making "a sudden noise like thunder'' (793), appears to offer evidence of divine judgment. It certainly epitomizes a view of Providential intervention which Dickens had defended against Wilkie Collins; a preference for that which Jerome Meckier describes as "a single climactic revelation'' (97). However, on closer examination, the event which provides the climax to *Little Dorrit* subverts the allusion to special providence by using the language of general providence. Early on in the novel, the first description of the house indicates that it is in a bad state of repair: "Many years ago, it had had it in its mind to slide down sideways; it had been propped up, however, and was leaning on some half-dozen gigantic crutches: which . . . appeared in these latter days to be no very sure reliance'' (31). As the novel progresses, the reader is given further clues regarding the natural state of the house: "The debilitated old house in the city . . . leaning heavily on the crutches that had partaken of its decay and worn out with it, never knew a healthy or cheerful interval . . . '' (178). Having been given this information, the reader subsequently realizes that it was only a matter of time before the laws of nature took effect and the house collapsed. Not only can the fall be accounted for by general providence; the novel carefully resists any attempt to attribute the incident to special providence. In the Old Testament, God's special judgment on Judah is prophesied by Jeremiah. In *Little Dorrit*, the prophetic mantle is transferred from Jeremiah to Affery Flintwinch because there are no longer any supernatural signs to interpret. Affery's awareness of the natural warnings that signal the house's demise is evident when Arthur asks her to explain the cause of her fear. She replies: ''Because the house is full of mysteries and secrets; because it's full of whisperings and counsellings; because it's full of noises. There never was such a house for noises'' (688). Her ability to listen to these signs leads to Rigaud's half-joking recognition of her prophetic status: ''Assuredly, Madame Flintwinch is an oracle!'' (773).

The nineteenth century's increasing support for general rather than special providence can partly be explained by the rise of science. Phenomena that had once been seen as evidence of God's direct intervention in the world became increasingly subject to natural explanations, and many felt that it was best to interpret God's providence in terms of natural laws.[4] Yet there was considerable concern in some quarters that this might ultimately undermine belief in providence. In his book, *Divine Providence, Considered and Illustrated* (1850), Charles Hargreaves complained that: ''Some have endeavoured to set aside the providence of God, and to account for the operation of all things, without the agency of an ever-present, active, and controlling deity'' (27). In response, he simply affirmed the necessity of a Deity for the continual operations of nature, arguing: ''Were He for one moment to withdraw or suspend his agency, confusion would immediately take place, the whole system of nature would fall into ruins'' (28). Dickens incorporates a similar argument into *Little Dorrit* by showing the inability of natural determinants, particularly political economy, to replace providence. This is visible in the financial collapse that results from society's willingness to trust their wealth to one man's financial acumen. Mr. Dorrit highlights this misplaced trust when he assures his daughter that ''I—hum—can, with the—ha—blessing of Providence, *be* taken care of'' (611). Mr. Dorrit is obviously thinking of Mr. Merdle, for only a few pages later, he finds himself ''relieved by Mr. Merdle's affable offer of assistance'' (616). Even the established church is involved in this debacle—Bishop has Mr. Merdle in mind when he talks about the ways of Providence: ''Surely the goods of this world, it occurred in an accidental way to Bishop to remark, could scarcely be directed into happier channels than when they accumulated under the magic touch of the wise and sagacious, who, while they knew the just value of riches . . . were aware of their importance, judiciously governed and rightly distributed, to the welfare of our brethren at large'' (251). In her reading of *Little Dorrit* as a novel that relies on the interplay between two biblical texts (Revelation and Ecclesiastes), Janet Larson explains the religious significance of the widespread ruin that follows Bishop's attempt to locate Mr. Merdle as the benevolent and righteous center of society: ''Merdle's reversal is polar and total: as in the fall of Babylon, 'in one great hour so great riches is come to nought' (Rev. 18: 17) and the false messiah is acknowledged as antichrist'' (190).[5]

Merdle's downfall causes problems for the rest of society because he is at the center of a web of economic speculation, but he is not the only human determinant to replace providence in the novel. Throughout *Little Dorrit* a system of patronage encourages individuals to look to their sponsor rather than trusting a divine figure to provide for them. From the worthless support that William Dorrit bestows upon the inmates of the Marshalsea, to Little Dorrit's inability to provide for all of Maggy's needs, the novel continually affirms the limitations of human benevolence and care. This is powerfully illustrated when Daniel Doyce refers to Meagles as ''my Nurse and protector'' (190); the advice he subsequently receives from Meagles about the suitability of Arthur Clennam as a business partner culminates in financial ruin.

Although the novel recognizes that patronage is often well meant, it also hints at the presence of a darker element, primarily through the character of Miss Wade, who rejects the ''swollen patronage and selfishness'' which call themselves ''kindness, protection, benevolence, and other fine names'' (671). Miss Wade is powerless to break out of this cycle, as her corruption of Tattycoram reveals, but her insight into the true nature of the patronage system is a perceptive one. Recounting her past, Miss Wade describes her employment as a governess who is asked to work alongside an incumbent nurse in the family of a poor nobleman. Despite the fact that the two carers are both appointed to support the children, Miss Wade describes their relationship as one of ''constant competition'' (666), a comment that alludes to the driving principle of political economy. If patronage is to be seen in these terms, as an activity grounded in self-interest, it is little surprise that a system designed to provide for dependents dehumanizes them instead. This is evident in Mr. Dorrit's professed benevolence towards Old Nandy: ''The most striking of these [wonders of Mr. Dorrit's protection of Old Nandy] was perhaps the relishing manner in which he [Mr. Dorrit] remarked on the pensioner's infirmities and failings. As if he were a gracious Keeper, making a running commentary on the decline of the harmless animal he exhibited'' (373).

The loss of human agency that accompanies, paradoxically, the replacement of general providence with man-made systems is epitomized by the Circumlocution Office. Indeed, the language that Ferdinand uses to describe the bureaucratic workings of this institution also anticipates the erosion of human distinctiveness implicit within evolutionary theory: ''It is there with the express intention that everything shall be left alone. That is what it means. That is what it's for. No doubt there's a certain form to be kept up that it's for something else, but it's only a form. Why, good Heaven, *we are nothing but forms*! Think what a lot of our forms you have gone through. And you have never got any nearer to an end? [italics mine]'' (736).

As far as *Little Dorrit* is concerned, the Circumlocution Office undermines human agency by turning the workings of Providence into an exercise in *"how not to do it"* (104). The novel is quite explicit about the way in which this negative version of providence "went beyond" (105) the attempt by some to invoke providence as an excuse for inactivity. The Office is not passive in its attempt to maintain the status quo; but active in being "down upon any ill-advised public servant who was going to do it . . . with a minute, and a memorandum, and a letter of instructions, that extinguished him" (105). In this institution, mystery is inflated to the extent that those who enter its labyrinth are not merely confused, but "lost" (105).[6] Having been "referred at last to the Circumlocution Office," they "never reappeared in the light of day" (105). This negative parody of divine providence is described as the demonic "Legion" (106) by the narrator and, among other things, seeks to undermine the very possibility of human freedom. Thus the young Barnacle, speaking on behalf of the Office, offers Arthur an empty choice between a course of action that will go nowhere, and doing nothing at all: "Try the thing, and see how you like it. It will be in your power to give it up at any time, if you don't like it" (116–17).

One of the techniques that the novel uses to point to a providential order beyond the material is mystery, or bewilderment.[7] Mr. Plornish has no explanations to offer which might account for the suffering endured by the inhabitants of Bleeding Heart Yard: "They was all hard up there, Mr. Plornish said, uncommon hard up, to be sure. Well, he couldn't say how it was; he didn't know as anybody *could* say how it was; all he know'd was, that so it was" (142). His response to this state of affairs is one of resignation: "He only know'd that it wasn't put right by them what undertook that line of business, and that it didn't come right of itself" (143). The willingness of Mr. Plornish to submit to the mystery of providence and accept the status quo is particularly striking. While it initially seems at odds with Dickens's general desire for social reform, the confusion can be resolved by viewing the communal atmosphere in Bleeding Heart Yard as a contrast to the individual greed that consumes various members of the Dorrit family. Both before and after the discovery of their fortune, some in the Dorrit family exemplify the consequences of a commercial society in which individuals are obsessed with their own interests. In contrast to this materialistic paradigm, Bleeding Heart Yard embodies the value of a continuing belief in providence. Even a providence that is shrouded in mystery is seen as preferable to the dangers that Dickens identified as inherent within materialism.

A similar point emerges from the contrast between Affery and Jeremiah Flintwinch. Affery is aware of a providential force at work in the noises that she hears, but she is unable to interpret these signs correctly until after the house collapses: ''The mystery of the noises was out now; Affery, like greater people, had always been right in her facts, and always wrong in the theories she deduced from them'' (794). Nevertheless, despite the limitations of Affery's understanding, her recognition of the providential signs encourages her to intervene on Arthur's behalf, whereas Jeremiah's unwillingness to heed the warnings of the house is accompanied by a continual desire to further his own interests without regard for others.

Little Dorrit reveals the tension in Dickens's attitude towards providence. On the one hand he affirms its importance by demonstrating the problems that result from any attempt to replace it, and yet on the other, he is wary of being left with an inexplicable concept that paralyzes the agency of the individual. Either way, Dickens's primary interest is in affirming the potential for human agency amid a world in which a complex web of determinants is at work. This is evident in an article entitled "Nobody, Somebody, and Everybody," published in *Household Words* on 30 August 1856. Dickens exclaims: "And yet, for the sake of Everybody, give me Somebody! I raise my voice in the wilderness for Somebody. My heart, as the ballad says, is sore for Somebody. Nobody has done more harm in this single generation than Everybody can mend in ten generations. Come, responsible Somebody; accountable Blockhead, come!'' (146–47). In an attempt to come to terms with providence in a manner that protects the role of "Somebody" Dickens explored three models in *Little Dorrit*: determinism, deism, and agent causation.

The character of Mrs. Clennam provides the reader with a deterministic model of providence.[8] Although she is not explicitly labeled as a Calvinist, there is no doubt that this is the case. Perhaps the clearest indication is to be found towards the end of the novel when she implies to Amy that Arthur is not one of God's elect: "I have seen that child grow up; not to be pious in a chosen way (his mother's offence lay too heavy on him for that), but still to be just and upright, and to be submissive to me'' (791).[9] Both here and elsewhere, it is significant that the references to Mrs. Clennam's Calvinism dwell on aspects of that belief which are essentially negative. For example, Mrs. Clennam reminds Rigaud of the depravity of the created order: "If I forgot that this scene, the Earth, is expressly meant to be a scene of gloom, and hardship, and dark trial, for the creatures who are made out of its dust, I might have some tenderness for its vanities'' (357), while later on, Mrs. Clennam's narrative insists on drawing attention to the "depravity" of Arthur's mother (776).

Calvin's model of providence, in which "all things are divinely ordained" (183),[10] left no room for human free will, and Mrs. Clennam exemplifies this belief. When Jeremiah Flintwinch tells her that she is "the most determined woman on the face of the earth" (182), there is a certain irony regarding his choice of words. Jeremiah's use of the word "determined" suggests that she is strong willed, but the other meaning of the word is equally pertinent: the character of Mrs. Clennam has been determined by her religion. The negative consequences of this are apparent in the effect that it has upon Arthur, "a grave dark man of forty" (17), who explains his upbringing as follows:

> "I have no will. That is to say," He coloured a little "next to none that I can put in action now. Trained by main force; broken, not bent; heavily ironed with an object on which I was never consulted and which was never mine; shipped away to the other end of the world before I was of age, and exiled there until my father's death there, a year ago; always grinding in a mill I always hated; what is to be expected from *me* in middle life? Will, purpose, hope? All those lights were extinguished before I could sound the words."   (20)

In addition to using negative language to describe Mrs. Clennam's deterministic beliefs, the text calls the viability of these beliefs into question. Despite her apparent rejection of the existence of free will, Mrs. Clennam still feels the need to oppose it actively. In doing so, she echoes the Murdstones in *David Copperfield*: "The creed, as I should state it now, was this. Mr. Murdstone was firm; nobody else in his world was to be firm at all, for everybody was to be bent to his firmness" (49). The relationship between deterministic belief and the assertion of power raises an interesting point. From the first occasion on which Dickens establishes Mrs. Clennam's determinism, he simultaneously subverts her creed. The imposition of her harsh and rigid views on others involves an act of the same will that she is trying to deny. Dickens takes this one stage further by showing her actions as being vengeful and spiteful. She defends her cruel treatment of Arthur's mother by insisting that "it was appointed to me to lay the hand of punishment upon that creature of perdition." She continues: "I was but a servant and a minister" (775). Yet one is struck by the zealousness with which she goes about this service, a zealousness which appears to contradict the Calvinistic belief in the inability of the individual will to alter the decrees of providence.

Jeremiah is the character who finally articulates the inconsistencies of Mrs. Clennam's determinism, insisting: "call yourselves whatever humble names you will, I call you a female Lucifer in appetite for power!" (782). Mrs. Clennam's desire for power leads to her self-appointment as the final arbiter and instrument of justice. In a perceptive analysis of the real motivation behind Mrs. Clennam, Janet Larson argues that she should be understood as a device for critiquing the subjective nature of dogmatic religious claims: "In portraying Mrs. Clennam, however, Dickens does not satirize only a Calvinist mythos that he found abhorrent. Mrs. Clennam also personifies a modern moral psychological type of unbeliever Carlyle had dissected in 'Characteristics,' who 'knows she has a system' " (199–200).[11] While the anthropological religion that lies behind the distorted beliefs of Mrs. Clennam might appear to be the real issue at stake here, it would be wrong to separate it from the satire on Calvinism. Mrs. Clennam's insistent attempts to retell the narrative in a way that substitutes her own efforts for God's redemptive role, for example, "I devoted myself to reclaim the otherwise predestined and lost boy [Arthur]" (777), can be seen as a natural response to the loss of agency that arises from a deterministic model of providence. Unable to live with a belief-system that allows no room for human agency, Mrs. Clennam ends us swapping her previous trust in God's providence for a reliance upon human beings. This explains why, faced with the collapse of her worldview in the face of Rigaud's threatened exposure at the climax of the novel, she turns to Little Dorrit as a divine surrogate. Kneeling before Little Dorrit, Mrs. Clennam begs forgiveness and addresses her "petition" and "supplication" to Little Dorrit's "merciful and gentle heart" (792).

Dickens not only rejected the viability of a model of Providence in which the agent was allegedly determined by the deity; he was also unwilling to accept a second model in which deism left the agent with complete autonomy in a universe of chance. Although the influence of deism had gone into decline during the eighteenth century, the increasing interest in the scientific explanations that were emerging in the 1840s and 1850s, culminating in Darwin's theory of natural selection, "minimized the possibility of a benevolent God's interference and brought men dangerously close again to a Deist philosophy" (Jay 97). As a result, figures such as Rev. Rupert J. Rowton identified deists as one of the groups of people who did not believe in the providential faithfulness of God: "The name of Deist is applied to a few more, who, like the Hindoos, believe that 'a supreme Deity' (such is their cant phraseology) exists, but lets the world alone, reposing calmly in some distant region, and leaving chance or fate to govern all" (15–16). In *Little Dorrit* the association between deism and chance is manifest through the character of Rigaud, whose nationality and skepticism is suggestive of one of the best known deistic thinkers, Voltaire. Unlike Mrs. Clennam, Rigaud does not believe that he is subject to anyone or anything, hence his continual insistence on being treated as a gentleman: "A gentleman I am, a gentleman I'll live, and a gentleman I'll die! It's my intent to be a gentleman. It's my game. Death of my soul, I play it out wherever I go!" (9). Although Rigaud claims that the game is his own, his subsequent death from the collapse of the House of Clennam suggests otherwise.

Rigaud refers to life as a game on a number of occasions, and it is a game that he is happy to participate in: "I am playful; playfulness is a part of my amiable character" (769). In his continual desire to play games, Rigaud implicitly rejects the Victorian belief in self-help. As Wilfred Stone explains in an article on *Daniel Deronda*: "Gambling is a form of 'play,' and play, in the catechism of proper Victorians, was suspect, since it was the antithesis of work" (42). Rigaud boasts about his inactivity to Cavalletto with the following rhetorical questions: "Have I ever done anything here? Ever touched the broom, or spread the mats, or rolled them up, or found the draughts, or collected the dominoes, or put my hand to any kind of work?" (8). If play is to be seen as the antithesis of work, it is because it relies upon chance rather than action and effort. Certainly, chance is central to Rigaud's thinking, as the explanation of his presence at the Marseille Prison suggests: "Here I am! See me! Shaken out of destiny's dice-box into the company of a mere smuggler . . ." (9).

Despite Rigaud's tendency to see life as a game of "dice" (745) in which he is the only determinant, he frequently refers to his desire to beat his opponents. At one point he reflects to himself: "You shall win, however the game goes. They shall all confess your merit, Blandois [i.e., Rigaud]" (352). The way in which Rigaud strives to outwit his competitors in the game that they are playing contradicts the image of a chance universe that he offers elsewhere. Rigaud's annoyance at finding that his plans have been "interrupted" (747) shows an implicit awareness of the vast web of related causal determinants that affect the universe. Moreover, it undermines the chance universe of deism by positing a state of affairs in which one constantly has to anticipate the possibility of providential intervention.

Throughout the novel the complex interactions between individual agents and external determinants require more than determinism or deism is able to offer. Even Little Dorrit, the redemptive heroine who manages to assert her own identity amid the determining pressures of her society, fails to provide a solution. Her comment to Flora—"I have always been strong enough to do what I want to do" (286)—reveals a strength of character that coexists with providence rather than interacting with it. While Little Dorrit serves as the novel's heroine, it is the character of Mr. Pancks who provides us with a third, and ultimately successful, model of providence.

Theological discourse on providence has frequently made use of the concept of agent causation, in which a first cause (God) introduces a secondary cause (human agents), to combine a notion of causality and design with a meaningful conception of human freedom (and responsibility). Thomas Aquinas explained that God had determined a universe in which human beings had the ability to make free choices: "God, therefore, is the first cause, Who moves causes both natural and voluntary. And just as by moving natural causes He does not prevent their acts being natural, so by moving voluntary causes He does not deprive their actions of being voluntary: but rather is He the cause of this very thing in them . . . " (Vol. 1, 418). A similar understanding informs mid-nineteenth-century discussions of providence, as Charles Hargreaves illustrates:

> The agency of God, however, is seldom *direct* . . . Even in things purely spiritual, and where the result is so manifestly his own, he uses means to produce it. Paul plants and Apollos waters, though *He* giveth the increase, and worketh in all. And thus it is in temporal things; instruments are employed: but instrumentality supposes and requires agency . . . Thus agents act of themselves; yet are God's servants: they follow their own inclinations but fulfil his purpose.
>
> (23–24)

In *Little Dorrit* Pancks embodies the concept of agent causation and, in doing so, provides the novel with a successful model of providence. Although his contingency is never in doubt, Pancks has the ability to act freely and alter the fortunes of those around him. This is illustrated by the image that Pancks cultivates for himself of a mysterious gypsy who can look into Little Dorrit's future. As soon as Pancks begins his fortune-telling, Little Dorrit's life changes, as he begins "to pervade her daily life" (290). Pancks's appropriation of the fortune-teller metaphor involves a reworking of determinism to make room for human agency: rather than simply foretelling her future, Pancks's "industry" makes it happen (319). The influence of Pancks on those around him can be seen in another reworking of a previously mentioned metaphor. Rigaud is seen as a card player, but Pancks is described as a card dealer. This occurs during a dinner that Pancks holds in the course of his search for the Dorrit fortune: "When Mr. Pancks, who supported the character of chief conspirator, had completed his extracts, he looked them over, corrected them, put up his note-book, and held them like a hand at cards" (300). Pancks subsequently distributes the cards among John Chivery, Mr. Rugg, and himself, a course of action that eventually leads to the Dorrits' inheriting a large sum of money, and in doing so, he reveals the extent of his influence within the providential order.

However, although Pancks is able to exert influence, he does not perceive himself to act in the same autonomous manner as Rigaud. Upon discovering the information that frees the Dorrits from Marshalsea Prison, Pancks immediately defers to Arthur Clennam: "That matter I place in your hands. I authorise you, now, to break all this to the family in any way you think best" (412). In addition to his willingness to submit to individuals, Pancks has the ability to defer to providence in general, but he is able to do so without losing his personal identity. When Pancks loses his investment in the aftermath of Merdle's ruin, he takes responsibility, albeit melodramatically, for the part that he has played in giving ruinous advice to Arthur: "Reproach me, sir, or I'll do myself an injury. Say, You fool, you villain" (712). Pancks's attitude towards his own "calculations" reveals both a submission to Providence and an affirmation of his own powers as a human agent, as in puzzlement, he repeats his claim "to prove by figures . . . that it ought to have been a good investment" (765).

During the events that unfold in *Little Dorrit*, Pancks confirms the contingency of his nature (in terms of the novel) by admitting, during his exposure of the Patriarch, that: "Pancks is only the Works; but here's the Winder!" (800). Pancks's agency is emphasized by the modified mechanical imagery that is used to describe him. On the one hand, he is seen as a piece of machinery, hence the fact that it is typical to find him "feverishly unfolding papers, and speaking in short high-pressure blasts of sentences" (387). At the same time, his willingness to sacrifice his own interests on behalf of others offers a model of sacrifice which contrasts with the materialistic individuals found elsewhere in the novel. Early on in the novel, Pancks admits to his "inclination to get money" (160), and yet later we discover that this motivation is subservient to an altruism that places the interests of humanity above commercial concerns and mechanical efficiency.

Ultimately, Pancks acts as a free agent within the providential order, reconciling the dilemma between freedom and determinism which, as John Reed tells us in *Victorian Will*, concerned Dickens "from his earliest days as a writer" (246). As such Pancks is neither determined nor autonomous, and is capable of asserting his individuality amid a world in which various determinants exert a powerful influence. The consequence of this is that Pancks plays an active part in helping to release others from the imprisoning motif that overshadows the novel: it is Pancks who helps discharge the Dorrits from the Marshalsea Prison; Pancks who leads the rebellion against the economic oppression endured by the inhabitants of Bleeding Heart Yard; and Pancks who, through his commitment to human relationships, helps to create the hopeful future with which the novel concludes: "They [Little Dorrit and Arthur Clennam] went quietly down into the roaring streets, inseparable and *blessed* . . . [italics mine]" (826).

NOTES

1. Thomas Vargish declares that in "nineteenth-century England there were perhaps two major versions of the providential worldview" (20). Vargish's description of these as transcendence and immanence is related to the distinction being made here between general providence (transcendence) and special providence (immanence).

2. It is interesting to note the article on George Mueller by Henry Morley that appeared in *Household Words* on 7 November 1857. George Mueller firmly

believed in special providence and recounted numerous occasions on which he believed that God had answered his prayers. While Morley's article is clearly suspicious of Mueller's belief in the power of prayer, it is favorably inclined towards Mueller on the basis of his other attributes: "A precarious subsistence—one obtained by living upon prayer—is a safe one in his eyes, but it is accompanied by him with the most energetic labour to do good work in the world. It will be seen, too, as we tell the main facts of his story, that, whatever error we find in his theology, his view of a Scriptural life tallies with some of the best precepts of worldly wisdom" (434).

3. In his letter to William Henry Wills (27 April 1856), Dickens wrote: "Get Epidemics as near the opening (the usual poetical place) as you can, because it has a purpose in it" (99).

4. G. Combe explained: "Here, then, an important revolution has been effected in the views of profound thinkers, in regard to the mode in which Providence administers this world. Science has banished from their minds belief in the exercise, by the Deity, in our [day], of special acts of supernatural power as a means of influencing human affairs, and it has presented a systematic order of nature, which man may study, comprehend, and obey, as a guide to his practical conduct" (411).

5. As Larson suggests, Merdle can be seen as an antichrist figure, who, in opposition to the providence of God, stands at the center of a vast economic system of corruption and exploitation. For a more detailed reading of the economic system of an empire that comes under the judgment of God in Revelation 18, see chapter 10 of Richard Bauckham's *The Climax of Prophecy.*

6. The way in which the Circumlocution Office is spoken of here resembles the depiction of the law in *Bleak House.* As Gordon Bigelow notes, "most ambitious critical studies of *Bleak House* have focused on the novel's interest in systems" (590).

7. Religious awareness of the theological significance of mystery gathered momentum in the late 1850s with the publication of Henry Mansel's 1858 Bampton lectures, entitled *The Limits of Religious Thought Examined.* In these lectures Mansel emphasised a transcendent and mysterious God who could only be known through supernatural revelation.

8. As many critics have pointed out, the determinism of Mrs. Clennam is also present in the cyclical pattern that marks the House of Clennam: "Morning, noon, and night, morning, noon, and night, each recurring with its accompanying monotony, always the same reluctant return of the same sequences of machinery, like a dragging piece of clockwork" (339). John R. Reed discusses this theme briefly in his *Dickens and Thackeray: Punishment and Forgiveness* (236–37), and Soultana Maglavera comments that: "In the end, it seems to me that the novel offers two solutions to the problem of how to react against a deadening and inhuman cyclicity" (120).

9. Calvin's doctrine of predestination distinguished between the "elect," who were destined for salvation, and the "reprobate," who were destined for damnation.

10. Significantly, Calvin's emphasis on God's providence at the end of book one of the *Institutes* provides the foundation for his refutation of human free will at the start of book two.

11. Larson's reading is supported by the following observation regarding Mrs. Clennam from the narrator in *Little Dorrit*: "Verily, verily, travellers have seen many monstrous idols in many countries; but no human eyes have ever seen more daring, gross, and shocking images of the Divine nature, than we creatures of the dust make in our own likenesses, of our own bad passions" (775).

WORKS CITED

Aquinas, Thomas. *Summa Theologica*. 3 Vols. Trans. English Dominican Fathers. London: Burns & Oates, 1947–48.

Bauckham, Richard. *The Climax of Prophecy: Studies on the Book of Revelation*. Edinburgh: T&T Clark, 1993.

Bigelow, Gordon. "Banking and Domesticity in *Bleak House*." *ELH* 67.2 (Summer 2000): 589–615.

Butt, John, and Kathleen Tillotson. *Dickens at Work*. London: Methuen, 1957.

Calvin, John. *Institutes of the Christian Religion*. Trans. Henry Beveridge. Grand Rapids, MI: Eerdmans, 1989.

Combe, G. *On the Relation between Religion and Science*. Repr. in *Religion in Victorian Britain Vol. III: Sources*. Ed. James Moore. Manchester: Manchester UP, 1988.

Dickens, Charles. *Bleak House*. Oxford: The New Oxford Illustrated Dickens, 1991.

———. *David Copperfield*. Oxford: The New Oxford Illustrated Dickens, 1996.

———. *The Letters of Charles Dickens*. Ed. Graham Storey et al. Oxford: Clarendon. The Pilgrim Edition. 11 vols. to date. 1965–.

———. *Little Dorrit*. Oxford: The New Oxford Illustrated Dickens, 1994.

———. *Martin Chuzzlewit*. Oxford: The New Oxford Illustrated Dickens, 1991.

———. "Nobody, Somebody, and Everybody." *Household Words* 14 (30 August 1856): 145–47.

———. *A Tale of Two Cities*. Oxford: The New Oxford Illustrated Dickens, 1994.

Hargreaves, Charles. *Divine Providence, Considered and Illustrated*. London: Ward and Co., 1850.

Jay, Elisabeth. *The Religion of the Heart: Anglican Evangelicalism and the Nineteenth-Century Novel*. Oxford: Clarendon, 1979.

Larson, Janet L. *Dickens and the Broken Scripture*. Athens: The U of Georgia P, 1985.

Lynn, Eliza. "Epidemics." *Household Words* 13 (10 May 1856): 397–400.

Maglavera, Soultana. *Time Patterns in Later Dickens*. Amsterdam: Rodopi, 1994.

Meckier, Jerome. *Hidden Rivalries in Victorian Fiction: Dickens, Realism, and Revaluation*. Kentucky: The UP of Kentucky, 1987.

Morley, Henry. "Brother Muller and his Orphan Work." *Household Words* 16 (7 November 1857): 433–38.

Reed, John R. *Dickens and Thackeray: Punishment and Forgiveness*. Ohio: Ohio UP, 1995.

———. *Victorian Will*. Ohio: Ohio UP, 1989.

Rowton, Rev. Rupert J. *The Lights and Shadows of Divine Providence*. London: B. Wertheim, Aldine Chambers, 1847.

Stone, Wilfred. "The Play of Chance and Ego in *Daniel Deronda*." *Nineteenth-Century Literature* 53.1 (June 1998): 25–55.

Swinburne, Richard. *Providence and the Problem of Evil*. Oxford: Clarendon, 1998.

Vargish, Thomas. *The Providential Aesthetic in Victorian Fiction*. Charlottesville: UP of Virginia, 1985.

Walder, Dennis. *Dickens and Religion*. London: George Allen and Unwin, 1981.

Help Wanting: The Exhaustion of a Dickensian Ideal

Daniel Siegel

Though he has come to personify the greatest ambitions of Victorian philanthropy, Dickens, at the height of his career, abandoned the very image of charity that he had so fiercely advocated throughout his early works. Initially, Dickens elaborates an ideal of "personal charity" as one that can inspire extreme acts of social recognition and class conciliation. This ideal becomes most profound in the novels of his middle period, in which personal encounters between rich and poor expose prior histories of abuse and neglect, and, through such exposures, provide an avenue for restitution and recovery. Yet, beginning in Little Dorrit, *a charity based on personal relation loses its power to reconcile; intimacy itself becomes a tool whereby the poor and disaffected are better manipulated. Through the dissolution of the Meagles household and the anti-philanthropic thrust of Amy Dorrit's eventual ascendancy, Dickens dismantles the ideal of personal charity, insisting that even the exertions of the most earnest benefactors are finally performed in the interest of their own security.*

> When you have sat at your needle in my room, you have been in fear of me, but you have supposed me to have been doing you a kindness; you are better informed now, and know me to have done you an injury.
>
> —Dickens, *Little Dorrit*

In July 1860, Dickens published a piece in *All the Year Round* containing a

Dickens Studies Annual, Volume 32, Copyright © 2002 by AMS Press, Inc. All rights reserved.

devastating scene of philanthropy gone wrong. The article relates Dickens's own experiences as, during a night of insomnia, he rambles "houseless" through central London and Southwark. A bell tolling three o'clock finds him on the steps of St. Martin's:[1]

> Suddenly, a thing that in a moment more I should have trodden upon without seeing, rose up at my feet with a cry of loneliness and houselessness, struck out of it by the bell, the like of which I never heard. We then stood face to face looking at one another, frightened by one another. The creature was like a beetle-browed hair-lipped youth of twenty, and it had a loose bundle of rags on, which it held together with one of its hands. It shivered from head to foot, and its teeth chattered, and as it stared at me—persecutor, devil, ghost, whatever it thought me—it made with its whining mouth as if it were snapping at me, like a worried dog. Intending to give this ugly object money, I put out my hand to stay it—for it recoiled as it whined and snapped—and laid my hand upon its shoulder. Instantly, it twisted out of its garment, like the young man in the New Testament, and left me standing alone with its rags in my hands.
>
> (*Uncommercial Traveller* 133)

What is gained, what even is learned, in this encounter? Imagine the cold March night in Trafalgar Square, a young man in rags, harried by the elements and by his imagination, faced suddenly by—not a Brownlow or a Cheeryble, but the father of all the Brownlows and Cheerybles, the very conscience of philanthropy. For decades Dickens had urged readers to reach out to lost souls like this beetle-browed youth. Yet now his own helping gesture comes to nothing. It *doesn't matter* that Charles Dickens passed by; an alderman or policeman, or an actual devil or ghost, would have done just as well. The futility of the scene seems to forfeit the social mission of the earlier Dickens, for there can be little hope for charity when the poor recoil from help as they would from harm. The benefactor too is called into question as a possible "persecutor," his companionship becoming theft as he inadvertently seizes the youth's only garment.[2] Philanthropy is no longer a solution to the failures of society; it has proven itself a failure as well. And yet while this scene is a testament to that failure, it contains traces of the hope that has been abandoned: the ideal of personal charity.

I use the phrase "personal charity" to denote a particular strain in Victorian discussions of philanthropy. Proponents of personal charity held that the primary (or exclusive) function of philanthropy should be to multiply the points of contact between rich and poor, a contact that had been increasingly attenuated by the stratifications of modern urban life. Rather than contribute to the economic relief that was the sole province of the state, philanthropists should personally visit hospitals, prisons, schools, workhouses, and of course the homes of the poor. Through individual scenes of personal contact, each class would exert a salutary influence on the other. The rich would advise the poor on matters spiritual (Scripture, doctrine, prayer) and temporal (economic and domestic management, health, hygiene), while the poor would remind the rich of the necessity of Christian charity, and would often provide examples of fortitude, dignity, and (paradoxically) independence.

Dickens embraced the personal approach to philanthropy, particularly in what I will call his middle period, from *Dombey and Son* (1846–48) to *Bleak House* (1852–53).[3] During these years, Dickens moves away from the vision of general benevolence he had supported in his earlier novels, and looks for solutions that draw rich and poor into a much tighter scheme of relation. Yet Dickens's brand of personal charity reaches beyond the regular philanthropic ideas of familiarity and influence to incorporate the idea of *restitution*—action that proceeds from a recognition of another's claims. In Dickens's middle novels, charity leads directly to restitution through the exposure of shared personal histories between rich and poor, histories that hinge on a primal moment of injury or failed paternity. Far from merely activating the powers of influence, charity effects an actual or symbolic resumption of paternity or reversal of some prior wrong.

Dickens's narratives of restitution temporarily find their expression in the operations of personal charity, but in the later novels, restitution presents a serious challenge to the entire philanthropic enterprise. This new attitude reflects the incipient socialism which, in the decades after Dickens's death, would convince the nation at large that philanthropy was an insufficient means of maintaining the social welfare. The proponents of state regulation (in matters such as housing and wages) argued that relief to the poor must not be seen as a philanthropic measure at all, but as an assertion of economic justice. Charity was a palliative for the consciences of the rich, who could thereby demonstrate their solicitude for the poor without compromising the foundations of their own economic dominance. As an example of the new socialist thinking, I cite Arnold Toynbee's famous 1883 confession (which I've excerpted from Beatrice Webb's autobiography):

> We—the middle classes, I mean, not merely the very rich—we have neglected you; instead of justice we have offered you charity, and instead of sympathy we have offered you hard and unreal advice; but I think we are changing. If you would only believe it and trust us, I think that many of us would spend our lives in your service. You have—I say it clearly and advisedly—you have to forgive us, for we have wronged you; we have sinned against you grievously—not knowingly always, but still we have sinned, and let us confess it; but if you will forgive us—nay, whether you will forgive us or not—we will serve you, we will devote our lives to your service, and we cannot do more.
>
> (176–7)

Toynbee's account names charity the enemy of restitution, a designation that is forecast by Dickens's own late-career change of heart. In *Little Dorrit* (1855–57) and afterwards, Dickens attacks the very form of personal charity that had previously proven so vital, showing it to perpetuate precisely the kinds of failures that it had earlier served to expose and expiate. The following pages will consider the uses to which Dickens put the idea of personal charity during his middle period, and the reasons he later abandoned it.

1.

When Alice Marwood, a fallen woman, angrily rejects the alms offered her by Harriet Carker, she performs an act that will be frequently rehearsed throughout Dickens's later novels. Jack Maldon, Jo, Richard Carstone, Amy Dorrit, Miss Wade, Lizzie Hexam, Betty Higden, and even Silas Wegg find occasion to refuse or resist offers of charity. And yet Alice's refusal of help, conventional as it is to become, is far from automatic; it takes her several hours to return the money, hours which bring her into and back out of London, and involve her in emotions ranging from intense gratitude to agonized rage. The whole transaction can be charted as follows:

1. Alice is "contemptuous and incredulous" toward Harriet's kindness;
2. Alice relents, becomes grateful;
3. Harriet gives Alice money, which Alice accepts as a *token* of her benefactor;
4. Alice delivers the money over to her mother;
5. Alice learns that Harriet is the sister of her enemy;
6. Alice seizes the money from her mother;
7. Alice returns to Harriet and replaces her gratitude with a curse;
8. Alice throws the money to the ground.

By opening a significant gap between Harriet's offer and Alice's refusal, Dickens suggests that the rejection of charity is not the spontaneous expression of a particular attitude, but the culmination of multiple motives, attitudes, and effects.

One conspicuous aspect of the transaction is that, whether Alice accepts or returns the alms, the money cannot stay in her hands. At the instant Alice arrives in the city, her mother asks her for money: "The covetous, sharp, eager face with which she asked the question and looked on, as her daughter took out of her bosom the little gift she had so lately received, told almost as much of the history of this parent and child as the child herself had told in words" (491). The demands of an avaricious mother are surely meant to signify the inescapable cycle of criminal poverty—the idea that, when one is forced continually to revisit her degraded origins, she has little chance to reform. But the profits of charity are ephemeral in a more mundane sense as well, as they are quickly lost to the hard contingencies of urban survival.[4] A little money can do nothing to improve Alice's connections, erase her crime, find regular work for her. Rejecting the donation therefore becomes a way for her to repossess it. As she seizes the money from her mother, Alice ensures that it will nourish a private and sacred cause—the cause of her anger and vengefulness—instead of feeding the parasitic demands of her ordinary life.

It is not just the money that Alice repossesses at that moment; she instantly returns in her mind to the very moment of the donation, so that she can construct a new image of what actually happened:

> "Stop!" and the daughter flung herself upon her, with her former passion raging like a fire. "The sister is a fair-faced Devil, with brown hair?"
> The old woman, amazed and terrified, nodded her head.
> "I see the shadow of him in her face! It's a red house standing by itself. Before the door there is a small green porch." (493)

The scene unfolds anew before Alice's eyes, but differently; Harriet is now a fair-faced Devil. Such an epithet may well have suggested itself to Alice in her initial "contemptuous and incredulous" apprehension of Harriet. If so, it has remained with her, ready to resurface if her interpretation of the scene should require it. The rejection of charity, then, involves not only a repossession of the alms, but a reconstruction of the past. Once arrived at Harriet's house, Alice further exercises the drive to reconstruct: "If I dropped a tear upon your hand, may it wither it up! If I spoke a gentle word in your hearing, may it deafen you! If I touched you with my lips, may the touch be poison to you! A curse upon this roof that gave me shelter!" (495). The battle for the present—who will have the money?—is revealed to be a battle over the past. To refuse charity Alice must look backward.

For Dickens, acts of charity are fundamentally concerned with this backward-looking reconstruction of the past. Harriet cannot look at Alice's "reckless and regardless beauty" without imagining the state she has fallen from, and Alice, in describing her own abjection to her mother, links together scenes of her past history as a child, then a girl, then a criminal, now a woman. In the same novel, Polly Toodles fears that Biler's tenure at a charity school will sever him from his family, and wants to reach him before he loses hold on his past: "She spoke, too, in the nursery, of his 'blessed legs,' and was again troubled by his spectre in uniform. 'I don't know what I wouldn't give,' said Polly, 'to see the poor little dear before he gets used to 'em' " (60). Both the desire to help out and the willingness to be helped are connected with memories of the past. Thus John Carker takes an interest in Walter, who reminds him of the hopeful days of his own youth; Edith Dombey looks after

Florence, a daughter who may still, unlike herself, be rescued from parental neglect; the prostitute Martha (*David Copperfield*) helps rescue Emily after she too falls; and Redlaw (*The Haunted Man*) finds, through Edmund Longford, a way to forgive the injuries of his own past. A study that wishes to integrate Dickens's scenes of charity with the most profound aspects of his narrative and social imagination, must begin by asking what charity has to do, specifically, with reconstruction and revision.

Critics have noted that Dickens's class aspirations, and the hopes and fears generally held by a precariously mobile lower middle class, make the question of origins a vexed one.[5] For those struggling upward, the past supplies alternating images of shame and security, images available to be sorted, selected, forgotten, and recovered. Complementing these impulses is the novelist's conventional turn to the personal past as a setting for the most outrageous fantasies of suppressed identity and improbable affiliation—not just in the sensation novels that surrounded Dickens in his final decade, but in the great novels of his youth, in Jane Fairfax's secret love affair and Roland Graeme's hidden ancestry. But it is Dickens's brazen innovation to use such a past—the personal as opposed to the cultural past—as a framework for the utopian reconstruction of social relations in the present. Dickens removes the act of charity from the utilitarian realm of policy and measured outcomes, and reveals it to be the reenactment of some primal and specific scene of alienation. The benefactor and the needy are invariably linked by a set of concrete circumstances that take three characteristic forms: (1) the object of solicitude sparks a remembrance in the benefactor of his or her own early life, as with Martha and Emily; (2) the benefactor turns out to share a suppressed kinship with the needy, as with Alice's eventual intercession on behalf of Edith Dombey; (3) the benefactor has had some actual role in causing the suffering of one she intercedes for, as with Mrs. Clennam and Amy Dorrit. Personal charity in Dickens advances far beyond the standard philanthropic program of forging a better acquaintance between rich and poor, and instead thrusts both classes upon an imaginary landscape in which they are always already related, whether through identification, kinship, or criminal culpability.

The Haunted Man (1848) bears out Dickens's conviction that the success of charity depends on the reconstruction or recovery of a shared past. At the story's opening, Redlaw (a chemist) is a haunted man, suffering from the memory of a past injury. Redlaw is granted his wish to forget the sorrow of his past life and remember only the good, but he gradually finds that, in the process of forgetting injury, he has lost his ability to compassionate others' sorrows.[6] Meanwhile, the chemist passes on his forgetfulness to all who come near him, always with the same effect: as soon as the sorrows of the past vanish, so does the compassion of the moment. This reprieve from sorrow proves fatal to the capacities both to help and to be helped. A mother loses interest in her infant children; a father has no pity for his dying son; a patient cannot tolerate his nurse; a prostitute slips beyond the pale of recovery. The hauntedness (shame, guilt, indignation, regret, loss) that had seemed a problem turns out to be a desirable condition, the only possible means to a constructive benevolence. While trying to escape his sorrowful past, Redlaw comes to realize that he has endangered his moral integrity—"integrity" in the chemist's sense of the word—and has cut himself loose from the community of suffering humanity. The story thus vindicates hauntedness and denounces any cure that would sever the ethics of the present from the trauma of the personal past.

The practical consequences of such a break are serious indeed, and the story traces these consequences, in allegorical fashion, across the diverse landscape of human life. For instance, Redlaw meets a fallen woman who is haunted by sorrowful memories of better days, but who loses all of her qualms of conscience once she begins to forget her past. " 'Sorrow, wrong, and trouble!' he muttered, turning his fearful gaze away. 'All that connects her with the state from which she has fallen, has those roots!' " (367). The chemist is "afraid to think of having sundered the last thread by which she held upon the mercy of Heaven" (367). Similarly, when Redlaw encounters a criminal who, softened by the pleadings of his father, is at the point of renouncing his career, Redlaw's presence restores to the man the boldness to eschew repentance and salvation. In another scene that is less sensational but even more pointed than these, Mrs. Tetterby, a mother of eight, ceases to care for her children, and grows contemptuous of her husband. As she is later to describe it, "I couldn't call up anything that seemed to bind us to each other, or to reconcile me to my fortune. All the pleasures and enjoyments we had ever had—*they* seemed so poor and insignificant, I hated them" (349). Mrs. Tetterby's indifference to her family is wrenchingly portrayed in Tenniel's illustration, which shows her surrounded by her clambering children who try to get her attention as she sits motionless and stares vacantly out of the frame.

The mother has drifted away from her family, and can only recognize afterwards that it was her sorrow, sweetened by memory, that had anchored her to her home. Severing the link to sorrow, then, does not only impair a person's benevolence; it reconfigures her whole ontology, such that she becomes a creature of the moment. As in Dickens's other Christmas tales (such as the earlier *A Christmas Carol* and the later *What Christmas Is as We Grow Older*), the authentic life is shown to be the one that holds past, present, and future together at every moment, and along with these includes failed hopes, lost ambitions, pasts that might have been but weren't.

" 'The past is past,' said the Chemist. 'It dies like the brutes. Who talks to me of its traces in my life? He raves or lies! What have I to do with your

Figure 1. "Mrs. Tetterby"

distempered dreams? If you want money, here it is. I came to offer it; and that is all I came for. There can be nothing else that brings me here' '' (356). With these words Redlaw reprimands Edmund Longford, the sick student to whom the chemist has paid a visit. Longford has just revealed his own hidden association with Redlaw's sorrowful past—a past that Redlaw can no longer remember—and welcomes the chemist's visit as a fulfillment of his long-nurtured hopes and expectations. But Redlaw rejects this account. He wishes to give a gift, but refuses to enter into (or to be implicated within) a cycle of reciprocity, a process that has prepared for his participation before Redlaw ever thought of offering it. This cycle would be most famously described a half-century later by Marcel Mauss, who saw the process of gift-exchange as constantly rehearsing the three phases of giving, receiving, and reciprocating. In Mauss's analysis, every aspect of the gift cycle is performed in response to an obligation. Correspondingly, in *The Haunted Man*, the escape from the past serves to liberate one from the burdens of the reciprocity cycle, making it possible to give without feeling obliged to do so, and to receive without feeling compelled to repay the gift.[7] Once Longford is infected by Redlaw's forgetfulness, he too resists the gift cycle (described below by Milly Swidger) that would extend the act of charity beyond its immediate circumstances:

> "When I have seen you so touched by the kindness and attention of the poor people down-stairs, I have felt that you thought even that experience some repayment for the loss of health, and I have read in your face, as plain as if it was a book, that but for some trouble and sorrow we should never know half the good there is about us." . . .
> "We needn't magnify the merit, Mrs. William," he rejoined slightingly. "The people down-stairs will be paid in good time, I dare say, for any little extra service they may have rendered me; and perhaps they anticipate no less."
> (359)

The student objects to the "drag" of a charity that, even as it heals him, demands that he always remember his illness—a charity that far exceeds the moment of necessity, and wishes to take back as much as it gives.

The hauntedness of Dickens's story is therefore the hauntedness of Mauss's gift, a sense in which every new encounter somehow recapitulates a moral drama that has come before. Redlaw's mistake is to think that he can become part of the solution without ever having been part of the problem. He enters Longford's sick chamber intending to relieve a stranger's distress, only to discover that he was present at the primal scene of catastrophe, and that he has suffered by it for years alongside the student. Indeed, it is Redlaw's desire to help that sets the story in motion; as he contemplates Milly Swidger's seemingly untroubled benevolence, he becomes fixated on his own troubles, which seem to remove him from the community of others. If he could forget his sorrows, he could train his efforts outwards, providing for others' peace and comfort as Milly does so easily. But the story's final revelation is that Milly is not untroubled—that she is in fact haunted by the greatest of sorrows, the loss of a child. Milly is the paradigmatic benefactor of Dickens's middle period, an avatar of personal charity whose itinerant social activism never ceases to look backward, attempting to recover an earlier scene of interrupted maternity. Figures like Milly and the reconstructed Redlaw are absent from Dickens's earlier novels, in which natural benevolence—of the kind demonstrated by John Browdie (who defends Smike), Mr. Garland (who employs Kit Nubbles), and the schoolmaster who takes care of Nell—does not have its sources in trauma. And yet the perfect solution represented by Milly and Redlaw would be short-lived; with later figures like Arthur Clennam, Miss Wade, and most importantly Miss Havisham, Dickens loses all confidence in the effects of a haunted solicitude that proceeds from suffering.

The beginnings of this shift can be traced to the philanthropic discourse of *Bleak House*. Like the other books of the middle period, *Bleak House* rigorously examines the motives and strategies that comprise personal charity, suggesting at every point that, rather than pursuing the "telescopic" course of philanthropy, benefactors should place their own intentions and interests under the microscope. As in *Dombey* and *The Haunted Man*, the sufferers of *Bleak House* harbor secret histories of criminal neglect or failed paternity. Consider the case of Gridley, who, as the Man from Shropshire, has witnessed the dissolution of his property by the Court of Chancery; or the case of the Neckett children, whose father's untimely death casts them upon the mercy of their neighbors; or the case of Jo, who doubles as a figure for the wandering orphan (his parentage comes under investigation) and a figure for the semi-criminal class of vagrant poor (the police call him "Toughey"). Acts of help uncover prior moments of abandonment, and "casual" interference reveals the inexorable pattern of identification that binds rich to poor, an identification crystallized by Lady Dedlock's impersonation of Jenny. But while the logic of personal charity continues to cast those who would help back upon their consciences, *Bleak House* ultimately doubts whether refinements of conscience can produce a constructive charity.

Personal charity is primarily endorsed within the context of the novel's multiple attacks against the impersonality of institutional philanthropy. Dickens's treatment of the shortcomings of his London philanthropists can easily be read as a general complaint against the narcissism of charity at large, but in fact his complaint is much more specific than that. The real problem is that, because of the flamboyance (and simply the scope) of the philanthropic enterprise, philanthropists are inevitably caught up in the commotion produced by their colleagues, in much the same way that the American social elite in *Martin Chuzzlewit* are caught up in the enthusiasm of their mutual idealism. Certain of *Bleak House*'s philanthropists hold their colleagues' missions in contempt (423), while others do not: "nothing respecting them was half so clear to us, as that it was Mr. Quale's mission to be in ecstasies with everybody else's mission, and that it was the most popular mission of all" (203). But whether contemptuous or ecstatic, the philanthropists are too concerned with one another. John Jarndyce finds the "noise" of the whole enterprise intolerable:

> Mr. Jarndyce had fallen into this company, in the tenderness of his heart and his earnest desire to do all the good in his power; but, that he felt it to be too often an unsatisfactory company, where benevolence took spasmodic forms; where charity was assumed, as a regular uniform, by loud professors and speculators in cheap notoriety, vehement in profession, restless and vain in action, servile in the last degree of meanness to the great, adulatory of one another, and intolerable to those who were anxious quietly to help the weak from falling, rather than with a great deal of bluster and self-laudation to raise them up a little way when they were down; he plainly told us.   (204)

Against a philanthropy spasmodic and loud, Jarndyce makes it *his* mission to keep quiet—and here already we can see the double bind. If personal charity is to be explicitly constructed as an alternative to other forms of philanthropy, it must become concerned with itself—with its own justification—in a way that duplicates the self-centeredness of every other philanthropic agenda. In its passage from feeling to form, from the pre-articulate to the deliberately silent, Jarndyce's tenderness becomes merely another philanthropic style.

Throughout the novel, Jarndyce awkwardly navigates between participation and self-effacement: he works to put the family legacy to rights, but he won't attend the Court of Chancery; he throws in with a fleet of philanthropists, but keeps his contributions secret; he looks after the welfare of Esther, Ada, and Richard from their early childhood, but only gradually (and sometimes reluctantly) reveals his own role in their lives and his intentions for their future. His generosity forces him into contortions:

> The notes revived, in Richard and Ada, a general impression that they both had, without quite knowing how they came by it, that their cousin Jarndyce could never bear acknowledgments for any kindness he performed, and that, sooner than receive any, he would resort to the most singular expedients and evasions, or would even run away. Ada dimly remembered to have heard her mother tell, when she was a very little child, that he had once done her an act of uncommon generosity, and that on her going to his house to thank him, he happened to see her through a window coming to the door, and immediately escaped by the back gate, and was not heard of for three months.   (61)

It is not only the united chorus of the philanthropic mob that Jarndyce cannot tolerate; he cannot, in fact, "bear acknowledgments for any kindness" at all. Jarndyce pursues the absolute purification of the philanthropic act, an act that cannot be acknowledged without being compromised.[8] But his qualms cause problems greater than an occasional disappearance. For instance, Richard finds it easy to resent Jarndyce's concealment and effacement of his own interests, interests which Richard's imagination can readily supply. Jarndyce's unwillingness to ingratiate others—to lay them under obligation—thus becomes a convenient avenue for Richard's defection. Somewhat more unsettling is the phenomenon of Harold Skimpole, a kind of emanation of Jarndyce's obscure benevolence. A Derridean impossibility, Skimpole accepts gifts *as* gifts and yet makes no return at all—of gratitude, recognition, or substance—to the giver. Skimpole short-circuits the gift cycle, deciding that every offer of charity is, at its *source*, a boon to the giver, and thus depriving the gift of its compulsion to be repaid. As he explains, "I almost feel as if *you* ought to be grateful to *me*, for giving you the opportunity of enjoying the luxury of generosity. I know you like it. For anything I can tell . . . I may have been born to be a benefactor to you, by sometimes giving you an opportunity of assisting me in my little perplexities" (71). The "luxury of generosity" without recognition or thanks is indeed a rare and welcome gift to John Jarndyce, but it is a luxury that can accomplish nothing, a pure but stillborn philanthropy.[9]

All of Jarndyce's work to manage the "noise" of philanthropy compensates for, and sometimes competes with, the more difficult problem of constructive social action. The novel thus fears that the personal charity which Dickens has so ardently defended, might be no more than a science of attitudes. Rescue operations may be able to keep their integrity, but what if that is all they can do? As Esther and Ada realize in the brickmaker's cottage, "between us and these people there was an iron barrier, which could not be removed by our new friend. By whom, or how, it could be removed, we did not know; but we knew that" (108). Here Esther's social astuteness attunes her to a broader narrative phenomenon, whereby the restitution plot has separated itself from the drama of benefaction. No longer is society restored through the relenting of a Scrooge or Dombey, or through the intervention of a Harriet or Martha. The fall of the Dedlock dynasty and the dissolution of the Jarndyce estate are inevitable. In the midst of this, charity struggles to keep its conscience clear. Like the walker in "Night Thoughts," the helpers of *Bleak House* come under the hard scrutiny of those they would reach. Increasingly, the complaints of people like Jo, Gridley, Miss Flite, and the brickmaker cannot be satisfactorily met. To recognize the claims of the distraught—to be haunted—is unproductive concern, unredeemed guilt. It remains for *Little Dorrit* to transform that guilt to resentment; to reveal a philanthropy in which benefactors are at war with their dependants; to propose that charity is (as Toynbee would have it) not a recognition, but a denial, of the claims of the poor.

2.

The third number of *Little Dorrit* concludes at sunrise outside the Break of Day inn, where we spot "John Baptist Cavalletto running away from his patron" (134). The chapter is called "Let Loose," and the new morning—inaugurated by John Baptist's flight "among the flaming pools of rain-water" (134)—is an unmistakable image of transformative liberation. In this context the choice of words is conspicuous; why "his patron" rather than "his tormentor"? Dickens's irony requires us momentarily to suppose that patrons wish to hurt and exploit their dependants, rather than help them. Echoing Cavalletto's italianized English, Dickens invokes the most sinister connotations of the Italian "padrone," connotations of covert negotiation and cruel mastery. Cavalletto himself certainly considers Rigaud a threat, frequently addressing him with the "conciliatory" expression, "my master" (7–8).[10] Patron and master are interchangeable.

The novel abounds with such mobile authority figures—patrons, patriarchs, benefactors, masters, and proprietors, whose "helping" gestures betray their intentions to command. Authority is universally mistrusted in the novel, in a way that causes charity, even when it is not intentionally exploitative, to forfeit all of its effectiveness. Attempts at social reconciliation actually work to sustain authority conflicts. This reconstitution of the problem is most explicitly realized in Miss Wade, as David Suchoff explains:

> False sympathy and cheer, and the will to spurious social reconciliation, thus become Miss Wade's avowed enemies. . . . Given the primacy of goodwill and benevolence in the appeal of Dickens' fiction, this set toward exploding the fictions of middle-class amity explains Dickens' assertion of her importance to the novel, since she constitutes a strong part of its challenging voice. . . . Ascetic discipline in Miss Wade's character is, as for Kafka, less pathology than a commitment to live without any social illusions, and a social skepticism that renders her unable to cherish the myths of middle-class home that Dickens himself produced.
> (81–82)

The "will to spurious social reconciliation"—a reconciliation that inhabits "the myths of middle-class home"—is everywhere present among Miss Wade's social betters. Yet gestures of reconciliation only frustrate Miss Wade; they are now indistinguishable from the root causes of her degradation. And so throughout the novel: when authority relents in any way, it is instantly suspected of doing so in order to maintain its own dominance. Failed acts of help make the very project of reconciling authority conflicts seem self-defeating and even perverse.

The British novel is deeply rooted in the tradition of misguided authority, a tradition which is manifest but perverted in *Little Dorrit*. Many of the great novels deal with the problems that arise when authority figures (such as fathers, landlords, and aristocrats) neglect or underestimate those situated below them. *Tom Jones* is the paradigm case; Squire Allworthy banishes his adopted child out of a mistaken idea about Tom's character. In *Guy Mannering* (1815), the laird of Ellangowan evicts the gypsies from his estate, but when his son is kidnapped, he is forced to seek help from an old gypsy woman. In Edgeworth's *The Absentee* (1812), Lady Clonbrony removes her family to London, disregarding the fact that her social position depends on her family's income from their tenants back in Ireland. But while the authority figures of *Little Dorrit* abuse their dependents, they do not forget or underestimate them. In *Little Dorrit*, authority is fascinated with the poor and the needy, and authority figures programatically cultivate their relationship with those below them. Unlike Ellangowan, *Little Dorrit*'s well-established householders and men of business are intensely aware of the disaffected multitudes on the streets and under their own roofs, and devote considerable attention to the proper management of these disaffected. Yet with this new awareness on the part of the authority figure, the novel propounds a dismal antithesis to those earlier books: now careful attention to the poor and disaffected is a mercenary activity of political prudence; charity is the most effective means of exploitation and self-exaltation.

The novel's great virtuoso of self-exaltation is William Dorrit, who receives charity as if it were homage, and treats others as beggars in order to exalt himself. Dorrit is at his characteristic best in his conversation with his ''pensioner,'' Old Nandy. Clennam notices

the relishing manner in which [Dorrit] remarked on the pensioner's infirmities and failings. As if he were a gracious Keeper making a running commentary on the decline of the harmless animal he exhibited.

''Not ready for more ham yet, Nandy? Why, how slow you are! (His last teeth,'' he explained to the company, ''are going, poor old boy.'')

At another time, he said, ''No shrimps, Nandy?'' and on his not instantly replying, observed, (''His hearing is becoming very defective. He'll be deaf directly.'')

At another time he asked him, ''Do you walk much, Nandy, about the yard within the walls of that place of yours?''

''No, sir; no. I haven't any great liking for that.''

''No, to be sure,'' he assented. ''Very natural.'' Then he privately informed the circle (''Legs going.'') (373–74)

Besides the intangible benefit that Dorrit derives from the homage of such as

Old Nandy and Henry Gowan are the important financial "contributions" he collects from Arthur Clennam and others. Dorrit, like Harold Skimpole, makes his very begging appear to be a form of patronage, and any exposure of the illusion becomes a concrete threat to his livelihood. Thus, when Tip plans to attack Clennam for refusing him money, Dorrit lashes out in protest, on the logic that the Dorrit family must demonstrate a nobility of Spirit by "forgiving" Arthur's temporary indisposition, and hitting him up once again. In constantly reducing the claims of the people around him, William Dorrit echoes Henry Gowan, who sees bankruptcy everywhere. "The worst class of sum worked in the every-day world," says the narrator, "is cyphered by the diseased arithmeticians who are always in the rule of Subtraction as to the merits and successes of others, and never in Addition as to their own" (488). Gowan, reasoning thus, makes a companion of Blandois, whom he thoroughly detests. Like Dorrit, Gowan perceives himself to be elevated by the degradation of the people around him.

Much criticism of *Little Dorrit* has discussed the novel's gallery of mystifications; "their purpose," explains George Holoch, "is to conceal the sources of wealth and the past histories of the characters" (336). Yet the connection between mystification and philanthropy hasn't been drawn as tightly as it might be. Holoch notes that "benevolence itself, in the person of Mr. Casby, is nothing but a fraudulent disguise for exploitation" (336), and others agree that generosity, when it appears, is often simply a mask for self-interest.[11] But we must recognize also the degree to which the prosperous *need* to exercise benevolence in order to maintain their authority. In other words, while it is true that philanthropy is grounded in self-interest, it is also true that self-interest cannot survive without the philanthropic gesture.

Consequently philanthropy pervades even the mind of the solipsist, in the form of self-torment. The impulse to self-torment is infectious and ubiquitous in this novel. Tattycoram, tearing at her own face, reflects the "self-tormentor" Miss Wade, even as Arthur reflects his mother's relentless self-torment when he refuses to leave the Marshalsea for a better prison. And yet self-torment is at best a degenerate form of philanthropy, in that it amplifies the value of renunciation to such an extent that it loses sight of an object of charity. The authority figure no longer even pretends to be a benefactor, but simply makes sacrifices as if her own spirit required it. For instance, Mrs. Clennam understands "reparation" only as it afflicts herself; she has no thought for those who might benefit from her reparation. Self-torment, like mystification and diseased arithmetic, is finally performed for the sake of the self-tormentor; it is another means by which a fragile authority empowers itself. The self-tormentors of *Little Dorrit* use their own suffering as a vehicle for legitimation (or, in religious terms, justification).

The advantages of suffering are elaborated in Mrs. Clennam's Calvinism, which threatens all worldly authority as a usurpation of Heaven, and holds out affliction as man's best security. For Mrs. Clennam, to have power is to owe a debt, and to suffer is to be redeemed. Mrs. Clennam keeps a balance-sheet, where those on top are always bound to fall and those below are always ascendant. She deplores any philanthropy which leaves the benefactor unimpaired, which emphasizes the raising up of the weak at no cost to the strong. This explains her mysterious hatred for Frederick Dorrit who, she claims, "was the beginning of it all" (779). Mrs. Clennam elaborates:

> "If [Frederick Dorrit] had not been a player of music, and had not kept, in those days of his youth and prosperity, an idle house where singers, and players, and such-like children of Evil, turned their backs on the Light and their faces to the Darkness, [Arthur's mother] might have remained in her lowly station, and might not have been raised out of it to be cast down. But, no. Satan entered into that Frederick Dorrit, and counselled him that he was a man of innocent and laudable tastes who did kind actions, and that here was a poor girl with a voice for singing music with."

In the transaction described, the real criminal is the girl's patron; along these lines, when Gilbert Clennam wishes to take pity on the girl, he does so by rewarding her patron. It is as though, for Mrs. Clennam and her father-in-law, patronage itself is on trial, and it cannot coexist with the balance sheet.

For all of his family resentment, Arthur is too much his stepmother's son, accepting wholeheartedly the balance sheet ideology.[12] Arthur imagines every part of his life to be integrated with every other in his great scheme of restitution. Thus, on his first approach to Twickenham, his thoughts fly from his occupation, to his inheritance, to his concerns about a family debt, to his relations with his mother, to Little Dorrit, to Pet (187–88). For Arthur, all thought of charity and social service are subsumed by thoughts of debt and reparation. We learn more of his state of mind in the eighth number:

> The shadow of a supposed act of injustice, which had hung over him since his father's death, was so vague and formless that it might be the result of a reality widely remote from his idea of it. But, if his apprehensions should prove to be well founded, he was ready at any moment to lay down all he had, and begin the world anew. As the fierce dark teaching of his childhood had never sunk into his heart, so that first article in his code of morals was, that he must begin, in practical humility, with looking well to his feet on Earth, and that he could never mount on wings of words to Heaven. Duty on earth, restitution on earth, action on earth; these first, as the first steep steps upward.   (319)

Although the text contrasts Arthur's world-view with his childhood lessons, we must remark how closely the two are aligned. Like his mother, Arthur sees the whole world around him for the claims it makes upon himself, just as he sees self-inflicted restitution as a ladder to absolution. It must be a relief to Arthur when his amorphous sense of obligation is replaced by the tangible debt that sinks him in the Marshalsea.

Despite their impulses to self-punishment, Arthur and Mrs. Clennam both pursue courses of self-acquittal which compete with the novel's restitution plot. Having suppressed Amy's claims to inherit, Mrs. Clennam assuages her guilt by taking the girl on as a servant. Meanwhile Arthur—whose suspicions of wrongdoing at first caused him to abandon the family business—eventually becomes the chief defender of the House of Clennam, working to silence the claims of Rigaud. And yet it is finally Rigaud's extortion, not Arthur's reparation, that restores Amy to her fortune. From a narrative point of view, Arthur and Mrs. Clennam are allies in one struggle, and Amy and Rigaud are allies in another. While one of the novel's trajectories centers on the enlightenment, repentance, and reparation of the Clennams, another trajectory—which supersedes the first—involves the destruction (by Rigaud) and forgiveness (by Amy) of the House of Clennam from the *outside*. The guilt-ridden self-torment of the Clennams is finally at odds with the restitution plot, which is accomplished instead by Rigaud, who has no guilt, and by Amy, who bears no blame.

Thus in *Little Dorrit* the refinement of the philanthropic conscience proves unconstructive, fulfilling a pattern that had begun in *Bleak House*. The "haunted philanthropy" of the middle period, through its revelations of shared histories and suppressed crimes, enabled authority figures to transcend interests narrowly personal or particular to their own class. But in *Little Dorrit* Dickens recognizes that hauntedness (or, in one manifestation, liberal guilt)[13] does not necessitate an emergence into the social—that it harbors its own private life. Authority may be self-serving (Casby, Gowan) or it may be self-punishing (the Clennams), but in neither case does it pursue a social aim. Real restitution must indeed come at the *expense* of the authority figure, but it is not within the hands of authority to achieve, whether by help or by sacrifice. The novel's central question becomes whether it is possible to perform an act of charity for the sake of the object, an act that is neither a vehicle for personal gain nor an exaction of penance. And while *Little Dorrit*'s indictment of the hollow show of benevolence is clear and bracing, its attempts to preserve the ideal of philanthropy are profoundly complex.

3.

So far we have examined *Little Dorrit*'s deep skepticism toward the idea that poverty and social alienation can be constructively addressed by the exertions of a benefactor. We might notice at this point that the failure of philanthropy takes much the same form in family life as it does in public life. William Dorrit's delusional patronage is extended to the Marshalsea prisoners and to his children alike; Casby's patriarchal mystification is equally active in Bleeding Heart Yard and under his own roof. Likewise, Mrs. Clennam runs her domestic affairs with the same balance sheet she uses for her business associates. On Arthur's homecoming, the narrator muses, "Woe to the suppliant, if such a one there were or ever had been, who had any concession to look for in the inexorable face at the cabinet" (47). Just as Dickens uses family life to add poignancy to his depictions of subjection and sham philanthropy, he also looks to the family for a possible justification of the philanthropic ideal. The whole philosophy of paternalism is, of course, built on the model of a parent's solicitude for a child, so the parent-child relationship is the ultimate testing ground for an attack against charity. If the parent has the power to ameliorate the child's distress, then charity cannot be altogether dismissed as a principle of social action. If, however, parental care is subject to the same failings as public philanthropy, then the whole principle of personal charity loses its grounding. In the character of Mr. Meagles, who is both an itinerant philanthropist and the head of a household, Dickens analyzes the capacities and the costs of an earnest, active charity.

By confronting the parent with the same set of issues that face the philanthropist, Dickens departs from the strategy, common to his late novels, of constructing domestic life as an alternative to the marketplace. This is not to say that the homes of these novels are impervious to outside forces. Lucie Darnay hears her conjugal peace disrupted by the footsteps of the Revolutionary Army; Pip's home with Herbert is invaded by Provis; and Lizzie Hexam's cottage is papered with the unwholesome documents of her father's trade. Yet in each case there is a tension between the domestic and the economic, a struggle that finds temporary relief in such abodes as Wemmick's castle, Boffin's Bower, and John and Bella's Greenwich house. In *Little Dorrit*, by contrast, domestic life does not exist in tension with economic life.[14] Essentially, *Little Dorrit* uses the family not as a sanctuary from social abuse, but as a laboratory for social experimentation. In the process, parental care becomes subject to the same dangers that beset philanthropic interest.

The most important participant in this experiment is Mr. Meagles, not because he abuses his authority, but because, even with the best intentions, he finds it impossible to exercise his authority in a way that elicits the "right" response from the people closest to him. "I am like a sane man shut up in a madhouse," he complains (15). Meagles's authority fails most visibly in his unsuccessful attempts to integrate Tattycoram into his household, attempts directly tied to the economics of philanthropy. In Tattycoram, Meagles is able to perceive most starkly the greatest danger that besets his household: the defection of the child. Meagles tries to manage Tattycoram through the exercise of parental charity, a practice that is premised, as we shall see, in the belief that the parent can intervene usefully to solve problems that are not of his own creation. But Tatty, in the course of her rebellion against the Meagleses, challenges this idea of intervention, suggesting that the parent is much more responsible for the suffering of the child than the logic of charity will allow. While it is perhaps impossible to determine the justice of Tatty's challenge, it is most significant that Mr. Meagles cannot actually recognize her claims for what they are; his generosity requires him to imagine Tattycoram as a suffering girl who doesn't know her own mind. This particular blindness becomes even more marked as Meagles tries to understand the defection of his own daughter. Rather than view Pet as a danger to his household, Meagles submerges her in a series of displacements and projections, all in the attempt to imagine a daughter who could be a proper object of charity.

Meagles is a philanthropist in the literal, public sense of the word; it is, in large degree, what he means by describing himself and his wife as "practical people." Of course, his (and Mrs. Meagles's) adoption of Tattycoram stands out as his great act of philanthropy. But Meagles's charity ranges beyond this act. He is the novel's primary meddler, intervening on behalf of Daniel Doyce, Miss Wade, and the incarcerated Arthur Clennam.[15] Meagles also falls prey to the busy gluttony of schemers who lay traps for philanthropists: when he advertises for Tattycoram, Meagles is flooded by responses from eligible young people, and he is solicited by a "swarm of begging-letter writers" for enterprises completely irrelevant to his search.[16] Beyond his deeds, Meagles has what we might call a philanthropic temperament. When he faces dissent or insurgency, he does not circumvent it in the manner of the Circumlocution Office, nor does he ignore it in the manner of William Dorrit, nor is he destroyed by it in the manner of Mr. Merdle. Meagles disarms such conflicts simply by being magnanimous. He is constantly pardoning the affronts of those around him; his signature is the munificent handshake, which he deploys on every possible occasion.[17] Meagles instinctively forgives Tattycoram for running away, altogether disregarding the injury to himself:

> "Yes, assuredly; I want to give her another chance; Mother and Pet want to give her another chance; come! You yourself," said Mr. Meagles, persuasively, as if the provocation to be angry were not his own at all, "want to give the poor passionate girl another chance, I know, Clennam."
> "It would be strange and hard indeed if I did not," said Clennam, "when you are all so forgiving." (323)

Meagles expects his forgiveness to be met with contrition and gratitude. The process of philanthropy is able to set his home to rights because his own spirit of generosity is met (among his subordinates) with a spirit of patience and a conciliatory hope. "Patience" and "duty" are Meagles's lessons to Tattycoram; with these, conflicts can be managed without any final cost. " 'Here we are, you see,' said Mr. Meagles, 'boxed up, Mr. Clennam, within our own home-limits, as if we were never going to expand—that is, travel—again. Not like Marseilles, eh? No allonging and marshonging here!' " (192)

Like Toynbee's philanthropists, Meagles intercedes so readily and good-naturedly as to put his own authority and intentions beyond doubt. While he does not pretend to have a share in—or even to understand—the suffering around him, he'll happily forgive it and provide what relief he can. Here we see the limits of personal charity, a paternalist practice that makes no actual claims of paternity. Whereas Dickens had once used charity as a means of revealing the actual claims of the poor upon the rich (or the child upon the parent), he now describes a charity that denies or defers those claims. The philanthropist is a not a father but a paternalist, intervening in a situation that is in fact the province of someone else. Mr. Meagles is by nature such a caretaker, ready to intervene in troubles that are not his own.

Miss Wade attacks Meagles for just this philosophy of intervention, which is used, in her view, as a way for culpable authority to exonerate itself. "You can be," she tells Tattycoram, "a toy in the house showing the goodness of the family. . . . You can recover all these advantages . . . by telling these gentlemen how humbled and penitent you are, and by going back to them to be forgiven" (328). Every act of forgiveness is also an attribution of blame; the weakness of the child is invoked in order to obscure the fault—or even the cruelty—of the parent. Wade articulates this strong charge in her "History of a Self-Tormentor," which explicitly references Mr. Meagles's constant concern for Tattycoram's bad temper:

> Did [Charlotte] say, "It is I who am wearing [Miss Wade] to death, I who am keeping her on a rack and am the executioner, yet she tells me every night that she loves me devotedly, though she knows what I make her undergo?" No . . . She began sobbing and weeping (to secure the aunt's sympathy to herself), and said "Dear aunt, she has an unhappy temper; other girls at school, besides I, try hard to make it better; we all try hard." (664)

According to this account, Charlotte is blind to her own instrumentality in Miss Wade's dejection; Charlotte's sympathy is predicated on (or productive of) this blindness. Likewise, throughout the "History," the philanthropist—in the aspect of friend, foster parent, or employer—sees herself as taking measures to mollify Miss Wade's intractable temper. Wade asserts that this language of intervention disguises the power that the benefactor has over the afflicted. In Wade's formulation, the one who intervenes becomes responsible for the welfare of the other. There is no portable paternalism: helping gestures lead to a full emotional custody, a principle that Miss Wade adheres to in her own "adoption" of Tattycoram.

Meagles's sympathetic recognition of Tatty's difficult origins allows him to assign the sources of her present discontent securely to her tattered past, a past that has nothing to do with him. When things go wrong with Tattycoram, according to Meagles, it is due to a defect in the girl's temper. He explains:

We are practical people. So if we should find her temper a little defective, or any of her ways a little wide of ours, we shall know what we have to take into account. We shall know what an immense deduction must be made from all the influences and experiences that have formed us—no parents, no child-brother or sister, no individuality of home, no Glass Slipper, or Fairy Godmother.

(18)

While in Meagles's account Tattycoram's bad temper has social causes, it is a thing already established by the time he adopts the girl; it does not occur to him that its causes may originate or persist under his own roof. "Temper" is not a quarrel; it is simply a condition. From the beginning, Tattycoram's unfortunate temperament is presented as an affliction—more specifically, as a disease. It is fitting that she makes her first appearance in quarantine. When Miss Wade finds her by herself, Tatty is "freshly disfigured with great scarlet blots" (26), having torn at her skin in an outbreak of ingratitude. If Tattycoram is ill, then her complaints are significant not for what they say about the Meagles family, but what they say about herself. They are the symptoms of her disease, the empty inarticulate signs of suffering: "The girl raged and battled with all the force of her youth and fulness of life, until little by little her passionate exclamations trailed off into broken murmurs as if she were in pain" (27). Yet while Meagles may succeed in casting the child's insurrection as a fault of her bad temper, Tatty's defection is ruthlessly—for Meagles, unaccountably—recapitulated in the devastating action of Pet, the good daughter.

Although Tattycoram questions what the Meagles family feels for her, she is convinced that they are happy among themselves. Her own exclusion only further convinces her of the contentment that the Meagleses find in each other. The family does, indeed, come onto the novel's stage as a harmonious group. For instance, when Pet privately offers Miss Wade her father's assistance (24), Meagles steps in to sanction the offer, having overheard the conversation. The whole interaction plays out as a choreographed scene, in which Pet acts as her father's operative. Pet, in her maid's eyes, is the idol of her parents' affection: "I am younger than she is by two or three years, and yet it's me that looks after her, as if I was old, and it's she that's always petted and called Baby!" (26). Tatty leaves the household just after Mr. and Mrs. Meagles have "said Good Night to Pet in her presence (very affectionately, I must allow)" (322). By Meagles's account, the burden of Tattycoram's complaint is her jealousy of Pet:

She was younger than her young mistress, and would she remain to see *her* always held up as the only creature who was young and interesting, and to be cherished and loved? No. She wouldn't, she wouldn't, she wouldn't! What did we think she, Tattycoram, might have been if she had been caressed and cared for in her childhood, like her young mistress? (322–23)

Miss Wade supports Tattycoram in the view that the Meagles family is content without her. In fact, Miss Wade goes a bit farther and claims that the Meagleses have purchased a sort of complacency and family unity at Tatty's expense: "You can be, again, a foil to his pretty daughter, a slave to her pleasant wilfulness, and a toy in the house showing the goodness of the family. . . . You can again be shown to this gentleman's daughter, Harriet, and kept before her, as a living reminder of her own superiority and her gracious condescension" (328). Wade sees the girl not just as neglected, but as exploited in order to showcase the family's "goodness," and to give them an object upon which to practice their condescension.

But Tattycoram and Miss Wade are both wrong to think that the only negotiations taking place in the Meagles house are between the family and the maid. Despite appearances, all is not well between Pet and her parents. Ever since the infant death of Pet's twin sister, Mr. and Mrs. Meagles have struggled to manage Pet properly. The family habit of international travel was originated for Pet's health and amusement, and the decision to adopt Tattycoram was similarly motivated. Much as she pleases her parents, Pet sharply opposes their wishes by committing herself to Henry Gowan. When Gowan visits Twickenham, Meagles is stricken to the heart. Despite Pet's attempts at conciliation (to be repeated three numbers later), Meagles cannot come to terms with her decision, and he and his wife are torn over the issue of managing Pet: "Mother and I have tried all we could to get the better of it, Clennam. We have tried tender advice, we have tried time, we have tried absence. As yet, of no use" (321). In fact, Tattycoram disappears on a night when the Meagles household is particularly fraught, Meagles having upset Pet by stating his desperate intention to take her abroad once more. We must assume from Meagles's account that the several nights preceding Tatty's disappearance have been especially uncomfortable. This challenges Tattycoram's account of the Meagleses' tender devotion to Pet; it is significant that Tattycoram runs away when Meagles's tenderness has given way to helpless frustration, and when his devotion seems most fragile.

Pet's discomfort with her parents' orchestrations causes a particular problem for the magnanimous Meagles. In general, when Meagles's amnesty is not met with gratitude—when his authority is rejected—he is completely disarmed. He is removed from a position to forgive others' resentment, and forced to cope with the resentment within himself. "To suspect me of the plague is to give me the plague," Meagles says (15). He grows agitated as he recounts Tattycoram's rebellion, becoming "almost as flushed and hot by this time as he described her to have been" (323). As much as Meagles wants to help Doyce, in doing so he must maintain his own superiority—in this quality, Arthur famously detects the "mustard-seed that had sprung up into the great tree of the Circumlocution Office" (194).[18] As soon as Mrs. Gowan affects superiority over the Meagleses, all of Mr. Meagles's schemes of magnanimous reconciliation are thwarted, leaving him paralyzed with resentment at having been suspected of strategy.

We can now understand why Meagles is at once so sensitive and so incapacitated with respect to his daughter. Meagles is very ready to acknowledge Pet's unhappiness and to give her his sympathy. But Meagles will not acknowledge his strong sense that Pet is a threat to his home and his authority. Pet is his image of calm obedience; her touch immediately curbs his temper (29). Meagles is outraged by the suggestion that Pet could be considered dangerous: "DID you ever hear of such damned nonsense as putting Pet in quarantine?" (16). Yet even while raising this objection, Meagles himself quarantines Pet in the image of her dead twin sister. Since this twin died, Meagles has nourished her image alongside Pet's. She is like Pet in every way, only she, unlike Pet, is safe. The twin has matured in her parents' imagination, but she has also remained the same, a daughter "who died when we could just see her eyes—exactly like Pet's—above the table, as she stood on tiptoe holding by it" (19). Her infant image is a perfect object for Meagles's parental condescension. She is well below him, very much needing his support, but at the same time standing on tiptoe and looking up, acknowledging the favor that is to be conferred and the authority of the one who confers it. This twin is Meagles's elect child, standing tiptoe as his inheritor but still holding by the table as a pet would.

Growing up in the Meagles home, Tattycoram has long been aware of the spectral presence of the dead twin. Insofar as Tatty sees herself as Pet's counterpart, the twin is a counterpart to both girls. Tatty's involvement with the twin is evident when Arthur first visits Twickenham, as he looks at a double portrait of the two sisters: "The picture happened to be near a looking-glass. As Arthur looked at it again, he saw, by the reflection of the mirror, Tattycoram stop in passing outside the door, listen to what was going on, and pass away with an angry and contemptuous frown upon her face that changed its beauty into ugliness" (194). Tatty does not, as one might suppose, simply envy the twin for being Pet's equal in her father's eyes. For although Tattycoram so often complains that Meagles favors Pet over herself, Tatty actually identifies closely with Pet. On the night Tattycoram runs away, she objects that the Meagleses do not "have a right to name her like a dog or a cat" (323); here she could just as well be speaking of Pet's own name. Tatty does not run away during an episode when Pet is being "spoiled"; she leaves exactly when Pet is most in conflict with her parents. "I hate you all three," Tatty says. "I am bursting with hate of the whole house" (322). It is the revolution in the Meagles house that frightens Tattycoram. Without understanding the particulars of Meagles's struggle with Pet, Tattycoram feels it

all intensely. She is frightened by the fierce insistence of Meagles's solicitous-
ness, and by her own sense that this generosity, particularly as it is extended to
Pet, conceals the father's profound doubts about the security of his household.

With his invocation of the dead twin, Meagles illustrates a tendency inherent to philanthropy: the imaginative projection of a certain kind of dependant.
As we've seen, the sham philanthropists of Little Dorrit are masters of mystification, advertising their exploitative schemes as helpful measures. But with
Meagles, Dickens suggests that projection is not merely a strategy of deception, but that it is in fact a necessary prelude to any charitable act at all. By
this logic, constructive intervention is not possible unless both benefactor and
dependant play their roles appropriately.[19] The question of the benefactor's
fault must never come up; the needy must never make demands. The benefactor cannot understand the plight of the needy from their perspective, since to
do so would be to abandon the superior perspective of the outsider, to cede
the mastery over the situation that the philanthropist requires.[20] Mr. Meagles
actually alerts Clennam to the difficulty of understanding Tattycoram on her
own terms: "As to how it happened, it's not so easy to relate: because you
must have the unfortunate temperament of the poor impetuous girl herself,
before you can fully understand it" (320). In order to help Tattycoram,
Meagles must project a particular image of her, that of the mistempered child.
Likewise, in order to benefit from Meagles's kindness, Tatty must capitulate
to that projection, must acknowledge it to be true—as indeed the novel itself
must do if it is to cede a victory to Meagles's benevolence. In order, too, to
help Pet, Meagles must project onto her the image of the grateful supplicant,
an image which Pet, for better or for worse, will not inhabit.

The gap between Meagles's projection and the actual, dangerous Pet, is
inhabited for a time by the fantasy of the dead twin, but by the end of the
novel it comes to be inhabited by Amy Dorrit, Meagles's ideal of the obedient
child. This displacement, which is prepared over the whole course of the
novel, is actualized in the last number. Tattycoram has just absconded from
Miss Wade and returned to the Meagleses,[21] at which point Meagles refers
her to the passing figure of Little Dorrit and urges Tatty to make a model of
her behavior. Moments later, Meagles offers Amy his continued intervention;
she leans forward and kisses his cheek, just as Pet had always done. Meagles's
associations instantly fly to Pet: " 'You remind me of the days,' said Mr.
Meagles, suddenly drooping . . . " (814). Meagles believes that Amy exemplifies the perfect object of charity—which, in fact, she does not. The rest of
this essay will look at the ways in which Amy undoes Meagles's narrative
of philanthropy.

4.

To what degree does Amy Dorrit support a philanthropic ideal? The moment that best seems to capture the character of Amy's charity is in her last encounter with Mrs. Clennam, in the novel's last number. Mrs. Clennam describes herself as "hard," and calls Amy "merciful" (twice), "gentle," and "kind" (790). These attributes cast Amy in the image of Christ, an association that she makes explicit in her plea to Mrs. Clennam: " '[A]ngry feelings and unforgiving deeds are no comfort and no guide to you and me. . . . [L]et me implore you to remember later and better days. Be guided, only by the healer of the sick, the raiser of the dead, the friend of all who were afflicted and forlorn, the patient Master who shed tears of compassion for our infirmities' " (792). Amy's plea supports the practice of compassion, intervention, care; but it is a care that bears an uncertain relationship to philanthropy. The progress of the passage—showing Christ as healer, then as friend, ultimately as compassionate Master—moves away from help and toward sorrowful identification, with the suggestion that the highest capacity of the master is to take the sorrows of the servant upon himself. This is a far cry from the sponsorship of the Cheeryble brothers; it is, too, rather different from the ministry of Mr. Meagles. Amy's benevolence exists apart from charity in a conventional sense; she has been neither the object nor the agent of philanthropy. When Mrs. Clennam kneels to Amy in supplication, the younger woman becomes uncomfortable: " 'Not in that posture,' said Little Dorrit. 'It is unnatural to see your grey hair lower than mine. Pray rise; let me help you' " (790). Rather than grant forgiveness in a way that would secure her own authority, Amy wishes altogether to disregard (or erase) Mrs. Clennam's crime, lowering herself to the level of her supplicant. Here—and afterwards, with the burning of the codicil—Amy removes herself from the negotiations of a philanthropy in which both parties ultimately pursue their own interests, yielding as much as they can afford in order to purchase their own security. As we have seen, *Little Dorrit* establishes such negotiations as charity's inevitable course, even a charity as well-meaning as that of the solicitous father. But Amy, first as a prison-child and later as an heiress, resists the relations of charity—a resistance that is formulated most explicitly in her story of the Princess and the cottager.

If Arthur Clennam is usually placed at the center of *Little Dorrit*—resembling the novel's author and readers, with respect to both his own social agency and his normalizing comprehension of the world around him—Amy Dorrit has always been placed at the novel's limits. For some critics, Amy introduces the possibility of responsible social action into the novel; for others, she occupies an exclusive perspective (marked by her gender, class, size, and family history) which uniquely enables the novel to transcend the usual limits of popular social analysis. Traditionally, Amy has been seen to provide an escape clause in the rigid logic of abuse that governs most of the novel's social relationships. Hillis Miller sees her as a figure for a preserved childhood, "the one stage of life which escapes the shadow of the prison."[22] Amy has been called the perfect servant.[23] She has been shown to be immune to the taint of acquisition that marks the novel's property-seekers.[24] She has been seen as embodying the ideal of the domestic woman, an alternative to the male authority figures of the liberal, paternalistic order.[25] In fact, critics have traditionally answered Clennam's desperate injunction that Amy not call the prison "home" (258) with a sense that such an identification with the lower world of the novel is not, after all, a danger to which Amy is susceptible. More recently, the critical focus has shifted away from claims that Amy is a moral resource for untainted action within the novel, toward claims that she is a touchstone by which the world of *Little Dorrit* is made to reveal itself for what it is.[26] In this formulation, Amy makes visible (by virtue of her compulsive submission and conspicuous silences) the violence common to the conditions of working-class life and to the repression of women in an economy of liberal, middle-class paternalism.[27] The difference between these two critical positions depends largely on opposing characterizations of the novel itself as a fantasy of reform or as an analysis of an existing situation; both positions, though, make strong arguments for Amy Dorrit's marginal status.

In all of these arguments, Amy is treated as a static image. However inscrutable her motives, however inexplicable her peculiar sensibility, and however ambiguous the effects of her actions, Amy's identification as an "image" is never questioned. The novel itself fosters this approach to Amy, drawing and redrawing her portrait within the Marshalsea walls, in Arthur's quarters, in the streets, and on the Iron Bridge. Various characters question the effect of Amy's very presence: Fanny says that Amy carries with her the prison's "tone and character" (262); Arthur says that Amy has brought the spirit and influence of the outside world into the prison (260); William Dorrit feels Amy's presence to be a reproach.[28] The nature of this reproach is theorized by Suchoff, who claims that the novel's descriptions of Amy "serve the function that Benjamin found in the dialectical image: fetishized visions identify their own escape from the culture of the marketplace, and point out the very urban history they evade" (61). For Suchoff, the popular novel's attempts to describe and account for a pauper's daughter expose middle-class blindness both within the novel and within its readership.[29] This characterization of Amy as a "dialectical image" accords well with other critical assessments of Amy as an image, a figure, a model, or an ideal. Yet to treat her exclusively as such is to assume that Amy's marginal relationship to the common humanity of the novel—that her subordination within the abusive authority structures that dominate the novel—is consistent throughout the narrative.

Is this assumption justified? Amy's experiences within the space of the narrative proper are more completely heterogenous and transformative than those of any other character in the novel. She graduates from extreme poverty to extreme wealth, from emotional isolation to friendship, love, and marriage, from a life of ritual repetition inside a prison to a whirlwind excursion through France, Switzerland, and Italy. Her night (in the fourth number) outside the prison walls is said to be literally epochal to her. She loses a father, wins a husband, and gains control of a fortune that derives from neither. The Amy of the final number is not the Amy of the early numbers, and her new scope of action has significant consequences for any attempt to understand the social principle behind her behavior. Amy's transformations enable Dickens to dismantle the ideal of charity from the perspective of rich *and* poor, presenting her at first as a sacrificial victim who reveals the poverty of her benefactors, and later as an authority figure who resists the temptations of philanthropy.

Amy fills the role of a kind of household sacrifice for the first third of the novel, and continues in this capacity up through the conference on the Iron Bridge (no. 6). She is called the Child of the Marshalsea, a badge of abjection which causes even the prisoners to pity her. Her domestic operations are figured as a kind of extremism, rather than a common filial attitude: ''It is enough that she was inspired to be something which was not what the rest were, and to be that something, different and laborious, for the sake of the rest. Inspired? Yes. Shall we speak of the inspiration of a poet or a priest, and not of the heart impelled by love and self-devotion to the lowliest works in the lowliest way of life!'' (71). Amy's family affections are thus distinguished from the usual set-pieces of the Victorian hearth. She is inspired, otherworldly—like the poet or priest, perhaps, only that Dickens never drew an inspired poet or priest.[30] As the Child of the Marshalsea, Amy is ''born and bred, in a social condition, false even with a reference to the falsest condition outside the walls'' (71). She lives below the threshold of gain, with no real prospect of domestic or social tranquility. The extremism of her psychic life corresponds to the extremity of her situation.[31] Her ''self-devotion to the lowliest works'' is possible because she has nothing to hope for. Amy's sacrifice—that is, the sacrifice *of* Amy—purchases her no security, no reward.

In this phase of the novel, several attempts are made to help Amy, but those who try to help are exposed as lacking either the ability or the intention of doing her any good. As early as the second number (where Amy is first introduced), the turnkey struggles to find a way to leave some money to the girl such that the father cannot get at it. It is an unsolvable riddle, and the man dies intestate. Other attempts to help fare no better. Arthur cannot intervene without encouraging William Dorrit's rapacity. Flora gives Amy work, but torments her with a fabricated account of Arthur's renewed devotions. Meanwhile, Mrs. Clennam's attentions to Amy constitute an elaborate subterfuge, as indicated in the epigraph to this paper.

Most interesting of all are the efforts of Pancks, whose inquiry uncovers the vast wealth of the Dorrit family. Even as the agent's charitable efforts begin to bear fruit, Amy expresses her skepticism toward his investigations: " 'I have heard him called a fortune-teller,' said Little Dorrit. 'But I doubt if he could tell many people, even their past or present fortunes' " (295). This verdict aptly follows Amy's own fortune-telling episode, a story she invents for Maggy—and one which, I will argue, implicitly challenges Pancks's philanthropic enterprise. The story (292–95) concerns a "poor tiny little woman" who lives by herself in a cottage, spinning at her wheel and guarding a secret "shadow of Some one"—a man—"who had gone long before." She is confronted by a Princess who "had the power of knowing secrets." The Princess continues to visit the cottager until her death, and the cottager's secret is interred in her grave.

The fable is most remarkable for what it *doesn't* include, for the narrative possibilities that are introduced but never realized. In particular, the "Some one" who is the primary object of memory and desire never returns to the cottage, and the story comes to focus much more on the interaction between the cottager and the Princess than on the absence of Some one. Even more mysteriously, the Princess, in her repeated visits, never helps the little woman; she simply looks in to "see what came of it." Essentially Amy has rewritten the Cinderella story, an important action since Cinderella has been invoked several times in the novel already in reference to the daughter's fortune. Tattycoram, according to Meagles, has had "no Glass Slipper, or Fairy Godmother" (18). Three numbers later, in a chapter entitled "Little Dorrit's Party," one of the running titles of the 1868 edition reads "Cinderella's Shoes," referring ironically to Amy's "thin, worn shoe" (167). Amy has told her father she is out at a party—a reversal of Cinderella's ball, which Cinderella attends under the pretence of having stayed home. Like Tattycoram in her early childhood, Amy is without Glass Slipper or Fairy Godmother, and the novel suggests that these things are the sign of rescue. In this light it is significant that Amy's fable features no Fairy Godmother and no change of fortune. It is offered up in explicit contrast to the lucrative godmothering of Pancks. In effect, Amy offers her fable as a truer vision than Pancks's; the attentive Princess and the settled cottager replace the bountiful Godmother and Cinderella ascendant.

If Amy's fable is not the Cinderella story, it is in fact not a story about charity at all. What the Princess discovers, when she looks in at the door, is not a scene of need but a scene of contentment. The cottager's shadow "was bright to look at; and when the tiny woman showed it to the Princess, she was proud of it with all her heart, as a great, great, treasure'' (294). The strange fact is that the cottager already has a treasure, and so the Princess has nothing more to offer, no crisis to rectify. While Diane Sadoff has argued that the shadow signifies a secret shame associated with incest and molestation,[32] Amy describes it as an object of pride, explaining that the reason the cottager keeps it hidden is that she is afraid someone will take it away (a condition that recalls the turnkey's conundrum). The revelation is that condescension is unnecessary—that, when the Princess looks into the cottage, the cottager can look back at the Princess not with vacant submission, but with a secret treasure of her own.

In fact, the primary activity of the fable is this back-and-forth looking, which is so insisted on that Maggy decides that the two woman are "trying to stare one another out" (293). The Princess and the cottager are thus linked by identification, not charity. Amy reiterates this: on the cottager's death, the Princess muses that "there was nobody to look at her now, and nobody for her to look at . . . '' (294). The fable's trajectory of fulfillment is not inheritance or fortune but the development of a fuller identification between rich and poor. Amy emphasizes the power of identification in the first encounter between cottager and Princess:

> The Princess was such a wonderful Princess that she had the power of knowing secrets, and she said to the tiny woman, Why do you keep it there? This showed her directly that the Princess knew why she lived all alone by herself spinning at her wheel, and she kneeled down at the Princess's feet, and asked her never to betray her. So, the Princess said, I never will betray you. Let me see it. So, the tiny woman closed the shutter of the cottage window and fastened the door, and, trembling from head to foot for fear that any one should suspect her, opened a very secret place, and showed the Princess a shadow.''   (293)

The nature of the communication between the two women is cryptic and extraordinary. The Princess mysteriously demonstrates her knowledge by asking a question, and goes on to duplicate the cottager's speech ("she asked her never to betray her"; "I will never betray you"). Basic communication acts are transformed into an erotically charged secret-sharing that obliterates the limits of identity. Of course this passage maintains the language of subjection, but it is an image of subjection without power and exposure without threat, a fantasy in which the stares of the Princess can be fully returned by the cottager. Amy's suggestion is that when the rich look at the poor, they are looking into a mirror, and that, once identification takes place, the purpose of charity falls away. For Little Dorrit, the pretenses, projections, and mystifications of charity are themselves the crisis; in response she creates a narrative of intervention without help.

The story of the Princess serves as a narrative hinge, linking the trials of poverty to the trials of wealth. The story can be read, and usually is, as Amy's synthesis of her own prior experience, a narrative both describing and enacting her feelings of guilt and desire. In this reading, Amy *is* the tiny woman, and the story is about her "state of mind" (to borrow the novel's terms). Of course it is natural to identify Amy with the cottager, and Phiz's illustration endorses this association.

Amy is drawn (as she tells the story) in the attitude of the little woman, peering out the window of her shabby room. But by telling a story rather than making a confession, Amy simultaneously invokes a powerful image of the sacrificial victim and casts some doubt as to her own immersion *within* this image.

With this in mind, it's surprising that so many readers see, in the Amy that emerges in the second book of the novel, the tiny woman of the cottage. Although throughout her continental travels she remains more concerned for others (such as Fanny, her father, and Pet) than for herself, her concern is no longer offered on the altar of her self-sacrifice. Her authority is predicated entirely on her personal qualities—particularly her keen observation—in the manner of an Anne Elliot or a Daniel Deronda. Amy becomes newly important as a vehicle for *articulating* the truth;[33] her carefully stated "advice" (so referred to in the chapter title) that Fanny not marry sharply contrasts her short, qualified statements to Fanny after the *first* meeting with Mrs. Merdle. I would suggest that, especially in relation to Pet, Amy's "dream-life" should be taken as an exact complement to her fable to Maggy. Now in the role of the Princess, Amy, the powerful knower of secrets, dips in and out of Pet's life as both comforter and observer. In a letter to Arthur, Amy keenly describes the Gowans' uncomfortable lodgings in Rome, and proceeds to analyze the deep sources of Pet's unhappiness: "She is so true and so devoted, and knows so completely that all her love and duty are his for ever, that you may be certain she will love him, admire him, and conceal all his faults, until she dies. I believe she conceals them, and always will conceal them, even from herself" (552). The reversal is remarkable: Pet has become the ill-fated harborer of secrets, while Amy has assumed the role of the Princess—with reference not only to her external social situation, but to her entire presentation as a knower of secrets and a conveyor of articulated wisdom. Like the Princess, Amy carries out a program of observation and identification, never entering into the negotiations of power that inhere within the economy of the gift.

Accordingly, when Amy burns the Clennam codicil, she reiterates the futility of charity. Amy is poised between poor and rich—she has inheritance within her grasp, but hasn't inherited yet—and this position allows her to correct what Dickens sees as the necessary failures of both parties to the philanthropic exchange. She chooses destruction over donation: she will neither receive nor give a legacy. Also, by choosing not to inherit the money that should have been hers from childhood, Amy is effectively choosing never

Figure 2. "The Story of the Princess"

to have had—a choice unavailable to the wealthy. Most importantly, Amy counteracts the mutability of philanthropy: the philanthropist always leaves the homes of the poor, but Amy will stay. If, as Suchoff claims, "the tiny woman's isolated 'cottage' evokes the Marshalsea prison" (62), then Arthur Clennam finally plays the role of the cottager, imploring Amy to leave him: "You belong to much better and brighter scenes. You are not to look back here, my Little Dorrit; you are to look away to very different and much happier paths" (761). Arthur's torment exposes the yearnings of the philanthropic imagination at its most tragic, most sublime. To the mind of philanthropy, the intimacy between poor and rich is fleeting; the gift is a reminder of difference, and the visit must give way to the real state of things. Like Dickens, it is Arthur's fate to believe in but despair of the gift. Of course this is why Amy cannot tell him about the codicil, cannot offer the inheritance to him, cannot even let him see her renounce. Amy must not help her husband—not because the *property* is corrupt, but because her act of charity would live on as a conquest ever afterwards.[34]

To destroy a codicil, erase an inheritance—what sort of agency do such acts indicate? What is left after charity fails? With Charles Darnay and Lucie Manette, Dickens will revive the predicament of *Little Dorrit*. Like Arthur, Charles is burdened with a superfluous reformism; his efforts to repair his family crimes are rejected, and he (like Arthur) can do nothing more useful than place himself in custody. Lucie, like Amy, waits, watches, and hopes; she is a reader of portents, a domestic savante. Restitution will come of its own accord. It has ceased to be the province of the charitable conscience. Debts can no longer be paid; they will be collected, and with interest. The trajectory of Dickens's career thus anticipates the trajectory of late-Victorian poor relief, which determined that the claims of the poorer classes could be met neither by the workhouse nor by the generosity of philanthropists and volunteer workers. To say that charity disappears from Dickens's later novels would be to overstate the case. But where acts of charity *do* succeed—of the sort performed by Biddy, Riah, and Jenny Wren, for instance—they are removed from the realm of authority. Dickens continues to marvel at "what the poor are to the poor" (*Bleak House* 109), but at the same time decries the effects of social paternalism. So, too, is there a place left below the radar for Amy and Arthur, who "went down into a modest life of usefulness and happiness . . . went quietly down into the roaring streets, inseparable and blessed" (826). Beyond the far fringe of Dickens's narrative, Amy and Arthur resuscitate simple helpfulness; they pick up the pieces of paternity, raising "Fanny's neglected children" along with their own, and watching over Tip. In a home without foundlings or "parricides," without pensioners or runaways—without authority—help works. It's hard to imagine, though, that Mr. and Mrs. Clennam will attempt to be helpful in the roaring streets, if they have learned the lesson of *Little Dorrit*. The thing for the streets is to go quietly.

NOTES

1. The passage that follows is one of the most commonly cited episodes of Dickens's later journalism; see, for instance, the introductions to *Charles Dickens: Selected Journalism, 1850–1870* and to *Homes and Homelessness in the Victorian Imagination.*
2. The threat inherent in sympathy is discussed by Audrey Jaffe, who argues that sympathetic encounters between rich and poor create a "phantasmatic opposition between images of cultural ideality and degradation" (8).
3. Dickens's attitudes toward philanthropy have often been invoked in studies of his life and works, particularly with reference to Urania Cottage and the ragged school movement. However, there has been little Dickens scholarship that takes philanthropy as its primary subject. The notable exception is Pope's *Dickens and Charity*, a useful reference work which is nonetheless limited by its exclusive focus on evangelical reform. For the most sustained discussions of Victorian philanthropy in general, consult Owen's *English Philanthropy*, Prochaska's *Women and Philanthropy in Nineteenth-Century England*, Himmelfarb's *Poverty and Compassion*, and Mandler's *The Uses of Charity*.
4. See Lynn Lees for a discussion of the ways in which charitable donations to an individual were often used to support other (sometimes "undeserving") members of the recipient's family.
5. Pam Morris compellingly argues that the return to an illicit past signifies the impulse of those at the margins "to unmask, even violate, the object of desire—genteel respectability." According to Morris, Dickens's later novels cast doubt not only on respectability, but on the entire project of securing that responsibility through a break with the past: "This involves a pattern of doomed circular flight, in which illicit love and illegitimacy centre increasingly upon the impossibility of escape from one's past, from shame, guilt, and the physical force of sexual desire. Again and again in these novels the hegemonic myth of causal progress is challenged, as origins assert their physical claims, and men and women are forced to recognize the impossibility of flight from the bondage of their own flesh into the frozen safety of genteel posturing" (12–13). Andrew Sanders has also recently written about the influence of Dickens's "novelty"—his rise in class—on his social imagination.
6. Dickens conveys a part of his premise in a letter to Forster: "Of course my point is that bad and good are inextricably linked in remembrance, and that you could not choose the enjoyment of recollecting only the good" (November 21, 1848).
7. In fact, the reciprocity cycle extends beyond the story's thematics to its very structure. The narrative is divided in three parts: "The Gift Bestowed" (where Redlaw is made to forget his sorrow), "The Gift Diffused" (where Redlaw passes

his forgetfulness on to others), and "The Gift Reversed" (where memory is universally restored). The strange terms—bestowed, diffused, reversed—show the sense in which Redlaw's fantasy (as it is realized by the ghost) distorts the principles of gift-exchange. Redlaw never "receives" the gift of forgetfulness, since once it is upon him he is a different man; likewise, he does not "reciprocate" the gift, but passes it on inadvertently through diffusion.

8. Derrida agrees: "*At the limit, the gift as gift ought not appear as gift: either to the donee or to the donor*" (14). He further explains, "The simple consciousness of the gift right away sends itself back the gratifying image of goodness or generosity, of the giving-being who, knowing itself to be such, recognizes itself in a circular, specular fashion, in a sort of auto-recognition, self-approval, and narcissistic gratitude" (23).

9. Bruce Robbins and Kathleen Blake provide cogent readings of the problem of social 'effectiveness' in *Bleak House*. Robbins focuses on the novel's discourse of professionalism, claiming that while the professions have generally been held to value *system* over *ethics*, they are in fact the embodiment of an agency that attempts to become analytically aware of social processes. "Through the intermediaries of Comte, Spencer, and Durkheim, a common attention to the disparity between the morality of individual actions and their eventual social value or function provides a historical link between Dickens and Foucault" (223). Like Robbins, Blake rejects the notion that, in the novel, individual ethics transcends social analysis or systemic action; against the Foucauldian "disparity" between individual actions and social value, however, Blake argues that *Bleak House*'s attack against social abuses falls in line with classical (i.e., Benthamite) political economy, an affiliation that has been obscured by critical suspicions of Victorian liberalism.

10. Avrom Fleishman aptly discusses Rigaud and Cavalletto in the terms of Hegel's master-slave dialectic.

11. Anny Sadrin puts the critique most crisply: "The great paradox of the patriarchal system that Dickens dramatizes here is that it magnifies a relationship that does not exist. The fatherhood of the fathers is exalted everywhere, but the fathers are not fatherly. They ooze benevolence, and they tyrannize" (84).

12. Holoch correctly calls Arthur's code "a barely secularized version of his mother's" (341).

13. The crucial discussion of liberal guilt in *Little Dorrit* belongs to Lionel Trilling, who sees this novel as the one in which the pressures of society are most fully carved out upon the will of the individual.

14. Catherine Waters deftly discusses "the ideological function of the family in the novel's analysis of social and economic transformation" (89).

15. His intervention in Arthur's plight is expounded in comic detail: "With no other attendant than Mother, Mr. Meagles went upon his pilgrimage, and encountered a number of adventures. Not the least of his difficulties was, that he never knew what was said to him, and that he pursued his inquiries among people who never knew what he said to them. Still, with an unshaken confidence that the English tongue was somehow the mother tongue of the whole world, only the people were too stupid to know it, Mr. Meagles harangued innkeepers in the most voluble

manner, entered into loud explanations of the most complicated sort, and utterly renounced replies in the native language of the respondents, on the ground that they were 'all bosh.' Sometimes interpreters were called in; whom Mr. Meagles addressed in such idiomatic terms of speech, as instantly to extinguish and shut up—which made the matter worse. On a balance of the account, however, it may be doubted whether he lost much; for, although he found no property, he found so many debts and various associations of discredit with the proper name, which was the only word he made intelligible, that he was almost everywhere overwhelmed with injurious accusations. On no fewer than four occasions the police were called in to receive denunciations of Mr. Meagles as a Knight of Industry, a good-for-nothing, and a thief, all of which opprobrious language he bore with the best temper (having no idea what it meant), and was in the most ignominious manner escorted to steam-boats and public carriages, to be got rid of, talking all the while, like a cheerful and fluent Briton as he was, with Mother under his arm'' (806–07).

16. One such petitioner presents to him an "entirely novel description of Pump" (332).

17. So resolved is Mr. Meagles on his handshake, that he forces it: "[Miss Wade] would not have put out her hand, it seemed, but that Mr. Meagles put out his so straight before her, that she could not pass it" (25).

18. That mustard-seed has caused Mr. Meagles a good deal of trouble among many critics, who pronounce him a snob. So he is, although Dickens means to show nothing especially insidious about Meagles himself, but a much larger problem attached to social patronage generally.

19. Peter Mandler argues that the poor of Victorian London routinely developed the skill of telling philanthropists what they wanted to hear, all the while using the charity of the rich toward ends that they would not typically have condoned or understood.

20. William Myers correspondingly claims that Mr. Meagles's "failure with Tattycoram points to a complete breakdown, in terms of sympathy, understanding and charity, between the classes" (85); in this failure, Myers argues, the novel's author and readers are inevitably implicated.

21. Waters demonstrates how Tatty's return, and her reappropriation within the Meagles household as a "family member," disguises the economic character of her relationship with the Meagleses. Because Tatty's appropriation is thus "smoothed over," Waters claims, Pet's "commercial value" to the family becomes visible (100–01).

22. Miller, 239. "The tragedy of *Little Dorrit*, then, is the tragedy of childhood distorted, betrayed, forgotten, buried so far down that it no longer seems to exist" (239). According to Miller, Amy is able "to carry the innocence and spontaneous love of childhood into adult life" (241).

23. Fleishman, 581.

24. Nunokawa, 32–34.

25. Waters, 91.

26. This position is well articulated by Myers: "Without explanation [Amy] is introduced into a totally unredeemed world as a rebuke both to smug quietism and

the distortions of revolutionary anger. She is at the center, in other words, of a literary rather than a practical appreciation of intransigent political and human problems; through her they are felt and judged; but she is not an instrument of change, a solution to the novel's problems'' (102–03).

27. Sadoff, 240; Suchoff, 58.
28. In this, Dorrit should be compared to Mr. Meagles, who at first feels Pet's presence as a consolation, but cannot finally keep her fixed in his image of her.
29. ''Little Dorrit becomes a dialectical image for the infantilizing force of conventional Victorian expectations on a woman who, like the novel, retains her socially critical and imaginative power.''
30. The young Amy Dorrit, most pointedly in her dialogues with the turnkey, is best compared to the otherworldly Paul Dombey.
31. Suchoff believes that the ''facts'' of Amy's life as a prison-child are manifest in Clennam's constructions of her as a moral ideal: ''[Clennam's] praise of Little Dorrit's virtue is exaggerated to the point of becoming lurid, encouraging readers to seek the social history that lies beneath his fetish and its social mask'' (59).
32. ''If the story of a son relates the search for a father's authority, the story of a daughter tells of incestuous structures of desire'' (240).
33. Amy fulfills this role most completely in her final dialogue with Mrs. Clennam.
34. This is a modification of Nunokawa's claim that property is tainted by the fact of its acquisition; it is not only acquisition, but also donation, that confers a taint.

WORKS CITED

Baumgarten, Murray and H.M. Daleski, ed. *Homes and Homelessness in the Victorian Imagination*. New York: AMS, 1998.

Blake, Kathleen. *''Bleak House*, Political Economy, Victorian Studies.'' *Victorian Literature and Culture* 25 (1997): 1–21.

Derrida, Jacques. *Given Time. I, Counterfeit Money*. Chicago: U Chicago P, 1992.

Dickens, Charles. *Letters*. Ed. Madeline House, Graham Storey, et al. Oxford: Clarendon, 1965–.

———. *The Oxford Illustrated Dickens*. Oxford: Oxford UP, 1989.

———. *Selected Journalism, 1850–1870*. Ed. David Pascoe. New York: Penguin, 1997.

Fleishman, Avrom. ''Master and Servant in *Little Dorrit*.'' *SEL* 14 (1974): 575–86.

Himmelfarb, Gertrude. *Poverty and Compassion: The Moral Imagination of the Late Victorians*. New York: Knopf, 1991.

Holoch, George. "Consciousness and Society in *Little Dorrit*." *Victorian Studies* 21 (1978): 335–51.

Lees, Lynn. "The Survival of the Unfit: Welfare Policies and Family Maintenance in Nineteenth-Century London." *The Uses of Charity: The Poor on Relief in the Nineteenth-Century Metropolis*. Ed. Peter Mandler. Philadelphia: U Pennsylvania P, 1990.

Mandler, Peter. "Poverty and Charity in the Nineteenth-Century Metropolis: An Introduction." *The Uses of Charity: The Poor on Relief in the Nineteenth-Century Metropolis*. Ed. Peter Mandler. Philadelphia: U of Pennsylvania P, 1990.

Mauss, Marcel. *The Gift: Forms and Functions of Exchange in Archaic Societies*. Trans. Ian Cunnison. New York: Norton, 1967.

Miller, J. Hillis. *Charles Dickens: The World of His Novels*. Cambridge: Harvard UP, 1958.

Morris, Pam. *Dickens's Class Consciousness: A Marginal View*. London: MacMillan, 1991.

Myers, William. "The Radicalism of *Little Dorrit*." *Literature and Politics in the Nineteenth Century*. Ed. John Lucas. London: Methuen, 1971.

Nunokawa, Jeff. *The Afterlife of Property: Domestic Security and the Victorian Novel*. Princeton: Princeton UP, 1994.

Owen, David. *English Philanthropy 1660–1960*. Cambridge, MA: Harvard UP, 1964.

Pope, Norris. *Dickens and Charity*. New York: Columbia UP, 1978.

Prochaska, Frank. *Women and Philanthropy in Nineteenth-Century England*. Oxford : Clarendon, 1980.

Robbins, Bruce. "Telescopic Philanthropy: Professionalism and Responsibility in *Bleak House*." *Nation and Narration*. Ed. Homi Bhabha. New York: Routledge, 1990. 213–30.

Sadoff, Diane. "Storytelling and the Figure of the Father in *Little Dorrit*." *PMLA* 95 (1980): 234–45.

Sadrin, Anny. *Parentage and Inheritance in the Novels of Charles Dickens*. Cambridge: Cambridge UP, 1994.

Sanders, Andrew. *Dickens and the Spirit of the Age*. Oxford: Clarendon, 1999.

Suchoff, David. *Critical Theory and the Novel: Mass Society and Cultural Criticism in Dickens, Melville, and Kafka*. Madison: U Wisconsin P, 1994.

Trilling, Lionel. *"Little Dorrit."* Rpt. in *Dickens: A Collection of Critical Essays*. Ed. Martin Price. Englewood Cliffs, N.J.: Prentice-Hall, 1967.

Waters, Catherine. *Dickens and the Politics of the Family*. Cambridge: Cambridge UP, 1997.

Webb, Beatrice. *My Apprenticeship*. London: Longmans, Green and Co., 1926.

Sucking the Empire Dry: Colonial Critique in *The Mystery of Edwin Drood*

Miriam O'Kane Mara

Many critics have considered Charles Dickens's attitudes about imperialism to be unified throughout his career. Citing his fiction and letters, they find ethnocentrism and intolerance for colonial subjects. While this perspective on the colonies was indeed present, it may be qualified by investigating Dickens's later work, in particular The Mystery of Edwin Drood. *Dickens's unfinished novel moves away from his previous colonial position and instead criticizes colonialism by juxtaposing British domestic consumption with the effects of empire. By examining the characters in the novel and their consumption of colonial commodities, including opium, I argue that Dickens's last novel subtly critiques such consumption. The critique suggests, then, that the appetites of the British themselves, rather than some taint or infection from the colonies, adulterates the colonial system and, in turn, England itself.*

> *"reduce to a smashed condition all other islands but this island, and all continents, peninsulas, isthmuses, promontories, and other geographical forms of land soever."* (147)
> —The Mystery of Edwin Drood

Scholars alternately admire Charles Dickens for casting light on the problems of the Victorian capitalist system in England and denigrate him for supporting the racist, ethnocentric policies of colonialism. His critics often claim that Dickens presents a unified vision about imperialism throughout his career. David Suchoff asserts that "Dickens supported Empire . . . and the subjection

Dickens Studies Annual, Volume 32, Copyright © 2002 by AMS Press, Inc. All rights reserved.

233

of colonial peoples, in accord with popular norms'' (43). In his celebrated
critique of colonial texts, *Rule of Darkness*, Patrick Brantlinger also cites
Dickens as an ardent imperialist, documenting Dickens's letters which address
the Jamaica Rebellion of 1865 and referring to his "Noble Savage" essay.
He claims: "Dickens' sympathy for the downtrodden poor at home is reversed
abroad, translated into approval of imperial domination'' (207). Dickens's
1865 letter to Cerjat seems to support their position: "That platform-sympa-
thy with the blacks—or the native, or the devil—in the midst of bloodshed
and savagery, makes me stark wild'' (11:115). He appears to blame the
natives rather than imperial presence or policies for any unrest in the colonies.
Edward Said also claims, "even Dickens had definite views on race and
imperialism, which are quite easy to be found'' (12). But their criticism
presents a congruent, unproblematized vision of Dickens's work as pro-em-
pire and racist. Moreover, the criticism of *The Mystery of Edwin Drood*
(hereafter referred to as *Edwin Drood*) often ignores the unfinished novel's
treatment of imperialism and focuses on solving the mystery of Edwin's
murder.[1] While some scholars note the tensions of empire in the incomplete
novel , they read it as a continuation of Dickens's inexorable attitudes about
the need for strict controls in the colonies. Ina Rae Hark notes that in *The
Mystery of Edwin Drood* the East is a "malignant . . . force" which functions
to infect or destroy Cloisterham (166). In *Reaches of Empire*, Suvendrini
Perera also observes that Dickens was "interested in empire's impact on the
domestic life of the metropolis'' (108). Both Hark and Perera recognize the
colonial connections in *Edwin Drood*, but they believe Dickens viewed these
effects as unidirectional, unwholesome Eastern influences visited upon Great
Britain. Their criticism asserts that Dickens indicts colonial influence as an
infection of England by the lazy, unclean natives and the commodities they
produce.[2]

It is important, then, to qualify their approach to Dickens by analyzing
Dickens's unfinished final novel where he appears to be condemning the
colonial system. Following the work of David Faulkner, who labels the attention to colonialism in *Edwin Drood* "neither a subordinated theme nor exotic
grace-note, but a transformative historical and psychological pressure, a para-
digm-shift legible in the deep structure of the novel'' (186), I propose that
Dickens foregrounds imperial tension. The text, begun four years after the
letter to Cerjat, often suggests that colonial infection begins, not in the colonies, but with the British themselves and their attempts to ingest other cultures. The novel also presents many characters in England, the center of
Empire, who experience the colonies by touching, eating, drinking, smoking,
or otherwise ingesting their luxuries. These consumptive characters become
increasingly *addicted* to commodities, while the most extreme of them become
savages, in effect, British cannibals. Indeed, contrary to the contentions of

Hark and Perera, Dickens's novel problematizes the cause and effect of Oriental infection to create a paradigm of British decay and dissoluteness, which ultimately connects to the greed and insatiable appetites of the Victorian consumer culture. Hobsbawm recognizes the new necessity of consumption in his explication of the era: "Their [bourgeois] problem was spending rather than saving . . . how else except by spending was the successful bourgeois, whether or not he held political power as a class, to demonstrate his *conquest*?" (236, my emphasis). Spending and consuming for Victorians became ways to differentiate the middle class from their working class compatriots. For Victorian England imperialism is increasingly necessary to this consumptive capitalism, and so Dickens's critique imbeds colonial issues into late nineteenth-century capitalism.[3] As his last and unfinished novel, *Edwin Drood* makes a tentative move away from Dickens's previous uncritical approval of the colonial system by his interpolation of Eastern cultural symbols and products, his critique of the abuses of conspicuous consumption, and his treatment of opium as the meeting point of these phenomena.

Opium, Dickens's clearest link between oriental *infection* and consumption obsession, contextualizes the discourse of imperialism by revealing its inherent addictive quality and its links to imperial policy. In 1830 London allowed colonials in India to extend the cultivation of the opium poppy there in order to create a more reliable source for the cash crop than Turkey. Forcefully grown in one colony to feed demand both in England and other colonies, this substance, which also contains the power to protract its own consumption, metaphorically exemplifies the colonial experience. Furthermore, opium represents the quintessential exotic product with its Eastern origins and mysterious uses and abuses. In *Edwin Drood*, an opium consumer becomes the most destructive character, and his habit is implicated in the heart of the mystery.

Edward Said's concept of Orientalism, which calls into question the way that the Orient is defined by Europeans as "a *place* of romance, exotic beings, haunting memories and landscapes" (1), helps to problematize Dickens's last novel and its extensive treatment of opium and other Eastern commodities, because the Orient becomes part of England rather than a separate place. In *Edwin Drood*, the boundaries between England and those exotic other places begin to dissolve as Cloisterham's characters prefer Turkish candy and candied peel. Faulkner recognizes the Oriental texture of the novel: "On Christmas Eve, Cloisterham's shops boast of luxurious, Oriental excess: 'Lavish raisins, spices, candied peel, and moist sugar' " (186). As I argue, Dickens manipulated and redeployed those Orientalist images and assumptions, especially the anxiety about exotic Eastern imports and of opium in particular. It is difficult to miss the Eastern flavor of the novel; he provides the Oriental essence in the very first lines:

English cathedral town. . . . Maybe it [spike/bedpost] is set up by the Sultan's
orders for the impaling of a horde of Turkish robbers, one by one. It is so, for
cymbals clash, and the Sultan goes by to his palace in long procession. Ten
thousand scimitars flash in the sunlight, and thrice ten thousand dancing-girls
strew flowers. Then, follow white elephants caparisoned in countless gorgeous
colors, and infinite in number and attendants.   (37)

Words like "Sultan," "Turkish," "scimitars," "dancing girls," and "elephants" place the text in an Orientalist conception of John Jasper's fantasy.
Yet Jasper conflates these Eastern images with Englishness by placing the
images in an English cathedral town, which illustrates the text's collapse of
the boundaries between "Occident" and "Orient." The attention to foreign
and especially Oriental and exotic commodities demonstrates a subtle indictment of the domestic consumption that fueled the colonial presence of England in the colonies and the colonies in England.

Even the ostensibly sympathetic characters in this novel are implicated in
colonial consumption. Their presence highlights the complexity of Dickens's
treatment of the imperial system, because even these relatively likeable people
are indicted as participants in some level of consumption of the products
of Empire. Canon Crisparkle outwardly appears a healthy, moral character.
Cordery observes: "Crisparkle is the healthiest man in Dickens; he revels in
early morning dips in the icy weir, shadow boxes in front of the mirror, and
climbs hills like a mountain goat. He is a deliberate contrast to the dark,
brooding Jasper, who frequents the opium dens in London" (102). Cordery
reads Crisparkle as a way out for the evil of Cloisterham, finding "in his
ethic of the natural healthy life, the possibility of redemption and salvation"
(97). Yet one of the most sympathetic characters in the unfinished novel
indulges in abundant collection and consumption. At breakfast the reverend
and his mother drink "Superior Family Souchong" (82), a rare, (often pine-
smoked) large-leafed, black tea from China, and in their home at Minor
Canon Corner, Crisparkle's mother keeps the amazing tiered closet filled
with pickles, jams, cookies, and cordials. He partakes of the contents, when
his mother encourages it: "the good Minor Canon took his glass of Constantia
with an excellent grace" (124).[4] The Crisparkles' cabinet is filled with exotic
Oriental dainties such as "tamarinds and ginger" (123), probably brought
from India and Malaysia.

The cabinet itself, called "a most wonderful closet, worthy of Cloisterham
and of Minor Canon Corner" (123), provides a clue to the real mystery of
Edwin Drood, the insidious seeping of consumption and, thus, empire into a
quiet English town. It contains a disguised structure with almost sinister
complexity: "this rare closet had a lock in mid-air, where two perpendicular
slides met . . . the upper slide, on being pulled down (leaving the lower a
double mystery), revealed deep shelves" (123). The multiple tiers with hidden

slides are like the multiple layers of consumption that progress from Crisparkle's tea and Constantia all the way to hidden opium addiction.

In combination with the consumption of these products, Dickens's text
alludes to the involvement of the church and clerics like Crisparkle in the
annexation and oppression of the colonies. When he first meets them, the
reverend composes "rough mental notes" about Helena and Neville Landless,
referring to their "very dark" skin tone and "a certain air upon them of
hunter and huntress," calling them "untamed" (85). His response to the
visitors from Ceylon indicates a subtle attitude of superiority that is com-
pounded in more consumptive characters like Mr. Sapsea and John Jasper.
Moreover, the Reverend Crisparkle's willingness to take the Landlesses under
his wing, becoming Neville's tutor (in Britishness?), subtly echoes the paternalism of missionary efforts in the colonies. Representatives of the church
often paved the way for commercial enterprises in the colonies, and in fact,
the missionary agenda provided a *legitimating* front for commercial activity.
Religion also intimates another layer (or tier) to the imperial project, because
sending Christian representatives to colonial areas highlights British attempts
to eradicate the language and religion of indigenous cultures.[5] Crisparkle's
character exposes the multileveled entanglement of colonialism into the
household consumption of the British in his "rare closet" (123), with its
multiple tiers of Eastern delicacies, and his problematic (religious) association with empire.

Like the reverend, Edwin Drood's fiancée, Rosa Bud, appears to be guiltless in the dark secrets of Cloisterham. Yet Rosa Bud, who prefers Eastern
commodities to kisses, becomes complicit in the consumption that underlies
the novel's mystery. Her innocent devouring of Turkish sweetmeats implicates her in the problematic consumerism of Cloisterham. During her "detest-
ably unhappy" (60) walk with Drood, the narrator pointedly mentions Rosa's
enthusiasm for the candy: "So he [Edwin] is gloomily borne off to the Lumps-
of-Delight shop, where Rosa makes her purchase, and, after offering some to
him (which he rather indignantly declines), begins to partake of it with great
zest" (58). Rosa eats the Orient while she and Edwin discuss her unwillingness to travel to Egypt; she glibly discards the pyramids and the history of
Egypt as boring and unimportant. Part of her unwillingness to marry Edwin
is connected to her imagined abhorrence of Eastern lifestyle. Rosa's fear of
the reality of colonialism underscores her fearless consumption of Turkish
delight; she refuses to understand anything about the Orient except consumption of its commodities.

In the same scene, she refuses to let Edwin kiss her, saying, " 'Eddy, no!
I'm too stickey to be kissed' " (61). Her stickiness and unwillingness to be
kissed at this moment of conspicuous consumption indicate that eating the
fruits of empire disrupts traditional patterns of gender relations in England.

Rosa is more interested in the delicacies made available by imperialism than in satisfying her fiancé. Her fetishization of Eastern exotic sweets indicates an inappropriate appetite for women. As Donald Hall notes: "hunger implies an emasculating ability," which contrasts with "the anorectic, child-bodied, and correspondingly docile heroines that appear throughout the Dickens canon" (36).[6] We see her tendency to favor such imported treats again in Tartar's rooms and when she describes: "a dazzling enchanted repast" (192) and "wonderful macaroons, glittering liqueurs, magically preserved tropical spices, and jellies of celestial tropical fruits" (192). The exotic banquet that Mr. Tartar serves to Rosa draws her inexorably to him. Its similarity to her Turkish Lumps-of-Delight signals that Rosa's apparent development toward a traditional sexual role remains connected to her appetite for Eastern commodities.

Princess Puffer, who has "opium-smoked herself into a strange likeness to the Chinaman," (38), is another female character who consumes Oriental commodities. Yet the novel implicates Puffer more than Rosa in the consumer system that plagues England. Not only does she smoke opium like the villain, John Jasper; she trades in it as well. She evinces this tension between consumption and production in her description of her method of mixing of opium as "mother[ing]" (266) her customers. Puffer's distortion of the nurturing role of women—trading upon that domestic role by professing to nurse or foster her customers—connects consumption with production. Rather than purchasing products to care for a home and children, this woman ventures out of the home to sell products in the market. Indeed, Puffer is not content to work in a factory as other working class women do, but she braves the public sphere of the marketplace usually reserved for men. In doing so Puffer collapses gender and class boundaries that keep middle-class women in the home caring for the children. Thus, Puffer's double consumer and merchant stance implicates her all the more in the imperial capitalist system that the novel indicts.

Yet, for Puffer, consumption (ingestion) has caused consumption (chronic respiratory illness). She complains of poor lungs resulting from sustained opium use for years. Her cough and "weak lungs" mimic the tuberculosis that ravaged England in the nineteenth century, causing one-fourth of London's deaths during that era (Houston 197).[7] Additionally, Puffer connects her own medical condition to the market: " 'O me, O me, my lungs is weak, my lungs is bad! . . . I ses to my poor self "I'll have another ready for him, and he'll bear in mind the market price of opium, and pay according" ' " (38). By conflating the poor performance of her body with the downward turn of the commodity market, the text correlates the consumptive body of Princess Puffer with the consuming body politic of England. In this case, the English body and its appetites create infection in the body politic. Hark's and Perera's analyses, conversely, blame imported products for infecting England from the outside. Puffer's willingness to engage in smoking and selling opium has begun to eat away at her organs, just as the consumer society of British colonialism destroys English culture. The disease imagery here indicates that England is sick, infected by Oriental commodities like opium, but, like Puffer's addiction, the British have invited infection through their demand for and exploitation of the "exotic" products.

Like Princess Puffer, Mr. Sapsea encounters the colonial system and the places of empire only through merchandise, but the text clearly marks his character as negative, "the purest Jackass in Cloisterham" (62). His dual position as auctioneer and Mayor of Cloisterham highlights the association between distribution, consumption, and the government bureaucracy of British imperialism. As a professional auctioneer, Sapsea experiences the colonies by handling their exports, marking him as a principal consumer and distributor. By his own declaration Sapsea understands the Orient exclusively through its products: "If I have not gone to foreign countries, young man, foreign countries have come to me. . . . It is the same with Japan, with Egypt, and with bamboo and sandal-wood from the East Indies; I put my finger on them all" (64). In this way Sapsea will "speak for and tell his readers" how these objects are " 'typically' Oriental" (Said 6). He, more than anyone else we see, except Jasper perhaps, acquires products, especially merchandise from Eastern colonies of England. He desires these curios of the Orient as disembodied artifacts, which cannot threaten him in the same way that native people and dangerous landscapes might. In a scene that mirrors opium smoking, he also indulges his body with the consumption of Orientalized mind-altering substances. In this scene the future Mayor ingests the sherry voraciously: "Mr. Sapsea, in a grandiloquent state of absence of mind, seems to refill his visitor's glass, which is full already; and does really refill his own, which is empty" (65). His gluttonous guzzling of the sherry, perhaps imported from a colony, aligns Sapsea with Jasper and with a British consumer culture that never feels satiated.

The priggish auctioneer may even have consumed his wife and collected her in the graveyard, relegating her memory to an artifact (her gravestone) he can control. His wording for the epitaph is entirely in regard to himself, not the wife he lost: "Ethelinda, Reverential wife of Mr. Thomas Sapsea" (67). Additionally, the text hints that his overbearing disposition and complete domination of his spouse, including selling her business and rendering her speechless, may be linked to her surrender of her life. Mr. Sapsea nearly admits to his negative effect on his wife—"I have asked myself the question: What if her husband had been on a nearer level with her?" (66). This question intimates that his forceful personality may have hurried her to her death. John DeWind unwittingly establishes Sapsea's ability to devour his fellow man:

"pure Englishman Mr. Sapsea, forever at his ease on dry land, has no mois-
ture in him; he even possesses the frightening ability to dry up others—indeed
to 'sap' the 'sea' from them'' (174, my emphasis). DeWind perhaps does not
intend to accuse Sapsea of consuming people, but his characterization of the
mayor as someone who depletes the moisture/life of others, in effect ingesting
them, implicates the collector in his wife's death. The insinuation that Sapsea
has symbolically consumed his wife intersects with the ingestion of foreign
commodities by the British and points toward another consumption, cannibalism. Of course, colonial powers charged indigenous people with eating hu-
mans to render the natives savage and evil (Other), but Sapsea's figurative
disposal of his wife seemingly places cannibalism inside England.

Dickens's narrator clearly indicts the over-consumption of British savages,
who like Sapsea, devour not just commodities, but people. He creates the
most spectacular example of the consumptive Englishman in John Jasper the
opium addict, like Puffer using opium to sub[con]sume his dread at the decay
in his life and because he cannot consume Rosa. Jasper presents his conflicted
attitudes in the first scene of the text when he dreams of beautiful, exotic
"dancing girls" and "white elephants" (39). Then, upon waking, Jasper
castigates the Chinaman and Lascar for their inarticulateness: " 'What do
you say?' . . . 'Unintelligible!' " (39). Jasper resents the shabbiness of the
Orientalized inhabitants of the opium den in opposition to his fantastic
dreams, and he protests his inability to understand or contain them as he
believes he can contain opium.

As the ideal Oriental commodity, opium connotes both sides of his feelings,
including "sensuality, promise, terror, sublimity, idyllic pleasure, intense energy" (Said 118). His addiction to opium, in turn, reflects Jasper's erotic
obsessions with Rosa, and on some level he has an addiction to his nephew,
Edwin, as well: "a look of *hungry,* exacting watchful, and yet devoted affection—is always, now and ever afterwards, on the Jasper face whenever the
Jasper face is addressed in this [Edwin's] direction" (44, my emphasis).
Jasper's habits of consumption have graduated from commodities to a wish
to cannibalize the people around him. The opium den, therefore, represents a
site where consumption of commodities from colonies turns inward, creating
physical dependence, and deepens into a paradigm of consuming as the only
(inter)action. The Oriental drug reifies the desire of consumer capitalism that
teaches people that they must always attempt to fill some lack, for "all
economic activity in a consumer society depends on the principle of scarcity
or insufficient material means" (Houston 10). Just such a need/lack infects
the Englishman with ostensible *savage, native* appetites like cannibalism. The
novel indicates that the infection begins in England, since Jasper constructs his
addiction (an additional appetite) to opium through persistent consumption.

The consumption, then, reduces Jasper's functioning to pursuit, possession,
and destruction. His anthropophagous desire for Rosa also commodifies her

as exotic merchandise to be exchanged. Jasper's claim that "No one should come between us. I would pursue you to the death" (231), emphasizes the colonial paradigm within which Jasper exists. Even the name Rosa Bud makes her a symbol or object, referring explicitly to her genitalia: "The sexual interpretations of the names Rosebud and Pussy are reinforced by the fact that within the development of the story Rosa is little more than the power of female sexuality" (Bleiler 91). Rosa is thus reduced to parts of her body, and represented as an object that Jasper wishes to devour (as, perhaps, do Neville and Tartar). To Jasper she is a commodity worth killing for. Only by violently taking her from his nephew (her fiance) can Jasper ingest the beautiful Rosa Bud; he cannot be satisfied by admiring her from afar: "I don't ask you for your love; give me *yourself* and that hatred; give me *yourself* and that pretty rage; give me *yourself* and that enchanting scorn; it will be enough for me" (229, my emphasis). His consuming desire to possess Rosa, facilitated by his addiction to opium, obviates any alternative to consumption.

In addition to his passion for opium and his obsession with Rosa, John Jasper becomes fixated on and addicted to the mental visions (reiterating his plan to murder Edwin), which assail him during his drug reveries. He replays his hallucinatory crime again and again in his opiated dream states. Each time Jasper dreams, he recreates the identical episode, confounding Princess Puffer's ideas about fantasy. She expresses disbelief at Jasper's unchanging meditation: " 'Did you never get tired of it, deary, and try to call up something else for a change?' " (270). His dream, however, acts as another commodity or drug to be consumed. As John De Wind notes, "Yet if Jasper finds freedom in the unconscious, his experience of it oddly mirrors his conscious life, for at least in part his unconscious life is one of endless and exact repetition" (179). Jasper repetitively consumes his fantasies, which resemble mass-produced consumer products, and still needs more. As with capitalism, Jasper's dreams become a repetition compulsion, which can never be fulfilled. In mimicry of his need for opium, which controls him, the dreams create false needs in him to relive his transgression. Consumer culture induces the same compulsion in buyers to consume incessantly the same things and more things and bigger and better things. When Jasper's only form of contact becomes consumption, he turns on his family, savagely murdering his nephew Edwin.

As a result of his addictions, Jasper is consumed by his own fixations. He feels trapped in the double life he has created for himself as he admits to his nephew early in the text: "The cramped monotony of my existence grinds me away by the grain" (48). Jasper's bifurcation into a consumer of opium and an uninteresting Cloisterham choirmaster may allude to the split condition of the capitalist subject who must continually produce in order to consume. He hates his respected job, the *production* of sacred music, and he escapes it through consumption of opium and dreams. Fragmentation of self becomes a recurrent theme in post-modern works, but it begins in the Victorian period when capitalism comes of age.[8] The constrictions of his own previous decisions for livelihood and residence leave John Jasper feeling *"consumed* by the past" (DeWind 176, my emphasis). When Jasper reveals his unhappiness to Edwin, he displays a sense of claustrophobia and inability to breathe (a symptom of medically defined consumption). Jasper can never leave, however, because his fissured reality allows him to feed his addictions and continue consuming; his career and income create the ability to consume opium, but the conflicting roles initiate an internal destruction of his viability as a subject. The choirmaster's split consciousness, his paradigm of over-consumption, and his symbolic cannibalism towards Edwin and Rosa represent the potential destructiveness of addiction to colonial goods.

Jasper's savage Britishness contrasts with the characters from the colonies, a space that to the British imagination might conceivably contain cannibals. Neville and his twin sister, Helena, travel to Cloisterham from Ceylon, and they do not quite fit into small English towns or England itself. Dickens's narrator represents these two as strong, moral characters in opposition to their consuming British counterparts. Neville Landless, however, seems lost and easily overwhelmed in England as his name indicates: "ne" is the negative in French, so his first name translates to no town and his last name denotes without land. The text represents Neville and Helena as colonized subjects who have already been negatively affected by British colonialism. Their early years under the guardianship of "a[n English?] stepfather" who was "a miserly wretch, who grudged us food to eat, and clothes to wear" (88) hint at the relentless, paternal role of England in the colonies. For Neville the influence of British imperialism has "always tyrannically" held him "down by the strong hand" (90). Abusive treatment has produced the unfortunate effect of a quick temper for Neville, and his resultant anger serves to question England's (step-parental) role in Ceylon.

As an *import* from Ceylon, Neville represents an Eastern or Oriental commodity to Jasper, who plans to use him. As Jasper's need to consume (opium, people, fantasies) multiplies, Neville becomes merely an expendable person on whom to blame his crime. Opium is again implicated as Jasper slips both Edwin and Neville the drug in their drinks. Jasper next provokes a quarrel between them in order to accommodate his plans to kill Edwin. Subsequently, Jasper endeavors to utilize Neville by placing him under suspicion for Edwin's murder, thereby exonerating himself. Neville himself feels "marked and tainted" (209) by Jasper's evil design. Thus, representatives of the system of British Empire like the Landlesses travel to England and become used up by its consumer culture (John Jasper).

The strongest link between Jasper and Neville, indeed, between all of Cloisterham and the Oriental other, becomes Edwin Drood. As heir to his father's firm overseas, Drood plans to "wake up Egypt a little ... Doing, working, engineering" (96–97). Such unabashed imperial intentions upset the balance between unthinking consumption and unpleasant colonial practice. Yet Edwin's views about the Orient are absent from the latter part of the novel, because he disappears, slain by Jasper. The disappearance or mystery of the eponymous character and the ring that he carries provides a clue to Dickens's evolving attitude about the colonies. Since the premier Victorian novelist places this novel *about* empire in the troubling context of a murder mystery, it indicates that the problems of empire must be solved. Ronald Thomas suggests that the guilt of empire "may have found a displaced expression in the murder of the heir to empire in *Edwin Drood*, a violently repressed wish for the end of the violence of empire" (232). Dickens kills off the character most directly connected with empire, but he does not provide an alternative or replacement for the colonial system. The social significance of the act of murder and its effect on a community immersed in imperial practices reflect increasingly complex notions about the social implications of imperial power overseas.

Just as Edwin is the character who represents the (re)connection between violent colonial activity (including production) and domestic consumption of those products, the ring is a product from the periphery that is not easily consumed. The most important piece of Eastern merchandise in the plot of this Dickens mystery is the ruby and diamond heirloom that Mr. Grewgious gives to Edwin Drood for sealing the engagement to Rosa. Each of the ring's components is an oriental product. Diamonds were mostly exported from India until their discovery in South Africa in 1867, and the most ancient and famous source of rubies was Burma, also a British colony. Additionally, the British imported gold from Australia after its discovery in 1851. Mr. Grewgious intimates the immutability of the beautiful circlet: "rose of diamonds and rubies delicately set in gold . . . . See how bright these stones shine! . . . I might imagine that the lasting beauty of these stones was almost cruel" (144). By describing the jewelry as "lasting" Grewgious seems to remove it from the realm of consumable commodity. Moreover, the non-consumable ring made from colonial resources operates in the center of the mystery, both because colonial trade abroad interpenetrates a domestic murder mystery and because the jewelry from that colonial trade provides a possible space for investigating Jasper's foul play. Since the heirloom is excluded when Crisparkle finds Edwin's personal items in the weir, Dickens may have meant for the ring to reappear later in the text, perhaps by materializing unconsumed in the quicklime. In any case, the mystery hinges on a colonial product, which is not easily consumed or contained. The ring's confusing role(s) may mirror Drood's uncomfortable reflection of the colonial system.

In his final, incomplete novel *The Mystery of Edwin Drood*, Charles Dickens examines the perplexing interdependence between domestic British desires to consume and the unsavory effects of the imperial project. Through their negligent craving for and expending of colonial and especially Oriental commodities, many characters in the work avoid any examination of the system through which these wares are procured and the people whom it may affect. These cloistered British country townspeople implicate themselves in a system that Dickens seems to censure to some degree. Thus, the novel creates, but refuses to solve, a *mystery* about Dickens's stance on colonialism. Both the continual allusion to Eastern imports and the emphasis on opium as indicative of consumer capitalism in his final text reveal Dickens's evolving negotiation of the troublesome implications of colonial narrative. They imply that his previous unquestioned acceptance and support of British imperialist policies may have become more fluid, creating questions about how much more his attitudes towards empire may have changed, if he had lived longer.

Notes

I am indebted to Jesse Alemán and Gail Turley Houston for their counsel and direction during various stages of this paper.

1. My reading of *The Mystery of Edwin Drood* begins with the assumption that Edwin's disappearance is a result of his death, and John Jasper is the murderer.
2. Barry Milligan's text, *Pleasures and Pains,* documents these fears in detail. He reads fear of infection in authors like Samuel Taylor Coleridge, Thomas De Quincey, and includes a section on Dickens's *ED*. In an early chapter, Milligan formulates his model on the subject of Oriental infection: "the pollution is linked most overtly with tainted Eastern commodities, the 'pestilent Luxuries' that enter the British body politic and 'leave an indelible stain on our national character' " (31–32). For Milligan, Jasper's corruption from the London opium den eventually suffuses the ill effects of that environment into Cloisterham. While the chapter on *Drood* acknowledges the conflation of the Orient with Domestic England, the "insidious foreign influence has already infected the seemingly upright citizen" and threatens to do the same to "the fundamental fabric of the *invaded* culture" (emphasis mine 105). Milligan's apparently non-ironic use of "invaded" underscores his reading of cultural influence traveling in only one direction.
3. See Smith's *Creating a World Economy.*
4. The beverage Crisparkle ingests in this scene is indeed a product of a colony, since Constantia valley was the cradle of South African wine.
5. See Winfried Baumgart's *Imperialism,* especially 13–17.
6. See Houston, who argues that in Dickens's work as in Victorian England the heroines must restrain their appetites (for food) in order to allow men to maintain and satisfy theirs (12–13).

7. The Porters advise that consumption represented more than just the disease of tuberculosis. Instead, the term carried a variety of medical meanings precariously connected to lung or respiratory complaints (146). Again, the term "consumption" sustains a number of shifting meanings.
8. Jameson maintains that late capitalism produces schizophrenia within the consuming subject as a result of the intense, accelerated replication of products and images (71–73). See also Miyoshi's *The Divided Self*, which describes the Victorian age as a time when the self divided and doubled. Miyoshi identifies this divisiveness in texts that use "the doppelganger, the double, and the Romantic ideal, or the self-division of the gothic villain" (x).

WORKS CITED

Baumgart, Winfried. *Imperialism: The idea and Reality of British and French Colonial Expansion, 1880–1914.* Oxford: Oxford UP, 1982.

Bleiler, Everett F. "The Names In *Drood.*" *Dickens Quarterly* 1:3 (1984): 88–93.

———. "The Names In *Drood* (Part Two)." *Dickens Quarterly* 1:4 (1984): 137–42.

Brantlinger, Patrick. *Rule of Darkness: British Literature and Imperialism, 1830–1914.* Ithaca: Cornell UP, 1988.

Cordery, Gareth. "The Cathedral as Setting and Symbol in *The Mystery of Edwin Drood.*" *Dickens Studies Newsletter* 10:4 (1979): 97–103.

DeWind, John S. "The Empire As Metaphor: England and the East in *The Mystery of Edwin Drood.*" *Victorian Literature and Culture* 21(1994): 169–90.

Dickens, Charles. *The Mystery of Edwin Drood* (1870), ed. Arthur J. Cox. London: Penguin, 1974.

Dickens, Charles. "Letter to W.W.F De Cerjat." 30 November 1865. *The Letters of Charles Dickens* Vol. 11 1865–1867 Ed. Graham Storey and Margaret Brown. Oxford: Clarendon, 1999.

Faulkner, David. "The Confidence Man." *Muscular Christianity,* ed. Donald E. Hall. Cambridge: Cambridge UP, 1994. 175–93.

Hall, Donald E. *Fixing Patriarchy: Feminism and Mid-Victorian Male Novelists.* New York: New York UP, 1996.

Hark, Ina Rae. "Marriage in the Symbolic Framework of *The Mystery of Edwin Drood.*" *Studies in the Novel* 9:3 (1977): 154–68.

Hobsbawm, E.J. *The Age of Capital, 1848–1875.* London: Weidenfeld and Nicholson, 1975.

Houston, Gail Turley. *Consuming Fictions: Gender, Class, and Hunger in Dickens's Novels*. Carbondale: Southern Illinois UP, 1994.

Jameson, Fredric. "Postmodernism, or The Cultural Logic of Late Capitalism." *New Left Review* 146 (1984): 53–92.

Milligan, Barry. *Pleasures and Pains: Opium and the Orient in Nineteenth Century British Culture*. Charlottesville: UP of Virginia, 1995.

Miyoshi, Masao. *The Divided Self*. New York: New York UP, 1969.

Perera, Suvendrini. "All the Girls Say Serve Him Right: The Multiple Anxieties of Edwin Drood." *Reaches of Empire: The English Novel from Edgeworth to Dickens*. New York: Columbia UP, 1991. 103–22.

Porter, Roy, and Dorothy Porter. *In Sickness and In Health: The British Experience 1650–1850*. London: Fourth Estate, 1988.

Said, Edward. *Orientalism*. New York: Pantheon, 1978.

Smith, Alan K. *Creating a World Economy: Merchant Capital , Colonialism and World Trade, 1400–1825*. Boulder: Westview, 1991.

Suchoff, David. *Critical Theory and the Novel*. Madison: U of Wisconsin P, 1994.

Thomas, Ronald R. "The Policing of Dreams: Nineteenth-Century Detection." *Dreams of Authority: Freud and the Fictions of the Unconscious*. Ithaca: Cornell UP, 1990. 193–253.

"Proud possession to the English nation": Victorian Philanthropy and Samuel Johnson's Goddaughter

Jude V. Nixon

From April 1855 to May 1856, Carlyle, Dickens, and Forster sponsored a benevolence on behalf of two Deptford spinsters, Ann Elizabeth and Frances Meliora Lucia Lowe, daughters to Mauritius Lowe, R.A., friend to Samuel Johnson. Knowledge of the Lowes Memorial remains scant, much of it veiled in hitherto unpublished letters. And the little that we can glean from the Dickens letters does not provide an altogether lucid picture. A more comprehensive portrait of this charitable venture will come with the release of volumes 29 to 31 of The Collected Letters of Thomas and Jane Welsh Carlyle. *Dickens's involvement is hardly surprising, considering his centrality to domestic charities and generosity to destitute individuals. The plan appealed to Lord Palmerston, whose inability to deliver a Civil List Pension prompted a public appeal in* The Times. *Approximately £300 was raised, reflecting some curious observations on which Victorians gave and how much. The Memorial reveals a complex set of ideas about Victorian philanthropy, demonstrating, among other things, the way Victorians rallied to support an exclusive pair whose ties to Samuel Johnson demanded national attention, urgency, and munificence. Additionally, the Lowes Memorial expands our understanding of Victorian charities—their goals, scope, and politics; the identity of their sponsors and donors; the interaction between sponsors and beneficiaries; and the ways monies were raised and disbursed.*

Dickens Studies Annual, Volume 32, Copyright © 2002 by AMS Press, Inc. All rights reserved.

Lost within the pages of David A. Wilson's multivolume *Carlyle* (1929) is "The Two Misses Lowe," an entry recounting a benevolence sponsored by Carlyle on behalf of two destitute spinsters from Deptford south of the river. Dickens, correct on all but the relation to Johnson, announced the discovery in an 8 May 1855 begging letter to Miss Coutts: "Two old ladies have turned up at Deptford, who are the last descendants (I think Great Grand-daughters) of Samuel Johnson. Mr. Carlyle has found them—in great poverty, but unde-monstrative and uncomplaining, though very old—with nothing to speak of in the wide world, but the plain fir desk on which Johnson wrote his English Dictionary" (*Letters of Dickens* 7: 614). The women were daughters to Mau-ritius Lowe, member of the Royal Academy and friend to Samuel Johnson. The two men were sufficiently intimate for Johnson to be named godfather to Mauritius Lowe's only son and elder daughter, Ann Elizabeth, to whom Johnson left a legacy. Whenever the Memorial is officially acknowledged, Johnson is named, forging as it were an unbroken line of succession between him and his beneficiaries. It suggests that the enterprise was more a memorial (to preserve the memory, an act of commemoration, *OED*) to the dead literary patriarch than a subscription effort to benefit the living women.[1] Carlyle, one could argue—a point I do not wish to pursue here in any great detail—perhaps also wanted to use the benevolence to help rehabilitate Johnson's "*Ulysses*" reputation which he felt was compromised in Croker's *Boswell's Life of Johnson*, where Johnson appears as someone needful of praise and given to sentimentalism: "that which we thought noble in old Samuel, was vulgar, base."[2]

Wilson cites a 30 June 1855 letter from Carlyle reprimanding Lady Ashbur-ton for not being on the scene to assist him with the benevolence: "The Johnson's God-daughter affair has not gone a good road, chiefly perhaps for want of you on the scene." Despite a £20 annuity from Miss Coutts for the benevolence, Lady Ashburton was "a Better who was equally munificent at an earlier stage,—to whom I will still apply in extremity." Carlyle lamented her absence: "I wish you had been here; I wish you were here" (161).[3] These two published entries—the Wilson citation and the Charles Sanders reference—based on a very public 1 November 1855 *Times* notice shed little light on this "benevolent adventure" (Florence Nightingale's term), shaped profoundly by Carlyle's personality and politics.[4] Examined closely, the Lowes Memorial registers Carlyle's concerns for English pauperism, contex-tualizes the New Poor Law, and evinces Carlyle's low tolerance for public philanthropy, which (between 1850 and 1860) added some 144 new organiza-tions.[5] The Memorial also suggests an identity politics of nationness, coming as it does at the height of the Balkan crisis, the changing racial and ethnic feature of overcrowded London, and Victorian concerns about foreign philan-thropic excess. Additionally, it expands our understanding of Victorian chari-ties—their goals, scope, and politics; the identity of their sponsors and donors;

the interaction between sponsors and beneficiaries; and the ways monies were raised and disbursed—and reveals the politics of Victorian benevolence, restricted, in this case, to the destitute from a narrowly imagined sense of community. Thus, while the Lowes Memorial touches on issues relating to the New Poor Law—squalor and poverty—it was a bad-faith gesture to the Condition-of-England Question.

Knowledge of the Lowes Memorial remains scant, much of it veiled in hitherto unpublished letters. Some hint of it might be gleaned in the Dickens letters, not enough, though, to provide a clear picture.[6] All three architects of the project—Carlyle, Dickens, and Forster—preferring an "unostentatious and sensitive benevolence" (Pope 11), desired an extravagant gift rather than having to appeal to the nation. In a culture committed to generosity, the word "philanthropic" had become a pejorative, defined as Exeter Hall's softness for the working poor and people of color. Benevolence, which flourished in a culture of "social distress and political uncertainty," had degenerated into sentimentality (Houghton 275, 277). Rejecting "the cult of benevolence" (Houghton), Carlyle wanted sanity, restraint, and reform. Ordinarily, the success of benevolent endeavors such as this of the Lowes is difficult to "measure or evaluate," given the paucity of evidence of such "scattered personal activity" (McCord 95). That Carlyle would undertake the Lowes benevolence is not unexpected, given his history of assistance to individuals he found in distress. He deeply resented philanthropy, but just as earnestly emphasized mutual accountability, the kind of ideological divide that so aptly characterizes Carlyle. His repeated allusions to Dr. William Pulteney Alison's Irish Widow disclose his commitment to communal responsibility based on something other than cash nexus; there is more to a "brother's keeper" than *"Cash-payment" (Past and Present, Works* 10: 146–47). But Carlyle's own attitude to philanthropy reflects much ambiguity. That conflict shows up in a 12 December 1850 letter Carlyle sent Forster on some "begging impostor; or a poor old woman of some merit endeavouring to escape the Atropos scissors a little longer." He wanted Forster's advice on how to handle the solicitation. "The story sickens one's hand. On the whole, what is one to do; or can nothing properly be done,—except perhaps send a few shillings and say, 'God help you, go?' " (*Letters* 25: 306). Helpful to specific individuals, Carlyle resented what he has called a "blind loquacious pruriency of indiscriminate Philanthropism." When "we pierce through that rosepink vapour of Sentimentalism, Philanthropy, and Feasts of Morals," we find behind it "one of the sorriest spectacles" (*Latter-Day Pamphlets, Works* 20: 51; *The French Revolution, Works* 2: 36).

Carlyle's aversion to public philanthropy was also politically informed. Anticipating the Hungry Forties, his essay on "Chartism" (1839) addressed the welfare of the working poor, like those Scotsbrig's ploughmen "toiling in the red furrow, their ploughshares gleaming in the sun," and whose "whole existence looking sad almost pathetic to me. They are very poor in purse; poor in purpose, principle, for most part, in all that makes the wealth of a man" (*Letters* 14: 178). The New Poor Law, he believed, was "but a temporary measure; an anodyne, not a remedy . . . and yet human beings cannot be left to die" (*Past and Present* 3). Carlyle's indigent, however, constituted a select group, white Lancashire weavers rather than "whole gangs of Quashees" across the sea: "O Brothers! O Sisters!" he lamented, "It is for these White Women that my heart bleeds and my soul is heavy" ("Occasional Discourse," *Works* 29: 366, 369). London's economically destitute, in Carlyle's account, although fewer in number than in other industrial cities, is yet quite visible: "you cannot walk along the street without seeing frightful symptoms of it." But the "Eleven thousand souls" whose plight he laments were Paisley's destitute, and *Past and Present*, that "red-hot indignant thing," voices Carlyle's concerns for "the two millions of men sitting in poor-law Bastilles [who] seem to ask of every English soul, 'Hast thou no word to say for us?' " (Froude 1: 243–44). The Lowes Memorial intended, then, to express the "grief and shame and manifold inarticulate distress and weariness" not of working and non-working English but of distressed gentlewomen.

If the growth of pauperism was, as Carlyle thought, a social sin, the effort to assist the Lowes was a means of expiation. But though a charitable act, the Memorial lacked a broad appreciation for philanthropy. Indeed, like so much of nineteenth-century philanthropy, it comprised "an essential sphere of politics and social relations" (Prochaska, *Royal Bounty* 67). Carlyle saw the Memorial as both an English cause and expressive of his paternal duty to a literary family, which explains his endorsement of the Civil List Pension, a dole for the literary destitute. Assuming the mantle of a Jeremiah, mourner for the poor, he wanted to abate suffering, reduce inward discontent, and extend lives. It is curious whether in this enterprise Carlyle was mindful of Johnson's *Rasselas*, a moral fable on the pursuit of the good life and whether it is attainable here on earth. He was, we know, impressed by Johnson's generosity: "he finds the wretched Daughter of Vice fallen down in the streets; carries her home on his own shoulders, and like the good Samaritan gives help to the help-needing, worthy or unworthy. Ought not Charity, even in that sense, to cover a multitude of sin?" As important to Carlyle, Johnson, involved in silent acts of charity, was not a Lady Bountiful, a mere cog in the machinery of public philanthropy: "No Penny-a-week Committee-Lady, no manager of Soup-Kitchen, dancer at Charity-Balls, was this rugged, stern-visaged man: but where, in all England, could there have been found another soul so full of Pity, a hand so heavenlike bounteous as his? The widow's mite, we know, was greater than all the other gifts" ("Boswell's Life of Johnson" 127–28).

But Carlyle's involvement in the Lowes benevolence, while compassionate, reveals very little genuine passion. He took it on, he told Forster on 25 October 1855, because of "a great deal of sorrowful stuff in this world, much ugly scavengerage to do, and we must not grumble to take our share of it on occasion."[7] The "social imperative" driving philanthropy, David Owen has observed, emerged from a sense of obligation "widespread among the upper and upper-middle classes" (165). To Prochaska, it was "a moral obligation or a test of faith." And in an era of government parsimony, "the needs of the community bound the citizenry together in a web of kindness, obligation and expectation" (*Royal Bounty* 67). Even Christian acts of charity were not "the spontaneous expression of a good heart," but mere "performances of religious duty" (Houghton 275).

How the benevolence originated is not entirely unknown. It might have been prompted by one of those patent Victorian begging letters, like the 5 July 1849 appeal to "The Editur of the Times Paper" at the height of the second cholera epidemic. A veritable blueprint for the Carlyle plan, the letter with fifty-four subscribers was published in the *Times* "just as it has reached us." It identifies the epidemic of limited space and the lack of mobility among the poor who could not, unlike the economically privileged, migrate to uninfected regions. In London during the 1831 cholera outbreak, Carlyle and Jane, for example, could "*forthwith bundle our gear* . . . return to Puttock till it is over" (*Letters* 6: 43).[8] The *Times* letter ends with an empathetic appeal: "Preaye Sir com and see us, for we are livin like piggs and it aint faire we shoulde be so ill treated" (5).[9] Also unclear is exactly when and how Carlyle found the Lowes. The Carlyles, we know, did employ a Deptford servant, one Elizabeth, whose quarrelsome disposition and stormy and abbreviated relationship with them did not occasion even a deathbed visit from the always more sympathetic Jane. Carlyle might also have picked up on references to the Lowes in Johnson's will while he was preparing his review of Croker's *Boswell's Life of Johnson*, where Mauritius Lowe is mentioned. Recently, however, Aileen Christianson, while working on volumes 29 and 30 of *The Collected Letters of Thomas and Jane Welsh Carlyle*, came across some information that perhaps prompted Carlyle's interest in the Lowes, a 12 April 1855 letter from Thomas Erskine of Linlathen to the Rev. Thomas Wright Mathews (whose identity is still unknown, perhaps a Deptford clergyman): "I wish you would get from that goddaughter of the old lexicographer some documents authenticating her relationship as goddaughter to him. Do you think that, in the parish register of her baptism, any record of the fact could be found? For, if the history could be fairly made out, there can be little doubt but that something could be done for her. I mentioned the matter to Carlyle, who immediately said that the Prime Minister would feel that the bestowment of a small pension, at least to the extent of keeping her from want, would be recognised by the whole country as a right use of power."[10] "The meeting with Erskine," Christianson tells me, "is not referred to at the time, although he had gone for a drive with JWC on 21 March" (*Letters* 29: 274). On 19 November 1855, Carlyle told his brother John: "Erskine saddled me with that" (*Letters* 30: 1 [forthcoming]). These Deptford spinsters, once found, must have recalled for Carlyle Alison's Irish widow, "hidden from all but the eye of God," and whose death by typhoid created a lethal "economy" (*Past and Present* 3, 149). Her story had become legendary, not only because of its emotional appeal, but also because it articulated the all-too-familiar trope of the female body as both site and agent of disease.[11] "No topic," as Bruce Haley has observed, "more preoccupied the Victorian mind than Health—not religion, or politics, or Improvement, or Darwinism" (3). And to Victorians especially, "physical health was not perceived in clinical isolation from religious, ethical and political concerns" (Alderson 47).

Carlyle's was a checkered history of charitable endeavors. He exhibited a "generosity" like his own in an " 'inverse ratio' to his means." Froude saw Carlyle's "expenditure on himself . . . thrifty, even to parsimony. . . . [H]e gave away profusely in his own family, and was liberal beyond his means elsewhere" (1: 100; 2: 138). Froude was perhaps responding to Carlyle's kindness toward the likes of Lady Bulwer Lytton, Delia Bacon, and tolerance of James Baillie, all of whom were connected intimately to him.[12] Spurred by Robert Chambers's "Samaritan endeavour on behalf of Burns's Sister," he dished out his "poor guinea; a kind of widow's mite," and volunteered to "gather a few guineas more in my home circle, if you send me a half dozen of your subscription papers." His 23 May 1842 letter to Monckton Milnes, suggesting an appeal to the premier, Robert Peel, for "a pension of £100 to this poor Widow" and "£50 each to her two meritorious Daughters," reflects the plan he would later adopt in the Lowes Memorial. At a time when Carlyle showed little interest in Edwin Chadwick's *Sanitary Report*, he found time and energy enough from April to July 1842 to sponsor this fundraising effort. This, clearly, was a more private matter ("this of the Pe[nsion to be] *kept totally secret* . . . [without secre]cy *it* will do no great feats") that bound friends of Burns together in a legitimate endeavor, "Hero-worship, of Divine (that is) and Humane" (*Letters* 14: 116, 193). The enterprise could not exclude Forster. "Did you not tell me," Carlyle appealed to him, "you had generously got together a few guineas for me in behalf of what we call the 'Begg Subscription,' Great Britain's gift to the sister of Burns? Milnes and I are . . . to combine the several fractions into some integer amount, and, sending it off to Chambers, wash our hands of the affair" (*Letters* 14: 115–16, 223). Carlyle's philanthropic activities were confined strictly to those he knew or those who came highly recommended. Such a narrow focus, and add to it Carlyle's personal habits, would not have appealed to recognized charities.

For example, the Lowes Memorial failed to attract the attention of such relief agencies as the Friendly Female Society, the Metropolitan Visiting and Relief Association, the Female Aid Society, and the Ladies' Royal Benevolent Society. Dickens's role (marginal for him) in the Lowes Memorial reflects perhaps his response to its exclusivity, however much he valued "well-intentioned, orderly experiments in coping with the destitute of London" (Welsh 91).[13]

From April 1855 to May 1856, with the Athenaeum as the base of operations, Carlyle undertook this charitable venture on behalf of Ann Elizabeth and Frances Meliora Lucia Lowe, destitute sisters from Deptford ("deep ford") south of the river. What little we know of the women concerns their relationship to Samuel Johnson and their father's discovery of J. M. W. Turner. And never lost on the framers of the benevolence are the women's ties to Deptford, considering what the name meant even to the most casual observers of metropolitan London. The politics informing the initiative cannot be separated from Deptford's social history, a place and a people who "bore the criminal brand on their faces" (Steele 91).[14] Deptford struggled to relinquish that reputation, wanting to be remembered not as the site where in 1593 Christopher Marlowe was stabbed in an altercation over his tavern bill but as the stately locale where Samuel Pepys dined royally. Wharfside commerce profoundly influenced Deptford's character, making the area home for transients of all hues (Sheppard 11–12). "He who wishes to behold one of the most extraordinary and least known scenes of this metropolis," the preeminent Victorian slum photo-journalist, Henry Mayhew wrote, "should wend his way to the London Dock gates at half-past seven in the morning" to see "congregated within the principal entrance masses of men of all grades, looks, and kinds." One can secure employment "without either character or recommendation, so that the labourers employed there are naturally a most incongruous assembly" (3: 301, 303). Raphael Samuel found the area an asylum for refugees wintering in London, including entire families of gypsies who took advantage of Deptford's cheap, temporary lodgings (143). Boasting social squalor, from high unemployment and large patches of slum housing, Deptford took on the term "rough," which meant "a complex mixture of bad conditions and perceived immorality."[15] But "rough" and "respectable," Steele warns, are more like "emotional labels attached by observers to certain ways of life" than actual "sociological categories describing real people or neighborhoods" (113).

Cheap housing sprung up when the Admiralty (in 1807) opened the Royal Victualling Yard to service vessels that would play a "significant role in London's privateering ventures," including that of John Hawkins, father of the Atlantic slave trade, who lived in Treasure's House at Deptford Dockyard (Anim-Addo 7). The Yard also served repatriation efforts in the Sierra Leone experiment. Docks built to advance trade and stockpile colonial spoils all barnacled around Deptford, Greenwich, and Woolwich, and were named after the colonies whose resources were warehoused there (the West India Docks and the East India Docks). One Scottish visitor to the Carlyles came fresh from the West Indies, speaking a mixture of Annandale accent and Dock English. To most observers, Deptford was rough and fast becoming racially toxic. Along the quay one can often encounter "a black sailor, with a cotton handkerchief twisted turban-like round his head," and from American ships entering the docks hear "sailors . . . singing boisterous nigger songs" (Mayhew 3: 302–3).[16] According to Anim-Addo, many of the vessels "enriched by the African Caribbean trade began and ended each trip at Deptford. They brought with them slaves, symbols of wealth. Deptford became a key area for these newly arrived individuals whose number would increase as the trade developed. . . . Pepys recalls several bouts of drinking which included the swapping of stories about blacks and slavery."[17] Plans in the 1830s to extend the horse tram to Deptford from the center of London were "rigorously and successfully opposed" on what were clearly class and racial grounds: it would lower "the character of the thoroughfare" (Porter 227). Deptford's other notable improvement were two intercepting sewers (from Putney and Balham) pumped from a large reservoir on the Erith marshes into the Southern Outfalls and discharged untreated into an already polluted Thames. This arterial flow of raw sewage meandering through densely populated areas generated frequent complaints of atmospheric impurities, "a temporary problem" at Greenwich, but a "fact of life" at Deptford. One angry Greenwich resident complained:

> There is always a disagreeable smell . . . at Deptford, of what appears to be the sewage, and now it seems we are to have it extended to Greenwich. If private residents are not to be driven away, it is time the local authorities bestirred themselves. It would seem, on the face of it, that they are exceedingly apathetic, as the smell referred to at Deptford has been going on for a long time. If it arises from the pumping station there . . . steps should be taken to stop it.
>
> (qtd. in Steele 95.)

To assist women with familial ties to an English patriarch and to counter England's domestic inattention, Carlyle initiated the benevolence on behalf of the Lowes, recruited Dickens, and conscripted Forster. Drafting Dickens required little forethought. Deptford was, after all, central to his life and fiction.[18] He was also a known supporter of countless domestic charities as well as public subscription efforts. And, moreover, by now he had become publicly averse to telescopic (foreign) philanthropy, opposing the Niger Expedition of 1841 and satirizing in *Bleak House* (1853) philanthropic enterprises on behalf of "the welfare of Africans," Borrioboola-Gha on the banks of the Niger, at the neglect of "those living in wretchedness at home" (Pope

105).[19] Forster's conscription resulted from his enthusiastic response to the initiative. "I am positively ashamed of having dragged you into this matter," Carlyle told him on 12 November 1855, "but in fact it was your own movement when I first spoke that encouraged me to move and (bravely speaking) that set the whole enterprise in motion. So [for] that fault you have only yourself to thank." In fact, in the entire management of the benevolence, Carlyle regularly encumbered Forster and fretted when he envisioned no easy exit. With a long history of spearheading such charitable ventures and eager to please Carlyle, Forster willingly shouldered those duties: were it not for an "obliging fellow called Forster, who took the whole thing on his back for me, I know not what would have become of me with it!"[20]

But Carlyle had to prod himself always, attributing his ennui not, as perhaps he might, to the demands of *Frederick the Great*, which robbed him of "spirit left to meet my fellow creatures or their daily topics" (*Letters* 29: 303), but, rather, to the emotional tax from the Crimean War—the two often conflated in Carlyle. Fred Kaplan sees him at the time in a bout of depression over the recent death of friends and acquaintances, including his mother. "By March 1855 the bitter cold of the 'severest winter' he had 'ever experienced' did not seem quite as piercing as his own sense of depression and desolation" as he struggled over *Frederick* (397), that "sad dusty dreary work" and "mass of immeasurable confusion" (*Letters* 29: 303). On 1 May 1855, he assured Forster: "I have not been idle in the poor Lowe case; tho' I have shuddered much to draw up anything in the Memorial . . . having indeed no *spunk* in me at all for writing anything." But while Carlyle valued secrecy, he wanted public appeal, more so than Dickens and Forster content to solicit funds from acquaintances and known government officials. From the very beginning, going public was Carlyle's idea, with early plans to make an appeal in the *Examiner* with "all these Letters &c &c from Boswell should be stuck into it *in extenso*; and in that way it might serve there too." The propaganda is clear. Carlyle wanted to shame the nation into giving, that patent Victorian appeal to social guilt: "Here however is a thing, off my hand at last, capable of being manufactured into what will perhaps [do?]. I get varieties of counsel as to whether the matter shd be kept absolutely private *till* Palmerston have been applied to, *or* should be made public, and blown into some *popularity*, as the only sure method of acting on Palmerston. . . . Consider it [the Memorial] and them [the Lowes]; and then let us meet . . . *without* either *meat* or drink, for I am far below all that in the days that now run!" Carlyle urged Forster to assume primary responsibility: "in fact you must think of it, you are a chari[t]able man, deliver poor lame *me* from the pressure of it!" Palmerston's officials were skeptical of the proposal's merit, which failed to dishearten Carlyle; "merely mentioning the case" to the Bishop of Oxford, "Soapy Sam," earned from a fund he administered "an annuity of £10 for the joint lives of these two poor women."

The plan appealed to Lord Palmerston, prime minister (1855–58), for a worthwhile pension from the Civil List. Carlyle informed Forster on 13 May that he had no additional subscribers other than Macaulay; "indeed you know far better than I who they are that ought to sign, and how to get them and make them do it.—more power to your elbow!" Someone, he felt, ought to get a decisive answer from Palmerston. On 12 May, Carlyle had already heard from Dickens regarding a "beautiful and excellent" donation (£20) from Angela Burdett-Coutts, baroness, Highgate socialite, and the doyenne of Victorian philanthropy, which he hoped "may be made the *nucleus* (if you can so contrive it) for others from other quarters." The gift came after Dickens, only two days earlier, had sent her Carlyle's draft of the Memorial. "You need not mind the pencil-marks, which have been observed in putting the Memorial into shape," he told her. "I think you will be interested in his [Carlyle's] own account of the case, given in his own odd way." Dickens wanted Miss Coutts to "empower" him to notify Carlyle of her contribution, "that small allowance you have with your usual kindness thought of." He then informed Carlyle that Miss Coutts "has given me Twenty Pounds for the immediate necessities of the two poor old ladies; having been greatly interested in your draft of the Memorial, which I shewed her. . . . In the meantime here it is, and you can anticipate it for the benefit of the good old souls in any way you think right" (*Letters of Dickens* 7: 615–18).[21]

To his credit, Carlyle wanted a woman's largess as bedrock for the benevolence. I do not wish to explore here the significant role women played in nineteenth-century philanthropy and the opportunity it offered them for meaningful and sustained activity ("spheres of actions," says Florence Nightingale, in *Cassandra*), personal growth, and a way to position themselves in society: "In an age in which women found so many doors closed, they discovered a crack in the doors of the charitable societies" (Prochaska, *Women and Philanthropy* 222).[22] I want merely to indicate that though it had become routine for women to serve on or manage charitable agencies, they had no such roles in the Carlyle plan.[23] Like the largely male sponsored (Chambers, Carlyle, and Milnes) Widow Begg subscription of 1842, the Lowes Memorial had an exclusively male supervisory committee, which perhaps explains why the percentage of women subscribers and subscription to the Memorial was comparatively less than that realized by other Victorian charities. Of the thirteen identified donors to the Widow Begg subscription, there were only three women (the most notable of whom is Mrs. Gaskell), and they were the most generous. In the case of the Lowes, Carlyle easily could have involved Ladies Ashburton, Stanley, and Palmerston, as well as Angela Burdette-Coutts, all of whom from the outset expressed great interest in the Lowes cause. But these women were brought in not so for their savvy, organizing skills, or presumed sensitivity to the afflicted, but only for their political connections and resources.[24] Of the Lowes, Carlyle urged Forster, "the only preoccupation is, not to flurry these poor old souls out of their old heads, or this to the least degree possible."[25] A subsequent meeting with "human wit (aided by tobacco) ought to be able to settle many things." Forster felt an immediate affinity with the project, which Carlyle sensed: "I owe you I know not what for having taken that Palmerston business on your own back so to speak: really a kind and charitable act, you may believe *me* as well as the ancient Goddaughter!"

Around the middle of May 1855, the three men petitioned Palmerston. Endorsed by the likes of Tennyson, Thackeray, and Disraeli, the Memorial surveys Johnson's will, forges familial ties between an English patriarch and the Lowes, isolates the aristocratic nature and quiet dignity of these women, and portrays the elder as a relic touched by Johnson's sacred hands, admitting once again his Midas touch: "all that our Johnson *touched* has become illuminated for us" (*Boswell's Life of Johnson* 66). The appeal depicts a family who suffered an unfortunate fall, emphasizes Johnson's manly, English character and the importance of cultural memory, and appeals to a nation's duty to a fallen hero, himself a national relic:

> The Undersigned beg respectfully to submit to Lord Palmerston a statement of reasons which appear to them to constitute, on behalf of the two aged surviving daughters of Mauritius Lowe, therein described, a claim to such small yearly pension as in his Lordship's judgment may consist with other claims and demands for the ensuing year, upon the fund appropriate to literature.
> In Dr. Samuel Johnson's last Will is this passage:
> "I also give and bequeath to my godchildren, the son and daughter of Mauritius Lowe, painter, each of them 100L. of my stock in the Three per Cent." Consolidated Annuities, to be disposed of by and at the discretion of my executors in the education or settlement in the world of them my said legatees."[26]
> The Mauritius Lowe mentioned here, who was once a man of great promise in his art, favourably known in the Royal Academy and in the world as a man of refined manners and real talent and worth (though probably with something of morbid or over-sensitive in his character), died ten years after Johnson without fulfilling the high hopes entertained of him. The godson, or younger Lowe, mentioned in the will, who at one time (1810–13) appears to have held some small appointment in Barbadoes, creditably to himself, but with loss of health—the crown and consummation of various other losses he had met with—is also long since dead. Of these Lowes and their hopes and struggles there is now nothing to be said. They are sunk under the horizon. Nor can they pretend to have any hold of the world's memory except what is derived from the father's intimacy with Johnson, of which and of Johnson's helpfulness and real esteem and affection for the man there are still abundant proofs, printed and not printed, besides this of the Will.
> But the goddaughter mentioned in the Will has not yet sunk under the horizon. She still survives among us, a highly respectable old person, now in her seventy-eighth year, with all her faculties about her, living with her younger sister, aged

seventy-two, the only other remnant of the family, in a house they have long occupied—No. 5, Minerva Place, New Cross, Deptford—with numerous memorials of Johnson in their possession, which vividly bring home to us and present as a still living fact, their connection with that great man. They have lived there for many years in rigorous though not undignified poverty, which now, by some unforeseen occurrences, threatens to become absolute indigence in these their final years.[27]

They are gentlewomen in manners; by all evidence, persons of uniformly unexceptional conduct; veracity, sense, ingenuous propriety, noticeable in them both, to a superior degree. The elder, especially, must have been a graceful lively little woman, something of a beauty in her younger days, and by no means wanting for talent. She still recollects in a dim but ineffaceable manner the big, awful figure of Samuel Johnson, to whom she was carried shortly before his death, that he might lay his hand on her head and give her his blessing; her awe and terror were great on the occasion. Both sisters are in perfect possession of their faculties—the younger only is slightly hard of hearing; the elder (on whose head lay Johnson's hand) has still a light step, perfect erect carriage, and vivacious memory and intellect. The younger, who is of very honest and somewhat sterner features, appears to be the practical intellect of the house, and probably the practical hand. They are very poor, but have taken their poverty in a quiet, unaffectedly handsome manner, and have still hope that, in some way or other, intolerable want will not be permitted to overtake them. They have an altogether respectable, or, we might say (bringing the past and the present into contact), a touching and venerable air. There, in their little parlour at Deptford, is the fir desk (capable of being rigorously authenticated as such) upon which Samuel Johnson wrote the "English Dictionary": the best dictionary ever written, say some.

It is in behalf of these two women, of Johnson's goddaughter fallen old and indigent, that we venture to solicit from the Government some small public subvention, to screen their last years from the worst misery. It may be urged that there is no public fund appropriated for such precise objects, and that their case cannot, except in a reflex way, be brought under the head of "literary pensions"; but, in a reflex way, it surely can; and we humbly submit withal, that this case of theirs is, in some measure, a peculiar and unique one.

Samuel Johnson is such a literary man as probably will not appear again in England for a very great length of time. His work and his life, looked at well, have something in them of heroic, which is of value beyond most literature, and much beyond all money and money's worth to the nation which produced him. That same "English Dictionary," written on the poor fir desk above spoken of, under sternly memorable circumstances, is itself a proud possession to the English nation, and not in the philological point of view alone. Such a dictionary has an *architectonic* quality in it; and for massive solidity of plan, manful correctness and fidelity of execution, luminous intelligence, rugged honesty and greatness of mind pervading every part of it, is like no other. This, too, is a *Cathedral of St. Paul's*, after its sort; and stands there for long periods, silently reminding every English soul of much that is very necessary to remember.

Samuel Johnson himself is far beyond the reach of our gratitude. He left no child or representative of any kind to claim pensions or distinctions from us; and here, by accident, thrown upon the waste sea beach, is something venerably human with Johnson's *mark* still legible upon it; Johnson, as it were, mutely bequeathing it to us, and to what humanity and loyalty we have, for the few years that may still be left. Our humble request, in the name of literature withal is, that the English nation will, in some small adequate way, respond to this demand of Johnson's.

Palmerston found himself with a difficult decision, compelled by a fabulous appeal but with little capital. In letters of 5 and 7 June, Carlyle acknowledged being shown a letter by Lady Stanley from Lord Granville, Palmerston's Secretary, concerning "those poor Lowes: his Lordship decides that there is no specific fund &c &c,—that, in short, he will give the poor women £100 once for all, and have done with him." Ladies Stanley and Palmerston agreed to work together to secure a £10 annuity for Frances Meliora, which would augment what Ann Elizabeth had been receiving. Carlyle had earlier rejected that idea, convinced they could do better and wanting also to shape public debate on the condition of the literary poor in the current politics of economic reform, especially the reorganization of the Privy Purse. He had come to believe that only Tennyson had been benefiting from the Civil List, "a sad thing if a true one," and felt that "a few touches about the literary Pension Fund might not be amiss." But for now, the plan was to await word from Lady Palmerston before appealing to "the world *out* of Downing Street":

> it seems the Premier's *Wife* has some small public fund which she can dispose of in small doles of that kind. . . . Lady Stanley will ask on the first opportunity: but whether there is a vacancy, and then whether there is a will, are questions;—and in brief this £100 is all that we can count upon. Even with the £10 annually, much more without it . . . I consider it rather an ineffective result; clearly *in*adequate by itself.

On 7 June, Carlyle told Lady Stanley that he wanted the women "saved from absolute want by the English Nation, without bursts of Newspaper balderdash being needed in such a case" (*Letters* 29: 325). But he still felt that "Wide publicity and no delay, seem to be the rules. It seems beyond doubt, if the Public were once stirred up, the Public would give abundantly. I do not think the old Dames will much mind the *noise*." He wanted Palmerston to escape censure, "least of all while the *Lady* Pn has not yet said no to us! . . . Well, do your best and assist, dear Forster;—ask Dickens and he will help!" Carlyle sent Forster "the Palmerston despatches" and instructed him to "read, and lock in your drawer till we see what further is to come of it."

But Palmerston could not deliver. His 8 June letter to Secretary Granville expressed regret that the Lowes case did not fit the purview of the Civil List,

> restricted to the cases of persons who have rendered literary or other service to their Country, and in some peculiar and special instances to the cases of

surviving relatives, who by the death of such persons have been left destitute. Now although Miss Lowe and her sister appear to have enjoyed the good will and regard of Dr. Johnson, yet they cannot be said to have been dependent upon or related to him; and I regret therefore that I should not be justified in holding out the expectation that a Civil List Pension could be granted to them. In consideration however of the destitute position in which these Ladies are placed, and the strong testimony borne in their favour, I have had much pleasure in recommending that one hundred pounds be granted to them from the Royal Bounty Fund.

Aware of Palmerston's refusal, Carlyle had already planned his response. The £100, he felt, hardly afforded the women a quality life, showing that it was now no longer a matter of survival for women who had in fact shrewdly devised an effective economic system of sustenance, able to live twice the age of the annual mortality rate for women in their district.[28] Whether or not Carlyle recognized it, and well intentioned as his efforts were, they helped subvert an economy of female self-sufficiency. The women can be observed abandoning their effective system of economic self-determinism to hunger after the elixir ("very cheery over it") of Goblin money, which would consign them to a slavish desire for male-generated commodity.

Carlyle's 15 June letter, totaling eight crammed pages, revealed some of his first signs of benevolence fatigue. He thanked Forster "for the trouble you take: I wish we all had done with this business; and hope we shall soon," and felt that "Dickens's idea" to pursue "private help" is "well worth attention . . . better that the big public be kept quite apart" and with "the *minimum of noise*, which is the rule in all cases, will be especially welcome in this," only "if it will suffice. But that is the question." Carlyle wondered whether an individual or a small group "would be ready to furnish the sum necessary, and to whom one could with a clear mind recommend such an act of beneficence?" He no longer expected the requisite annuity from Lady Palmerston; but with the funds already raised, £20 annually would be enough "for the *longest* of Two Lives (78 and 72)." But Carlyle still dreamt of a Lady Bountiful, who "will at once undertake to pay that annuity sum, and execute some Deed, so as to make it a finished thing, and let *us* wash our hands of it?" Without the talent for fund-raising, he felt that his own "powers of private begging are at this moment as good as zero. . . . Let Dickens then question himself; for it will turn all on that, on his capabilities on how he judges of them." Carlyle also felt that the Lowes could easily trade in Johnson's hero-as-man-of-letters reputation, "The largest soul that was in all England" (*Heroes, Works* 5: 179): if their case and "their relation to him were fairly made known to them;—the Palmerston Memorial (with such additions as you could soon make) with the Names attached to it, were conspicuously published in the Times," and a codicil that the British Government could not perform it, and so "will you, O English Nation do it?—the English Nation surely would not fail to come down with their dust to the due extent." Forster was asked to appoint a receiving committee from the subscription list: "I somehow feel confident there would be subscription in abundance." Carlyle remained apprehensive about a conspicuous *Times* application. Should it fail, he would adopt Dickens's appeal to benevolent ("Noble") individuals. With increasing demands from the epic biography, *Frederick the Great* ("extremely stiff-jointed and otherwise heavy-laden"), Carlyle, understandably, wanted short work of the Memorial. Lady Stanley had suggested that 100 guineas could be raised from raffling Johnson's desk. But Carlyle still held to Dickens's hope: "Truly, if Dickens knows a 'Single Person' (as the Commonwealth Politicians used to say) who is ready to do it in the handsome spontaneous way, that will be infinitely better! But let him consider and you, whether we ought not in any case to try the Nation first? . . . but till the Nation has been tried, I am . . . good for nothing in the begging way." To convince himself of his commitment to the benevolence, Carlyle provided Forster a comprehensive account of the Lowes' condition, "the Exact State of the Lowe Finance": ownership of their dwelling; monies raised; the need "to renew their stock of clothes, and set them up again, we might leave them with a kind of safe conscience"; and their need of a servant. He surmised that the women "were of a humour to suffer much rather than borrow," and probably had "little debt."

Ironically, the Lowes were modeling Carlyle's ethic of suffering, exhibiting a "rigour and reclusion traceable in the physiognomy of their house" (in "great poverty, but undemonstrative and uncomplaining," says Dickens). They also had not solicited assistance from Deptford's charitable agencies—the Deptford Soup Institution (est. 1809) and the Deptford Coal Institution (est. 1837). His actions moved to change all that. Carlyle recommended a servant and a new wardrobe, signs of upward mobility from the ranks of the destitute to middle-class standing.[29] He wanted to retailor these Johnsonian women in the garb of the socially respectable, as in fact they were but for their current economic distress. Unless Lady Palmerston provides the annuity or Dickens produces a benefactor, Carlyle opined, "we shall really have to try the public. I beg a million of persons; but what can I do except, lame as I am at present, cry for help. If Dickens and you will do whatever *you two like* in the matter, I shall be most grateful. Lady Pm's decision you shall instantly have, when it comes; and then—your own course will have become clear in the interim." June 23 saw them still awaiting her response before Forster, with "fresh copies of the Memorial," could proceed to the *Times*. All that remained now was consensus on the list of names to receive subscription and a banker, "if an honest & safe individual of that species may be found."[30]

The second half of 1855 saw the proposal go public. By 13 August, and mainly through word of mouth, monies were already coming in. On 30 August, Carlyle heard from Ann Elizabeth, "Chancellor of *their* Exchequer," he called her. "I own also to a kind of surmise (along with Dickens) that we shall have to make the thing public before he [Palmerston] will effectively stir in it," he told Forster. Ann Lowe had granted him exclusive rights ("as you think proper") to Johnson's desk. At the end of October, the three sponsors met at the Athenaeum to finalize the Memorial. With some disappointment ("one cannot quit it with a safe conscience in that *half-done* state," Carlyle admitted to Lady Stanley [*Letters* 29: 338]), they went public, submitting the Memorial to J. T. Delane, famous editor of *The Times*. On 28 October, Carlyle again expressed gratitude to Forster who was devoted to a cause frequently disconcerting to Carlyle: "you are the helpfullest of men! A pleasure to [work?] with in such promptitude and generous alacrity in the muddy thoroughfares of this world!" Entitled "Samuel Johnson's Goddaughter," and shot through with nostalgia and the politics of national identity (Carlyle believed that honoring Johnson is honoring England [see "Boswell's *Life of Johnson*" 133]), the Memorial was published on 1 November 1855:

> The following document, and the proposal or appeal now grounded on it, require to be made known to the British public, for which object we, as the course is, apply to the Editor of the *Times*.
> In the month of May last there was presented to Lord Palmerston, as head of her Majesty's Government, a memorial on behalf of a certain aged Miss Lowe and her sister, which memorial will sufficiently explain itself, and indicate who the Miss Lowes are, to those who read it here.

Here the notice incorporates the letter to Palmerston, and continues:

> To this memorial his Lordship made answer, with great courtesy and without undue delay, that the fund set apart for encouragement of literature could not be meddled with for a pension to the goddaughter of Johnson; but that in consideration of the circumstances, his Lordship, from some other fund, has made her a donation of £100. Which sum of £100 was accordingly paid to Miss Lowe in June last—a very welcome gift and help—all that the Prime Minister could do in this matter, and, unfortunately, only about the fifth part of what it was, and is, indispensable to get done.
> It was still hoped that the last resource of an appeal to the public might be avoided; that there might be other Government helps, minute charitable funds, adequate to this small emergency. And new endeavours were accordingly made in that direction, and new expectations entertained; but these likewise have all proved ineffectual: and the resulting fact now is, that there is still needed something like an annuity of £30 for the joint lives of these two aged persons; that, strictly computing what pittances certain and precarious they already have, and what they still want, their case cannot be satisfactorily left on lower terms—that is to say, about £100, to purchase such an annuity, is still needed for them.

If the thing is half as English as we suppose it to be, a small pecuniary result of that kind is not doubtful now when the application is once made. At all events, as the English Government is not able to do this thing, we are now bound to apprise the English nation of it, and to ask the English nation in its miscellaneous capacity—Are you willing to do it?

Messrs. Coutts, bankers, will receive subscriptions from such as feel that this is a valid call upon English beneficence; and we have too much reverence for Samuel Johnson, and for the present generation of his countrymen, to use any soliciting or ignoble pressure on the occasion. So soon as the requisite amount has come in, the subscriptions will cease: of which due notice will be given.

We are, Sir, your obedient servants,
Thomas Carlyle
Charles Dickens
John Forster

The Memorial saw an immediate response, overcoming the limited public resistance to it, like the one in the 3 November 1855 *Athenaeum*, whose "Weekly Gossip" column argued a distinction between the sentimental and the real, the private and the public. The Lowes' "claim on the charitable may be strong, for anything we know," it opined, "but the literary ground of appeal fails in this case absolutely." Johnson's friendship with Mauritius Lowe, notwithstanding, "it will scarcely be contended that the private regards of a man of letters constitute a claim on the public purse." The column did not discourage general support from the stereotypically female philanthropic: "If any Lady Bountiful should please to extend to the Misses Lowe on other grounds a part of her superfluous wealth, everybody will rejoice. But we object to the circulation of the hat in the name of literature."[31] The remonstrance, however, only increased awareness of the appeal. On that very day Dickens heard from a Lichfield banker, Richard Greene, who anticipated a substantial donation from Johnson's birthplace: "I am happy to acknowledge the receipt of your kind letter, and to assure you that Mr. Carlyle, Mr. Forster, and myself, hail with the greatest interest and satisfaction the prospect of our appeal being responded to by the citizens of Lichfield. No help rendered to these poor ladies could possibly be so graceful and welcome as aid coming from the place that boasts of having given Johnson birth." Preferring spontaneous acts of generosity (as did Carlyle, who on 5 June 1855 admitted to Forster that he feared "that my own visible urgencies might in some measure have interfered with the spontaneity of things"), Dickens discouraged coercion: "I should have had a great desire to excuse myself from obtruding any personal appeal of mine upon your citizens. I feel it so much more natural and becoming in me to leave them to their own generous impulses." On 4 November Dickens promised Carlyle donations ("Johnson letters") and, to show that he was being faithful to the Carlyle plan, enclosed the Greene letter with word that he had suggested that donations "should be composed of Lichfield citizens only, and should have *no such foreigners in it*" (*Letters of Dickens* 7: 736–37, my italics). Surprising to all, the Greene plan failed, forcing him to cough up £5, a substantial amount from someone so disconnected from the benevolence. Even the celebrated Victorian paleontologist, Richard Owen, became involved. On 7 November, Carlyle wrote Owen grateful for "the Cheque; and will duly deliver it at Coutts's tomorrow afternoon." The money Owen had sent him was a £10 contribution from Robert Slaney. Showing a measure of detachment from the benevolence, Carlyle wanted Slaney to know that "the Subscription is understood to be going on rather handsomely; and that there is little doubt the needful sum will gradually be got for these poor old women."[32]

As the Owen letter reveals, the months following the appeal were met by a flurry of donations, requiring no "further solicitation by Circular or otherwise" (HC). On 5 November, Forster submitted a Carlyle note to the *Times* thanking an anonymous donor for a £5 contribution. The gift came "from some friendly correspondent, who signs no name and gives no date of place." Forster had emended the note ("otherwise it might have been fancied that this single letter was the only one received") to reenergize the appeal. "Hardly had I dispatched my note to you on Saturday when letters began to tumble in." One letter proposed "admission for our clients into some 'free' cottages at Gravesend—which I have told my correspondent was exactly (as he might have perceived from the Times article) what the poor ladies did *not* want." Readers familiar with Deptford's social history and the Lowes' conformity to Carlyle's natural aristocracy felt that the women needed a place suitable to their heritage. No goddaughter of Samuel Johnson deserves a penury existence in backwater Deptford. On 27 November, an always munificent Ruskin donated £10 "for Turner's sake," aware that were it not for Mauritius Lowe, a member of the R.A., Turner quite likely would have remained obscure.

The Carlyles spent Christmas with Lady Ashburton at the Grange. Dickens was vacationing in Paris during November 1855 and from January to April 1856. Forster was left to manage the benevolence. "I perceive it must just stand ar[oun]d for a while, and take the benefit of your excellent industries in behalf of it," Carlyle wrote on 20 December. On his return he expected that "the thing will be about mature. . . . So that if we had Dickens's sanction (which I hope he will soon return to give us) we may at once knit up that [torn?] sleeve." On 28 December, Forster was appointed Secretary of the Lunacy Commission, which brought congratulations from Carlyle on 2 January 1856, along with the announcement that he had received from "three different hands (unsolicited) the sum of £9.2 for the old Lowes, which shall be paid on my arrival." He wrote to Bridges, the actuary, "to expedite the requisite settlement of date, and let us be ready to *wind up* shortly after we meet" (F48E18). Carlyle did not anticipate delay from Bridges, the financial adviser he had selected. "I know a tolerable man," he had informed Forster months earlier, "to take accurate knowledge of the old women's ages, long annuities etc.; and tell us what exact sum (say £400 low but a rough guess) will be rigorously needed for them and us."

Carlyle returned to London around mid-January 1856 and wanted, he told Forster on 22 January, to terminate the Memorial with a meeting at the Athenaeum, "where we shall then be able both to settle at once what is to be done with the cash gathered, and how and at what date or by what stages we are to withdraw ourselves from the gaze of a discovering public,—the brooding of which fill me (I must say) with more and more reverence the longer I live." English generosity had revived Carlyle's faltering faith in nation and allayed his angst about failure. But unexpected delays and Ann Elizabeth's relentlessness exasperated Carlyle, causing him to regret having undertaken the benevolence. "The faithless Actuary Bridges, for the second time, does not keep his promise," he complained to Forster on 27 January; "he was to send me, or bring me, on Friday evg last, his answers to my three simple questions, that I might be ready for you next night." Carlyle had asked Bridges to determine the women's exact age and to establish annuities appropriate to their expected longevity. With little progress by 4 February, Carlyle's impatience peaked.

Bridges was a bad bargain, leaving Carlyle, with Dickens's help, to shop around for another actuary. The goal was to end the project by 12 March. On 6 March, Carlyle wrote to Forster: "Next Monday,—I need not remind so vigilant a man,—is the ultimatum of the Lowe Subscription. I have sent various tolerable sums since we last met." They had hoped to raise about £400, but felt that the nearly £300 raised "will do perfectly well." Carlyle wondered whether Forster had secured another insurance company, "for the old Dames will be upon me again directly after the 12th." Although anxious to "terminate handsomely and soon!" he failed to see Forster at the Athenaeum, then again at the London Library Committee. On 5 April Ann Lowe, wanting their immediate hardship relieved, requested a single annuity of £300. "It seems to me this whim of hers, if she produce it, ought to be mildly *rejected.* . . . But the grand point is that we get, now at last, *done* with her affair. . . . We shall then have nothing but the Times Advertisement to be despatched, and wash our hands of the business to all eternity."

Carlyle's numerous references to handwashing, to tidy up things, but troping nonetheless on the Dickensian signature of de-contamination, disclose his anxiety to sanitize himself against philanthropic contagion. Carlyle was his usual indecisive self over the *idea* and the *thing*, attracted to the idea of benevolence more than benevolence itself. Ann Lowe's biweekly appeals kept him dispassionately involved. "I am sensible of your wish to promote our welfare," she wrote on 9 April, "and sincerely thank you for all trouble you have taken to serve us." She fretted that their "principal support" was a mere £10.16.7. On 12 April, Carlyle felt "*perfectly indubitable*, that the Lowe business will end on Saturday the 19th," then "we will with pleasure be over to rejoice and dine, with you upon that blessed event." They vowed Lenten-like austerity until relieved of this albatross "hanging round one's neck." Only then will they " 'dine' to any purpose" (F48E18). On 18 April, Carlyle, Dickens, and Forster scheduled another meeting at the Athenaeum for 24 April to "correct the Proof Advertisement of Names. . . . We will come and dine and be joyful;—but absolutely we must not till this sorrowful business is finished." Dickens's 8 February letter on behalf of all three sponsors officially terminated the subscription drive. Published in *The Times* on 11 February, it summarized their activities, noted the amounts raised at the time (£250), identified Mauritius Lowe as the "benevolent painter" who discovered Turner, remained silent on Ruskin's gift memorializing Turner, emphasized the voluntary nature of the initiative and how monies were derived ("like the dew on Gideon's fleece of this, our day," Dickens's analogy reads in an early draft of the letter), and promised that the books will be closed on 12 March, after which a full disclosure (a list of contributors and amounts donated) will be published in *The Times* (*Letters of Dickens* 8: 729).

True to his word, Dickens, on 23 April, drew up and subsequently published the subscription list in the 12 May issue of *The Times*. Discounting expenses, approximately £304 was raised and invested in a Government Annuity "for the joint lives of Miss Lowe and her sister." The donor list remains a curiosity of Victorian social politics. It reveals a number of 10s contributions, and a few of £1, generous amounts, indeed. Consistent with mid-nineteenth-century benevolence, women were the most charitable—Miss Coutts (whose name nor donation, not surprisingly, does not show up in the list of donors) and Lady Ashburton each contributed £20—and might have given more had the enterprise been more inclusive of women. Several individuals gave £10, among them Ruskin (who quite likely contributed more), Russell Sturgis, Lord Overstone (Samuel Jones Loyd), famous banker and one of England's richest men, and Robert Slaney, from Lichfield, who was active on the 1840 Sanitary Committee, was a strong advocate for public health reform, and lamented the slow pace of Chadwick's *Sanitary Report*. Carlyle, Dickens, Forster, Macaulay, FitzGerald, Lord Shaftesbury, and Lord Goderich contributed £5 each, as did Emily Baring. There was also a generous Indian connection: two British military officers stationed in Madras gave gifts of £10 and £5. Other Victorian notables were equally generous. Erasmus Darwin gave £1.1s, and Tennyson £1. Averse to the New Poor Law, though not the poor, Bulwer Lytton apparently did not contribute, nor did Kingsley, an active crusader for sanitary reform and against the spread of infectious disease among the poor living in overcrowded city dwelling. The project was highly politicized. Exeter-Hall sympathizers, like John Stuart Mill, for whom spontaneous voluntary acts, partisan politics notwithstanding, evince personal development and social liberalism, are not listed among the donors, indicating that support for the Memorial meant endorsement of Carlyle's social politics. In fact, one anonymous donor of 10s called himself "A Carlylist," another from Manchester donating 10s identified himself as a friend of Carlyle's, and a third who gave £5 did so on behalf of "Germanica." Indeed, "the citizenship of entitlement and the citizenship of contribution did not exist in isolation from each other," but were part of "the same 'complex intermixture' " (Finlayson 12–13).

Not surprisingly, the benevolence discloses no participation from known women suffragists such as Isabel Knox, Frances Power Cobb, Anna Jameson, Barbara Bodichon, Emily Davies, Bessie Parkes, and Lady Pauline Trevelyan. Not that Carlyle craved their participation, considering his antagonism to the machinery of public philanthropy, with such bizarre expenditures as drinking fountains for dogs. No more than nine of the 117 identified donors were women, all of them prompted by their personal and social ties to the framers of the benevolence. The sole exception was the arch-philanthropist, Miss Coutts, whose indiscriminate acts of charity are estimated to have been no less than one million pounds. The Lowes Memorial was to the last an exclusively male patronage in an age where, with Victoria as model, women were at the vanguard of philanthropy, "founding and joining sisterhoods" to aid the indigent (Nightingale 10).[33] What is said of Marcella Boyce easily describes socially conscious Victorian women: "A large and passionate humanity plays about her" (Ward 63).

Dickens's farewell letter, however, was hardly the last word on the Memorial. Carlyle continued to hear from Ann Elizabeth who, on 7 May, complained of exhaustion (could barely climb to the second floor of the house), and pleaded for assistance, for which she had "not money to pay." A week later, on 13 May, she wrote to inquire "when I may receive the benefit of the property," and cited rumors that the matter had long been settled: "The false reports I have heard are dreadful." Mystified that the financial settlement continued to experience unexpected delays, and harassed weekly by the Lowes, Carlyle lamented the benevolence. No longer a "noble Healing Act," it had become an affliction: "I began (in my despair) to feel as if this wd never end at all! What on earth can be the meaning of it?" He was sure the "unfortunate old creatures had *got* their money; and that we (thrice unfortunate) *had* heard the last of them—Or is it they have gone mad?" He suggested to Ann that she consult Coutts's. For not entirely clear reasons, perhaps the death of Ann Elizabeth (c. 1779–1860), Carlyle wrote Forster on 24 January

1860: "We none of us ever heard a whisper from the Old Lady after she got her money tho' she was so diligent before it."

The Lowes Memorial manifests a complex of ideas on Victorian philanthropy. It shows that what mattered most was the identity of the subjects deserving of the public dole. It also demonstrates the way Victorians rallied to support their own. For Carlyle, the Lowes project, like the two Begg Subscriptions, discloses his complex personality—humane yet selective; charitable yet wanting. How much can be made of Carlyle's noninvolvement in an 1857 subscription (sponsored by Thackeray, Dickens, and Forster) to benefit Maguerite Power, the destitute niece of Lady Blessington, Irish novelist, society figure, and founding editor of the *Keepsake* whom the Carlyles knew only socially, is unknown yet puzzling. Robert Buchanan saw in him the rugged Scotchman, the "hard and almost aggressive identity" masking "a kindly man" (795). Indeed, concerning the Lowes Carlyle was generous, but overly discriminate in his generosity, and torn between keeping the benevolence private, all the while attracted to its potential for propaganda, more important, often, than the "simple wish to relieve the suffering or to uplift the benighted" (Prochaska, *Royal Bounty* 67). His efforts disclose indifference to the greater public need, the kind that inspired Lady Pauline Trevelyan's lacemaking initiative among Seaton's poor (1858), Craig Knox's *Victoria Press Lancashire Volume* of poetry (1863) supporting distressed cotton districts, and *English Lyrics* (1865), an anthology to promote a charitable enterprise. Instead, "elitist rather than egalitarian"—the hallmark of most voluntary initiatives (Finlayson 11)—the Lowes Memorial benefited an exclusive pair, who, were it not for the unveiled kinship relations to Samuel Johnson, would have received no such national attention, urgency, nor munificence. Ultimately, the image of the women evolved from that of destitute spinsters rescued from the contagion of Deptford to that of a younger sister and Samuel Johnson's goddaughter, beneficiaries of a legacy Carlyle, Dickens, and Forster fabricated in the consciousness and conscience of charitable Victorians.

NOTES

1. Even Ruskin's generous contributions were a memorial, this to J. M. W. Turner, whose discovery was due to Mauritius Lowe.
2. Carlyle saw John Wilson Croker's edition of *Boswell's Life of Samuel Johnson* (1831) in much the same way critics have come to see Froude's Carlyle. Carlyle held a low estimate of Croker's edition, believing that "The whole business belongs distinctly to the lower ranks of the trivial class." He felt that the work

"missed Johnson's life" and that its greatest disappointment is the absence of a truly historical sense, whereby we can "in the full sense of the term, *understand* [Johnson], his sayings and his doings" ("Boswell's Life of Johnson," *Works* 28: 63–66).

3. In another letter to Lady Ashburton, dated 13 November 1855, Carlyle reported hurrying off to a meeting on the Lowes at the Athenaeum (see 188–89). I am extremely grateful to the staff of both the Victoria and Albert Museum and the Armstrong Browning Library for assistance on the unpublished letters and documents relating to the benevolence, and to the Victoria and Albert Museum for permission to publish the letters. I am also grateful to Aileen Christianson for providing me access to the page-proofs of volume 29, for 1 May to 30 June 1855, of *The Collected Letters of Thomas and Jane Welsh Carlyle.* Volume 29 covers 1854 to June 1855. Volume 30, from July to December 1855, and volume 31, covering perhaps the first half of 1856, are scheduled to appear in 2002 and 2003, respectively. All the Lowes material, Aileen Christianson and Sheila McIntosh inform me, should be completed in volume 31. I am also indebted to Aileen and Sheila for their helpful emendations in the manuscript.

4. But for the short Wilson entry, the Sanders acknowledgment ("the effort to raise money for Miss Lowe, Dr. Samuel Johnson's god-daughter, and for her sister") and Rodger L. Tarr's entry on the *Times* announcement, nowhere in Carlyle scholarship is the Lowes benevolence mentioned.

5. See Finlayson 62. "If philanthropy was ascendant in Georgian Britain, it was triumphant in the reign of Victoria" (Prochaska, *Royal Bounty* 67). According to Norman McCord, "The nineteenth century was probably the classical period of the work of organised charitable societies" (90), and could, says Keith Laybourn, "still lay claim to be one of the most philanthropically oriented of societies." Britain's "charitable contributions was immense and . . . focused upon the need to tackle the problem of poverty and the various crisis points in life that could lead to social and economic decline of the 'respectable' working classes" (129–30).

6. Norris Pope is also silent on Dickens's involvement with the Lowes, so much has the benevolence escaped critical attention. Pope, however, cites a number of charitable acts Dickens undertook on behalf of individuals whose plight approximates the Lowes': providing financial assistance to John Overs, Bertha White, and John Poole; establishing a fund in 1843 to aid the family of the drowned actor Edward Elton; and organizing relief in 1857 for the family of the dead Douglas Jerrold. Feeling that he owed so much to William Hone, editor and infamous blasphemer/parodist, Dickens also sought relief from the Literary Fund for "the Destitute widow and children of the late Mr. Hone. . . . They are very poor, and he was not a common man" (*Letters of Dickens* 3: 366, 373).

7. The Forster Collection, F48E17. Quoted by permission of the Victoria and Albert Museum. References to the Forster Collection will be cited by pressmark. Unless otherwise indicated, all references to the unpublished letters from Carlyle to Forster are from the manuscript F48E17.

8. On Carlyle's overall concerns with issues of health, see Bruce Haley.

9. "Every subscription to a benevolent scheme," Humphry House observes, "was in part an insurance premium against a revolution or an epidemic" (49). In *The Sanitary Evolution of London*, Henry Jephson observes that "Overcrowding and disease mutually act and react upon each other" (qtd. in Welsh 16).

10. I owe this to Aileen Christianson.

11. The account resonates with any number of instances of Victorian disease-bearing women. Reverend Brocklehurst introduces Jane Eyre to a community already infected with pestilence, though he mistakenly thinks it a place of healing, "the troubled pool of Bethesda" (58). He warns the Lowood community to avoid Jane and not "allow the waters to stagnate around her" lest she should "contaminate their purity." Jane is also a potential carrier because both of her parents succumbed to the disease. Brontë engages much of the contemporary debate about sanitation. Published in 1847, *Jane Eyre* historicizes Edwin Chadwick's *Sanitary Report* (1842), and even employs to the letter its recommendations for sanitary reform: improving drainage, water supplies, nutrition, clothing, and reducing overcrowding. Dickens also echoes the Irish Widow in *The Chimes* (1844), which Carlyle reviewed before its publication. For more on this see *The Chimes* 148; see also Oddie 114–15. Kingsley, the "apostle of cleanliness," referred to the Irish Widow in "Who Causes Pestilence?" a sermon delivered to his Eversley congregation in 1848, five years after *Past and Present* (1843) was published and only a year before the cholera epidemic struck Eversley. He placed the myth in Edinburgh and not Liverpool, and forgot the source text, a proclivity of Kingsley's (Kingsley 2: 24). Thanks to Carol Collins for providing me with this source. For Kingsley and cleanliness, see Haley 116.

12. Lady Bulwer Lytton was the wife of a close friend; Delia Bacon "of the mythic Shakespeare" was the American purveyor of the spurious Shakespeare authorship theory ("tragically *quixotic*," Carlyle describes it) whom Emerson introduced to Carlyle; and Lt. James Belial Baillie, true to the Belial part of his name, was Jane Welsh's disgraced cousin described as "a bankrupt dandy living, unmarried, with a woman for the sake of her money." Jane wondered: "It were a curiosity of rascaldom to know how that man lives, and gets his washing done" (*Letters* 15: 71n, 137; see also *Letters* 12: 196 and the *Reminiscences* 49–55, 74–75).

13. Dickens has an impressive history of involvement with numerous charities, among them the Metropolitan Drapers' Association, the Poor Man's Guardian Society, the Birmingham and Midland Institute, the Metropolitan Sanitary Association, the Orphan Working School, the Metropolitan Improvement Association, the Royal Hospital for Incurables, the Hospital for Sick Children, and the Newsvendors' Provident and Benevolent Institution. I owe this to Norris Pope.

14. Mothballed vessels and convict hulks, including Captain Cook's *Discovery*, were moored off Deptford.

15. In June 1875, Matthew Arnold "scraped together money enough" to assist in the publication of a collection of poems by one Charles P. O'Conor, "a working man down at Deptford." Arnold hoped that sales of the collection, which recalled for him Burns's poetry (possessing "real gaiety, tune and pathos . . . but of Burns infinitely less educated"), would help improve the man's depressed economic

condition. For more on this endeavor and the way the collection reflects O'Conor and Deptford alike, see *Letters* 4: 268, 270.

16. On the relationship between the Dickens and Mayhew accounts of London, see F. R. Leavis and Q. D. Leavis 184–86.

17. Deptford's links to the navy and centrality to the African-Caribbean trade contributed immeasurably to "the black presence in the South East London area," which "became established locally at the same time as esteemed members of the local community were building up increasing profits from the slave trade" (Anim-Addo 26, 28). Many transient blacks soon settled in Deptford and were pressed into service in the homes of the wealthy. With such notable residents as Olaudah Equiano and Ignatius Sancho, Deptford became a launching ground for emancipationist activities. William Penn frequented Deptford Quaker Meeting House, and John Wesley, avoiding the politics of abolition in his sermons, preached at Turner's Hall in Deptford. Deptford held other connections to slavery. One of the places Thackeray visited during his first tour of America (1852–53) was a Negro settlement on a cotton plantation in Georgia owned by one Robert Habersham. The plantation, formerly called Lapithlowly, was renamed Deptford (*Letters of Thackeray* 3: 241, n127). Deptford, where he was sold into slavery by his English master, is also memorialized in Equiano's autobiography, *The Life* (1789). Deptford's connection to the criminal element is also recognized in Defoe's *Moll Flanders* (1722). When Moll's life sentence was commuted and she was being transported to Virginia, she described the journey as "riding . . . in *Deptford Reach*" (306), a reference to Deptford as the port of departure for all such penal ships to the colonies.

18. See Collins 538. In the fall of 1842, Dickens arranged for the visiting Longfellow a tour of the slums of London, "the worst haunts of the most dangerous classes," says John Forster, who recalls that one of their companions, Daniel Maclise, soon grew sick of the experience and had to discontinue the excursion (1: 297–98).

19. The zealous Mrs. Jellyby, obsessed with African coffee and the natives of Borioboola-Gha, becomes blind to the misery and suffering around her. Her passion—"the momentous importance of Africa, and the utter insignificance of all other places and things"—caused her to ignore the human wreckage in her home. Esther Summerson observes: "perhaps she was a little unmindful of her home. . . . it is right to begin with the obligations at home. . . . while those are overlooked and neglected, no other duties can possible be substituted for them" (34–45, 61). See Tarr, "The 'Foreign Philanthropy Question' " 275–83. While the twenty-six chartered foreign philanthropic organizations raised over £1 million annually for Africa and the West Indies, only about one-seventh went to support local charities. These foreign efforts, it was believed, impinged upon the livelihood of London's indigent population (Tarr 275–76). The Colonies were vital to England's economic and political muscle. James Macqueen authored no fewer than six essays on "The British Colonies" in *Blackwood's* from February 1830 to August 1833. *Fraser's* also saw an explosion of essays connecting England's stability to the economics of the colonies, especially in issues spanning the years 1830 to 1849.

20. For a study of the Carlyle-Forster relationship, see Nixon.

21. Miss Coutts was easily the most charitable Victorian. There is hardly a nineteenth-century charity untouched by her benevolent hand. In October 1854, Florence Nightingale appealed to her for medical assistance in the Crimea, which raises a number of provocative issues on women and the military, the kinds that Tennyson's *Maud* merely sketches.

22. See, for example, the ways these aspirations are played out in Mrs. Humphry Ward's *Marcella*, the preeminent Lady Bountiful novel.

23. See Prochaska, *Women and Philanthropy*.

24. Carlyle's might have modeled the Memorial after the charitable initiatives on which Dickens and Miss Coutts collaborated to benefit diverse bodies of England's disenfranchised. The two collaborated on the Ragged School movement (1843), and together founded Urania Cottage, a reformatory for women (1846–47). They also joined forces on the Columbia Square project, a working-class housing in Bethnal Green (1852), a working-class housing in Hickman's Folly, adjacent to Jacob's Island (1853), and a home for fallen women in Shepherd's Bush (1855).

25. The editors of *The Collected Letters of Thomas and Jane Welsh Carlyle*, Aileen Christianson and Sheila McIntosh are convinced that the warning should read, "not to flurry these poor old souls out of their old track," of which I am not convinced.

26. A variant of the codicil reads: "to be applied and disposed of by" (*Boswell's Life of Johnson* 4: 402–03). The elder Miss Lowe, Ann Elizabeth, recalled as a toddler sitting on Johnson's knee. Her father and Johnson first became acquainted in early 1779.

27. No such street currently exists in either Deptford, Lewisham, or New Cross. Either the street was destroyed during the many renovations Deptford experienced, or else No. 5 Minerva was a house located on New Cross Street, separating Lewisham to the south from Deptford to the north.

28. According to the *Sanitary Report*, women in the Greenwich section of the city, the South District, lived to about thirty-eight years (Chadwick 321). Of the five city districts, the Deptford region had the highest mortality rate; the lower laboring class was the most vulnerable.

29. Carlyle also was concerned with the social status of Isobel Begg and with how the benevolence might improve it, or worse return her and her daughters to their more customary existence. He suggested to Chambers that she be provided a "better task than sewing clothes at Tranent," unless, that is, "she is *safe* at Tranent, and not unhappy;—rather well off, one may say, as welfare goes in the world. I reckon it one of the best features of this Begg business that your conquest for them is not one that lifts them out of their old state at all; but simply renders soft and light for them a set of conditions they were from the first used to" (*Letters* 14: 236–37), a curious observation, indeed, in light of the Lowes and Carlyle's plan to rehabilitate them.

30. Quoted from the Aurelia Brooks Harlan Collection by permission of the Armstrong Browning Library. Hereafter, all references will be cited as HC.

31. The *Athenaeum*, however, did not object to the appeal made by Walter Savage Landor on behalf of James Defoe, great-grandson to the novelist, which it considered "a solid ground of sympathy," and Landor's gesture "benevolent" (1275). Thanks to Rodger Tarr for providing me this source.

32. Ms. National Library of Scotland (Add. 39954, Vol. 1, f. 325–325v). I am extremely grateful to John Ulrich for bringing this letter to my attention and for providing a copy of it.

33. *The English-woman's Yearbook*, edited by Louisa Hubbard and Miss Coutts, estimates that by 1893 some 500,000 women labored ''continuously and semi-professionally'' in philanthropy (qtd. in Prochaska, *Women and Philanthropy* 224). ''In an age in which women found so many doors closed,'' Prochaska observes, ''they discovered a crack in the doors of the charitable societies'' and ''were increasingly called upon to be agents of social improvement'' (vii, 222).

WORKS CITED

Alderson, David. *Mansex Fine: Religion, Manliness and Imperialism in Nineteenth-Century British Culture.* Manchester: Manchester UP, 1998.

Anim-Addo, Joan. *Longest Journey: A History of Black Lewisham.* London: Deptford Forum, 1995.

Arnold, Matthew. *The Letters of Matthew Arnold.* Ed. Cecil Y. Lang. Vol. 4. Charlottesville: UP of Virginia, 2000.

Boswell's Life of Johnson. 6 vols. Ed. George Birkbeck Hill. Oxford: Clarendon P, 1971.

Brontë, Charlotte. *Jane Eyre.* New York: Norton, 1987.

Buchanan, Robert. ''Wylie's Life of Thomas Carlyle.'' *The Contemporary Review* 39 (1881): 792–803.

Carlyle, Thomas. *The Collected Letters of Thomas and Jane Welsh Carlyle.* Eds. Kenneth J. Fielding, Ian Campbell, Aileen Christianson, David Sorenson, and Sheila McIntosh. 29 vols. Durham: Duke UP, 1970–2001.

———. *Reminiscences.* Eds. K. J. Fielding and Ian Campbell. New York: Oxford UP, 1997.

———. *The Works of Thomas Carlyle.* Centenary Edition. Ed. H. D. Traill. 30 vols. 1896–99; rpt. New York: AMS, 1980.

Chadwick, Edwin. *Report on the Sanitary Conditions of the Labouring Population of Great Britain.* Ed. M. W. Flinn. Edinburgh: Edinburgh UP, 1965.

Collins, Philip. ''Dickens and London.'' *The Victorian City: Images and Realities.* Eds. H. J. Dyos and Michael Wolff. Vol. 2. London: Routledge & Kegan Paul, 1973. 537–57.

Defoe, Daniel. *Moll Flanders.* World's Classic. New York: Oxford UP, 1998.

Dickens, Charles. *Bleak House*. Eds. George Ford and Sylvère Monod. New York: Norton, 1977.

———. *The Chimes. Christmas Books*. New York: Oxford UP, 1954.

———. *The Letters of Charles Dickens*. 10 vols. Eds. Madeline House, Graham Storey, and Kathleen Tillotson. Oxford: The Clarendon P, 1993.

"The Editur of the Times Paper." *The Times* 5 July 1849: 5.

Finlayson, Geoffrey. *Citizen, State, and Social Welfare in Britain, 1830–1990*. New York: Oxford UP, 1994.

Forster, John. *The Life of Charles Dickens*. 2 vols. London: Chapman and Hall, 1899.

Froude, James Anthony. *Thomas Carlyle: A History of the First Forty Years of His Life*. 2 vols. New York: Scribner's, 1882.

Haley, Bruce. *The Healthy Body and Victorian Culture*. Cambridge, Massachusetts: Harvard UP, 1978.

Houghton, Walter. *The Victorian Frame of Mind*. New Haven: Yale UP, 1986.

House, Humphry. *The Dickens World*. London: Oxford UP, 1965.

Kaplan, Fred. *Thomas Carlyle: A Biography*. Ithaca: Cornell UP, 1983.

Kingsley, Charles. *The Sermons*. London: Richard Griffin, 1854.

Laybourn, Keith. *The Evolution of British Social Policy and the Welfare State*. Staffordshire: Keele UP, 1995.

Leavis, F. R. and Q. D. Leavis. *Dickens: The Novelist*. London: Chatto, 1970.

McCord, Norman. "The Poor Law and Philanthropy." *The New Poor Law in the Nineteenth Century*. Ed. Derek Fraser. New York: St. Martin's, 1976. 87–110.

Mayhew, Henry. *London Labour and the London Poor*. 4 vols. London: Frank Cass, 1967.

Nightingale, Florence. *Cassandra Other Selections from Suggestions for Thought*. Ed. Mary Poovey. New York: New York UP, 1992.

———. *Letters from the Crimea*. Ed. Sue M. Goldie. Manchester: Mandolin, 1997.

Nixon, Jude V. " 'Return Alphias': The Forster-Carlyle Unpublished Letters and Re-Tailoring the Sage." *Carlyle Studies Annual* 18 (1998): 83–122.

Oddie, William. *Dickens and Carlyle: The Question of Influence*. London: Centenary, 1972.

"Our Weekly Gossip." *The Athenaeum* 3 Nov. 1855: 1275.

Owen, David. *English Philanthropy, 1660–1960.* Cambridge, Massachusetts: Harvard UP, 1964.

Pope, Norris. *Dickens and Charity.* New York: Columbia UP, 1978.

Porter, Roy. *London: A Social History.* Cambridge, Massachusetts: Harvard UP, 1994.

Prochaska, Frank. *Royal Bounty: The Making of a Welfare Monarchy.* New Haven: Yale UP, 1995.

———. *Women and Philanthropy in Nineteenth-Century England.* Oxford: Clarendon P, 1980.

Samuel, Raphael. "Comers and Goers." *The Victorian City: Images and Realities.* Eds. H. J. Dyos and Michael Wolff. 2 vols. London: Routledge & Kegan Paul, 1973.

Sanders, Charles. "Carlyle's Letters." *Bulletin of the John Rylands University Library of Manchester* 38 (1955): 199–224.

Sheppard, Francis. *London 1808–1870: The Infernal Wen.* Berkeley: U of California P, 1971.

Steele, Jess. *Turning the Tide: The History of Everyday Deptford.* London: Deptford Forum, 1993.

Tarr, Rodger L. *A Bibliography of English Language Articles on Thomas Carlyle: 1900–1965.* Columbia: U of South Carolina P, 1972.

———. "The 'Foreign Philanthropy Question' in *Bleak House*: A Carlylean Influence." *Studies in the Novel* 3.3 (1971): 275–83.

Thackeray, William Makepeace. *The Letters and Private Papers of William Makepeace Thackeray.* 4 vols. Ed. Gordon N. Ray. London: Oxford UP, 1945–46.

Ward, Mrs. Humphry. *Marcella.* New York: Penguin, 1985.

Welsh, Alexander. *The City of Dickens.* Oxford: The Clarendon P, 1971.

Wilson, David A. *Carlyle.* Vol. 5. London: Kegan Paul, 1929.

The Widowhood of Catherine Dickens

Lillian Nayder

This essay examines the cultural and legal significance of widowhood for Victorian women as well as the particular experience of widowhood for Catherine Dickens. It considers the effects of Charles Dickens's death on the wife from whom he separated in 1858, correcting the tendency of Dickens critics and biographers to engage in what Catherine Dickens's friend, the novelist Annie Thomas, termed "the suttee business." Despite the commonly held assumption that her life effectually ended with that of her husband in 1870, if not with their separation twelve years before, Catherine Dickens played a variety of meaningful roles in the nine years between her husband's death and her own, a period in which she enjoyed her improved status as Dickens's widow, strengthened her ties to a number of her children, and sought to move from the margins of her family to its center.

In 1870, the year of Charles Dickens's death, the most famous widow in England was undoubtedly Queen Victoria, the ever-grieving "Widow at Windsor." Victoria's beloved husband, Prince Albert, had died of typhoid fever in 1861, at the age of forty-two. After Albert's death, the queen entered a prolonged period of mourning that extended well beyond the conventional limits set for a widow's grief in the Victorian age.[1] Not until 1866, after an absence of four years, did the queen agree to attend the opening of parliament and exchange her widow's weeds for her robes of state. And even then, she remained silent, having arranged for the Lord Chancellor to read her speech for her (Hardman 101). As early as 1863, many of her subjects judged her self-imposed withdrawal from public life to be excessive and resented her

Dickens Studies Annual, Volume 32, Copyright © 2002 by AMS Press, Inc. All rights reserved.

willingness to abandon her political duties as monarch in order to indulge in her womanly grief. Public opinion was reflected, for example, in a poster that appeared outside Buckingham Palace in March 1864, announcing that "these commanding premises [were] to be let or sold, in consequence of the late occupant's declining business" (qtd. Homans 62).[2]

Historians and critics disagree over the political effects of Victoria's withdrawal into grief in the 1860s. Some argue that the queen's prolonged mourning weakened the authority of the crown by proving that the monarch was expendable; others characterize her withdrawal from public life as an effective political strategy. According to Margaret Homans, the invisibility of the queen may actually have augmented the sense of her power among the English (67), while Adrienne Munich argues that Victoria "staged" her widowhood so as to disarm anxieties about the political authority of a woman newly freed from her husband's control (99).[3] But whether Victoria's excessive mourning showed her political savvy or marked her political incompetence, her widowhood underscored her paradoxical position as a female monarch in a patriarchal culture—as a woman who was "expected . . . to mourn deeply" as a dutiful wife but also "to violate mourning practices and appear on display as usual" as England's queen (Homans 59).

A widow deeply grieved by the death of her husband and withdrawn into private life, Victoria could be seen as an "ordinary woman, subject to ordinary feelings" (Homans 71). Although she held a uniquely privileged position, the queen actively sought to identify with her widowed subjects, particularly those in the working classes. She commiserated with a cottager near Balmoral, whose husband had died soon after Prince Albert and with whom the queen was "thankful to cry," and she responded to the 1862 mining disaster in Hartley by expressing her "tenderest sympathy" for "the poor widows and mothers": "Her own misery makes her feel all the more for them," Victoria explained, speaking of herself in the third person (qtd. Weintraub 313, 312).

Despite this emotional link among women, high and low, the widowhood of Victoria's subjects differed from her own in one especially striking way. With the single exception of the queen, married Englishwomen were legally empowered by widowhood; it restored the rights they had lost when they became wives under English common law, rights that the queen alone retained as a married woman. In her famous 1854 critique of marriage law, entitled *English Laws for Women in the Nineteenth Century,* Caroline Norton bitterly contrasted the legal position of Victoria with that of her female subjects; as Norton observed, the queen was "the one Englishwoman in England whom injury and injustice cannot reach." Due to the "accident of regal birth," Norton argued, Victoria was invested "with sacred and irrevocable rights, in a country where women have no rights," "where the signatures of married women are legally worthless; where they cannot lay claim to the simplest article of personal property,—cannot make a will,—or sign a lease,—and are held to be *non-existent* in law!" (159). Although her tone is less indignant than Norton's, Barbara Leigh Smith Bodichon, writing in the same year, makes the same point: a married queen "is considered by the law as unlike other married women. She can herself purchase land and make leases, receive gifts from her husband, and sue, and be sued alone. She is the only wife in England who has these rights" (Bodichon 6).

Indeed, under the common law doctrine of coverture, all Englishwomen except for a "Queen Regnant" or a "Queen Consort" lost their property rights and their legal identity upon marriage, since husbands and wives were considered "one person," that person being the husband (Bodichon 6, 15). As Sir William Blackstone explained in his *Commentaries on the Laws of England,* the standard work of English jurisprudence, "the very being or legal existence of a woman is suspended, or at least it is incorporated or consolidated into that of the husband, under whose wing, protection and cover she performs everything, and she is therefore called in our law a *feme covert*" (qtd. Holcombe 25). Until it was undermined by two parliamentary acts passed in the second half of Victoria's reign, coverture gave men possession and control of their wives' earnings, their personal property, and any property they might inherit. A wife retained legal possession of whatever "real property" (that is, property in land) she brought to her marriage, since her husband could not dispose of it without her consent. But he was entitled to whatever income she might receive from it. Upon the death of her husband, however, a widow recovered her legal identity and her property rights. Unlike a *feme covert,* she was entitled to enter into legal contracts and to make a will, and was held responsible for her own debts. She lost the protection or "cover" provided by her husband but she was also freed from his control, and regained the legal and financial autonomy to which she had been entitled as a single woman.[4]

As Dagni Bredesen notes, the Victorian widow generated "societal unease" because of her financial autonomy and, more generally, the challenge she posed to "ideas of respectable femininity": "In an era when respectable single women were uniformly expected to be chaste and sexually naive, widows were respectable, single, yet sexually experienced. Similarly, despite the ideal of the subjection of a woman to a man . . . many widows were the heads of their own households. Further, although the notion of the fully privatized domestic sphere was widely approved, when forced by circumstances to support themselves, widows frequently turned the home into a source of income" (222). Victorian stereotypes of the widow, often represented as merry or emasculating, register the perceived threat posed by women liberated from the control of their husbands, possibly enriched by means of their deaths, and suddenly entitled to exercise some of the rights enjoyed by men. During the 1860s, a decade in which members of parliament hotly debated the laws governing married women's property, the figure of the widow assumed added significance—as a woman to whom the rights of the *feme sole* had been restored. Depending on their political sympathies, playwrights, poets, and novelists contrasted the idealized and subservient wife with the domineering widow or questioned such oppositions. In *The Merry Widow,* a play adapted from the French in 1863, Leicester Buckingham does the latter, vindicating the seemingly heartless widow in his final act. Although she appears merry after she learns of her husband's death abroad, her mirth is actually a ruse intended to protect her frail mother-in-law from the knowledge that the man they both love is dead. The widow is rewarded for her loyalty and kindness with the unexpected news that her husband is alive—imprisoned rather than buried—and the play is brought to an end with her joyful swoon.[5]

In her 1873 novel *The Two Widows,* Annie Thomas treats the stereotype of the merry widow with more complexity and ambivalence than does Buckingham. Instead of simply exonerating that figure, Thomas develops a counterpoint between an idealized widow, Mrs. Arthur Waldron, and her vain and callous sister-in-law, the widowed Mrs. George Waldron. After her husband's death, Mrs. Arthur defends the property rights of her son rather than her own and sacrifices her happiness to the memory of her dead husband. By contrast, Mrs. George quickly forgets her husband and looks to her own interests, toying with a host of suitors, whom she subjects to "coquettish caprices" (238). However, Thomas does not simply champion the ideal Mrs. Arthur at the expense of the conniving Mrs. George. Instead, she suggests that the ideal widow is all-too-anxious to "go through a little bit of the suttee business" (128), and justifies the behavior of the scheming widow, at least in part; as Thomas explains it, the widow's will-to-power is best understood as a reaction against the powerlessness of wives. "I really doubt if any woman of five-and-twenty feels anything but sore perplexity and half-repentence when she finds that she has gone into the bondage of a promise to marry," the narrator remarks (248), before explaining that the "feminine victories" won by Mrs. George over her suitors "are not utterly despicable": "When one considers how utterly powerless a woman becomes from the day of her marriage, who can marvel at her struggles to develop the attribute [of power] as fully as she can before she [again] goes into bondage? . . . The woman who has been once married knows that though she may shut her eyes to the fact, the fact remains—the man she is going to marry will be her master" (329).

Whether real-life Victorian women felt liberated or constrained by widowhood depended largely on their marital histories and the circumstances in which they were left. For all her newly-restored rights as a *feme sole,* an unwaged middle-class widow could find herself without any financial support or provided with an annuity too small for her to live in a respectable manner. Much depended on the terms and restrictions of a husband's will. When a married man died intestate in the Victorian period, his widow was automatically entitled to one third of his estate if the couple had living children, and to one half of his estate if they had none. But a husband who made a will could leave his wife as much—or as little—as he desired. As Leonore Davidoff and Catherine Hall reveal in *Family Fortunes,* nineteenth-century testamentary patterns indicate that, in increasing numbers, men chose to impose restrictions when making their bequests: by leaving their widows a life interest in property rather than the property itself, for example; by allowing them the use of property, but only for a limited time, until their children came of age; or by stipulating that property was to remain in their possession only as long as they remained unmarried (276).

Even before her own husband's death brought the point home to her, Catherine Dickens realized that men often placed heavy restrictions on the property they left to their wives. In the year preceding her husband's death, she read a novel in which just such restrictions provide the central theme: *Only Herself* (1869), written by Annie Thomas, who befriended Catherine Dickens in the 1860s.[6] Thomas's novel hinges on the status of a widow, Mrs. Bruton, whose husband "left every thing to his wife, subject to . . . one condition": "If she married a second time, she was to forfeit every shilling of the wealth with which he had endowed her" (25). Under the guise of protecting his widow from fortune hunters, Mr. Bruton's will is designed to test and control her from beyond the grave. In treating this theme, Thomas's novel is double edged. It identifies Mrs. Bruton as a transgressive woman who "rejoice[s] much in her recently gained power of doing whatever pleased her" (26). But it also criticizes the law that encourages widows to think as Mrs. Bruton does by subordinating them to their husbands and making them accountable for their every move. As Thomas puts it, the widowed Mrs. Bruton "almost purred to herself in her intense satisfaction with . . . every thing . . . that left her free. Free to move to the right, without explaining why she didn't move to the left. Free to welcome whom she pleased, and to turn the cold shoulder on whom she pleased. Free, in fact, to live any life she liked" (25).

Unlike such fictional widows as Mrs. Bruton, Catherine Dickens was not discouraged from remarrying by the terms of her husband's will; the very possibility of Catherine's remarrying after his death never seems to have occurred to Charles Dickens. Nonetheless, he imposed substantial limitations on the property he left to Catherine, using his will to maintain the restrictions that had been placed on her at the time of their marital separation in 1858.

Born in Edinburgh in 1815, Catherine Hogarth married Charles Dickens in April 1836, shortly before the first monthly number of *The Pickwick Papers* appeared. They lived together until May 1858, when Catherine was pressured to leave her home and her children by her husband, who had become infatuated with the eighteen-year-old actress Ellen Ternan.[7] Anxious to avoid a public scandal, Charles and Catherine Dickens arranged the terms of their separation by means of a deed rather than a court hearing. Accompanied by her eldest son, Charley, Catherine moved into her own home at 70 Gloucester Crescent, Regent's Park, while her unmarried sister, Georgina Hogarth, remained with Charles at Gad's Hill Place in Kent, to the chagrin of her own family members. Battling the scandals that ensued and that linked him to his sister-in-law as well as Ellen Ternan, Dickens published various statements in newspapers and periodicals, explaining his separation from Catherine in a way that justified his own behavior and unfairly disparaged hers.

The most notorious of these explanations—the so-called "violated letter"—was published in the *New York Tribune* on 16 August 1858 and quickly reprinted in various English and American newspapers.[8] Here, Dickens asserted that Georgina Hogarth rather than his own wife had devoted herself to their home and their nine living children. "From the age of fifteen," he wrote, "[Georgina] has been their playmate, nurse, instructress, friend, protectress, adviser and companion. In the manly consideration toward Mrs. Dickens which I owe to my wife, I will merely remark of her that the peculiarity of her character has thrown all the children on someone else." Elaborating on what he termed Catherine's "peculiarity," Dickens informed the reading public that she "sometimes labours [under] a mental disorder," "that she felt herself unfit for the life she had to lead as [his] wife," and that she herself had told him that "it would be better for her to go away and live apart" (Pilgrim 8:740).

Although Catherine suffered from postpartum depression after some of her childbirths, there is no evidence to support her husband's claim that she was mentally ill or "disordered." Her own letters as well as the accounts provided by others testify to her sanity, and she was neither dysfunctional nor "unfit." In 1851, suffering from "nerves," she took the water cure at Malvern—but so did Alfred Tennyson, Edward Bulwer Lytton, the Carlyles, George Henry Lewes, Florence Nightingale, and Charles Darwin, all "water patients" in the mid-Victorian period (Oppenheim 136). As Michael Slater has shown, most of Dickens's assertions about his wife in 1858 were simply false, including his allegation of Catherine's "mental disorder."[9] Hence a number of the Dickenses' friends and relations rallied to Catherine's defense, protesting against her husband's misrepresentations. The philanthropist Angela Burdett Coutts, an old friend and associate of Dickens, gradually broke off relations with the novelist, as did a number of other prominent figures. Although she did not know Catherine personally, Elizabeth Barrett Browning found Dickens's treatment of his wife "criminal"; in Barrett Browning's view, Dickens was "us[ing] his genius as a cudgel against . . . the woman he promised to protect tenderly with life and heart—taking advantage of his hold with the public to turn public opinion against her" (qtd. Pilgrim 8:648–49 n. 4). This view was echoed by William Thackeray, Harriet Martineau, Shirley Brooks, and other well-known writers. Yet Catherine herself remained virtually silent on the subject, maintaining what her contemporaries praised as her ladylike dignity. Accepting the deeded promise of "free access" to her children, over whom she had no custody rights under English common law, and agreeing to an annuity of six hundred pounds, Catherine moved into her new home on Gloucester Crescent. Struggling to overcome what she termed her "bitter . . . feelings," and "trust[ing] by God's assistance to be able to resign [her]self to His will" (Pilgrim 8:749),[10] Catherine left her youngest sons and her two grown daughters in the care of her husband and her sister Georgina. In the years that followed their separation, Catherine saw Charles only once, by accident at the theater one night; after 1858, the two never spoke in person again.

Because of the terms of Dickens's will, Catherine's condition did not improve with her husband's death, at least from a financial point of view. Using his will to reinforce the moral distinction he had drawn between Catherine and Georgina Hogarth twelve years before, Dickens left his sister-in-law the sum of eight thousand pounds, to spend or invest as she saw fit; by contrast, he left his wife a life interest in eight thousand pounds, placed in a trust administered by two of their sons, Charley and Henry. At the very moment in which Catherine regained her property rights as a *feme sole* under English common law, her husband curtailed her financial autonomy by keeping the eight thousand pounds out of her reach and by appointing their sons as her trustees. And because Catherine's trust fund was invested in the three percents, she would have to make do with considerably less money as a widow than she had as Dickens's estranged wife, with her annuity reduced to 240 pounds from 600. While Dickens denied Catherine autonomy by the terms of his will, he also berated her for the dependence he helped to ensure: "I desire here simply to record the fact that my wife, since our separation by consent, has been in the receipt from me of an annual income of £600," he wrote in his will, "while all the great charges of a numerous and expensive family have devolved wholly upon myself" (Charles Dickens, "Will" 859). How an unwaged lady such as Catherine was to help pay the "great charges" of their family, Dickens did not pause to explain. Exercising his prerogative as a father, furthermore, and reinforcing the myth of Catherine's incompetence, Dickens appointed Georgina as the guardian of Edward (or "Plorn"), his one underage child in 1870; whether married or widowed, Catherine had no custody rights if her husband chose to withhold them.

After her separation, Catherine claimed that she still loved her husband and she was clearly grief stricken by his death. She allegedly learned that she had been widowed from a poster on the street rather than from a family member, although her daughter Katey travelled from Gad's Hill to London to bring her the news (Panton 150; Storey 137). In August 1870, Catherine described to her Boston acquaintance, Mrs. Francis Alexander, "the great shock" she had "sustained" with her husband's passing, her need for "a change of scene," and the severe illness from which she was only gradually recovering.[11] Yet the loss of Charles Dickens proved to be a gain for his widow, though in a social and psychological rather than an economic sense.

Perhaps most obviously, widowhood freed Catherine from the continuous and cutting criticism implicit in Dickens's decision to live with Georgina instead of herself. She would no longer have to bear with the comparison between her alleged incapacities and the capabilities of an idealized Georgina. Furthermore, she could now speak with detachment of her painful separation, which had become a thing of the past: "I need not tell you," she wrote to Mrs. Alexander, "that unhappily for the last twelve years, I was separated from my late husband."[12] Three years later, at the opening performance of Andrew Halliday's "Heart's Delight"—a dramatic adaptation of *Dombey and Son*—Catherine spoke to the actor William Farren of her husband's "greatness" with a pride undimmed by feelings of rejection and injury.[13]

Dickens's death left Catherine with considerably less money than had been at her disposal since 1858, and with a new pair of male trustees to replace Mark Lemon and Frederick Evans, the two appointed at the time of her separation. But it also had the odd effect of improving her social status; it was considerably more prestigious to be the widow of Charles Dickens than to be his jilted wife. Although she had not been Dickens's companion for more than a decade, Catherine received a message of condolence from the queen, as did the widows of other famous men. "Deepest regret at the sad news of Charles Dickens's death," Victoria telegraphed the new widow from Balmoral ("Mrs. Charles Dickens" 694).

Whereas in years past, Catherine had watched in relative silence while Dickens shaped the public image of his "unfit" wife, she could now oversee and correct those shaping the image of the famous novelist. As Shirley Brooks noted in his diary soon after Dickens's death, Catherine was "resolved not to allow Forster, or any other biographer, to allege that she did not make D. a happy husband, having letters after the birth of her ninth child in which D. writes like a lover" (qtd. Slater 156). Rumor had it that Charley promised to "tell the story [of the separation] himself in *All the Year Round*" if he and his mother were dissatisfied with Forster's account (Pilgrim 1:xvii). Corresponding with John Camden Hotten in July 1870, Catherine requested a copy of his newly published *Charles Dickens: The Story of His Life,* agreeing to identify any errors and "to communicate them to Mr. Hotten," and prepared to monitor the way in which the author represented the novelist's private life.[14] Catherine was no doubt satisfied with Hotten's treatment of her separation, which he declined to discuss at any length, merely mentioning it as "a painful matter, which occasioned a great talk at the time, and led Mr. Dickens's warmest friends to marvel at the course he had thought fit to pursue" (243–44).

Considering her estrangement from Dickens as well as his romantic relationship with Ellen Ternan, it is not surprising that Catherine felt closer to her husband after his death than she had during the twelve years preceding it. She could lay claim to his memory in a way that she had not been able to lay claim to the man himself. Bessie Evans Dickens, the wife of Charley, suggested as much when writing to Charley's brother Alfred of their mother's state of mind in 1870: "Poor dear she is better than I dared to hope she would be, and I am sure that in a little time she will be more settled, and even happier than she has been for years, for she says what is true that she has already lived 12 years of widowhood, and now she feels that there is nobody nearer to him than she is."[15]

Catherine also had the vicarious satisfaction of seeing Charley, her faithful mainstay since 1858, inherit many of her husband's most prized possessions—his books, engravings, and prints—and she took pleasure in quoting from the portion of Dickens's will that included this bequest when writing to her friends. When Charley purchased Gad's Hill Place in 1870, and took up residence there the following year, Catherine's exile from the home of her late husband came to an end. From 1871 to 1878, she spent holidays with her eldest son and his family at what had long been Georgina's residence rather than her own.

At the time of her separation from Dickens, Catherine was also separated from her children, with the exception of the twenty-one-year-old Charley, who chose to join his mother on Gloucester Crescent. In 1858, Frank (14), Alfred (12), and Sydney (11) were away at school, although they soon returned to Gad's Hill Place for their vacation. Walter, seventeen years old, was serving with the 42nd Highlanders in India; Plorn (6), Henry (9), Katey (18) and Mamie (20) were at home. According to the deed of separation, Catherine was given "free access to all or any of her children at all places,"[16] yet this clause was never honored by Dickens, who did what he could to keep mother and children apart. Not only did he forbid the children to see or speak to Catherine's two trustees, Mark Lemon and Frederick Evans, and to Catherine's mother and her sister Helen, her staunchest allies during the marital breakdown. He labelled Catherine an unnatural and unfit mother, and pressured the children to avoid her. "[Catherine] is glad to be rid of [the children], and they are glad to be rid of her," he told Angela Burdett Coutts in August 1858 (Pilgrim 8:632).[17]

Until the publication of Slater's *Dickens and Women* in 1983, critics and biographers proved all-too-willing to accept Dickens's representation of Catherine as an unnatural mother, distant and uninterested in her own children. In Slater's view, Dickens "arraigned" Catherine in this way in order to "present his children as re-enacting his own childhood loss of mother love," suppressing the "mass of evidence . . . that Catherine was a loving mother . . . and that she was loved by her children" (147, 146). Like her husband, Catherine was closer to some of the children than to others, and she delegated many of the responsibilities for their care to her sister, who lived with the family, in part, for that purpose. Nonetheless, Catherine's performance of motherhood clearly fell within the middle-class Victorian norm, and any assessment of the children's feelings for her must take into account the pressure their father placed on them to "rid" themselves of their mother.

In his *Recollections,* Henry Dickens claims that he visited Catherine at Gloucester Crescent with his father's "full knowledge and acquiescence" (19), but his sister Katey provides a very different account of family dynamics during the separation. For nearly two years following the marital breakdown, Katey told her friend Gladys Storey in later life, her father "would scarcely speak to [her] because she visited her mother" (qtd. Parker and Slater 4). In calling at Gloucester Crescent, the children seemed to "reproach" their father, Katey felt, and most of them found it difficult to do so (Storey 219). Both before and after 1858, Dickens's authority in the family was paramount, and until the day of Dickens's death, Charley addressed him as "sir." "My poor mother was afraid of my father," Katey Dickens told Gladys Storey. "Ah! We were . . . very wicked not to take her part; Harry does not take this view, but he was only a boy at the time, and does not realize the grief it was to our mother, after having all her children, to go away and leave us" (Storey 219).

When they separated, Catherine and Charles each had their own allies among the children, one sign that Catherine was not simply the unloving and unloved mother that her husband made her out to be. Among the eldest children, Charley sided with his mother and Mamie with her father, while Katey was painfully divided in her allegiances. Henry clearly identified with his father, and Sydney with his mother, while Alfred claimed to "love them both equally."[18] As this summary suggests, the divisions among the children did not fall into any neat pattern—one correlated to birth order, for example—although the Dickens daughters seem to have had a deeper sense of attachment and obligation to their father than some of their brothers did.

As the terms of his will make clear, Dickens hoped to maintain the distance separating Catherine from the children after his death. To this end, he appointed Georgina rather than Catherine as the guardian of those who were underage, reminded his children of their mother's flaws, and "solemnly enjoin[ed]" them "always to remember how much they owe to . . . Georgina

Hogarth, and never to be wanting in a grateful and affectionate attachment to her'' (Charles Dickens, "Will" 859). Despite Dickens's efforts, however, Catherine managed to strengthen her ties to several of the children during her widowhood, even though her relations with some were still strained.

After Dickens's death, Catherine remained at 70 Gloucester Crescent while Mamie and Georgina found a house together near London's Hyde Park. Charley had established his own household in 1861, when he married Bessie Evans, but their eldest daughter Mary often visited her widowed grandmother and appears with Catherine on the 1871 census return for Gloucester Crescent. Henry chose to stay with his aunt and sister rather than with his mother during his breaks from Trinity College, Cambridge, helping to pay their household expenses instead of Catherine's. By contrast, Sydney, a sub-lieutenant in the Navy, lived with his mother during his leaves. From the distance of Melbourne, Australia, Alfred offered financial support to Georgina and Mamie, and confided in them rather than in Catherine. When he married Jessie Devlin in March 1873, Alfred announced the event to Georgina and Mamie but left his mother to learn of it at second hand. "I am hoping to receive by the post another of your dear and welcome letters soon," Catherine wrote to Plorn in May 1873, five years after her youngest son had joined his brother in Australia. "I suppose it will contain the news of Alfred's marriage, which he has *not* informed me of."[19]

Wounded by Alfred's failure to tell her of his marriage, Catherine was also pained by her exclusion from the second wedding of her widowed daughter Katey, who married the artist Carlo Perugini in June 1874. Because Katey's first wedding was organized and hosted by Dickens, Catherine could easily understand why she was left out when their daughter married Charles Collins at Gad's Hill Place in 1860. But history now seemed to be repeating itself, even though Dickens was dead. Katey's 1874 wedding was attended by Georgina, Mamie, brothers Frank and Henry, as well as John Everett Millais, but Catherine was not invited. Neither were the parents of the groom, although Katey and Carlo dined with them before leaving for their honeymoon in Paris (Storey 158; Adrian 176). Charley made a point of inviting his mother rather than his father to his wedding with Bessie Evans, a union of which Charles Dickens strongly disapproved, and celebrated his anniversary by dining at Catherine's home every year.[20] But Katey seemed equally determined to exclude her mother from such occasions, perhaps feeling that she was keeping faith with her father in doing so.

Nonetheless, Katey grew closer to Catherine after Dickens's death, visiting with her on less momentous occasions and trying to make up for what she later described as "lost opportunities" to be kind to her mother (Storey 220). Mamie continued to define herself as her father's daughter and insisted that "[her] love for [her] father has never been touched or approached by any other love" (M. Dickens 2). But she, too, visited Catherine in the 1870s, and both she and Katey nursed their mother through her prolonged, final illness in 1879. Like his sisters, Henry saw more of Catherine during her widowhood than he had during the separation and, unlike Katey, he invited his mother to his wedding in 1876. "I very often see dear Harry," Catherine wrote to Plorn in December 1873, shortly after her closest companion, her sister Helen Roney, moved away. "He is so kind in coming to cheer me in my solitary life."[21]

During her separation from her husband, Catherine was also separated from Georgina, twelve years her junior, as were the other members of the Hogarth family. Casting in her lot with the brother-in-law she adored and whose household she managed in Catherine's absence, Georgina cut herself off from her family, apparently missing the funerals of both her parents in the decade preceding Dickens's death. Estranged from Georgina, Catherine spent much of her time with her sister Helen, eighteen years younger than herself, who moved in across the street on Gloucester Crescent. Widowed in 1868, after only four years of marriage, Helen supported herself and her daughter May by giving singing lessons, and she and Catherine hosted informal concerts at their homes, inviting their circle of musical friends. Sadly for Catherine, Helen moved to Cheltenham in 1873, having accepted a teaching position at the Ladies' College. "I miss her so very much here," Catherine told Plorn that November, having returned to London after three weeks spent at her sister's new home. "However, it would be selfish in me to wish her back to the anxious life she had latterly in London, as her position in Cheltenham is an excellent one."[22]

After Dickens's death, Catherine was reconciled with Georgina, although their relationship never gained much warmth. As Georgina told her American friend Annie Fields in 1872, "[Catherine] comes to dine with us, and we go to her, from time to time. I cannot say we get much pleasure out of it, but it is better it should be so."[23] In effect, the two sisters learned to tolerate one another's company while remaining aware of their differences and what each saw as the other's flaws. The more outspoken critic of the two, Georgina continued to promote the idea of Catherine's "peculiarity," alleging that her sister lacked feeling for the children. For example, Georgina asserted that Catherine too readily overcame her grief over the death of Sydney Dickens in 1872. However, it is clear from Catherine's own letters that she felt Sydney's loss all-too-keenly—but confided her feelings to those closer to her than Georgina, who made no secret of her hostility toward the impecunious nephew she had lost.[24] When she considered Sydney's financial difficulties and his various "follies," Georgina told Annie Fields, she "fear[ed] we *must* feel that his being taken away early is the most merciful thing that could have happened to him."[25]

If the death of Sydney Dickens was "merciful" in Georgina's view, the death of Sydney's father was a cruel blow. Whereas Catherine had considered herself a widow since 1858, the year of her separation, and felt closer to her *dead* husband than she had been to the living man, Georgina found no such consolation in Dickens's death. Losing the man she served and worshipped, Georgina was forced to leave her home at Gad's Hill and entered a life-long state of mourning and commemoration that her biographer, Arthur Adrian, compares to Queen Victoria's (250). "I do not think the freshness of grief is the hardest to bear," Georgina told Annie Fields nearly three years after Dickens's death. "It is the continuance of living without *the* thing that made life interesting and *worth* living!"[26]

Feeling only the "blank . . . left in life,"[27] Georgina decided to revitalize Dickens by publishing a collection of his letters, an undertaking that occupied her and her niece Mamie in 1878 and 1879. Hoping to produce "a wonderful Book—like a new one from the dear dead Hand,"[28] Georgina collected and heavily edited the letters of Charles Dickens, obscuring the unadmirable features of his life and character. Georgina cut, pasted, and rearranged the contents of Dickens's correspondence so as to safeguard his reputation, suppressing passages in which he disparaged his parents, his brothers, and his sons, for example, and tallied the profits made from his public readings. With each of the three successive editions Georgina prepared for publication, her pruning became more extensive. Needless to say, Georgina omitted all mention of Dickens's marital breakdown from the volumes.[29]

Writing to Frederic Ouvry, the solicitor who administered Dickens's estate, in 1879, Georgina noted that Catherine "has taken the greatest interest and the greatest pleasure" in the forthcoming collection of Dickens's letters, the first two volumes of which were published the day before Catherine's death. "I really think it has been of much . . . comfort to her," Georgina told Ouvry. "Under the sad circumstances [of Catherine's final illness] this has been a real happiness to Mamie and me."[30] Catherine may, indeed, have taken pleasure in Georgina's project, hearing and discussing her husband's letters as she lay ill in bed and revisiting a past from which its most painful episode had been omitted. But she may also have felt that Georgina carried her excisions too far. In her two 1879 volumes, covering 1833 to 1870, Georgina included only 19 out of 140 letters written by Dickens to Catherine, and these were altered so as to obscure the intimacy as well as the difficulties between husband and wife. More significant than any particular omission from Dickens's letters to Catherine is the cumulative effect of Georgina's cuts, which make the relationship between husband and wife seem more distant, as well as less troubled, than it actually was. Deleting passages in which Dickens gossiped with his wife as well as those in which he criticized her, Georgina obscured Catherine's role as the friend and confidante of her husband. It may have been

Catherine's perception of this tendency on Georgina's part that led her to ask her daughter Katey to bring her *complete* collection of letters from Dickens to the British Museum after her death—so that, in Catherine's words, "the world may know that he loved me once" (Storey 164).

Typically, Catherine sought to defend herself by citing her husband's writings rather than producing her own, and she was often praised for suppressing her voice and silently enduring her wrongs. Newspaper articles set her apart from such outspoken "shrew[s]" as Lady Bulwer Lytton, who publicly attacked and rebutted her husband for decades following their separation (Pilgrim 8:648 n. 1). Unfortunately, Catherine's ladylike reticence to defend herself in her own words and tell her side of the story worked to her disadvantage in the twentieth century, encouraging even those sympathetic to her "cause" to treat her as a nonentity and unwittingly promote the logic of coverture—by suggesting that Catherine had no real existence or identity apart from her husband's. Thus, in her section on the Dickenses in *Parallel Lives* (1983), Phyllis Rose asserts that Catherine entered "a kind of living death" in 1858: "Deprived of her children, deprived of any role, Catherine lived for twenty years after the separation" (190). In her one-woman play, *My Dearest Kate* (1983), Jean Elliott presents a more carefully researched portrait of Catherine, and her work is much more effective in winning respect for her subject than Rose's. Nonetheless, Elliott charts Catherine's experiences largely by having her read from the letters her husband wrote to her. This strategy effectively contrasts Catherine's constancy with the mutability of Dickens yet it also suggests that Catherine's life ended with his; once Dickens stops writing, the play draws to its close.[31] Elliott relegates Catherine's widowhood to a single, concluding paragraph in her play, and in so doing, she unintentionally promotes what Annie Thomas terms "the suttee business."[32]

By paying due attention to Catherine's nine years as a widow, we can avoid consigning her to the flames of her husband's funeral pyre and cease to define her simply as "Mrs. Charles Dickens." Although Rose claims that Catherine was "deprived of any role" after she lost Charles Dickens, the fact is that Catherine performed multiple roles during her widowhood, at least some of which she found satisfying: as a sister, mother, and grandmother; as the member of an active social circle; and as the mistress of a female household that included two other women—Sarah Hatfield, her cook, and Matilda Albright, her housemaid.[33]

Furthermore, despite her reticence to defend herself publicly, Catherine *can* be seen to have answered Dickens's allegations against her in a narrative about her family that she herself authored in the late 1870s: her last will and testament, which provides a telling counterpoint to her husband's. Characterized by its inclusiveness rather than by its exclusions, the history Catherine relates in her will positions her at the center of her family, not its margins, and invites comparison with Dickens's representations.

As Davidoff and Hall observe in *Family Fortunes,* female patterns of property distribution within the English middle class differed markedly from male patterns in the Victorian period. Whereas men tended to consolidate their property in their wills, women often did the reverse, leaving a host of small legacies to a wide range of people. "Women tended to leave personal effects and small parcels of money to named individuals, many of them wider kin or friends, a pattern which emphasizes both the dispersion and the personal nature of their property" (276). Unlike her husband, whose estate was worth well over ninety thousand pounds at the time of his death, Catherine did not have much property to leave when she died nine years later. What she *did* possess, however, she distributed as *Family Fortunes* leads us to expect she would—among a wide range of kin and friends, with an emphasis on the personal rather than the financial value of her belongings. Catherine includes not only her relatives and oldest friends in her will but also her servants, past and present. Matilda Butler, Sarah Slade, Emily Brooks, and Maria Bywaters, employed by Catherine at Gloucester Crescent, are all mentioned by name: among the four, Catherine distributes brooches, sleeve studs, a photograph, as well as her sewing machine.

In distributing her property widely, Catherine acted as a typical woman of the Victorian middle class but also as an individual wife and mother who had been exiled from her family, who was anxious to defend her kinship ties, and who had found her husband's will particularly hurtful. In dispersing her property as she did, Catherine declined to use her will as Charles Dickens used his: to discriminate among survivors and pass explicit judgments upon them. In his will, Dickens divides most of his estate equally among his children, with two exceptions—he provides an extra one thousand pound legacy to his unmarried daughter, Mamie, as well as an annuity of three hundred pounds as long as she remains single; and he privileges his eldest son, Charley, by leaving him his library, his engravings and prints, his share and interest in the journal *All the Year Round,* and a number of personal and commemorative objects. However, the clearest distinction drawn in Dickens's will, as we have seen, is that between the beloved Georgina, given a legacy of 8000 pounds, and the burdensome Catherine, left a life interest on a trust in that amount.

Insofar as Catherine offers a commentary on *her* heirs, she does so implicitly, by leaving Georgina considerably fewer belongings than their sister Helen and nothing that has any association with the Hogarth name; Georgina has lost her claim to it, Catherine suggests. Together, Helen, their brother William Hogarth, and Helen's daughter May, inherit all the items significant to the Hogarth family—Helen receives the bracelet made from "the hair of [their] sister Mary," an 1837 sketch of Mary, their mother's prayer book, and a locket containing a photograph of their father; Catherine leaves Mary's album to her brother William and gives her niece May a gold brooch with the hair of her Hogarth grandparents (Catherine Dickens, "Last Will").

Catherine strives for equity—and feeling—in making her bequests to her direct descendents. Whereas her husband names only two of his children in his will, referring to the others as a group, Catherine makes a point of naming each of her surviving children and leaving objects with sentimental value to all of them, whom she lists according to their birth order; next come the spouses of her children, each named, and then her grandchildren. Her will, unlike that of her husband, is designed to demonstrate her family connections and acknowledge her personal attachments. At the same time, Catherine describes the origins of many of the items she bequeaths, leaving her heirs a sense of family history as well as the objects themselves and reinforcing the ties that exist among them, whatever their far-flung travels: "to my grandson Charles Walter Dickens[,] the bronze inkstand . . . brought me from Rome by his Uncle Sydney[;] the Ivory Elephant with Houdah sent me by his Uncle Walter. . . . To my Granddaughter Mary Angela Dickens[,] the Japanese Cabinet brought to me by her father from Japan" (Catherine Dickens, "Last Will"). With several of her sons "banished" to the reaches of the Empire by their father (Tomalin 185), Catherine distributes the Eastern curios they brought or sent to her among a new and more home-bound generation, positioning herself at a center to which some of her children could not return.[34] Having experienced her own form of exile, fated to go virtually unmentioned in the memoirs written by Mamie and Henry, and underrepresented in Georgina's editions of Dickens's letters, Catherine uses her bequests to position her descendants and also herself in a nexus of family relations. Representing herself as a Hogarth daughter, sister, and aunt, and as the loving mother and grandmother of the Dickenses, Catherine reminds her relations of their ties to the woman her husband wished to forget.

NOTES

I would like to thank Mark Charles Dickens for granting me permission to quote from the unpublished letters of Catherine Dickens and from the Ouvry papers. I am grateful to the following libraries and archives for allowing me to draw on material in their collections: Beinecke Rare Book and Manuscript Library, Yale University; Dartmouth College Library; Dickens House Museum; Fales Library, New York University; Rare Book Department, Free Library of Philadelphia; Huntington Library; Leeper Library, Trinity College, University of Melbourne; and Department of Rare Books and Special Collections, University of Rochester Library.

1. "The regulation period for a widow's mourning is two years," a writer explained in *Manners and Rules of Good Society* (1888): "Crape should be worn for one year and nine months . . . [and] during the last three months black without crape should be worn. . . . A widow is not expected to enter into society under twelve months, and during that time she should neither accept invitations nor issue them" (qtd. Mitchell 163).

2. The past decade has seen a boom in scholarship devoted to Queen Victoria, her cultural significance, and the meaning of her widowhood; see, for example, Munich's *Queen Victoria's Secrets,* Homans's *Royal Representations,* and *Remaking Queen Victoria,* a collection coedited by Munich and Homans. In *Becoming Victoria,* Vallone examines Victoria's girlhood.

3. As Munich observes, "had Victoria revived her early self-presentation as a single, unattached, autonomous queen, she would disrupt Victorian gender conventions. . . . What she provided by invoking a ghostly Albert—still there albeit marmoreal—was a husband, a ruler of the queen, someone who kept the woman—and the nation—in line" (96).

4. During Victoria's reign, the legal inequities affecting married women under English common law were gradually eliminated. With passage of the first Married Women's Property Act in 1870, wives were given control of their own earnings and certain types of investments and inherited property. The Married Women's Property Act of 1882 granted wives the same property rights enjoyed by unmarried women. As Mary Lyndon Shanley writes, "Passage of the Married Women's Property Act of 1882 was arguably the single most important change in the legal status of women in the nineteenth century. . . . In enabling married women to act as independent legal personages, it not only gave them the legal capacity to act as autonomous economic agents, but struck a blow at the whole notion of coverture and the necessary subordination of a woman's will to that of her husband" (103). For discussions of the legal reform of married women's property rights in the Victorian period, see Holcombe and Shanley.

5. Buckingham based his two-act play on *Jeanne qui pleure, et Jeanne qui rit.* For a description of its 1863 performance at the St. James's Theater, see Morley, 241–42.

6. Annie Thomas was known in private life as Mrs. Pender Cudlip. She and Catherine Dickens exchanged letters referring to Thomas's novels, in which Catherine was "*very much* interested" (autograph letter signed [ALS] to Mrs. Cudlip, 27 July 1872; Fales Library, New York University). Catherine was the godmother of Mrs. Cudlip's eldest child, Pender Gerald, born in September 1869.

7. For a detailed and compelling analysis of Dickens's relationship with Ellen Ternan, see Tomalin.

8. Dickens claimed that he never intended this letter, addressed to Arthur Smith, to be published, but a host of critics have disputed that claim. "You have not only my full permission to show this, but I beg you to show, to any one who wishes to do me right, or to any one who may have been misled into doing me wrong," Dickens told Smith in the letter (Pilgrim 8:568).

9. See Slater's two excellent chapters on Catherine in *Dickens and Women.* As Slater argues, Dickens created his "own 'plot' for the story of the marriage," one

generally accepted by Dickens critics and biographers, despite its self-serving distortion of Catherine as a "marital incubus" (114).

10. Here, Catherine is quoted by her maternal aunt, Helen Thomson, in a letter of [30] August 1858 to Mrs. Stark.

11. ALS to Mrs. [Francis] Alexander, 22 August 1870; Department of Rare Books and Special Collections, University of Rochester Library.

12. Ibid.

13. "Mrs. Dickens was greatly moved and the tears were falling," Farren recounted. "During the intervals she told me of the greatness of her husband, and one could see how great was her pride in him." See "A Dickens Memory," Farren's 1928 Letter to the Editor of the *Daily Mail*, written in response to Roberts's *This Side Idolatry* (1928), perceived by many as an unjust attack on Dickens's moral character.

14. ALS to J. Camden Hotten, 15 July 1870; Dartmouth College Library.

15. Alfred Dickens quotes Bessie Dickens in a letter (ALS) to Mr. [G. W.] Rusden, 11 August 1870; Leeper Library, Trinity College, University of Melbourne.

16. Deed of separation (draft); Ouvry Papers, Dickens House.

17. As Slater notes, Dickens's hostility towards Catherine intensified during the summer of 1858, perhaps because he suspected that she was helping to spread rumors about his liaison with Ellen Ternan (151–52).

18. ALS to Mr. [G. W.] Rusden, 11 August 1870; Leeper Library, Trinity College, University of Melbourne.

19. ALS to "Plorn" [Edward Bulwer Lytton Dickens], 6 May 1873; typescript, Beinecke Rare Book and Manuscript Library, Yale University.

20. Furious with Bessie's father Frederick for refusing to publish his *Household Words* statement about his separation from Catherine in *Punch*, his anger exacerbated by his sense that Evans (one of Catherine's two trustees) was his wife's advocate, Dickens broke with his publishers in 1858. He stipulated that his children were not to socialize with Evans or his family when he arranged the terms of his separation. ("I absolutely prohibit [the children's] ever being taken to Mr. Evans's house," Dickens told Charley in July 1858 [Pilgrim 8:603].) Charley's marriage to Bessie was thus a clear affront to Dickens.

21. Catherine Dickens to "Plorn" [Edward Bulwer Lytton Dickens], 16 December 1873; typescript, Dickens House.

22. ALS to "Plorn" [Edward Bulwer Lytton Dickens], 18 November 1873; Rare Book Department, Free Library of Philadelphia.

23. ALS to Mrs. [Annie] Fields, 18 June 1872; Huntington Library (qtd. Adrian 172).

24. "I am a little better than when I saw you," Catherine wrote to Mrs. Cudlip in June 1872, two months after Sydney's death, "but I need not tell you I am very miserable and depressed" (ALS to Mrs. Cudlip, 29 June 1872; Rare Book Department, Free Library of Philadelphia). "I am going shortly down to Gad's Hill, and I am looking forward to the change," Catherine informed her friend Mrs. Chester in July, thanking her for her sympathy. "I need not tell you how depressed and ill I feel" (ALS to Mrs. Chester, 27 July 1872; Rare Book Department, Free Library of Philadelphia).

25. ALS to Mrs. [Annie] Fields, 18 June 1872; Huntington Library (qtd. Adrian 171).

26. ALS to Mrs. [Annie] Fields, 21 February 1873; Huntington Library (qtd. Adrian 199).
27. ALS to Mrs. [Annie] Fields, 29 September 1870; Huntington Library (qtd. Adrian 161).
28. ALS to Mrs. [Annie] Fields, 11 August 1878; Huntington Library (qtd. Adrian 208).
29. The latest letter to Catherine that Georgina includes in her editions is dated 5 May 1856; after that date, Catherine simply disappears. For discussions of Georgina Hogarth's editorial practices and aims in *The Letters of Charles Dickens,* see the Pilgrim *Letters* (1:ix-xi); and Adrian (pp. 206–25). Adrian concedes that Georgina's "policy amounted, virtually, to canonization" yet he justifies her decision to use "comparatively little of Dickens's correspondence to his wife," claiming that "in writing to his spouse [Dickens] had seldom appeared as an Inimitable" (223, 221). Adrian blames this "sad fact" on the alleged "shortcomings" and "inadequacy" of Catherine rather than on Dickens's own qualities or the character of married life (24, 25). Unlike Adrian, Slater finds many of Dickens's letters to Catherine "highly entertaining": "Their joyous spontaneity of comic description may be contrasted with the determined jocularity or elaborate facetiousness so often characteristic of his letters to his friends" (110).
30. ALS to Mr. [Frederic] Ouvry, 14 November [1879]; Ouvry Papers, Dickens House.
31. For the performances and playbills of *My Dearest Kate,* Elliott used the stage and pen name "Ellie Dickens." I am grateful to her for providing me with a copy of the unpublished script.
32. Norman Holland valorizes what he imagines as Catherine's self-immolation in *Widow of Charles Dickens* (1953), a one-act play that compresses her widowhood into the single day following Dickens's death and represents the widow nobly sacrificing herself to her husband's memory and greatness. "Oh, my dear, I have every reason to be grateful," Catherine tells her daughter Katey after meeting Ellen Ternan at Gad's Hill. "Better twenty-two years with Charles Dickens than the happiest lifetime with any other man. . . . His greatness of spirit transcends the littleness of our loves" (18).
33. Catherine Dickens's servants are so listed on the 1871 census return for Gloucester Crescent. In her will, Catherine includes bequests to her "late faithful servant Sarah now the wife of Benjamin Slade" and her "late servant Matilda now the wife of William Butler." Catherine's letters to her housemaid reveal that Matilda married William Butler in 1876. By 1878, Catherine's cook had married as well. Matilda and Sarah were replaced by Emily Brooks and Maria Bywaters in Catherine's household.
34. Catherine was grieved by her husband's decision to send four of their children to the colonies to "begin the world"—Walter and Frank to India, Alfred and Plorn to Australia. Walter died in India at the end of 1863 and Plorn never returned to England. After Alfred left the country in 1865, Catherine never saw him again. As Tomalin notes, by the fall of 1868, when Plorn was "packed off" to Australia by his father, "Gad's Hill was . . . entirely free of boys": "Catherine

Dickens was not consulted on the fate of her youngest any more than that of the others'' (185).

WORKS CITED

Adrian, Arthur A. *Georgina Hogarth and the Dickens Circle.* London: Oxford UP, 1957.

Bodichon, Barbara Leigh Smith. *A Brief Summary, in Plain Language, of the Most Important Laws of England Concerning Women.* 1854; rpt. with intro. Marie Mulvey Roberts. In *The Disempowered: Women and the Law.* Eds. Marie Mulvey Roberts and Tamae Mizuta. London: Routledge/Thoemmes Press, 1993.

Bredesen, Dagni. "The 'Widdy's' Empire: Queen Victoria as Widow in Kipling's Soldier Stories and in the *Barrack-Room Ballads.*" In *Remaking Queen Victoria.* Eds. Margaret Homans and Adrienne Munich. Cambridge: Cambridge UP, 1997. 219–32.

Davidoff, Leonore, and Catherine Hall. *Family Fortunes: Men and Women of the English Middle Class, 1780–1850.* 1987; rpt., Chicago: U of Chicago P, 1991.

Dickens, Catherine. "Last Will and Testament." 31 January 1878. Typescript. Dickens House.

Dickens, Charles. *The Letters of Charles Dickens,* Pilgrim Edition. Eds. Madeline House, Graham Storey, and Kathleen Tillotson. 12 vols. Oxford: Clarendon Press, 1965–2002.

———. "The Will of Charles Dickens." In John Forster, *The Life of Charles Dickens.* Ed. J. W. T. Ley. New York: Doubleday, Doran and Co., 1928. Appendix. 857–60.

Dickens, Henry. *The Recollections of Sir Henry Dickens, K. C.* London: William Heinemann, 1934.

Dickens, Mamie. *My Father as I Recall Him.* New York: E. P. Dutton, 1898.

[Elliott, Jean]. "My Dearest Kate: The Marriage of Mrs. Charles Dickens." Typescript. [1983].

Farren, William. "A Dickens Memory: To the Editor of 'The Daily Mail.' " *Daily Mail,* 12 September 1928.

Hardman, William. *The Hardman Papers: A Further Selection (1865–1868) from the Letters and Memoirs of Sir William Hardman.* Ed. S. M. Ellis. London: Constable, 1930.

Holcombe, Lee. *Wives and Property: Reform of the Married Women's Property Law in Nineteenth-Century England.* Toronto: U of Toronto P, 1983.

Holland, Norman. *Widow of Charles Dickens: A Play in One Act.* London: Samuel French, 1953.

Homans, Margaret. *Royal Representations: Queen Victoria and British Culture, 1837–1876.* Chicago: U of Chicago P, 1998.

Homans, Margaret, and Adrienne Munich, eds. *Remaking Queen Victoria.* Cambridge: Cambridge UP, 1997.

[Hotten, John Camden]. *Charles Dickens: The Story of His Life.* London: John Camden Hotten, [1870].

Mitchell, Sally. *Daily Life in Victorian England.* Westport, CT: Greenwood, 1996.

Morley, Henry. *The Journal of a London Playgoer.* 2nd ed. 1891; rpt. with intro. Michael R. Booth. Leicester: Leicester UP, 1974.

"Mrs. Charles Dickens." *Athenaeum* (29 November 1879): 694.

Munich, Adrienne. *Queen Victoria's Secrets.* New York: Columbia UP, 1996.

Norton, Caroline. *English Laws for Women in the Nineteenth Century.* 1854; rpt. with intro. Marie Mulvey Roberts. In *The Disempowered: Women and the Law.* Eds. Marie Mulvey Roberts and Tamae Mizuta. London: Routledge/Thoemmes Press, 1993.

Oppenheim, Janet. *"Shattered Nerves": Doctors, Patients, and Depression in Victorian England.* Oxford: Oxford UP, 1991.

[Panton, Jane Ellen]. *Leaves from a Life.* New York: Brentanos, 1908.

Parker, David and Michael Slater. "The Gladys Storey Papers." *Dickensian* 76 (Spring 1980): 3–16.

Roberts, C. E. Bechhofer. *This Side Idolatry.* Indianapolis: Bobbs-Merrill, 1928.

Rose, Phyllis. *Parallel Lives: Five Victorian Marriages.* 1983; rpt., New York: Vintage, 1984.

Shanley, Mary Lyndon. *Feminism, Marriage, and the Law in Victorian England.* Princeton, NJ: Princeton UP, 1989.

Slater, Michael. *Dickens and Women.* 1983; rpt., London: J. M. Dent, 1986.

Storey, Gladys. *Dickens and Daughter.* London: Frederick Muller, 1939.

Thomas, Annie. *Only Herself.* New York: Harper & Brothers, [1870].

———. *The Two Widows: A Novel.* New Edition. London: Chapman and Hall, 1875.

Tomalin, Claire. *The Invisible Woman: The Story of Nelly Ternan and Charles Dickens.* New York: Alfred A. Knopf, 1991.

Vallone, Lynne. *Becoming Victoria.* New Haven, CT: Yale UP, 2001.

Weintraub, Stanley. *Victoria: An Intimate Biography.* New York: E. P. Dutton, 1987.

Impounding the Future: Some Uses of the Present Tense in Dickens and Collins

Susan Lynn Beckwith and John R. Reed

Both Charles Dickens and Wilkie Collins make interesting use of present-tense narration in their fiction. Collins imbeds a present-tense text within the main narrative of The Woman in White, *and Dickens alternates between present- and past-tense narration in* The Mystery of Edwin Drood. *Collins exploits the immediacy of the present tense in the conventional mode of the diary, but Dickens more experimentally uses a nondiegetic present-and-past-tense narrator. Both writers seek to create anxiety about the future in their readers while still implying a providential design at work in human affairs. Both Collins and Dickens use present-tense narration for enhancing suspense and increasing narrative authority through the withholding of information about the future, but Dickens is more inventive, using a single narrator who moves between* history *and* discourse *and employing a shifting focalization that includes the narrator.*

The present tense in fiction was not new when Charles Dickens and Wilkie Collins came to make use of it. *Clarissa* and other diary and epistolary novels had exploited the mode long before. Such novels gained the advantage, through present tense, of making the events of their narratives appear immediate.[1] Moreover, by restricting the narrative voice or voices to the present, there could be little chance for a premature revelation of what was to occur in the future of the narrative. Aside from these modes of present tense, the traditional novel did make use of present tense in third-person narratives. As

Dickens Studies Annual, Volume 32, Copyright © 2002 by AMS Press, Inc. All rights reserved.

Christine Brooke-Rose points out, however, "in nineteenth-century fiction, brief passages in the historic present are used for vivid scenes before safe returns to the past, and the present tense is favoured for universalizing moral or social comments from the author" (12).[2] Dickens and Collins in their use of the present tense anticipate experiments with tense in the twentieth century, including Modernist and *nouveau roman* fiction. But whereas twentieth-century narratives exploiting present tense are chiefly concerned to liberate the narrative from the tyranny of the narrator, as in the fiction of Alain Robbe-Grillet, Dickens and Collins used the device to strengthen the narrative voice's power by taking command of the future and withholding its secrets from the reader.

In what follows, we shall examine first how Collins and especially Dickens use present-tense narration in a way that violates recent thinking about "historical" narration and, how in doing so, they increase authorial control. Collins employs the traditional device of a present-tense text embedded in an otherwise past-tense narrative, but Dickens is more innovative. In fact, Christian Paul Casparis, one of a few critics to deal extensively with present-tense narration, credits Dickens with being the first novelist "to use the Present tense in a structured manner on a large scale" (62). Our discussion of Collins's and Dickens's use of present tense will require brief preliminary discussions of the role of tense in narration and of the providential esthetic of nineteenth-century literature.

*   *   *

In *Problems in General Linguistics*, Emile Benveniste drew a helpful distinction between two planes of utterance, that of *history* and that of *discourse*. *History* is delimited, in terms of tense, to three possibilities—the aorist (simple past), the imperfect, and the pluperfect. It excludes everything "autobiographical," especially the present tense (206–07). By contrast, *discourse* is free to use all tenses except the aorist (209). Benveniste defines present tense as " 'the time at which one is *speaking*.' This is the eternally 'present' moment, although it never relates to the same events of an 'objective' chronology because it is determined for each speaker by each of the instances of discourse related to it. Linguistic time is *self-referential*. Ultimately, human temporality with all its linguistic apparatus reveals the subjectivity inherent in the very using of language" (227). In associating *discourse* with subjectivity and language with the possibility of subjectivity, Benveniste seems to reinforce the separation of *history*, the narration of past events, and *discourse*, the more broadly conceived plane of language use. We shall argue, however, that it is precisely across the boundaries of *history* and *discourse* that Collins and Dickens achieve some remarkable effects, effects that, in our own day might be most closely identified with cinema.

Aside from a few writers like Christian Paul Casparis, few narratologists have paid much attention to present-tense narration. Seymour Chatman remarks that "verbal narratives in English are occasionally written in the present tense. But story-time is still usually the past" (83). He also observes that cinema is the medium most clearly associated with real-time narration (84). Shlomith Rimmon-Kenan cites one type of narration that "is simultaneous with the action, e.g. reporting or diary entries," and gives Butor's *La Modification* as an example. Rimmon-Kenan does not pursue this narrative possibility. Most narratologists seem to take for granted the position that Philip J. M. Sturgess, following Gerald Prince's treatment of the subject in *Narratology*, summarizes thus:

> To narrate is also to commit oneself to a tense of narration, with that of the past tense being overwhelmingly the elected mode. Unlike the present tense which has, so to speak, contingency and even the possibility of sudden closure or cancellation built into it, the past tense seems to offer a guarantee of narrativity since it denotes a certainty of temporal duration, extending to whatever (present) temporal vantage point the narrator may be understood to be narrating from. Within such duration, obviously enough, events and situations can be understood to have occurred, people to have lived and perhaps died. In other words the past tense is narrativizable in a way that the present tense does not suggest itself to be. (23)

But it is precisely the possibility of "sudden closure or cancellation," among other uncertainties, that makes present tense an attractive method for creating anxieties and exploiting uncertainty. Dorrit Cohn, picking up Gerard Genette's expression "simultaneous narrating," goes on to demonstrate how present-tense narration can avoid two prominent conventions of fictional realism, first-person fictional narration and the interior monologue, by "dissolving the semantic specificity that attends the historical present," thus encouraging the reader "to understand the present as a temporally indeterminate or 'absolute' narrative tense, for which the most appropriate term—highlighting its fiction-specificity—would seem to be 'fictional present' " (106). She explains that whereas the fictional diary or letter may shrink the temporal hiatus to hours or even minutes, simultaneous narration reduces it to zero, "the moment of narration is the moment of experience, the narrating self is the experiencing self" (107). As we shall see, this is the distinction between Collins's and Dickens's use of present-tense narration, the full impact of which does not seem to have registered with their critics.[3] Part of their narrative strategy was determined by what has been called the providential esthetic, which establishes a difference between their use of present-tense narration and its use by such modern authors as John Fowles, J. M. Coetzee, Margaret Atwood, and others.

There now exists a tradition of critical writing that accepts the significance of providence as a narrative ally in literature of the eighteenth and nineteenth century in England.[4] Generally this critical view admits that an assumption of providential design lies behind many of the ultimately positive narrative schemes produced by British novelists. Often the providential design was openly acknowledged. But developments during the nineteenth century, including the theory of evolution propounded by Charles Darwin and others, problematized the notion of providential control and introduced an anxiety about the future that was new in kind. Sir Arthur Conan Doyle remembered the mood of that midcentury time:

> [F]rom my reading and from my studies, I found that the foundations not only of Roman Catholicism but of the whole Christian faith, as presented to me in nineteenth century theology, were so weak that my mind could not build upon them. It is to be remembered that these were the years when Huxley, Tyndall, Darwin, Herbert Spencer and John Stuart Mill were our chief philosophers, and that even the man in the street felt the strong sweeping current of their thought, while to the young student, eager and impressionable, it was overwhelming.
>   (26)

In general, both Dickens and Collins employed the providential pattern to one degree or another in their novels, but the openness of the future also became for them an intriguing counterpoint to the directedness of providential designs. Because present tense is blind to the future, it was an excellent tool for exploiting anxiety about the outcomes of narratives.

*   *   *

Wilkie Collins's utilization of present-tense narration to manipulate his audience is relatively conventional. It is his insertion of Marian Halcombe's narrative in *The Woman in White* (1860) that is most relevant to our exploration of the inventive ways in which Victorian writers play with narrative structure in order to exploit their readers' fears about the future. Marian's voice is remarkably strong; the reader can hardly help but like her, and, in fact, some have even fallen in love with her.[5] However, rather than listening for *what* we hear in her voice, it will be more profitable for us to look at *how* we hear Marian's story. It is in this facet of the narration that we see both Collins's achievement with regard to narrative form and his genius for generating suspense. Peter Thoms points out that early detective fiction "not only reflects authorial exuberance in intricate plotting but also reveals an extensive critique of narrative patterns and the compulsions that generate them"(3). Collins's manipulation of the narrative was quite purposeful and it can be no accident that the revelation of Marian's story takes place under the very controlled circumstances that we shall now detail.

Before dealing specifically with Marian's testimony, it is worthwhile to provide a brief review of the structure of Collins's novel as a whole. *The Woman in White*, like *The Moonstone* (1868), consists of a series of first-person narratives compiled by one character in order to guide the reader through the unraveling of a mystery. It is constructed as if we are reading individual testimony and much has been written on the ways in which Collins's experimentation with this form resulted in a greater sense of mystery. Each eyewitness is allowed to reveal only his or her own firsthand experiences, thus effectively eliminating any problems Collins might have had with a third-person narrator who, if omniscient, would have had sometimes to withhold information in order to maintain suspense and mystery. But the analysis we are working toward has to move beyond discussing simply that brilliant aspect of Collins's novels. It is important to note that while we hear the voices of individual characters, they do not truly speak for themselves; they are, in effect, edited.[6] Individual testimonial texts, such as transcribed accounts, series of letters, diaries, and so forth, reach the reader only after they have passed under the pen of the editing character. In *The Woman in White*, this character is Walter Hartright, and it is only through him that we hear the voices of the other characters. Sometimes their stories, as in the case of Mrs. Catherick, are culled from letters that are addressed to Hartright himself. Most of the time the accounts are written as documents, as in the cases of Vincent Gilmore and Eliza Michelson. But these are still directed to Hartright, as is demonstrated by Gilmore who begins, ''I write these lines at the request of my friend, Mr. Walter Hartright'' (127). These submitted testimonies offer us interesting venues for investigating various aspects of narration, but here we are concerned with one specific aspect best explored in the portion of the text described as ''The Story continued by MARIAN HALCOMBE, in Extracts from her Diary'' (163).

Diary writing enters into a mixed temporality: it is neither fully present, nor fully past. The diary entry generally records the immediate past, oftentimes what has transpired over the course of that same day.[7] As it describes an incident, the tense tends toward the past—*we breakfasted*.[8] But diaries are also immersed in their own present: the author *is* writing. As entries depict the setting in which they are being created, they may allude to that very instantaneous temporality—*I am sitting in the window seat in the parlor as I write this down*—and then return to reflections upon the past, which are easier to sustain. The diarist may also venture into the time of the future, but it is generally only possible for the writer to do so in the most uncertain of terms—*tomorrow we depart: will I ever look upon these walks and gardens again?* In her work on both the diary (non-fictive) and the diary novel, Lorna Martens determines that the diarist ''cannot foresee what will happen or what he will think on any future date, and if he keeps his diary as a general record, he cannot predict what he will write about in the future. The diary is thus a form that eludes the author's full control" (33). Therefore, as the diarist records his or her present, there can be no true foreshadowing of what is to come: the writer has absolutely no idea of the way in which things will work themselves out or even which incidents are important.

Herein lies the brilliance of Collins allowing Marian to speak only in this medium. In a diary, all kernels of information are equal in that they have yet to be judged with an eye to the end. Even though a reader of the novel might be fully aware of the author's (Collins's) control of the diarist's entries, he/she cannot know what the author intends to reveal anymore than he/she can surmise what is unknown as yet to the diarist. The diarist might place greater emphasis on some happenings or observations than on others, but then readers must determine whether or not they trust the character's intuitiveness (a term which we are here differentiating from reliability) before they can decide if the diary's hierarchy of information is accurate. So, as the Victorian reader entered into the narrative of the diary, he or she would have been, as we still are, forced to question Marian's ability to record clues to the future. Marian herself questions this ability. In her self-examination of advice she has given to Hartright, she writes, "Except Laura, I never was more anxious about anyone than I am now about Walter. All that has happened since he left us has only increased my strong regard for him. I hope I am doing right in trying to help him to employment abroad—I hope, most earnestly and anxiously, that it will end well" (177).[9] Here, independent of an editorial time, Marian has access only to the near past and her immediate present as she attempts to analyze her situation and predict the outcome of her actions. Her diary provides a perfect medium through which the Victorian reader can be confronted with questions of knowledge and destiny. By examining what is important today, is it possible to find traces of what will be imperative in the future? Does Fate foreshadow? Does Providence guide?

Of course, Collins complicates this inquiry into the future by sometimes suggesting that this particular Victorian quest is an anxious occupation in its own right. Anticipating the marriage of Laura to Sir Glyde, Marian herself is conflicted by her construction of the tomorrows that stretch endlessly before her. "I am writing of the marriage and the parting with Laura, as people write of a settled thing. It seems so cold and so unfeeling to be looking at the future already in this cruelly composed way" (187). The pursuit of knowledge will continue as the marriage preparations unfold; and, again, the reader is put in a position parallel to that of the character speaking. Because Marian is recording her impressions as they occur to her, we are given mistaken and contradicting accounts of Glyde. "19th.—More discoveries in the inexhaustible mine of Sir Percival's virtues" (192); "20th.—I hate Sir Percival!" (194). However, this ambivalence does not erode Marian's credibility; it simply intensifies the reader's sense of sharing the present-tense temporality of the speaker. After Sir and Lady Glyde return to England and establish themselves and their guests at Blackwater Park, Laura confides her anxieties to Marian: "Every fresh thing he does, seems to terrify me about the future" (253). If central characters fear the future, what must the reader feel? Through the temporal form of the diary, one lacking the consistency and confidence of hindsight, readers are able to experience the same apprehensions and uncertainties as Marian and Laura. There is no frame that can establish a retrospective analysis of events, so when Marian writes, "I almost dread to-morrow," so too can the reader! (259).

Martens tells us that "the diary novel . . . emphasizes the time of writing rather than the time that is written about" (4). Thus while Marian's diary provides us with clues to what deviousness Fosco and Glyde are concocting, the emphasis is on Marian's vulnerability. The very introduction of her diary into the narrative heightens its suspense since the reader cannot be sure that Marian herself has survived from the time of her documenting into the time of the compiling. Todorov tells us that "the movement [in suspense] is from cause to effect: we are first shown the causes . . . and our interest is sustained by the expectation of what will happen" (47). Collins's suspense is not that of gangsters (cause) and corpses (effect), but of diary (the medium through which Marian speaks) and absent writer (why else would a woman hand over the record of her most private thoughts?). It is this twist that demonstrates Collins's ingenious understanding of what might frighten his audience—he played on their fears of not having the means to know the end. Marian's section of the narrative ends with the same insinuation of absence—"NOTE. At this place the entry in the diary ceases to be legible. . . . On the next page of the Diary, another entry appears. It is in a man's handwriting . . . " (343). The astute reader, by now fully able to recognize his diction, need not wait for Count Fosco's signature. His intruding comments offer a sinister picture of the now occluded future. "I breathe my wishes for her recovery. I condole with her on the inevitable failure of every plan that she has formed for her sister's benefit . . . Fosco" (344).

On January 28, 1860, readers would have received the tenth installment of the serialization which opens with Marian's diary. Tension would have begun to build at that point in time. However, it can be said that because of the ongoing sense of the entries, the crisis does not make itself overt until Fosco's violation of the diary. This would have occurred in the 22nd installment of the serialization, which was published on April 21, 1860. The revelation that Marian never left Blackwater ends the 25th installment on May 12, 1860. For almost five months, but most especially during this aforementioned three-week period, the reader would have been left in doubt as to whether Marian spoke through her diary by choice or by necessity. That is, whether she was still available to speak at all. As the 25th installment ends, Marian is presumably alive, although the Victorian reader would still have had to endure a painful anticipation before another installment verified this. In effect, the reader would have lived through a very convincing simulacrum of what the characters in the book were living through.

In general, the narrative constitutes a *history* in which the compilation of information by Hartright causes most of the "documents" to be a past-tense discussion of events from a time—the time of their creation *for* Hartright—which is actually forward of the time in which the mystery would have reached its climax. Thus the reader is assured that the story as a whole is one read through a retrospective filter which was constructed only after some conclusion (albeit one unknown to the reader) had been reached. Collins knew that his Victorian readers more than anything desired a sense of closure. They were searching for the meaning this would provide for their own lives—a reinforcement of the concepts of both providence and destiny. However, as Lonoff points out to us, Collins also wanted to write a suspenseful novel that would be more popular and profitable for its manipulation of his readers' anxieties. He does this most effectively through the *discourse* of Marian's diary by forcing the reader into a simulation of what it would have been like to live out the events in the story in the present tense of their happening, thereby exploiting their fears that some other force, such as chance or malign human intent, might prevail if not in the narrative as a whole, then in the fate of one of its most appealing characters.[10] However, as Cohn points out, no matter how immediate the temporal sensation of a diary might be, it cannot achieve the zero temporality she associates with simultaneous narration. The reader always knows that the diary is a document completed up to a certain point before the reader reads it. Despite Collins's skill in exploiting present-tense narration in order to enhance suspense and strengthen his narrative authority, his approach is nonetheless conventional. The same is not true of Dickens.

Dickens makes extended use of present-tense narration in three of his mature novels—*Bleak House*, *Our Mutual Friend*, and *The Mystery of Edwin Drood*.[11] In *Bleak House* the third-person narrative voice speaks in the present tense with a Jeremiah-like authority, which contrasts with Esther Summerson's humble and subjective first-person, past-tense narration. The third-person narrative voice's chapters are more panoramic than dramatic. They pass judgment and summarize actions. They address large issues concerning society. Now and then they become intensely dramatic, but often still remain without dialogue. The best example is the presentation of the events leading up to and following Krook's extinction by spontaneous combustion. In *Our Mutual Friend* there is no obvious division of narrative voices. The whole text is narrated in the third person. But now and then a chapter is narrated in the present tense. These present-tense chapters generally are concerned with public or quasi-public events, such as the activities of Veneering and his associates surrounding his decision to run for Parliament. These chapters consist almost entirely of panoramic presentation. But Dickens's use of the present tense in *The Mystery of Edwin Drood* is an advance in technique upon these two employments of the tense.

Like Collins, Dickens played upon his readers' anxieties about an uncertain future, while nonetheless endorsing a providential certainty about the nature of human existence, and in doing so both thrilled and entertained them. In *Bleak House* the subjective narrative of Esther Summerson is narrated in the traditional past tense of *history*, but surprisingly the third-person narrator records events in the present tense in a way that recalls Carlyle's experiments in historical writing.[12] The third-person narrator approximates the mode of cinema, where the camera, with all of its real-time immediacy, can show us surfaces in great detail, but makes few attempts to penetrate them. *Bleak House* forces *history* and *discourse* to inhabit a single text, leaving the reader to puzzle out the significance of the suspense and satisfaction created by this abutment. Ironically, it is Esther's ''autobiographical'' narrative that employs the presumably non-autobiographical and non-subjective past-tense mode of *history*, and the objective, historically-oriented third-person narrator who employs the subjective mode of *discourse*. *Our Mutual Friend* complicates this conjunction of planes of utterance by removing the ''simplification'' of having two distinct narrators. Now the same narrative voice shifts from the manner of *history* to that of *discourse*, from past tense omniscience to present-tense cinemantic exploration of surfaces. But in *The Mystery of Edwin Drood*, the device is taken to a new level because now one narrative voice slides between *history* and *discourse*, but the present-tense chapters permit a transcending of surfaces, so that internal conditions can be revealed, as, in cinema, voice-over, symbolism, fade-ins to mental states, and so forth can reveal unexpressed states of mental action, such as dreams and desires.[13] Dickens has finally established his past-tense narrative as *history* and his present-tense narrative as *discourse*, according to Benveniste's distinction, but he has done so in a single narrative in which the two modes continually, but covertly, manifest their mutual incompatibility.[14]

Another problem that surfaces when contrasting the use of present-tense narration in *Bleak House* and *The Mystery of Edwin Drood* is that of focalization, the means by which the events of a narrative are perceived. There is still no certain agreement about how to define focalization, but for our purposes here we may define it as the mediating vantage point from which events in the narrative are seen. Mieke Bal offers one of the broader explanations. ''When focalization lies with one character which participates in the fabula as an actor, we could refer to *internal* focalization. We can then indicate by means of the term external focalization that an anonymous agent, situated outside the fabula is functioning as focalizer'' (105).[15] Many narratologists, following Gerard Genette, argue that the focalizer must be a figure in the fabula, not a nondiegetic voice.[16]

In *Bleak House* there are essentially no focalizing characters in the present-tense narration, but the ideological position of the narrating voice located outside the fabula is so apparent that that voice occasionally cannot help but blurt them out, as in this notorious example just after Jo the crossing sweeper has died.

> The light is come upon the dark benighted way. Dead!
> Dead, your Majesty. Dead, my lords and gentlemen. Dead, Right Reverends and Wrong Reverends of every order. Dead, men and women, born with Heavenly compassion in your hearts. And dying thus around us every day.[17]

Something more complicated is happening in *The Mystery of Edwin Drood.* Like *Bleak House*, *Drood* begins in the present tense The first character introduced is John Jasper in an opium den. "Shaking from head to foot, the man whose scattered consciousness has thus fantastically pieced itself together, at length rises, supports his trembling frame upon his arms, and looks around. He is in the meanest and closest of small rooms" (1). But where is the narrator? Not only is he in the present tense, but he is also either in Jasper's head or else on some other spatial and temporal plane—the passage opens with a description of a cathedral and dissolves into fragmented references to a Sultan, Turkish robbers, and a royal procession complete with ten thousand scimitars and white elephants! The narrator and the narrative sustain this strange construction of temporality until the sixth and seventh chapters, when the narrative shifts temporarily to past tense.[18] This first present-tense narration's focalization is blurred from the outset. The narrator is capable of knowing what the dreaming John Jasper sees. Are we to understand that Jasper is the focalizer here even as he dreams? We think not. His vision is mediated through the narrator and we are prepared to call that focalization. But the focalization does not rest there. When Jasper comes to consciousness it shifts to him as he looks on with disgust at Princess Puffer and a drugged laskar. Moreover, in the last pages of the novel, focalization hovers between the narrator and Datchery. Dickens, in this novel, seems to be treating focalization as a version of free indirect discourse, where boundaries of definition can also blur and dissolve quickly. The present-tense narrator of *Bleak House* was a remote surveyor of surfaces. By contrast the narrative voice of *Drood* is so intimate and invasive that it can describe the images in dreams and can know what the characters think. In fact, in some of these instances it appears as though the simultaneous narration is compromised and that the narrator is providing an account of events that have already transpired, most notably in the chapter that describes events the night before Drood's disappearance. Here is an example:

> Edwin Drood passes a solitary day. Something of deeper moment than he had thought has gone out of his life, and in the silence of his own chamber he wept for it last night. Though the image of Miss Landless still hovers in the background of his mind, the pretty little affectionate creature, so much firmer and wiser than he had supposed, occupies its stronghold. (124)

A similar passage describes Jasper's day.

> John Jasper passes a more agreeable and cheerful day than either of his guests. Having no music-lessons to give in the holiday season, his time is his own, but for the Cathedral services. He is early among the shopkeepers, ordering little table luxuries that his nephew likes. His nephew will not be with him long, he tells his provision-dealers, and so must be petted and made much of. (127–28)

We would argue that this is not historical present—the present-tense narration of events already past—but a compacted version of simultaneous narration. It resembles the technique Dickens used in *David Copperfield* where David provides condensed accounts of his early history in present-tense chapters he calls retrospects. These are historical present accounts. But the condensed descriptions of Drood's and Jasper's days are condensed within the present-tense narration of ongoing experience, a characteristic emphasized by the parallel presention ("Edwin Drood passes . . . " "John Jasper passes . . . ").

We are suggesting that Dickens was making some remarkable advances in narrative craft and that an examination of his use of present-tense narration is one avenue through which to disclose them. However, whereas modern novelists have carried such experiments a long way for new purposes, Dickens remained committed to authorial control. He did this to a great extent in *Drood* by dwelling upon what is not known.

While a number of Dickens's novels deal with mystery as a crime that must be solved or as the unknowable destiny that awaits each character, only one of his works—as its title suggests—specifically sets out to be a suspense novel: *The Mystery of Edwin Drood*. Like his earlier work, this book also poses questions of how much control characters have over their own lives. Rosa Bud and Edwin Drood, for example, feel themselves trapped in an arranged betrothal that has determined the course of their futures in a way that they themselves might not have arranged those tomorrows. And John Jasper feels himself trapped in what to him is the trivial existence of a cathedral choir director. Present-tense narration, more specifically simultaneous narration, enhances this sense of entrapment at the same time that it increases immediacy. It emphasizes contingency.

The absence of a frame complicates and enriches *Drood*. As with the third-person narrators of *Bleak House* and *Our Mutual Friend*, there is no suggestion that the narrator exists within the story itself, despite his present-tense discourse.[19] There is also no reference that would allow us to read *Drood* as a memoir, for example, a text that can plausibly use the present tense to re-create past incidents. Instead, the reader is caught up in the moment as it actually occurs and experiences the events in the same temporality as do the characters. Of course, the reader cannot actually ever get past the fact that he or she is situated elsewhere, in the study or on the couch *reading* the story instead of living the events. But it is a compliment to Dickens's talent that the reader's reality rarely interferes with the development of the story and that no ruptures occur in the narrative which would jolt the reader back to the fact that it is highly implausible that someone would have been able to follow along with *all* of the events *as* they actually happened. Indeed, the shifts back to past tense emphasize the unusualness of the present-tense chapters. Dickens is calling attention to their transgressive nature. Working ostensibly toward a "mystery" narrative, Dickens has created an even deeper level of suspense in his creation of a third-person narrator who is able to pass judgment on characters and their actions, but who is never put into the position of seeming to withhold information from the reader. There is nothing in Dickens's text from which the reader can infer that the narrator holds the secret to the mystery; the reader simply accepts that he or she will follow the present-tense description of events until the conclusion (or, as should have been the case, the solution). Strikingly, the present-tense narration, with its blindness of the future, dominates the past-tense narration, which, because it is in the past tense and hence presumably subsequent to the events it describes, should overwhelm the present-tense narration through its supposed access to the outcome of events. That it does not is apparent in the opaqueness of *Drood*'s plot. No one has been able satisfactorily to finish Dickens's story. Dickens, an already astute judge of his audience's desire for social justice and personal security, has tapped into what would have been one of his readers' greatest fears: that life is a mystery enshrouding each individual and that no single clue exists which can lift that mantle and reveal the future.

Although the present-tense sections of *Drood* play upon the reader's anxiety by withholding any information about what is to come, they can nonetheless create an atmosphere of mystery and even dread. A relatively innocuous example occurs when John Jasper looks in upon his sleeping nephew, Edwin Drood. "His nephew lies asleep, calm and untroubled. John Jasper stands looking down upon him, his unlighted pipe in his hand, for some time, with a fixed and deep attention. Then, hushing his footsteps, he passes to his own room, lights his pipe, and delivers himself to the Spectres it invokes at midnight" (38). The apprehension experienced in reading this passage comes not only from previous knowledge of Jasper, but, even more deliberately, from the sense that nobody, not even the narrator, truly knows what is lurking and lying in wait and, thus, everyone who ventures into that next moment known as the future is vulnerable. By intimating that signs do exist, sometimes in the form of heavy thunderclouds and other times in the cast of a sunny day, Dickens is toying with his readers' desperate desire to read their own personal and cultural climate. Perhaps Dickens is directly addressing this desire when he describes, in a third-person section of the novel, Mr. Grewgious's meditation upon the heavens.

> [H]is gaze wandered from the windows to the stars, as if he would have read in them something that was hidden from him. Many of us would, if we could; but none of us so much as know our letters in the stars yet—or seem likely to do it, in this state of existence—and few languages can be read until their alphabets are mastered. (160)

Expounding upon the concepts of destiny and providence is one of the ways in which Dickens is able to create the sense that there is "something-about-to-happen" without having to allude directly to the event itself. Were Dickens to do this, were he to allow his present tense narrator to know things before they happen, Dickens would be breaking the narrator's temporal boundaries. One of the few theorists to deal with the present tense in narration is Gary Saul Morson. He writes of the professional requirements of a sportscaster that "in the temporality of his narration, there cannot be foreshadowing. On the contrary everything in his voice is oriented toward the present and the *unknown* future" (177, emphasis added). Christian Paul Casparis calls such activities as sports announcing "current report" and relates this category of present-tense usage to what he calls the historical Present by its inability to know the causal framework of the event in progress; the historical present narrative similarly manifests "a conscious or unconscious indifference to the causal linking of events" (151).

Past-tense narration can be mute about the future. It can forego prolepsis and limit itself to the events as they transpire, moving as close to sheer story (the chronological order of events) as possible, and avoiding the maneuvers of plot (the rearrangements of and refinements upon story). It can, in short, approach the condition of historical-present narration. It is even possible for present-tense narration to make use of prolepsis. That the narration is in the present tense does not mean that the future is not fully known to the narrator. An example of this possibility within Dickens's own work is *David Copperfield* where the present-tense retrospective chapters occur within David's autobiography of which he has complete knowledge. What is to prevent the narrator from writing something like this? "David sits at the window, watching travelers pass in the street. The day will come when he too will be one of those travelers. But now his wondering gaze rests upon a parade of strangers.'' This is present-tense narration resembling historical-present narration. Such a liberty would presumably violate the conventions of simultaneous narration, the method, we are arguing, of *Drood.*

What is striking about *The Mystery of Edwin Drood* is that both present- and past-tense chapters withhold knowledge of the future. It is the muteness about the future in the past-tense chapters that enhances a similar muteness in the present-tense chapters. The inability or refusal of Dickens's narrator to claim an already complete knowledge of the story would have disturbed a nineteenth-century reader more perhaps than grisly hints of horrors to come. The opaqueness of the future, rather than specific references to forthcoming adventures, would have unnerved the reader. It is the opposite effect to that created by the use of prolepsis, when a narrator anticipates an event to come, especially an unpleasant or even fatal event, as when a narrator says, ''If only he had known at that moment what was to occur the very next day.'' This disclosure of a future event can create suspense and anxiety in a reader, but it is a different order of suspense from the blank future of present-tense simultaneous narration.

One of the ways in which Morson differentiates between ''sports time'' and a novel is his claim that a reader can always close a book, read its last page, or perhaps read an introduction that explains the plot. He writes, ''the outcome has in a sense already happened . . . rather than [being] of real contingency in our own present'' (174).[20] Thus, no matter how mysterious or threatening the circumstances might appear, there is always the underlying suggestion that it is all already over, already done, and that nothing in the reading of the narrative can happen to change the ending of the story. Most readers have probably sensed an impending resolution, even when narrative events appear at their most tangled, simply because there is a diminishing number of pages separating them from where they are in the story and the last page of the book. When it becomes obvious that there is only one chapter or one page left, even the least savvy of readers can see that the finale draws closer and that the circumstances of the story must be resolved. Thus, by the sheer passing of turned pages, an adventure that began with an infinite number of possibilities must at last come down to only one—the end. However, because both Collins and Dickens first published their work in serial form, it is arguable that for their audiences there would have been a greater sense of an open ending. Since it would have been easily recognized that both authors alluded to current events, readers would have been aware that the stories were being written *even as they read.*[21] This would have undermined the reader's sense that the characters' futures were foretold—that the events were long over—and would have intensified the reader's anxiety as to what the next installment of the characters' lives might mean for them. Through the medium of serial publication, which would have reinforced the effects of the present-tense narration, a feeling of contingency would have been more firmly established in the text. Again, this would have mimicked the same tension that confronted readers in their anxieties over their personal lives and the future generally. Who could know what tomorrow might bring?

It is with regard to the very human desire to know the ends of our own stories that Kermode gives new meaning to the concept of literacy. ''The world is our beloved codex . . . we do, living as reading, like to think of it as a place where we can travel back and forth at will, divining congruences, conjunctions, opposites; extracting secrets from its secrecy . . . this is the way we satisfy ourselves with explanations of the unfollowable world—as if it were a structured narrative'' (145). Victorian readers would have found that any alterations in the conventions of the novel, such as the insertion of a present-tense narration that disallows a foretold future, would have been simply one more way in which the author could force them to acknowledge their inability to read or write the future. Collins and Dickens, in their different ways, made sure that readers could not read their texts in the old familiar way—with the comfort of past-tense temporality and the reassurances of an omniscient narrator. Instead, both authors insisted that their readers confront the characters' situations as if they were themselves living in, if not the same circumstance, at least the same temporality. And by interrupting the traditional *history* narrative with the real-time impression of *discourse*, they allowed for a further examination of the questions of providence and destiny—not simply as narrative constructions, but as actual forces in the working out of events. By withholding any hints of the future in their present-tense narrations, thereby increasing their audiences' anxieties about it, they strengthened their own command over it, thus conferring on themselves the power of providential or fateful control that the present-tense itself seemed to deny. Just as promises of religion and philosophy could only be hoped for, not known for certain, so the reader of these present-tense narratives received no proleptic promises of a comfortable conclusion. But, like the scientists examining the physical relics of the past to construct a narrative of human existence, they had to wait until the story was told before they could judge if it was providence, destiny, or chance that brought them to where they now stood. Ironically, it was by this, the most obviously contrived element of the narrative, the rude coupling of the supposedly discrete planes of utterance of *history* and *discourse*, that Collins and Dickens were able to make their stories that much more *real* to their readers.

NOTES

1. Lorna Martens's *The Diary Novel* examines this use of present-tense narration. The present tense was also often used clumsily to increase dramatic effect. In

John Henry Newman's *Callista*, for example, there are many awkward shifts in tense where Newman seems merely to be attempting to heighten dramatic effect. Chapter 35 opens with the sentence: "We have already had occasion to mention that there were many secret well-wishers, or at least protectors of Christians, as in the world at large, so also in Sicca" (343). The next paragraph begins: "The burning sun of Africa is at the height of its power" (344). But the next is back to standard past-tense narration: "She too thought it was the unwelcome philosopher come again . . . " (344).

2. Janice Carlisle similarly notes that unconventional present-tense narration became commonplace in the late Victorian period especially among second-rate or inexperienced writers (84).

3. Janice Carlisle and Randolph Quirk are two Dickens scholars who have noted Dickens's use of present-tense. Carlisle sees its use in *Dombey and Son* as a means of achieving immediacy by drawing the reader more forcefully into the narrative (77, 85).

4. Early studies that concentrate on the relationships between providence and narrative include Leopold Damrosch Jr.'s *God's Plots and Man's Stories*, Thomas Vargish's *The Providential Aesthetic in Victorian Fiction*, and John R. Reed's *Victorian Will*. These scholars examine how writers of the eighteenth and nineteenth centuries in Great Britain and elsewhere could assume on their readers' part a belief in a covert and sometimes apparent teleology in human affairs under the superintendence of a benign or baleful God. In many instances, novelists linked their own plots to the implicit tendency of Providence.

5. Sue Lonoff notes this peculiar reader response in *Wilkie Collins and His Victorian Readers* (144).

6. This technique may serve two purposes: Rosemary Jann writes that "although authors using third-person narrators can accomplish this by limiting their omniscience, there is always a certain amount of conscious concealment of important information on the author's part that may try the reader's patience" (23) and Tzvetan Todorov points out, with respect to his formulation of point of view, that "the tenor of each piece of information is determined by the person who transmits it, no observation exists without an observer" (46). Thus Collins's use of several first-person narrators also serves to disguise any objective truth that an omniscient narrator would have to provide; the eyewitnesses who speak for themselves may distort a clue that is the key to the mystery. However, should this happen within Collins's structure of the narrative, neither the "editor" nor the author would be held to blame for this misinterpretation.

7. Martens deals with this particular point in her excellent examination of diary writing (5), but, oddly enough, though she mentions Miss Clack's diary in *The Moonstone*, she entirely overlooks the more dramatic instance of Marian Halcombe's in *The Woman in White*.

8. It is also possible for the diarist to record recollections and memories of more distant pasts. And, as an aside, we should also note that diarists record not only their own stories, but the lives (past and present) of those around them.

9. But what does it mean to end well? Where is the end that is well? Frank Kermode emphasizes in *The Genesis of Secrecy* that human life is played out with a sense

that we are in the middle of events. He addresses this issue on the cosmic level, but it applies as well to individual lives. The person who writes an autobiography at the age of thirty comes to the end of things in her narrative and might even conclude that the story of her life has ended well. But the next few years might change that story considerably.

10. Although it is only tangential to our interests here, it is a note of some importance that Marian never speaks for herself outside of the medium of the diary. Hereafter, anything which she contributes is filtered through Hartright's narrative.

11. Dickens used present-tense narration elsewhere—in *Dombey and Son* and *David Copperfield*, for example—but his use of present tense in the three novels discussed here is systematic and extensive.

12. Carlyle made frequent use of present-tense narration in *The French Revolution*, thereby creating greater drama and what he himself regarded as a novelistic effect. Of course, Dickens claimed to have read *The French Revolution* many times and declared it a source for his own *A Tale of Two Cities*.

13. An extreme example of this penetration in cinema is *Last Year at Marienbad*, written by Alain Robbe-Grillet and directed by Alain Resnais.

14. What we are describing here using Benveniste's terms, Suzanne Fleishman explores in narratological terms, explaining that present-tense narrations are unstable because they erase the distinction between the two temporal planes of the past tense of narrated events and the time of narration.

15. Shlomith Rimmon-Kenan accepts the idea of external and internal focalization (74ff).

16. See Genette's response to Bal in *Narrative Discourse Revisited*, chapter 12. Seymour Chatman offers different terms to clarify the process others lump together as focalization. "I propose slant to name the narrator's attitudes and other mental nuances appropriate to the report function of discourse, and filter to name the much wider range of mental activity experienced by characters in the story world—perceptions, cognitions, attitudes, emotions, memories, fantasies, and the like" (143). Manfred Jahn offers a means to adjust this difference within the concept of focalization by employing the concept of field of vision and presenting the idea of narrators at the windows of James's House of Fiction.

17. Another notorious instance is in chapter 32, when the narrator associates Krook's spontaneous combustion with the injustice of the British courts.

18. Of the 23 chapters, those already mentioned as well as those numbered 9, 10, 11, 13, 15, 16, 17, 18, 20, 21, and 22 are in the past tense. The novel opens and closes (though we can never know if the later action would have been Dickens's intent) with a present-tense narration.

19. It would be interesting to consider the situation of the "implied" audience. This essay deals only with the fact that Dickens has set up a narrative that is being told in the present tense by an unknown narrator. But to whom is this narrator speaking, for this is speech and not written text? Does not the present-tense narrator imply an immediate present-tense auditor? The device that this most immediately resembles is the aside spoken by a living actor to a living audience in the theater, and there is no question but that Dickens's use of present-tense narration in *Drood* heightens the drama. Several authors have dealt with problems

of audience reception of present-tense narration from Genette on, but one of the most compelling is James Phelan's study of J. M. Coetzee's *Waiting for the Barbarians*, where the instability created by simultaneous narration acts as a means of involving the reader in a double sense of complicity, first in the events of the story and then in the way that we are obliged to process them.

20. Robin W. Winks makes a similar comparison in *Modus Operandi*, when he states that "In football . . . the variables at any given moment are enormous. To the spectator, suspense arises as much from not knowing what must happen next . . . - the huddle allows one's doubts, like private detectives, to search out weaknesses in the game plan . . . the beauty in sport . . . arises from the persistence of doubt, and its mounting repetitious nature . . . living with ambiguity is not easy. Most people like their History [sic] clear and plain" (8). In the Victorian era the variables themselves were not even fully known and history was being eroded by a new revolution—one which questioned not just the structures, but the very foundations upon which people laid their lives.

21. Morson unwittingly supports this picture of the serial reader when he says, "spectators have to be *simultaneous* with the events they watch" (176). *The Mystery of Edwin Drood* dramatically confirms the open-endedness of serial publication because Dickens's death before the narrative was completed has turned the novel into a continuing memorial of such open-endedness.

WORKS CITED

Bal, Mieke. *Narratology: Introduction to the Theory of Narrative.* Trans. Christine van Boheemen. Toronto: U of Toronto P, 1992.

Benveniste, Emile. *Problems in General Linguistics.* Trans. Mary Elizabeth Meek. Coral Gables, Florida: U of Miami P,1971.

Brooke-Rose, Christine, "Narrating without a narrator," *Times Literary Supplement*, December 31, 1999: 1213.

Carlisle, Janice. *The Sense of an Audience: Dickens, Thackeray, and George Eliot at Mid-Century.* Athens, GA: The U of Georgia P, 1981.

Casparis, Christian Paul. *Tense Without Time: The Present Tense in Narration.* Bern: Francke Verlag, 1975.

Chatman, Seymour. *Story and Discourse: Narrative Structure in Fiction and Film.* Ithaca: Cornell UP, 1978.

Cohn, Dorrit. *The Distinction of Fiction.* Baltimore: Johns Hopkins UP, 1999.

Collins, Wilkie. *The Woman in White.* Oxford: Oxford UP, 1998.

Damrosch Jr., Leopold. *God's Plots and Man's Stories: Studies in the Fictional Imagination from Milton to Fielding.* Chicago: U of Chicago P, 1985.

Dickens, Charles. *The Mystery of Edwin Drood,* ed. Margaret Cardwell. Oxford: Clarendon, 1972.

———. Bleak House, eds. George Ford and Sylvère Monod. New York: W. W. Norton, 1977.

Doyle, Sir Arthur Conan. *Memories and Adventures.* Boston: Little, Brown, 1924.

Fleischman, Suzanne. *Tense and Narrativity: From Medieval Performance to Modern Fiction.* Austin: U of Texas P, 1990.

Genette, Gérard. *Narrative Discourse Revisited.* Trans. Jane E. Lewin. Ithaca: Cornell UP, 1994.

Jahn, Manfred, "Windows of Focalization: Deconstructing and Reconstructing a Narratological Concept," *Style* 30:2 (Summer 1996): 241–67.

Jann, Rosemary. *The Adventures of Sherlock Holmes: Detecting Social Order.* New York: Twayne, 1995.

Kermode, Frank. *The Genesis of Secrecy: On the Interpretation of Narrative.* Cambridge: Harvard UP, 1979.

Lonoff, Sue. *Wilkie Collins and His Victorian Readers: A Study in the Rhetoric of Authorship.* New York: AMS Press, 1982.

Martens, Lorna. *The Diary Novel.* Cambridge: UP, 1985.

Morson, Gary Saul. *Narrative and Freedom: The Shadows of Time.* New Haven: Yale UP, 1994.

Newman, John Henry. *Callista: A Tale of the Third Century.* London: Longmans, Green, 1904.

Phelan, James. "Present Tense Narration, Mimesis, the Narrative Norm, and the Positioning of the Reader in *Waiting for the Barbarians." Understanding Narrative.* Eds. James Phelan and Peter J. Rabinowitz. Columbus: Ohio State UP, 1994, 222–45.

Prince, Gerald. *Narratology.* The Hague: Mouton, 1982.

Quirk, Randolph. *Charles Dickens and Appropriate Language.* Durham: Duke UP, 1959.

Reed, John R. *Victorian Will.* Athens: Ohio UP, 1989.

Rimmon-Kenan, Shlomith. *Narrative Fiction: Contemporary Poetics.* London and New York: Methuen, 1983.

Sturgess, Philip J. M. *Narrativity: Theory and Practice*. Oxford: Clarendon, 1992.

Thoms, Peter. *Detection and Its Designs: Narrative and Power in 19th-Century Detective Fiction*. Athens: Ohio UP, 1988.

Todorov, Tzvetan. *The Poetics of Prose*. Trans. Richard Howard. Ithaca: Cornell UP, 1977.

Vargish, Thomas. *The Providential Aesthetic in Victorian Fiction*. Charlottesville: UP of Virginia, 1985.

Winks, Robin W. *Modus Operandi: An Excursion into Detective Fiction*. Boston: David R. Godine, 1982.

Wilkie Collins's Villainous Miss Gwilt, Criminality, and the Unspeakable Truth

Maria K. Bachman
Don Richard Cox

The Foreword to Wilkie Collins's novel Armadale *warns that the book may offend some readers because it is a book "daring enough to speak the truth" Collins, however, does not mention specifically just how the book "oversteps, in more than one direction," the limits of what he labels the "Clap-trap morality" of the day. Critics who have focused only on the crimes of the novel's villain, the outrageous Miss Gwilt, have overlooked the book's undeniable emphasis on sexuality, specifically the homoerotic bond that exists between the novel's two protagonists, Allan Armadale and Ozias Midwinter. Collins repeatedly hints at the irrepressible passion between the two, a passion they can acknowledge privately, but not publicly. Indeed, given the attitude towards sodomy that was present in nineteenth-century England (it was a capital crime until 1861), it is clear that the frequent hysterical fits of Midwinter reflect his own homosexual panic as he contemplates the criminality of the love that "dare not speak its name." Lydia Gwilt, who appears on the scene as this relationship is nearing a climax, represents an unspeakable pathology of male homosocial desire, the signification of the criminal. The Armadale/Gwilt/Midwinter triangle that ensues reveals the love shared by the men as she attempts to come between them and inherit a fortune by marrying Midwinter and murdering Armadale. Miss Gwilt finally decides to kill herself instead, because she understands that the love the two men share will continue unabated. At the novel's conclusion Armadale marries the asexual Neelie Milroy, but*

Dickens Studies Annual, Volume 32, Copyright © 2002 by AMS Press, Inc. All rights reserved.

*he also vows that he will never part from Midwinter, thus preserving
homosexuality as an option which Collins depicts, but refuses to judge.*

In the center of Wilkie Collins's labyrinthine novel, *Armadale* (Bk. 3, ch. 9),
appears what must be regarded as one of the more curious conversations in
the novel, a conversation that, strangely enough, has apparently also gone
unnoticed by scholars and critics. The exchange takes place between one of
the book's protagonists, Allan Armadale (one of five characters in the novel
who bear that name), and Eleanor ("Neelie") Milroy, the young woman he
will eventually marry. Miss Milroy is obviously smitten with Armadale, and
wonders whether her feelings are reciprocated, so when the pair are momentarily alone while on a group picnic she flirtatiously proposes a little game
with him. "Should I be right or wrong, Mr. Armadale," she inquires, "if I
guessed that you were thinking of somebody?" "You know everything,"
Armadale responds, "I *was* thinking of somebody." Convinced that he has
been thinking of her, Miss Milroy continues the game. "I have been thinking
of somebody too," she says. "If I tell you the first letter of my Somebody's
name, will you tell me the first letter of yours?" (257). Armadale agrees, and
tells her the first letter of the name of the person he has been thinking of is
"M." She in turn tells him the first letter of the name of the person she has
been thinking of is "A." Allan Armadale, who apparently is less sensitive
than many other Victorian protagonists, does not seem to make any connections with the significance of her choice of the letter "A." Miss Milroy, on
the other hand, is first a little startled, because Armadale is apparently thinking
of her surname, "Milroy," rather than "Neelie," or "Eleanor." She gamely
persists, however, asking how many syllables are in this name, and is dumb-
founded when he responds "It's a name in three syllables" (258). The name
on his mind, as readers who are familiar with the novel know, is of course
"Midwinter," his best friend and companion, not, to Neelie's chagrin, Milroy. She stalks off in anger, her flirtation ruined, and he in turn is as startled
by her reaction as if she "had actually boxed his ears" (258). Miss Milroy
is surprised by his answer, and he is equally stunned by her response, but we
as readers should be surprised or stunned only if we have not been paying
attention to the text up to this point, for *Armadale* is a novel with a love
triangle that may very well be unique in Victorian fiction.

    The Victorian novel, as Dennis Allen has noted in *Sexuality in Victorian
Fiction*, is often characterized by a sense of interiority, hidden forces, and
meanings, and a truth that cannot be directly spoken. What Allen labels
the "erotic reserve" of Victorian fiction "reflects the difficulty of inserting
Victorian ideas of sex and sexuality into the larger ideological framework of
nineteenth-century English culture." According to Allen, "Victorian conceptions of sex and sexuality as anarchic reflect the actual ineffability of the

sexual, the tendency of sex and sexuality to resist and disrupt *any* attempt to represent them'' (4–5). This realm of the "ineffable" or "unspeakable" was corroborated by Wilkie Collins, who in his 1866 preface to *Armadale* suggested that "estimated by the Clap-trap morality of the present day, this may be a very daring book . . . daring enough to speak the truth" (5), although Collins does not specify exactly what "truth" he may have in mind. Collins's very language here, however, seems to anticipate Oscar Wilde's description of homosexuality as the "love that dare not speak its name."[1] Indeed, sexuality, or, more precisely, homosexuality—specifically, its signification in the nineteenth century as criminal—is at the center of Collins's *Armadale*, and it represents one of the "unspeakable" forces to which Collins may be directly referring when he speaks of the book's "daring truth."

Numerous critics have pointed out that the sensation novel of the 1850s and 1860s exploited the reading public's prurient interest in the crimes and scandals of the day.[2] According to Lyn Pykett, "private affairs were turned into public spectacle" (2) and novelists, fascinated by the annals of crime, were quick to draw upon the sensational cases of bigamy, adultery, divorce, and murder for their fiction. In *Armadale*, Allan Armadale's lawyer, Mr. Pedgift, emphasizes the criminality of the times: "Read your newspaper, Mr. Armadale, and you'll find we live in piping times for the black sheep of the community—if they are only black enough" (368–69). Indeed, allusions to real-life drama are a staple of Collins's fictional drama and have been frequently commented upon. The highly publicized domestic poisoning trials of the 1850s, for example, figure in *Armadale*; the 1861 Yelverton bigamy-divorce case laid the foundation for *Man and Wife;* and in *The Moonstone*, details such as the stained nightgown that incriminates Franklin Blake, and the dismissal of Sergeant Cuff from the investigation, are based on actual details of the notorious Road murder of 1860, for which Constance Kent was eventually convicted. Moreover, in the Appendix to *Armadale*, Collins insists on the verisimilitude of various occurrences in the novel on the basis of specific newspaper accounts; his use of such source material in which he has "spared no pains to instruct [himself] on matters of fact" (678), was not gratuitous.[3] Indeed, critics have noted that the sensation novel, as both a reflection of *and* response to contemporary social debates and scandals, offers a way of interpreting certain anxieties that plagued mid-Victorian culture (Pykett 9–11). Jenny Bourne Taylor's study, for example, *In the Secret Theatre of Home*, focuses on "instability of social and psychic identity" (8) as a strategy of tying Collins's sensation fiction to anxieties about cultural transformation and the blurring of class and gender boundaries.

Homosexuality was to be counted among the scandalous topics of the day,[4] yet the issue of homosexuality as fodder for sensation novelists has seldom been addressed.[5] We should point out, however, that homosexuality, for most of the nineteenth century, was literally and figuratively "unspeakable" (the word "homosexual" was not introduced into the English vocabulary until the 1890s with the translation of Krafft-Ebing's *Psychopathia Sexualis*, a study which incidentally begins with and from perversions),[6] but same-sex desire between men was nevertheless an issue that evinced great public antipathy. As Foucault and others have noted, the nineteenth-century persecution of homosexuals was the result of the identification of "homosexuality" as a concept, a perversion, and a type. "As defined by the ancient civil or canonical codes," Foucault states, "sodomy was a category of forbidden acts; their perpetrator was nothing more than the juridical subject of them. The nineteenth-century homosexual became a personage, a past, a case history, and a childhood, in addition to being a type of life, a life form, and a morphology, with an indiscreet anatomy and possibly a mysterious physiology" (*History* 43). Furthermore, as James Eli Adams points out, while "sex between men has been around from time immemorial," there is little evidence before the nineteenth century "that men who enjoyed such activity therefore thought of themselves as different *in kind* from other men" (134). Partly as a response to the "discovery" of this "new species," over fifty men were hanged on charges of sodomy during the first third of the nineteenth century. Moreover, efforts to remove the death penalty for sodomy during this period were generally unsuccessful: Sir Robert Peel *reaffirmed* it in his 1826 "reforms" and when Lord John Russell attempted to remove "unnatural offenses" from the list of capital crimes in 1841, he was forced to withdraw it because of lack of parliamentary support. Pearsall notes that during this time the existence of the death penalty for sodomy served as a grisly deterrent because there were reports of some "homosexually inclined" men committing acts of self-mutilation (548). During the years 1856–59 alone, fifty-four men were sentenced to death for sodomy, and, while capital punishment ultimately was not carried out, the fact that sodomy was still prosecuted as a capital crime indicates the level of anxiety mid-Victorian society experienced toward those phenomena which were "against the norm."[7]

Foucault has pointed out that, in the second half of the nineteenth century, the belief prevailed that "ever-present criminality is a constant menace to the social body as a whole. The collective fear of crime, the obsession with this danger which seems to be an inseparable part of society itself, are thus perpetually inscribed in each individual consciousness" ("Dangerous Individual" 12).[8] While there are no overt allusions in *Armadale* to this particular "crime," the text assiduously uncovers the homoerotic bond between Allan Armadale and Ozias Midwinter, and in doing so produces a "reverse discourse"[9] as it articulates and responds to the moral panic that arose from Victorian perceptions of transgressive sexualities. As a prefatory directive to both critics and readers, Collins warned somewhat cryptically in his Introduction that *Armadale* "oversteps, in more than one direction, the narrow limits within which [critics and reviewers] are disposed to restrict the development of modern fiction'' (5). How or where the novel overstepped these boundaries Collins left for the reader to decide. (Interestingly, Collins's original claim was that the novel overstepped *"in all directions"* [emphasis added], but perhaps in a move to uphold the novel's project of secrecy and deception, substituted "more than one direction" instead.)

Upon the novel's publication in 1866, there was no doubt that *Armadale* had offended some sensibilities. One reviewer for *The Spectator* declared that the novel "overstep[s] the limits of decency, and revolt[s] every human sentiment,''[10] and blamed the novel's red-headed villainess, Miss Gwilt, for these transgressions. Indeed, what outraged contemporary reviewers most in *Armadale* was the depiction of the novel's notorious heroine, Lydia Gwilt. Described by one critic as "the extreme form of the demonic sensation heroine" (Pykett 26), the flamboyant Miss Gwilt is a liar, murderess, poisoner, adulteress, bigamist, and forger. She is a femme fatale who personifies the guilt—both sexual and social—that her name connotes.[11] But more specifically, Lydia Gwilt serves as a signifier for the criminality and corruption that was perceived as threatening the moral fabric of Victorian society. Miss Gwilt's behavior is so *outré*, so deviant and dangerous in fact, that modern critics, though agreeing that she is the most "forceful" character in the novel, have scrambled to find a rationale for her outrageousness, at times labeling her behavior as "inexplicable," and at other times, identifying her as a "castrating woman" who possesses "all-embracing, disarming, and suffocating female power."[12] Lydia Gwilt's bizarre criminality, however, which cannot always be understood in terms of her personal motivation, becomes more clear when we understand her role emblematically as representing an unspeakable pathology of male homosexual desire.

Collins's convoluted novel opens in 1832 with the bizarre deathbed confession of one of the five characters named "Allan Armadale," who recalls events from the 1820s in the British West Indies. (That the recounted events are set in exotic and wild Barbados, a site of unlicensed debauchery, is, as we shall see, significant.) The confession takes the form of a dictated letter intended to "warn [his] son of a danger that lies in wait for him—a danger that will rise from his father's grave" (27). The confessor, Allan Armadale (*né* Wrentmore, godson and heir to the first Allan Armadale) recounts, without going into specifics, the depravity of his youth: "I doubt if there was ever a young man in this world whose passions were left so entirely without control of any kind, as mine were in those early days" (28). He inherits one of the largest estates in Barbados (the stipulation being that he change his surname from Wrentmore to Armadale) when his English cousin, Allan Armadale, is disowned by his father. This cousin can also lay claim to a particularly debauched life for he "had disgraced himself beyond all redemption;

had left his home an outlaw; and had been thereupon renounced by his father at once and for ever'' (28). For a novel that has been noted for its intricacy, complexity, and meticulous plotting—indeed, its strict attention, if not obsession, to details—it is uncharacteristic for Collins to withhold such information from his readers, unless of course, that information is significant to the novel's central puzzle. Herein, Collins introduces one of the novel's many mysteries, but this is a mystery that has heretofore gone undetected and hence, remains unsolved. What does such ''uncontrollable'' behavior suggest and what exactly is the nature of this depravity such that it remains unspeakable? This oblique suggestion of deviance does not end here.

Soon after Armadale has inherited his godfather's estates, a young man named Fergus Ingleby arrives; Armadale is immediately and indisputably attracted to him: ''My impulses governed me in everything; I knew no law but the law of my own caprice, and I took a fancy to the stranger the moment I set eyes on him'' (28–29). Disregarding Ingleby's ''unsatisfactory'' character references—the details of which also remain unspecified—Armadale hires him as his clerk, and finds the ''intimacy between [them] rapidly ripening'' (29). Armadale's mother, however, interprets this relationship as an unnatural alliance and makes a series of efforts to part the two men. She fails in every attempt but one. Apparently desperate to end this close and perhaps ''unnatural'' companionship, she provides a potential romantic distraction when she gives him a miniature portrait of a woman whom he has never met. He is affected profoundly, for the face in the portrait looks at him ''as no woman's face had ever looked at me yet'' (30). Having grown weary of his own (again, unspecified) ''base pleasures'' of the past few months—months he has presumably spent in the company of Fergus Ingleby—the feeling that is produced in Armadale by the young woman's face is ''something better in [his] nature than [his] animal-self'' (30). Here again, we might ask what sorts of ''base pleasures'' might Armadale be referring to and whether this debauchery involves Ingleby? Judging by Ingleby's ''mortified'' reaction to Armadale's unforeseen intention to marry the woman in the portrait, we might surmise that the ''intimacy'' that exists between the two men is more than male bonding. Shortly after disclosing his marriage plans, Armadale suddenly falls ill and Ingleby disappears.[13] When he recovers and travels to Madeira, he discovers Ingleby has impersonated him and married Miss Blanchard (Armadale's intended) with the help of her precocious young maid, who will be identified later in the novel as Lydia Gwilt. In an act of revenge, Armadale/Wrentmore murders his cousin, Armadale/Ingleby, by locking him in the cabin of a sinking ship. Shifting forward in time to 1832 to conclude the deathbed confession, the confessor (Armadale/Wrentmore) gasps his last few breaths; he explains that he has recounted these events because he believes his son will suffer for the sins of his father. With this confession comes an injunction to his son—an injunction that is repeated numerous times throughout the novel—to hide from the conspiratorial maid and to deny the man he will most desire:

> Avoid the widow of the man I killed—if the widow still lives. Avoid the maid whose wicked hand smoothed the way to the marriage—if the maid is still in her service. And more than all, avoid the man who bears the same name as your own. . . . Hide yourself from him under an assumed name. Put the mountains and the seas between you; be ungrateful, be unforgiving; be all that is most repellent to your own gentler nature, rather than live under the same roof, and breathe the same air with that man. Never let the two Allan Armadales meet in this world: never, never, never! . . .   (48)

And with this portentous injunction that does not reveal consequences, come two additional mysteries: Why must Allan Armadale avoid the "maid" and the man whose name he shares? And, what will happen if these warnings are not heeded?

To find the answers to these questions, we should understand that, in a sense, the plot of *Armadale* hinges on two types of inheritance—material and psychological.[14] Materially, the plot works to restore the rightful Allan Armadale as heir to the ancestral estates at Thorpe-Ambrose, and, psychologically, the plot traces the implications of hereditary transmission—in this case, the sins of the fathers. The belief that certain morbid physical as well psychological traits could be passed on from one generation to the next had not only gained widespread currency by midcentury, but also fed fears about inherited pathologies, particularly criminality.[15] In *The Principles of Psychology* (1855), Herbert Spencer stated, "It is not simply that a modified form of constitution produced by new habits of life, is bequeathed to future generations; but also that the modified nervous tendencies are also bequeathed: and if the new habits of life become permanent, the tendencies become permanent" (quoted in Taylor 66–67).[16]

These two notions of inheritance offer a way of questioning the motivation behind Armadale/Wrentmore's murder of Fergus Ingleby. Superficially, we might conclude that Armadale/Wrentmore murdered Ingleby to secure his inheritance (property). However, given the emotionally-charged narrative, it seems clear that there is more at stake. The real motivation is in fact jealous revenge, a case of spurned love—what Krafft-Ebing in *Psychopathia Sexualis* described as "lust-murder"—as Armadale admits of being seized by "violent passions rooted deep in [his] nature"(35).[17] Armadale/Wrentmore's sudden interest in a woman spawns an act of retaliation on the part of Ingleby, his equally sudden marriage to this very same woman. What other possible motive could Ingleby have for his instant marriage to someone who was previously a complete stranger to him? This retaliatory marriage is then followed by

Armadale/Wrentmore's own act of retaliation—murder. Krafft-Ebing postulated that "the homosexual urge may sometimes enforce satisfaction with such violence that control becomes impossible. It has even been said that the excitements and dangers entailed by the prohibition of homosexual acts may easily intensify nervous and sexual irritability" (quoted in Pearsall 547). Though neither supposition is conclusive, what we can say with confidence is that, throughout the novel, Midwinter is haunted by the "horror of his hereditary superstition" (104) that his father outlined in his deathbed confession:

> I see the vices which have contaminated the father, descending, and contaminating the child; I see the shame which has disgraced the father's name, descending and disgracing the child's. I look in on myself—and I see My Crime, ripening again for the future in the self-same circumstance which first sowed the seeds of it in the past; and descending, in inherited contamination of Evil, from me to my son.   (47)

The Crime and "vices" to which the dying Armadale refers are ambiguous, and here again another mystery opens up. Is he referring to the murder, and if so, why does he warn against those "vices which have contaminated the father"? Murder is not normally seen as a vice, but is frequently seen as an aberrant act. One is tempted here to recall Foucault's statement about aberrant sodomy being transformed into the pathology of homosexuality; Armadale seems not to be referring to something he *did*, a specific action, but rather something he has *become*. How are we to interpret Midwinter's sense of himself as the incarnation of his "murdering father's passions" (89)?[18]

    As the narrative shifts to the present, 1851, the three main characters, Allan Armadale (posthumous son of Armadale/Ingleby), Ozias Midwinter (the son of Wentworth/Armadale, who is legally "Allan Armadale," but has changed his name), and Lydia Gwilt, the maid and co-conspirator, are brought together by an unusual series of circumstances.[19] Pykett has postulated that "secretiveness is not only the structuring principle of the sensation plot, it is also its origin, and its subject" (14). *Armadale* and its project of concealment are no exception to this rule, for this is undeniably a novel of numerous secrets. The homoerotic bond that exists between Armadale and Midwinter, however, may hardly be counted among those secrets. Indeed, it seems almost redundant to point out the highly charged sexual relationship between Armadale and Midwinter, a relationship that has apparently hitherto gone unnoted by critics. The two men's intimacy—a relationship that seems to be a repetition of their fathers'—proceeds from an impetuous cordiality on Allan Armadale's part, a characteristic that he seems to have inherited: "Allan had followed his usual impulses in his usual headlong way. He had taken a violent fancy to the castaway usher; and had Ozias Midwinter to reside permanently in the neighbourhood, in the new and interesting character of his bosom friend'' (63). Not only does Armadale take a "violent fancy" to this stranger, but he "obliges" Midwinter to live with him at Thorpe-Ambrose as his steward, a position for which Midwinter is wholly unqualified. Moreover, Armadale stipulates that Midwinter will reside under the same roof with him—literally in the bedroom next to his—*not* in the cottage traditionally designated for previous stewards.[20] The friendship that is immediately struck between Midwinter and Armadale might simply appear as male bonding if we ignored the alarm with which others regard their not-so-innocent relationship. Mr. Brock, for instance, wonders "what had Allan seen in [Midwinter] to take such a fancy to?" Brock concludes that what Allan must find so attractive in Midwinter is that he is not like other men: he was "a man who was not cut out on the regular local pattern, and whose way in the world had the one great merit (in those parts) of being *a way of his own*" (66–67, emphasis added). Indeed, as far as Victorian cultural norms are concerned, Midwinter, "a slim, dark, undersized man" with a "sensitive feminine organization" (219–20) is undeniably *un*-masculine:

> He wasn't like all the other fellows in the neighbourhood. All the other fellows were cut out on the same pattern. Every man of them was equally healthy, muscular, loud, hard-headed, clean-skinned, and rough; every man of them drank the same draughts of beer, smoked the same short pipes all day long, rode the best horse, shot over the best dog, and put the best bottle of wine in England on his table at night. . . . They were no doubt excellent fellows in their way; but the worst of them was, they were all exactly alike. (66)

And while Brock along with Allan's mother, Mrs. Blanchard, regard Armadale's relationship with Midwinter as an "indiscretion" (67) and "perverse fancy" (82), the source of their alarm is never explicitly named. While Midwinter's darker skin could be an issue or a cause for alarm, this racial distinction is never mentioned by any of the characters, and it apparently goes unnoticed by all the novel's narrators.

The repeated description of their friendship as *indiscreet* and *perverse* denotes it as "outside the norm." If their relationship stayed within the boundaries of the "norm," efforts to break the two up would be unnecessary and unthinkable. Brock though, acting on behalf of Allan's mother, warns Midwinter to terminate his "intimacy" with Armadale, an injunction which leaves Midwinter in a "violent fit of crying" (69). And here again, if some readers remain skeptical of a homoerotic subtext, we might question Midwinter's passionate and distinctly *un*-masculine response to this injunction. In point of fact, however, such passionate outbursts are not limited to Midwinter. When Armadale learns of Midwinter's forced departure the next morning, his reaction—shouting and swearing, his face "all of a flame"—also registers more than just disappointment. He sets off in violent pursuit of Midwinter, insisting that he won't "give him up"; Armadale declares, "if my friend Midwinter doesn't come to *me*, I'll go to my friend Midwinter" (69–70). That Armadale's actions might be interpreted as suspect is corroborated by the fact that Mr. Brock demands that Armadale's scandalous conduct be kept a secret from the servants. Why is this veil of secrecy necessary for the master of the house and why exactly is his behavior perceived as scandalous? The force of their passion is irrepressible and undeniably suggestive. Midwinter unashamedly explains that it is his "love for Allan Armadale" that guides him to "the better feeling and the truer view." "Have I no right to speak of him in that way?" he asks Brock. "I do love him! It *will* come out of me—I can't keep it back. I love the very ground he treads on! I would give my life—yes, the life that is precious to me now, because his kindness has made it a happy one. . . . " (101–02) As Midwinter continues, "the *hysterical* passion rose, and conquered him . . . and he burst into tears" (102, emphasis added). Here, Midwinter's struggle to restrain his emotion is a case study in what one nineteenth-century psychiatrist identifies as the pathology of hysteria. In *On the Pathology and Treatment of Hysteria* (1853), Robert Brudenell Carter contends that hysteria is not a strictly female disease; rather, "in many cases of hysteria in the male, the sufferers are recorded to have been 'continent,' " deliberately restraining their sexual impulses. Because of nineteenth-century culture's insistence on female chastity, women are particularly prone to hysteria. Carter argues that the sexual impulse in men is normally and "speedily exhausted through the proper channel."[21] If this impulse is not released (as in the case of Midwinter), the result can be "paroxysm[s]," language which Collins repeatedly employs. When Collins refers to "the cruel necessity of self-suppression" (102), he is specifically alluding to Midwinter's attempt to remain sexually continent.

Thus, throughout the novel, Midwinter hovers on the brink of hysteria as he struggles not only to conceal his mysterious heredity, but also to separate himself from the man he most desires. In the chapter entitled "Midwinter in Disguise," we see him struggling with information he has received that Lydia Gwilt may soon appear on the scene. At breakfast he bursts into "a strange outbreak of gaiety," startling Armadale, and revealing to him what was apparently "a new side to the character of his friend." In fact, Collins assures us, Midwinter's behavior "was only a new aspect of the one ever-recurring struggle of Midwinter's life," and has been prompted by the possibility that he will soon be forced to part from "the one human creature whom he loved." As Midwinter's speech becomes more chaotic and his "artificial spirits" are "mounting hysterically beyond his own control," Collins tells us that Midwinter "looked and spoke with that terrible freedom of licence which is the necessary consequence, when a diffident man has thrown off his reserve, of the very effort by which he has broken loose from his own restraints'' (220–21).[22] Sure enough, in a few pages we see that his forced spontaneity, his ''sheer delirium,'' his ''paroxysms of laughter [that] followed each other with such convulsive violence,'' cause Armadale to drag him from the room into the park. The scene is virtually a textbook illustration of Carter's theory. There in the park, Collins notes,

> For the moment, Midwinter was incapable of answering. The hysterical paroxysm was passing from one extreme to the other. He leaned against a tree, sobbing and gasping for breath, and stretched out his hand in mute entreaty to Allan to give him time. . . . ''Don't stop here,'' he said; ''don't look at me—I shall soon get over it.'' Allan still hesitated, and begged hard to be allowed to take him back to the house. It was useless. ''You break my heart with your kindness,'' he burst out passionately. ''For God's sake leave me by myself!''
> (225–26)[23]

His extreme emotionalism and hysteria, the perpetual anxiety that characterizes Midwinter's ''battle against himself'' (106) as his ''love for Allan'' competes with his ''superstition'' could very well be deemed homosexual panic.[24] Although Dennis Allen notes that ''the ineffability of the sexual, the 'unspeakability' of sex is nonetheless reflected in Victorian culture precisely through the troping of sex and sexuality as chaotic and disruptive forces'' (34), the chaos that engulfs Midwinter—his hysteria and panic as well as his apparent inability to utter the unspeakable truth about Armadale—must not be interpreted simply as sexual repression. Midwinter is not conflicted about his ''unconquerable affection'' for Allan Armadale; rather, his hysteria, his perpetual anxiety and feelings of terror, stem from an unconscious awareness that his ''love'' for Armadale signifies death. It is a violation of the Law (not only of the father, but of nineteenth-century society's law) that registers homosexuality as criminal. Midwinter's homosexual panic anticipates Freud's claim that guilt exists prior to a transgression. That is, ''criminals'' suffer from a ''sense of guilt'' and a belief in having erred precedes and even causes misdeeds and criminal acts. In Christopher Lane's reading of Lacan, he argues that ''the subject is torn between several incommensurate demands: social law, psychic Law operating by injunctions and guilt, and an internal resistance to satisfaction'' (27). Collins, whose whole novel turns upon the notion of premonitory visions, translates these psychological fears into the hypersensitive Midwinter's belief that there is ''a fatality that follows men in the dark'' (105), a fatality that takes the form of a Woman (133).

And thus, into this highly charged relationship enters Miss Gwilt, the uncanny link between the two generations, with her own dangerous agenda. She represents the repressed legacy of a shameful past who has returned to incriminate the heirs.[25] Miss Gwilt is the prime source of Midwinter's haunted state just as the uncanny is "undoubtedly related to what is frightening—to what arouses dread and horror" (Freud 219). Midwinter's feelings of terror, his perpetual anxiety and occasional outbursts of hysteria, are unconsciously derived from Miss Gwilt's signification as the criminal. Freud has theorized that the uncanny is in reality nothing new or alien, but that which is familiar and old; it often appears as something dangerous which demands recognition. According to Freud, the figure of *jouissance* "always appears as a disturber of love." She is the intruder who always emerges at the moment when the subject comes close to fulfilling a sexual relation.[26] Indeed, the intensity of the two men's relationship does abate when Armadale (and later Midwinter) pursues Miss Gwilt.

When Midwinter first meets the strangely familiar Lydia Gwilt, he is "overwhelmed . . . by [an] immense, [and] instantaneous revulsion of feeling" (279). The horror that is initially evoked by Miss Gwilt serves as a necessary correlative to the psychological and social phenomenon of abjection. In *Powers of Horror*, Kristeva identifies this "horror" as "a massive and sudden emergence of uncanniness, which, familiar as it might have been in an opaque and forgotten life, now harries [the subject] as radically separate, loathsome. Not *me*. Not *that* " (2). When Armadale reluctantly tells Midwinter he is in love with Miss Gwilt, Midwinter is visibly unsettled. His face turns "ashy pale, and his glittering black eyes fixed full on Allan's face." Midwinter admits that he "is always in extremes"; when Armadale takes his hand at this moment it is "cold as ice," though he confesses that his hand was as "hot as fire the first time [Armadale] took it at the old West-country inn" (298). Shortly thereafter, Midwinter, who originally was repulsed by her, finds himself drawn to Miss Gwilt, a sudden change of heart which, for the reader, is unsettling and inexplicable:

> The pang that had wrung him when he heard Allan's avowal, had set the truth self-revealed before Midwinter for the first time. He had been conscious of looking at Miss Gwilt with new eyes and a new mind, on the next occasion when they met. . . . [H]e had been conscious of his growing interest thenceforth in her society, and his growing admiration of her beauty—but he had never until now known the passion that she had roused in him for what it really was.
> (301–02)

In her study, *Between Men: English Literature and Male Homosocial Desire*, Eve Sedgwick has shown how René Girard's schematization of the dialectic of power found in erotic triangles reveals a bond between males. Specifically, the bond that links two rivals is as intense and portentous as the bond that links either of the rivals to the beloved. It is such a triangle we find at work in *Armadale* in the relationship between Miss Gwilt, Armadale, and Midwinter. As Miss Gwilt schemes to "come between them," her attempts give rise to a violent rivalry between the two, and it is the intensity of this rivalry that assiduously affirms the real secret of *Armadale*—not so much the homoerotic bond between the two Allan Armadales, but rather the criminality associated with that bond that is registered in the unconsciousness of Midwinter.

The title of one chapter in particular, "She Comes Between Them" (Bk. 4, ch. 8) emphasizes Miss Gwilt's divisive influence. She tells Midwinter of how Armadale abused her, and it is this lie that creates a violent rift between the two men. When they next meet, Armadale, in a panic, declares, "there seems to be something strange between us!" (395) (a phrase which is repeated three times in the chapter). Midwinter is torn between his "instinctive loyalty towards Allan" and the "influence of Miss Gwilt." His confusion is such that his mind fills "with a sudden distrust of the governess's influence over him, which was almost a distrust of himself" (392). A violent conflict ensues in which "the truth" (Midwinter's interest in Miss Gwilt) was "stripped . . . instantly of all concealments and disguises, and laid . . . bare to view" (398).

Freud notes that the uncanny causes a vague sense that the conscious "I" is not fully self-contained or in control. Despite his confusion Midwinter pursues his strange attraction to Miss Gwilt; even she finds this pursuit lacking in self-control, as she recounts: " 'Ask me if I love you,' he whispered. At the same moment his head sank on my bosom; and some unutterable torture that was in him burst its way out, as it does with *us*, in a passion of sobs and tears" (418). In this emotional scene, Midwinter resignedly embraces, literally and figuratively, the Criminal, an act and an acknowledgment that is "unutterable torture." Shortly thereafter they marry, though Miss Gwilt not only insists on a secret wedding, she also insists that they marry using Midwinter's real name, the name he has also kept secret—Allan Armadale. Almost immediately, however, the relationship sours. The new Mrs. Allan Armadale declares to an indifferent Midwinter that "there is something wrong in our married life" and goes on to blame "some adverse influence" that she cannot trace (546). For Kristeva, the figure of *jouissance* is that which must be violently cast out, abjected, an operation fundamental to the recovery of subjectivity. In this case, Miss Gwilt must be cast out—literally killed—so that Midwinter can assert a subjectivity that is homosexual, but not criminal.

In a climactic meeting, all three characters significantly come together at a "sanatorium," a mental asylum that exists to "cure" nervous patients. The clinical significance of this location should not be overlooked. It is here presumably that Midwinter will be "cured" of his problem by casting out his demon, Miss Gwilt. Unaware of what is about to transpire, Miss Gwilt, however, has conspired to poison Armadale (so that she may seize control of an inheritance as Mrs. Allan Armadale),[27] but her plans are thwarted when Midwinter, sensing danger, substitutes himself in Armadale's room: "Confronted by actual peril, the great nature of the man intuitively freed itself from the weaknesses that had beset it in happier and safer times. Not even the shadow of the old superstition rested on his mind now—no fatalist suspicion of himself disturbed the steady resolution that was in him" (657–58). In exchanging rooms, Midwinter saves Allan and himself from certain death. Miss Gwilt discovers the room change that has thwarted her plans and drags the unconscious Midwinter into the corridor and out of the room containing the poison gas. She ascertains that he is in fact alive and realizes he has attempted to save Armadale's life with his own. Despite the fact that Miss Gwilt's initial motivation in marrying Midwinter is to legitimize herself and acquire the estate at Thorpe-Ambrose, she does in fact repeatedly demonstrate a genuine affection for Midwinter. Now she clearly sees that her affection will never be returned as long as his male lover lives. She intends to enter the death room and close the door, committing suicide. But before Miss Gwilt takes this step and her own life, she hovers over an *unconscious* Midwinter and admits defeat: "All your life is before you—a happy life, and an honoured life, if you are freed from *me*" (666).

The fact that he remains unconscious during this soliloquy is particularly significant. She has released Midwinter from making a conscious choice between herself and Armadale, a choice Collins wants us to realize will not be made in her favor if Midwinter is forced to make it. Collins will not then need Midwinter to reveal publicly his preference for his male lover over his wife. Hence, Midwinter is liberated from an unconscious signification of his dangerous criminality. The real secret that drives the plot of *Armadale* can remain unspoken.

In the final pages of the novel, Armadale anticipates his upcoming wedding to Miss Milroy, an event which might lead us to a Foucauldian conclusion that *Armadale* puts its homosocial pathology in the service of promoting a homosocial "cure"; ultimately, the protagonist and reader are disciplined to heterosexual norms as each renounces same-sex desire. Such a reading, however, would overlook Midwinter's words to Armadale: "No clouds, raised by my superstition, will ever come between us again. . . . I, too, am standing hopefully on the brink of a new life, and . . . while we live, brother, your love and mine will never be divided again" (677). This final affirmation of the love they share, though, does not necessarily fit neatly into Sedgwick's essentialist formulation that nineteenth-century novels frequently offer a queer critique of a homophobically patriarchal structure. We would be giving short shrift to Collins's novel if we subscribed to such polarized readings. Following Foucault, we know that "discourse transmits and produces power; it reinforces it, but it also undermines and exposes it, renders it fragile and makes it possible to thwart it" (*History* 101). This is precisely what Collins does—*thwart* nineteenth-century perceptions of homosexuality. Thus, we can see how the novel works to produce an alternative form of knowledge.

However, while one of the projects of the novel is to decriminalize the love that dare not speak its name, Collins has not necessarily invested in garnering sympathy for homosexuals; we must remember that "decriminalize" does not necessarily mean "legitimize." As his Foreword states, Collins realizes that this daring book will offend his contemporary critics; he does not aspire to change their hearts. But, he continues, "Time will help me if my work lasts. I am not afraid of my design being permanently misunderstood, provided the execution has done it any sort of justice."

NOTES

1. The term first appeared in a poem by Lord Alfred Douglas, "Two Loves," published in *The Chameleon* in December, 1894. In his second trial, Wilde was asked to explain the poem and the expression in detail.
2. See, for instance, Winifred Hughes (36–37); Patrick Brantlinger (30–57); and John Sutherland (75–90).
3. Collins's fiction does not simply draw upon real life; it also symbiotically helps to shape the culture's attitudes. Richard Altick, for example, comments extensively upon the public prejudices against red-headed women, attributing this attitude to Pre-Raphaelite art as well as popular fiction. For Victorian readers, Lydia Gwilt's flamboyant red hair would underscore both her sexuality and her villainy; at the same time, Collins's choice both reflects and strongly reinforces this popular contemporary bias. See Altick 315–29.
4. See, for instance, Pearsall, who details some of the century's more infamous cases involving homosexual scandal: the Banks Case of 1833, the Boulton and Park transvestitism case of 1870, and the Cleveland Street Scandal of 1889 (548, 559–76).
5. D.A. Miller is the only critic that we know of who has even broached the topic (but not topicality) of homosexuality in the sensation novel. In his discussion of *The Woman in White*, Miller argues that Collins calls sexual difference into question by feminizing the presumably male reader. The resulting hysteria or "homosexual panic" in his audience thus effects a type of disciplinary "heterosexual masculine protest."
6. The term was actually first coined in 1869 by Hungarian writer Karoly Benkert. The word first appears in the Supplement to the *OED*, with a citation attributed to Havelock Ellis in 1897. Krafft-Ebing himself contends that the "mental condition of the perpetrator" must be determined in judging whether homosexuality is a criminal act. Only "an anthropological and clinical judgment of the perpetrator," he claims, "can permit a decision as to whether we have to do with a perversity deserving punishment, or with an abnormal perversion of the mental and sexual life, which, under certain circumstances, excludes punishment." See *Psychopathia Sexualis* 382 ff.

7. While the 1861 "Offenses Against the Person Act," which removed the death penalty for buggery (thus revoking Henry VIII's statute of 1533 that criminalized buggery as "a crime against nature"), seemed to signal a relaxing of tensions towards homosexuals, this illusion was legally dispelled in 1885 when the Labouchere Amendment reaffirmed homosexuality as criminal. The amendment declared all homosexual acts to be "acts of gross indecency," punishable by law for two years (this was the law under which Oscar Wilde would be convicted and sentenced to two years of hard labor in 1895). While the law did not necessarily create public hostility toward homosexuality, Jeffrey Weeks points out that "as part of a wider restructuring of the social regulation of sex, it helped shape a new mood, particularly in its operation." Weeks suggests that what may have been even "more important than the individual prosecutions were the outbursts of moral panic that often accompanied some of the more sensational cases" (103). *The Yokel's Preceptor,* published in the 1850s as a kind of guide for "men about town," articulated gross indignation over the presence of homosexuals in a civilized city: "Why has the pillory been abolished? Would it not be found very salutary for such beasts as these? for can they be too much held up to public degradation and public punishment?" (Quoted in Pearsall 548).

8. This belief, according to Foucault, was perpetuated by a "literature of criminality" that included both "newspapers and sensation novels" ("Dangerous Individual" 12).

9. In *The History of Sexuality,* Foucault argues that "there is no question that the appearance in nineteenth-century psychiatry, jurisprudence, and literature of a whole series of discourses on the species and subspecies of homosexuality, inversion, pederasty, and 'psychic hermaphrodism' made possible a strong advance of social controls in this area of 'perversity'; but it also made possible the formation of a 'reverse' discourse: homosexuality began to speak in its own behalf ... " (101).

10. Rev. of Armadale, *The Spectator,* 39 (9 June 1866), 638–40. Quoted in Page 150.

11. Altick suggests her name connotes both "guilt" and "gilt" (323).

12. Taylor argues that Miss Gwilt is "the figure of all-embracing, disarming, and suffocating female power.... She is everything men desire in the feminine and everything they fear" (167). Donald Hall, while acknowledging that Miss Gwilt "is clearly something of a *femme fatale,*" contends that "she is no simplistic stereotype." He sees Miss Gwilt as a source of "energy, power, and narratorial force," dedicated to the disruption of gender roles and male autonomy" (165).

13. Although Armadale/Wrentmore speculates that he may have been poisoned by a "woman ... whom [he] had wronged," his very language—"I have no proof against Ingleby"—suggests that the spurned lover is in fact Ingleby (31).

14. Admittedly, distilling so succinctly what has been described as "the most labyrinthine of plots" and the most "overplotted novel in English literature" *is* an ambitious claim in and of itself.

15. In *Inquiries into Human Faculty and Its Development* (1883) Francis Galton stated unequivocally that "it is easy, however, to show that the criminal nature tends to be inherited" (Quoted in Taylor and Shuttleworth 331) and Havelock Ellis upheld this view in *The Criminal* (1890): "The influence of heredity ... in

the production of criminals, does not always lie in the passing on of developed proclivities. . . . [T]here is no doubt whatever that the criminal parent tends to produce a criminal child'' (104, 112).

16. We are indebted to Jenny Bourne Taylor's illuminating distillation of nineteenth-century psychology (27–70). In her discussion of *Armadale*, Taylor analyzes the way in which the various inheritances of one generation are psychologically internalized and passed on to the next generation through psychic phenomena such as the dream.

17. Such an interpretation would concur with Oscar Wilde's late-century declaration of despair: ''All men kill the things they love'' (*The Ballad of Reading Gaol*).

18. Krafft-Ebing, of course, also notes ''that antipathic sexual instinct as an anomaly of sexual life is only found in individuals who are tainted, as a rule, hereditarily'' (295).

19. The extent to which these circumstances are deliberately contrived, fated, or coincidental is a subject that would be disproportionate to include here.

20. Collins, in fact, makes a point of telling us that at the large Thorpe-Ambrose estate there are many ''bedrooms and dressing-rooms—light, spacious, perfectly furnished; and all empty, except the one bedchamber next to Allan's, which had been appropriated to Midwinter'' (169).

21. Quoted in Taylor and Shuttleworth 191.

22. Collins continually reminds us that Midwinter is attempting to ''restrain'' his emotions. See also 395, 491, and 647.

23. Needless to say, we do not accept Natalie Schroeder's assertion that Midwinter is a ''conventionally masculine hero,'' or that he ''possess[es] all the equipment and energy for some of the active male eroticism that was typically associated with male dominance'' (5, 8)

24. Indeed, Miss Milroy already perceives Midwinter to be her potential rival—''she was fond enough of Allan already to be jealous of Allan's friend'' (226).

25. Though Donald Hall briefly acknowledges a homosocial attachment between Midwinter and Armadale, he sees Miss Gwilt as both a transgressive *and* sympathetic force that works to undermine the male power structure (165–66).

26. For Freud, the uncanny (as figured in the reappearance of the Sand-man) bars the sexual relation. As the bearer of a terrible and lethal *jouissance*, the Sand-man ''separates the unfortunate Nathaniel from his betrothed and from her brother, his best friend; he destroys the second object of his love, Olympia, the lovely doll'' (231). While Freud says the uncanny effect of the Sand-man is linked to the ''anxiety belonging to the castration complex of childhood'' (233), we would argue that the anxiety that is produced by the (re)appearance of the criminal (Miss Gwilt) would render the same kind of uncanny effect.

27. Poison, which repeatedly is the instrument of choice for homicide in Collins's fiction, is also frequently alluded to as a ''woman's'' weapon. Collins relies on poison for his murderesses in order to make the feminine transgressive without overstepping the line and making them masculine. The crazed Bertha brandishing fire in *Jane Eyre*, for example, is not a ''proper'' woman, but is someone who appears to be more masculine than feminine. For obvious reasons, we do not need another masculine lover in *Armadale*.

WORKS CITED

Adams, James Eli. "Victorian Sexualities." *A Companion to Victorian Literature and Culture*. Ed. Herbert F. Tucker. Oxford: Blackwell, 1999. 125–38.

Allen, Dennis. *Sexuality in Victorian Fiction*. Norman: University of Oklahoma P, 1993.

Altick, Richard. *The Presence of the Present. Topics of the Day in the Victorian Novel*. Columbus: Ohio UP, 1991.

Brantlinger, Patrick. "What is 'Sensational' about the Sensation Novel?" *Wilkie Collins*. Ed. Lyn Pykett. New York: St. Martin's, 1998. 30–57.

Collins, Wilkie. *Armadale*. Ed. John Sutherland. London: Penguin, 1995.

Ellis, Havelock. *The Criminal*. London: Walter Scott, 1890. Rpt. Montclair, NJ: Patterson Smith, 1973.

Foucault, Michel. "About the Concept of the Dangerous Individual in 19th Century Legal Psychiatry." *International Journal of Law and Psychiatry* (1978): 1–18.

———. *The History of Sexuality, Volume I: An Introduction*. New York: Random House, 1978.

Freud, Sigmund. "The Uncanny." *Standard Edition of the Complete Psychological Works*. Trans. and ed. James Strachey. London: The Hogarth P, 1957. 17: 219–52.

Hall, Donald. *Fixing Patriarchy: Feminism and Mid-Victorian Male Novelists*. London: Macmillan, 1996.

Hughes, Winifred. *The Maniac in the Cellar*. Princeton: Princeton UP, 1980.

Krafft-Ebing, Richard von. *Psychopathia Sexualis*. Trans. Franklin S. Klaf. New York: Stein and Day, 1965.

Kristeva, Julia. *Powers of Horror*. Trans. Leon S. Roudiez. New York: Columbia UP, 1982.

Lane, Christopher. *The Burden of Intimacy: Psychoanalysis and Victorian Masculinity*. Chicago: University of Chicago P, 1999.

Miller, D. A. *The Novel and the Police*. Berkeley: University of California P, 1988.

Page, Norman. *Wilkie Collins: The Critical Heritage*. London and Boston: Routledge and Kegan Paul, 1974.

Pearsall, Ronald. *The Worm in the Bud: The World of Victorian Sexuality*. New York and London: Penguin, 1983.

Pykett, Lyn. *The Sensation Novel.* Plymouth: Northcote House, 1994.

Schroeder, Natalie. " 'A Book That is Daring Enough to Speak the Truth.' " *Wilkie Collins Society Journal* 3 (1983): 5–19.

Sedgwick, Eve. *Between Men: English Literature and Male Homosocial Desire.* New York: Columbia UP, 1985.

Sutherland, John. "Wilkie Collins and the Origins of the Sensational Novel." *Wilkie Collins to the Forefront: Some Reassessments.* Eds. Nelson Smith and R.C. Terry. New York: AMS Press, 1995. 75–90.

Taylor, Jenny Bourne. *In the Secret Theatre of Home.* London and New York: Routledge, 1988.

———. and Shuttleworth, Sally. *Embodied Selves: An Anthology of Psychological Texts, 1830–1890.* Oxford: Oxford UP, 1999.

Weeks, Jeffrey. *Sex, Politics and Society.* London and New York: Longman, 1981.

Charles Lutwidge Dodgson's Infatuation with the Weaker and More Aesthetic Sex Reexamined

Hugues Lebailly

Again and again, the Reverend C. L. Dodgson, better known under his pen name of Lewis Carroll, is described in the media as a more or less active child-lover, whose single lifelong source of pleasure would have been the company of prepubescent girls. If his most famous extant photographs indeed depict little girls in various attires, an objective examination of his unabridged diaries and published letters demonstrates that, far from deliberately dropping his young friends when they reached puberty, he was very intent on stretching his acquaintance with them as long and as far as they were willing, and as Mrs. Grundy would allow him. The actual ages of the recipients of his so-called letters to child-friends, and his repeated marks of satisfaction at being able to go around with older girls and women as he himself grew older, as well as massive evidence for his fascination with the adult naked female body, have all been overlooked by most of his biographers so far. In this day and age when pedophilia is widely condemned as an abominable crime, it is important the image of one of the greatest Victorian writers be cleared of such outrageous and ungrounded suspicions.

The still more or less universally accepted view of the extremely limited range of Charles Lutwidge Dodgson's interest in the opposite sex has been

Dickens Studies Annual, Volume 32, Copyright © 2002 by AMS Press, Inc. All rights reserved.

wonderfully encapsulated by Karoline Leach as an endless repetition of short-lived "friendships with prepubescent female children" in which he "invariably lost interest when they reached puberty." There is no denying that, not only in the media but in his most authorized biographies, his emotional life is presented, to quote Leach a little further, "as an ultimately sterile and lonely series of repeated rejections as the little ones grew up and inevitably left him behind." This purported obsession is regarded as "evidence of a repressed deviant sexuality," and "Lewis Carroll" described as "a man who struggled to master his differing sexual appetites" in academic papers, and as "a paedophile" in the popular press (Leach 11).

This quasi-unanimous tenet turns out to be grounded in just half-a-dozen ever-recurring quotations, taken at face value, often out of context, if not grossly misinterpreted, and belied by a far more considerable body of evidence, which has been there for everyone to see for at least thirty years, in the original, unedited, text of his manuscript diaries, and the various collections of letters edited and annotated by Morton N. Cohen.

One such old favorite is the disparaging judgment Lewis Carroll passed on thirteen-year-old Alice Pleasance Liddell on the eleventh of May 1865: "Alice seems changed a good deal, and hardly for the better, probably going through the usual awkward stage of transition." In his 1999 edition of the fifth extant volume of Dodgson's diaries, Edward Wakeling ascribes that harsh remark to the fact that strong-willed Alice (the only child who ever dared pester Dodgson until he wrote down the story whose heroine bore her name) "was becoming more independent in mind and manner" (*Diaries* 5: (74). Until then, most commentators had interpreted this as proof of Dodgson's disgust for the changes induced in her physical appearance by her dawning puberty. But Dodgson did not seem to mind the growing body of the much sweeter-tempered Lorina. He repeatedly gave vent in his diaries to his fear that she would be banned by her mother from their unchaperoned excursions at about the same age, thus demonstrating that he did enjoy Lorina's company though she was by then "so tall as to look odd without an escort" (Wakeling, *Diaries* 5: (192).[1] "Tall" could be a Victorian understatement for a process that might have involved more than vertical growth in the fourteen-year-old dark-haired daughter of a woman admired for her Spanish beauty.

Another quotation endlessly rehearsed in support of this view of Lewis Carroll's social life is Ellen Terry's famous remark that he was "as fond of [her] as he could be of any one over the age of ten" (qtd. in Cohen, *Interviews* 240). Leaving aside the fact that this could be interpreted as a mark of disappointment, if not frustration, from a very sensual and physical actress, Terry's judgment is not supported by the facts. She actually met Dodgson on numerous occasions when he was accompanied by teenage girls and young women in their twenties whom he proudly introduced to her. Her comment may say as much about her as about him. The two youngest girls he introduced to Ellen Terry, for example, were both fourteen: Agnes Hull in 1881 and Dolly Rivington in 1897 (Green, *Diaries* 2: 393, 537–38). In between, Ellen had also enjoyed opportunities to see him accompanied by seventeen-year-old Ethel Arnold (to whom she was introduced three times in a single day) (*Letters* 1: 479), then, two months later, by Ethel's twenty-five-year-old sister Julia (Green, *Diaries* 2: 415), as well as to send autographs at his request to eighteen- and nineteen-year-old Charlotte and Edith Rix, whom she oddly described as fulfilling the "little desires of little children," so that Dodgson felt compelled to reassure them he "DIDN'T tell Miss Terry that [they] were 'little children' " and that "that [was] entirely her own idea" (*Letters* 1: 604–05). This systematic misconception on Terry's part did not prevent her from introducing him to an actress-friend of hers, Violet Barnes, who was twenty by then, and the misconception was apparently not dispelled when he wrote to her afterwards that "it ha[d] been a great pleasure to make friends with Violet" (*Letters* 2: 681), nor when he turned up at the Lyceum with the by then twenty-three- and twenty-two-year-old flesh and blood Edith and Charlotte Rix (*Letters* 2: 726–27, 737).

Meanwhile, Dodgson had taken fifteen-year-old Muriel Taylor to *The Merchant of Venice* (Green, *Diaries* 2: 451) and same-aged Isa Bowman to *Macbeth* (Green, *Diaries* 2: 469–70), the latter a prelude to many more meetings with the teenage actress whom Terry generously accepted to coach one year later. Though Dodgson expressed his gratitude for her willingness to teach his "dear little friend" and vouched that Terry had won herself the "rapturous love of one enthusiastic child" (*Letters* 2: 812–13) (after all, at fifty-eight, he might have been Isa's grandfather), Ellen had to see his protégée was well over ten. In a letter of December 1892 to Charlotte Rix (his "dear Lottie," now twenty-five), he quoted Ellen's suggestion that "perhaps little Lottie would like to come and see *King Lear*" and her offer to make available her box, so that "she might bring some young friends, and then [Ellen] would see them all in [her] room after the play was over" (*Letters* 2: 940). Dodgson was a most diligent go-between, and Charlotte and her twenty-six-year-old sister Edith did take advantage of Ellen's offer: Ellen was so pleased with what she saw of these two rather mature "childfriends" that she asked their "old friend" to provide her with likenesses of various members of the Rix family (*Letters* 2: 943).

In 1894, he introduced to Ellen his twenty-six-year-old cousin Minna Quin, whose career on the stage he wanted to promote, and whom Ellen agreed to hire for a month as a "super" in *Faust* (Green, *Diaries* 2: 510). He also introduced her to nineteen-year-old Dolly Baird, to whom Ellen "stood talking for five or ten minutes, behind the curtain, while the 'Brocken' scenery was being put up" (Green, *Diaries* 2: 511), in probably too poor a light for Ellen to realize Dolly was twice the age she supposedly would have expected her to be. The following year, Dodgson took Agnes Wilson, nineteen, and Ethel Rowell, eighteen, to *The Merchant of Venice*. Nothing in the corresponding diary entry proves that they met Ellen in person, though it had become quite a ritual on such occasions.

Whatever one may think of how far Leach has stretched her reassessment of Dodgson's potentially active sexuality, it cannot be denied that she has most convincingly evidenced many of Dodgson's female friends common tendency to underestimate their age at their first meeting when they wrote, many years later, of their recollections of their friendship with him.

One example is provided by Isa Bowman. She asserts in *The Story of Lewis Carroll* that she was "only some ten or eleven years of age" when Dodgson, after having violently torn from her a small drawing of him she had been making on the back of an envelope and then thrown the pieces into the fire, "caught [her] up in his arms and kissed [her] passionately" (19). The snag is Isa was thirteen when they first met, in 1887 (Green, *Diaries* 2: 455). If this scene took place in his rooms at Christ Church, as she seems to imply, she must have been at least fourteen, as on the day when they were walking hand in hand in Christ Church meadows and he got quite "disturbed" when a male acquaintance suddenly "came round the corner." (Bowman 13).[2] To a Victorian mind, it was indeed a much more embarrassing situation if the girl was fourteen or over than if she had been under ten. Four years later, Dodgson confided uneasily to Mrs. Mallalieu that his "little friend Isa Bowman [wa]s rather apt to dress in GAUDY colours, which [he] d[id]n't much like, as it [made them] too conspicuous" (*Letters* 2: 913). Indeed, whereas Mrs. Mallalieu's daughter Polly was twelve when she came to stay with him at Eastbourne, Isa was eighteen by then, though she would still cling to his arm as innocently as five years earlier. The previous autumn, he had nonetheless proudly written to a woman friend: "Isa has been my guest here for four summers now (now that I am nearly sixty I venture to do VERY unconventional things) and on Monday I come to town to fetch her down for her fifth visit" (*Letters* 2: 862–63). The seventeen-year-old actress was joined for two days by twenty-four-year-old Violet Barnes, for whom an extra bed was put up in Isa's room.[3] This visit was deleted from the version of Dodgson's manuscript diaries that his nieces allowed to be published.

Isa's inclusion among Dodgson's "childfriends" is perhaps reflective of a time that had not yet invented adolescence as a bridge between childhood and adulthood. But it can be misleading to readers who would hardly imagine that the "millions of hugs and kisses" about which "Lewis Carroll" joked with relish for a whole page of a letter to "[his] darling Isa" had been sent to him by a sixteen-year-old actress and not by someone under ten (*Letters*

2: 785–86). Green's severely censored edition of Dodgson's diaries has many suggestions of Dodgson's distinctions between girls of 10 (or younger) and others. One is an excerpt from a letter to Mrs. Aubrey-Moore in which Dodgson asked whether her daughters were "invitable to tea, or dinner, SINGLY," as he didn't think "anyone knows what girl-nature is, who has only seen them in the presence of their mothers or sisters," and whether they were "kissable," as "nearly all his girl-friends (of all ages, and even married ones) [were] now on such terms with [him], who [was] now sixty-four." "With girls under fourteen," he went on, "I don't think it necessary to ask the question: but I guess Margery to be OVER fourteen, and, in such cases, with new friends, I usually ask the mother's leave" (Green, *Diaries* 2: 527). In fact, one of the very few occasions on which Dodgson got into major trouble with a mother was not when he photographed the Hatch or the Henderson sisters in the nude—a point to which I will come back later on—but when he kissed a girl of seventeen, Atty Owen, in front of her father, expecting her to be right below the above-mentioned age limit (Green, *Diaries* 2: 385). Mr. Owen did not mind much, but his wife did—and yet Dodgson was bold enough to write them a letter four months later, suggesting they might send him Atty to photograph (Cohen, *Kitchins* 40).

Similarly, it is not his playfulness with underage girls which brought him the often-quoted single letter of remonstrance he received from his sister Mary, in 1893, but yet another unchaperoned four-day visit from an unmarried woman, the twenty-seven-year-old Gertrude Chataway. He had in fact first met her at Sandown when she was nine, and much enjoyed being allowed to draw and photograph her in her unconventional "wading attire"—a fisherman's jersey and shorts that left her legs, knees, and even most of her thighs bare—but she had outgrown this costume without losing his affection. In his diaries, he described the four days they had spent together as "a really delightful visit" (Green, *Diaries* 2: 501), and, in his answer to his sister, he brushed aside other people's opinions of his actions as "worthless as a test of right and wrong," before perversely passing on to her the additional information that he was presently enjoying the company of twenty-three-year-old Edith Miller. In conjunction with his own conviction "to be entirely innocent and right, in the eye of God" in acting thus, he always secured "FULL approval" of his plans from the parents of his "girl-friends" (*Letters* 2: 977–78). Dodgson did not have ten- or twelve-year-olds in mind when he wrote that sentence, but young ladies twice that age. Some readers perhaps forget that Victorian middle- and upper-class women were to obey their parents to the very eve of their wedding, even when they were well into their twenties.

This confusion seems to have been mischievously fed with relish by Dodgson himself, who described another of his protégées, a painter for a change,

Theodosia Laura Heaphy, as "a mere child of four or five and twenty" in a letter to Maud Standen—who was twenty-seven herself at the time (*Letters* 1: 536). Another time he called his "dearest" Edith Rix "a wicked girl" for not returning to him one of Isa Bowman's letters and "a good girl" to have sent him Tolstoy's *What Men Live By* in a letter he sent her when she was twenty-three (*Letters* 2: 773–74). A young lady didn't need to have been noticed by Lewis Carroll as a fascinating prepubescent little girl and to be loved by him for what she had been and not for what she actually was to be granted such odd marks of tender intimacy. Edith was not a former childfriend, but a nineteen-year-old reader of *The Monthly Packet* who had sent him a solution to Knot X when they started corresponding. Even Morton Cohen, when he reported these circumstances in a note to his 1979 edition of the *Letters*, felt compelled to present them as unusual, writing that "although Edith was nineteen . . . she and Dodgson became fast friends" (*Letters* 1: 557).

The recollections Cohen collected for his later biography counter this implied position. Laurence Irving typically described Dodgson's friendship with Edith Lucy as having "begun, as was usual with him, when she was a child" but he added that "less usually it had survived her transition to adolescence" (Cohen, *Interviews* 151). But some confusion in twentieth-century readers is inevitable when Cohen adds in a note that the girl was sixteen when they first met. Edith was a pupil of the class in logic Dodgson taught at Oxford High School for Girls in 1887, then again in 1894: though he usually alluded to her and her fellows as "children," and though the only one of them mentioned by name in Cohen's biography, Dorothy Poole, was only fourteen,[4] most of them were anywhere from fifteen to nineteen, including Dorothy's best friend, Margery Aubrey Moore, who was sixteen. Three months later, Dodgson, who had taken Edith to Eastbourne with him, deplored that, after a single night there, "Edith was in such tribulation at being away from her mother that [he] took her back to town by the twelve o'clock train, her visit having lasted exactly seventeen hours" (Green, *Diaries* 2: 454). Who would expect such a crisis from a sixteen-year-old today, and not jump to the conclusion the young guest must have been half that age?

Though Dodgson shared part of the anxiety of his times about the possible damage overtaxing might cause to women's "frailer" brains, he was not afraid of female university students either: Edith Olivier was the Susan Esther Wordsworth Scholar at St. Hugh's, as well as twenty-four, when he struck up a friendship with her through his old childfriend Evelyn Hatch, twenty-five by then, and "enjoyed the evening [he] had with [that] very nice girl," to the point of regretting that, unlike Evelyn, she was not "on 'Kiss' terms" (*Letters* 2: 1110–11). Though it is a different point, I cannot resist mentioning in passing that Evelyn was so unconcerned by her intimate relationship with

Dodgson as a child nude sitter seventeen years before that she had shown the resulting prints to her cousins, who had been very "envious"—of her appearance as an eight-year-old odalisque or of the fascinating adventure Evelyn and her elder sisters had been lucky enough to live?

When Dodgson bitterly reproached Julia Arnold with kissing Ellen Terry and her sister Ethel goodbye in his rooms, while depriving him of the same pleasure, and likened the frustration it raised in him to watching someone drink "a large foaming tumbler of delicious cool lemonade" when you are yourself "half fainting with thirst" (*Letters* 1: 559–60), he was writing to a twenty-three-year-old. Edith Miller was twenty-four when he felt he had to give her "an EXTRA hug and kiss to make all right again between [them]" (*Letters* 2: 1030), twenty-five when he signed "yours lovingly" a flirtatious letter in which he complained that her mother would not let her dine in his room unchaperoned, and teased her that, if he went to try his luck at the door of her college, St. Kentigern's, and was not allowed to have her, he "would have to pick out some very nice girl to take instead, and how awfully jealous [she] would be" (*Letters* 2: 1056–57), and twenty-seven when he again harped on the same subject, professing his inability to understand how her mother could let her "go up to town, for a day, with [him] as her sole escort" but would not allow her to "come to [his] rooms for an evening," and concluded: "I HOPE it won't occur to her to forbid KISSING! That will be the next privilege cut off, I fear" (*Letters* 2: 1148). That bitter postcript, coming from a man who had flirtatiously signed himself her "sexagenarian lover" (*Letters* 2: 1035) three years earlier, convincingly demonstrates that whatever part physical contact played in his relationships with his female friends, these women at least were not children.

Among the letters "from childfriends" quoted by Stuart Dodgson Collingwood in his *Life and Letters of Lewis Carroll*, almost half were received when the girls were over fourteen, and more than a fourth when they were over eighteen. Though Cohen, in his 1995 biography of Dodgson, makes too much of the "man-with-different-sexual-attractions" aspect of his personality, especially under the unfortunate chapter heading, "The Pursuit of Innocents," he does occasionally attempt to bring to the reader's notice that, over the last ten years of Dodgson's life, "Charles cultivated the companionship of mature women more than before" (*Biography* 461). As Alice would have remarked during the Mad Tea-Party, how can you get more of something when you haven't had any so far? Cohen supports this assertion with a series of pertinent quotations from letters addressed to mothers of girl friends, pressing them to follow their daughter's example, and, "encouraged by the circumstance that [the latter] ha[d] returned alive, brave the ogre's den, and come and dine with [him]" (*Letters* 2: 1103–04). The recipient of this unconventional invitation, Mrs. R. L. Poole, did walk in the steps of her fourteen-year-old daughter, Dorothy. Three years earlier, Mrs. G. J. Burch had done something even bolder for a married woman, staying overnight at Guildford with him (and his sisters) after a very busy day in London (*Letters* 2: 955–56) What better conclusion to this long list of adult friends than to quote Dodgson's letter of invitation to Mrs. Poole: "Child-society is very delightful to me: but I confess that grown-up society is much more interesting! In fact, MOST of my 'child'-friends (specially those who come to stay with me at Eastbourne) are now about twenty-five" (*Letters* 2: 1104).

Apart from the harsh judgment passed on Alice's evolution at thirteen, which I quoted in my introduction, the case for the prosecution is essentially grounded in his profession to Arthur Burdett Frost that "a girl of about twelve [was his] ideal of beauty of form" (*Letters* 1: n. 307–08) and his plea to Emily Gertrude Thomson to get him a child-model to copy, but never to get a grown-up model any time she was expecting him, as he "like[d] drawing a CHILD best" (*Letters* 2: 805–06). It may not be a coincidence that, each time, this assertion was formulated to an illustrator of his works, in whose eyes the celebrated "author-for-children" in him had to look immaculately prim and proper, so that his rejection of any connection, however distant, with an adult professional model sitting in the nude—the kind of lower-class women deemed by his peers hardly any better than street-walkers—mattered much more to him than any hypothetical suspicion of exaggerated fascination with the prepubescent female body.

The Victorians, of course, were generally fascinated with the female child as an embodiment of purity and innocence.[5] John Everett Millais, for example, expressed in a letter to his fellow painter Charles Collins, that "the ONLY head you could paint to be considered beautiful by EVERYBODY would be the face of a little girl about eight years old, before humanity is subject to such change" (qtd. in Warner 137–38). The photographer Henry Peach Robinson asserted in his personal reminiscences that "the most delightful sitters are children." "A glow of happiness runs through me," he continued, "when I think of some of my little friends. I do not know a more charming occupation than photographing little girls, from the age of four to eight or nine. After that they lose their beauty for a time. . . . The result, when you get one, is so exquisitely beautiful that it repays you for all your labour" (qtd. in Harker 57). Even more to the point, as it straightforwardly refers to their bodies and not just to their faces, George Du Maurier's narrator professed that "all beauty is sexless in the eyes of the artist at his work—the beauty of man, the beauty of woman, the heavenly beauty of the child, which is the sweetest and best of all" (61).

What is far more ambiguous is where Dodgson drew the line between a child's body and a budding or grown woman's. The third most frequently cited piece of evidence for his dislike of the woman's body is not a direct quotation from his diaries or correspondence, but Mrs. Edith Shute's recollection of a letter in which he "confessed to having no interest in . . . grown-up female models, having the 'bad taste' to find more beauty in the undeveloped than the mature form'' (Cohen, *Interviews* 57). But he was far from consistent in such matters. For instance, his assertion, in the above-quoted letter to A. B. Frost, that ''[he] had rather not have an adult figure (which always look[ed] to [him] in need of drapery)'' (*Letters* 1: 307–08), is not only contradicted by his favorable reception of nude paintings by Dante Gabriel Rossetti and Frederic Leighton that will be established later, but also by his readiness to ''try an adult rather than lose the chance of such splendid practice'' (*Letters* 1: 592) when he got an opportunity to sketch in Henry Paget's studio in London. Granted, he did state beforehand that he ''HOPE[D] it would be a child,'' but this might again be interpreted as a shrinking from the prospect of a confrontation with an unknown adult professional model.

It would be not just dishonest but preposterous to pretend that Dodgson did not enjoy watching, photographing, and drawing little girls in various states of dress and undress, and to deny that he eagerly collected as many photographs and sketches of naked female children as he could get. But it is nearly as dishonest to claim that this was the alpha and omega of his fascination for the nude. In her above-quoted recollections, Edith Shute adds that he described twelve as his ideal age because ''children are so thin from seven to ten'' (Cohen, *Interviews* 57), which can legitimately make us wonder exactly what kind of thinness he had in mind, especially if we notice the relatively large number of fourteen-year-olds he came to draw in the 1880s and '90s. Oddly enough, most of them seem to have been provided by Mrs. Shute, who regularly stretched the upper age-limit they were supposed to have agreed on, to his apparently great pleasure. Such was the case with Ada Frost, a professional model aged 14, whom he sketched in Mrs. Shute's studio in 1888, an opportunity he described as ''quite a new experience [as] the only studies of naked children [he had] ever had opportunities for making were of . . . about five years old.'' He felt compelled to add that ''a spectator would have to be really in SEARCH of evil thought to have any other feeling about her than simply a sense of beauty, as in looking at a statue,'' a remark of self-justification, but one that shows he did not resent her age at all, describing her figure as ''quite lovely,'' and concluding that ''it was a real enjoyment to have so beautiful an object to copy'' (*Letters* 2: 692–93).

Another instance of acute self-contradiction is the case of Maud Howard, another fourteen-year-old model he had met at Mrs. Shute's, whom he described in his diaries as ''not very pretty in face, but certainly beautiful in figure'' (*Letters* 2: 805), and in a letter to Emily Gertrude Thomson as having ''a beautiful figure,'' and looking ''nice and modest.'' But he seems to give way to some sort of panic, maybe inspired by the reputation of young female models to have an early entry into sexual practice, and added: ''But she is turned fourteen, and I like drawing a child BEST. However, if you . . . CANNOT find a child, Maud would be well worth having for an hour'' (*Letters*

2: 805–06). Three years later, when he discussed with Miss Thomson the elder child in her "bower picture," he claimed that the child must be female, and hence was to be provided with longer hair and thinner wrists and ankles to "make a beautiful girl." He put forth as his main argument supporting this that the artist had "given her breasts just the curvature which [he] noticed in the last child-model (Maud Howard, aged fourteen) whom [he] had the privilege of trying to copy in Mrs. Shute's studio." The memory of this great occasion, or maybe the visual evidence he had sought out and consulted before writing that letter, evoked from him the quite lyrical profession that "one hardly sees why the lovely forms of girls should EVER be covered up!" (Letters 2: 947). This must of course be read in the light of his incredibly elastic use of the word "girl" demonstrated above, which can be further demonstrated by his wish to commission Miss Thomson to do a pastel of the head of "a lovely girl friend" (Letters 2: 981) staying with him at Eastbourne: twenty-seven-year-old May Miller.

Rather than losing interest in girls over the age of ten or twelve, Dodgson seems indeed to have been quite anxious to be able to photograph or sketch them as long as he could do so decently. When he insisted on Miss Thomson's photographing for him ten-year-old Iris Bell in the nude, in spite of an unsightly "scar" whose exact position we shall never know, he asked for the photograph not because as she got older, she would be less pleasant for him to look at, but because it was now "possible to get it: in two or three years, it will be impossible" (Letters 2: 981–82), which sounds more like regret than disgust. In his conclusion to his evocation of Maud Howard's sitting, after asking Emily Gertrude Thomson whether she had ever got "[his] little friend Maud Howard," he added: "(I'm afraid she is SIXTEEN by this time.)" (Letters 2: 948). This "afraid" can be interpreted in different ways: "What a pity she has now grown too old to be of any interest to me," "What a pity she is now too old for a mere amateur to sketch her for his private pleasure without breaking the current code of propriety," or "What a pity she is now too old for me to be able to pretend in the eye of God and of my own conscience that the pleasure I am taking in looking at her is wholly innocent," or else "What has become of her? What if she has a sexual life and is liable to behave in a provocative way?"

There is indeed ample proof of Dodgson's attraction to, rather than disgust with, budding womanhood. Some of the drawings by William Stephen Coleman that Dodgson was able to borrow from the artist and to send to be photographed for him by Henry Peach Robinson in 1882, now in the collection of British artist Graham Ovenden, are especially telling. Dodgson's visits to Coleman are recounted in his diary. But four out of the five diary entries mentioning Coleman's name have—not surprisingly—been edited out of Green's edition: in the earliest one, Dodgson reported having met "two of his models, girls of about sixteen and fourteen, the younger rather pretty.''[6] The second described his second visit to Coleman's place, where he stayed "from eight till about eleven, and had a very enjoyable evening, looking through the drawings.'' He selected twenty-two of them, among them two which were drawn from his child-friend Connie Gilchrist, a pantomime actress and notorious skipping-rope dancer, who also modeled for the painter and President of the Royal Academy, Frederic Leighton. Green's edition leaves out a parenthesis in which Dodgson describes them as "one dancing, and one with tambourine,'' as well as the whole of the following sentence: "Two (one crouching on pillow, and one with hands behind) from Frances Mace, and one (picking flower) from Ellen Feldon, who is painted by Dobson in the R. A. this year.'' (Green, *Diaries* 2: 406).[7]

Though the only girl picking a flower to be found in the "Coleman'' section of Graham Ovenden's *Nymphets and Fairies* looks quite young, it is definitely a teen-ager's body that Connie's see-through dress allows the viewer to perceive on the two Christmas cards mentioned—and treasured—by Dodgson (20, 27). This is even more blatantly the case with Frances Mace, if it is she who appears on two other drawings not included in *Nymphets and Fairies* but of which Graham Ovenden has sent me photographic reproductions, and which he assures me were part of Dodgson's collection. The age of the girl is referred to in a letter written by Dodgson to Emily Gertrude Thomson fourteen years later and less than two months before his death. In it, he asked her whether she would agree to hire a camera and pose a thirteen-year-old professional model named Isy Watson " (hands behind her back,'' which he thought "a very pretty arrangement,'' in imitation of "a lovely photo of a girl (of about fifteen)'' he sent her a tracing of, adding that, contrary to the original, "the picture need not include the knees'' (*Letters* 2: 1147), a requirement probably inspired by his belief, expressed in an undated letter to Emily Gertrude Thomson, that "plebeian models'' all had unsightly "thick ankles'' (*Letters* 2: 980–81).

Dodgson implied that such pictures were perfectly proper in his eyes by sending prints of those photos as gifts to fifteen- and eleven-year-old Agnes and Jessie Hull, through his artist friend Theo Heaphy, twenty-three, a present that was, according to his diary entry, gratefully accepted.[8] Mr. Coleman's name last occurs in Dodgson's diary in reference to one of his models, Nellie May, whom he met and befriended in March 1883, but unexpectedly found too young to be photographed yet: "She is pretty, and no doubt artists can make very pretty pictures of her, but I doubt her being a good photographic subject for a 'nude' study, and should guess her to be too fat, at present, though she is eleven and a half: in another year or two she might be more graceful.''[9] Who said puberty was Dodgson's nightmare?

Another even clearer piece of evidence of his fascination for the adolescent body and wish to portray teenage girls in minimal attire is to be found in a series of letters he exchanged with Xie Kitchin's very understanding mother just before he suddenly gave up photography. Xie was one of his favorite models, and he went on photographing her until she was fifteen. In a letter dated February 27th, 1880, he asked Mrs. Kitchin whether she would agree to sell him the bathing dress Xie had been wearing the previous summer rather than have a similar one made on purpose for him, as "new dresses never photo as well as those that have been worn some time," and he went on thus: "OF COURSE I shall not suggest anything so heartrending to your feelings as a mother, as that XIE herself should come and be done in it: but I shall use it for other young ladies, whose theories of life (crossed) dress are more (crossed) less Conservative" (Cohen, *Kitchins* 33).

These few lines reveal his emotional involvement in the daring open request he is making, as well as the indirect plea that lies behind it: crossed words are quite infrequent in this highly meticulous man's correspondence, and were very likely left deliberately in this case: Dodgson might obviously have started copying such a short letter again if he had not wanted Mrs. Kitchin to feel how hurt he was that Xie should deprive him of the pleasure of keeping forever such a delightful vision of her. He might also have wanted her to guess the reproof implied by the original wording, which would have been something like "whose theories of life are more open-minded." Also the emphasis laid on "OF COURSE" makes it even more obvious that he was dying to get the permission he pretended to rule out yet could not resist mentioning just in case Mrs. Kitchin might once more side with him and convince her now less pliable daughter to please her dear old friend once more. And finally, we can notice that, for once, Dodgson did not resort to his sempiternal and quite vague "girls," but used the much more direct "young ladies."

A month later, Mrs. Kitchin tried to assuage his disappointment by offering him a print of "a photo of three young ladies, friends of theirs, dressed as boys in a sort of acrobat dress, the eldest being about sixteen!" The exclamation point is once more quite telling as is the fact that when he sent his love to Xie in his next letter, he stipulated that it would have to be "not quite the BEST kind—but a sort of second-best—a good sound Civil Service sort of article." He wondered whether she would not be by now "too proud to write" and concluded that if she did, and was "in any doubt as to how to sign herself, 'yours faithfully' [would] do very well" (Cohen, *Kitchins* 34–35)—a rather bitter way to show the by now sixteen-year-old "young lady" that he still resented her refusal to pose for him in the sort of costume he would have loved to see her in rather than in the long black or white dresses in which she preferred by then to be portrayed, playing the violin.

Mrs. Kitchin was obviously far more compliant than her daughter, and Dodgson sent her on multiple errands on his account, as he did not dare purchase in person "young ladies' bathing-dresses" or "pairs of stockings" to match his "acrobatic" dresses, "in four sizes, for about the ages six, nine, twelve and fifteen" (Cohen, *Kitchins* 37). A few weeks later, he "mourn[ed] over the non-arrival" of the outfit, adding: "For though I have accepted with all resignation the fact that Xie won't be taken in one, yet there ARE other damsels in the world, and it is quite possible that I might find one not averse to figure as an acrobat. I must however admit that it is less likely I shall find one as beautiful" (Cohen, *Kitchins* 38). If that Machiavellian attempt to arouse Xie's jealousy and win her back through base flattery is not a typical case of desperate sentimental blackmail, then what is? Two days later, he could not resist pricking her again by parading that he had already "found ONE young lady of fifteen who [was to] come and be done in" the fateful dress (Cohen, *Kitchins* 40). It is no wonder that, after so much harassment, he was enjoined to drop the matter altogether, or forget about the Kitchins. He had no choice but to surrender, and send the line: "Don't stay away for clouds. Let there be no further allusion to Xie and the gymnasium dress." But he could not resist adding it merely "diminished [his] happiness by .0001—not more" (Cohen, *Kitchins* 42).

A month later, he sent Mrs. Kitchin what was to be the final letter of that series, apparently followed by a ten-year gap. In a postscript to it, he could not refrain from boasting that he had been able to use "one of the 'swimming-dresses' the other day for Gerida Drage, and got a very picturesque result [as] she is rather handsome" (Cohen, *Kitchins* 43). In a letter to Julia Arnold, at whose parents' home Gerida was a boarder, he had already stated his intention to "do Gerida in the Gymnasium-Dress" and to "have a vague hope Miss Dr- 'her sister' [Gertrud] may think herself not too old for the other Gymnasium-dress" (*Letters* 1: 382–83). Leach gives Gerida's age as sixteen—which means Gertrud was even older, hence Dodgson's doubts. His misgivings must have proved unfounded, as both sisters came to his studio unchaperoned, at three o'clock in the afternoon, on the fifteenth of July 1880, and he spent two hours photographing them (Green, *Diaries* 2: 388). But we shall never know whether both of them did pose in the controversial "swimming" or "acrobat" dresses, as the pictures taken on that day are most likely to have vanished forever.

What we do know is that they were the very last ever taken by Dodgson. There has been much debate about the reasons why he suddenly stopped photographing after that day. His above-mentioned letter to Mrs. Kitchin contains a clue in its last paragraphs in which he tells her of his recent meeting with Mr. Owen, the father of "unkissable" Atty. "He looked like a thunder-cloud. I fear I am permanently in their black books now: not only by having given fresh offence—apparently—by asking leave to photo Atty (WAS that such an offensive thing to do ?) but also by the photos I have done of OTHER people's children'' (Cohen, *Kitchins* 43). Misled by Dodgson's idiosyncratic use of the word "children," all commentators so far but Leach have taken for granted that the offensive pictures both parties had in mind were the nude photographs of nine- and eight-year-old Annie and Frances Henderson he had taken over the previous month. Yet the context points more convincingly in a different direction. Photographing "young little Misses Robinson Crusoe" was perfectly innocent in the eyes of those late Victorians who bought Christmas, New Year's, and birthday cards depicting naked children by the dozen, and found it perfectly proper to display them on the sitting-room mantelpiece or on the piano. The fuss was all about kissing a seventeen-year-old girl, and compulsively harassing sixteen- (and possibly eighteen-) year-old "young ladies" until they yielded to pose in "acrobatic" dresses and dark stockings that clung to their ankles, calves, knees, and thighs, and made them look like those vulgar circus artists whose shows Dodgson was so fond of watching.

Coincidentally—or perhaps quite logically—from the mid-1880s on, he became a regular and enthusiastic spectator of the various aquatic or underwater shows performed by winsome young ladies on Brighton's pier or at Eastbourne's Devonshire Baths. Even more than his description of "Miss Saigeman's Swimming Entertainment" as "a very pretty performance," it is the fond satisfaction with which he noted it was "the first year gentlemen ha[d] been admitted"[10] that testifies to the eagerness with which he had taken advantage of this new opportunity to quench his thirst for contemplating as much as he could of the adult female body without compromising himself too much. Such shows were to hold a considerable place among his seaside entertainments. He attended on four occasions Miss Louey Webb's during the summer of 1887, because "she [was] 18, and as she [was] beautifully formed, the exhibition [was] worth seeing, if only as a picture" (Green, *Diaries* 2: 452).[11] A few months before his death, he was still a devoted patron of "Miss Saigeman's Swimming Entertainment" and ready to go to the trouble of sailing from Eastbourne to Hastings just to applaud the feats of the Beckwith family, which featured a girl he had admired for the first time when she was nine in 1888, but who had by then reached the mature age of eighteen, and must have granted him the same visual pleasure as Louey ten years earlier (Green, *Diaries* 2: 493, 455–56).[12]

Because of the severe editing by Violet and Frances Menella Dodgson of the contents of the nine remaining volumes of their uncle's diaries when they prepared the typescript they allowed Roger Lancelyn Green to publish, Green was unable to indicate all the omissions. Half a century went by before we could see that what the Victorian old ladies were intent on hiding from the general public was not their uncle's interest in little girls, but his enjoyment of what they regarded as coarse performances starring pert young actresses, and the favorable impression various adult female nudes produced on him. Evidence of such vulgar tastes looked to them far more scandalous, and they suppressed it in a much more consistent and systematic way, than his attention to "girls."[13]

The scope of this paper does not allow me to list all the enthusiastic judgments he passed on the grace, agility, charm, or figures of young adult singers, dancers, and actresses in these deleted passages, nor all the depictions of women's faces and figures on portraits and genre paintings that he admired on his numerous visits to public exhibitions and artists' studios. I shall concentrate only on those adult female nudes that fell victim to his nieces' censoring of his diaries.

Some of the references to painters that remain in the edited texts are as suggestive as those censored. Nothing but the failure to actually view some of the pictures to which Dodgson paid a brief tribute, as well as an ignorance of the pictures' exact context, can account for the presence of Dante Gabriel Rossetti's *Venus Verticordia*, Edwin Long's *The Search for Beauty* and *The Chosen Five*, or Frederic Leighton's *Psamathe* and *Crenaia* in the nieces' typescript. If the ladies had known the pictures to which Dodgson was referring, they never would have allowed his favorable comments on them to be printed.[14]

Long's diptych, depicting two successive steps in the Greek sculptor Zeuxis's quest for five models worthy of lending some of their beauty to his ideal Venus, ranked second to his *Anno Domini* among Dodgson's favorite pictures at the 1893 Edwin Long Gallery, and had its pagan theme redeemed perhaps by the proximity of the famous holy "flight into Egypt." Violet and Francis Menella were possibly unaware that the two Zeuxis paintings came from the brush of the master of the picturesque exoticism that had perpetrated the scandalous *Babylonian Slave Market* (Green, *Diaries* 2: 497).[15]

Leighton's works, hardly better known half a century ago than Long's, appeared within narratives of Dodgson's flattering private receptions at the President of the Royal Academy's prestigious house. Moreover, Leighton's uncompleted *Crenaia* was mentioned as a curiosity, "a female figure which look[ed] very queer . . . as the (unfinished) drapery only reach[ed] to the waist," and the quasi-telegraphic style used by Dodgson to describe his "Psamathe," "a sort of 'Hero' on the shore (nude figure, seated, back view)" (Green, *Diaries* 2: 381) in no way pointed to the fullness of her generous curves, worthy of a Rubens, which F. G. Stephens described in the *Athenaeum* as "exuberant, and therefore not severe in their character, . . . studied from the life, and . . . less classical than those usually affected by Sir F. Leighton" (No. 2740), a sight that should have been repulsive if Dodgson had been exclusively addicted to the slender outlines of pre-pubescent girls.

Just as unexpected is his enthusiasm over Dante Gabriel Rossetti's *Venus Verticordia*, an interest that was reasserted on his two successive visits to the ill-reputed painter's studio. In June 1864, the picture was still unfinished when Dodgson judged that it would certainly be "very beautiful" (Green, *Diaries* 1: 217). One year later, the completed work again met with his approval when, in Swinburne's presence, the artist showed him "many beautiful pictures, two quite new: the bride going to meet the bridegroom (from Solomon's Song) and Venus with a background of roses" (Green, *Diaries* 1: 230). Once again, the biblical reference appended to *The Beloved* came just where needed to temper the alluring sensuousness of the pagan goddess, Rossetti's single bare-breasted "stunner," whose gaze looks straight into the viewer's eyes in a provocative way. Even if Dodgson had only been confronted, on that second visit, with a watercolor version R. L. Megroz deemed "rather sentimental [and] quite inoffensive, which is more than one can say about the oil" (197–98), that "tall, massively-built [Venus], no spiritual goddess of beauty" (Marillier 100), of whom F. G. Stephens wrote in October 1865 that "she reck[ed] not of the soul" and that "there [was] more of evil than of good in her" (No. 1982) should have aroused Lewis Carroll's reprobation and disgust, had his repulsion for "fully developed" bodies been so complete as usually alleged.

Perhaps such disconcerting infatuations, in full contradiction with the generally accepted view of his tastes and interests, have been overlooked by many scholars for half a century because most of the other expressions of Dodgson's admiration for adult female nudes had been eradicated out of the only printed version of the diaries then available. For example, John Collier's *Pharaoh's Handmaidens* was one of his five favorite paintings at the 1883 Grosvenor Gallery, none of which depicted little girls (Green, *Diaries* 2: 417).[16] F. G. Stephens saw in the painting only "three saucy ladies of the modern ballet who ha[d] been dyed brown," whose only assets were their "plump contours" (No. 2898), and Cosmo Monkhouse, who condemned their "wholly unredeemed" nudity, liked much better a "pretty naked little girl playing with her father's palette" by a P. R. Morris, which does not seem to have caught Lewis Carroll's eye (316–17).

The "unmentionable" works also included Jean Alexandre Joseph Falguière's *Madeleine*, which Dodgson praised as a "wonderfully life-like picture"(Green, *Diaries* 2: 455),[17] and which appeared to have disturbed him enough to make him misattribute it to Emmanuel Benner, another French artist whose sylvan nymphs adorned the walls of the 1887 Bond Street exhibition of Salon pictures; Thomas Riley's *After the Chase*, shown at Burlington House in 1888, which Dodgson remembered with pleasure as "a beautiful 'nude' study,"[18] an impression shared by F. G. Stephens, who described it as "an elegant group of nude girls, deftly designed and painted" (No. 3163); and, finally, most embarrassing of all, Marceli Suchorowski's *Nana*.

That Dodgson should have noticed Anna Lea Merritt's *Eve*, "seated, with hands clasped round her knees, bowed head and face hidden in her hair" was not that objectionable.[19] The female hand that had produced it absolved it of any suspicion of lewdness, as did the biblical theme and the repentant and decent attitude of the first sinner. Dodgson's introductory sentence, in describing the painting, pointed out the "unusual number of pictures of the nude" (Green, *Diaries* 2: 435) at the 1885 Royal Academy without necessarily deploring this fact.

But while everything concurred in ascribing to *Eve* a respectability, Dodgson's acknowledged viewing of a lurid depiction of Zola's infamous heroine was different. Not only had the painting itself, by a Russian emigrant living in Paris named Marceli Suchorowski, been described by *The Magazine of Art* (in an anonymous entry within the regular feature enttled "The Chronicles of Art") as "a cheap, clever and singularly impudent Salon picture of the vulgarest type" (xxxviii) and by *The Art-Journal* as "a revoltingly sensual picture" (92), but it was exhibited at the Egyptian Hall in a sensational setting aiming at increasing its success of scandal. Standing by itself on an easel raised on a platform, in the center of a room dark enough to protect its viewers' anonymity, but also to bring out the brilliantly lit canvas, the painting with its outrageous subject was further enhanced by two mirrors placed on either side of it, reflecting endlessly, as in a brothel room, the voluptuous curves of its protagonist's body. No wonder *The Magazine of Art*'s critic concluded his review with a paraphrase from the Gospel, stating that "no great work of art shuns the light of the day; and 'Nana' appeals not so much to lovers of art as to lovers of M. Zola's work, two very distinct divisions of mankind" (xxxviii).

For Dodgson to have seemingly included himself among the latter, even on the ill-advised commendation of a friend of his, the actor Lionel Brough, who must have been aware of his interest in adult nudes, was for his nieces an unforgivable faux pas that had to be concealed from posterity. The moderation of the judgment Dodgson passed on it sharply contrasted with the indignant curse called down on the painting by the author of an untitled review in the March 1885 issue of *The Art-Journal*, who wished "the authorities who look[ed] after [the country's] morals [would at last] be roused to action" against such an ignominious show (92). Dodgson, on the other hand, wrote that he "did not like the feeling of [this] very life-like picture of a reclining woman, nude, except for a little drapery covering one leg from knee to foot," and, true to his conviction that only complete nudity could look natural, healthy and innocent, added that "it would have been better entirely nude, but even so rather 'French' in feeling."[20] Such a degree of tolerance, highly typical of a man who was anything but the "prudish and pernickety" average Victorian that Virginia Woolf claimed him to be (47–48), is yet further proof that, contrary to John Ruskin, Dodgson did not find adult nudes shocking as such, but only when they seemed to make dangerously attractive the barely enviable position of the prostitute.

If I have so far supported my thesis that Dodgson found the whole of the female sex, not just underage little girls, more aesthetic than his own, I have not yet justified my use of the adjective "weaker" in my title.

In November 1881, Dodgson wrote in his diaries that he "wear[ied] more and more of dinner-parties, and rejoice[d] that people ha[d] almost ceased to invite [him]" (Green, *Diaries* 2: 401). In a letter he sent to Mrs. Walford, in 1892, he informed her that she was to "excuse [him] from accepting any DEFINITE invitation, even to tea [as he] decline[d] ALL invitations without exception" (*Letters* 2: 924–25). Unlike Phyllis Greenacre, who interpreted this as proof that Dodgson "had become solitary [and] given up much of his always moderate social life" (316–19), James Playsted Wood seems closer to the truth when he writes that "Dodgson was never shy, and he was seldom a recluse. He was aloof only when, for reasons of his own, he wished to be" (172–73).

This emphasis on his unshakeable independence might well be the major key to Dodgson's so often misunderstood relationships with members of the opposite sex. He was neither selfish nor self-centered. He was far too generous for these responses. He spent his time putting into practice his fervent advocation that "one of the deep secrets of Life [is] that all, that is really WORTH the doing, is what we do for OTHERS" (*Letters* 2: 813). But his altruism also sprang from the fact that he belonged to a category of people who derive much more pleasure from giving than from receiving, so long as they get plenty of love and gratitude in return. He never wanted anything to be imposed on him, not even a prearranged meeting with someone whose company he sought, hence his wanderings in London, from locked door to carriage on the leave, especially on his unlucky Fridays. These disappointments were far outbalanced in his eyes by the utter freedom he enjoyed. And perhaps, because, like the cat in Kipling's *Just So Stories*, he hated nothing more viscerally than the slightest risk of being led where he did not want to go, he renounced any deep and lasting emotional involvement that would have made him passive—as the word passion etymologically implies—when he always wanted to be in control of the situations in which he lived. Who is more controllable indeed than a fascinated little girl, and less liable to demand anything from you that you are not willing to do?

There is a mathematical proportionality to his own age in Dodgson's professed favorite age in a girl. Cohen briefly hints at this by referring to two of Dodgson's letters: one to Macmillan in 1877 in which Lewis Carroll claimed that his "views about children [were] changing, [as he] NOW put the nicest age at about seventeen" (Cohen and Gandolfo 462) and another, sent in 1894 to a Mrs. Egerton, whose two daughters, aged eighteen and sixteen, he was keen on adding to the list of his childfriends, provided that she would let them come to his lodgings for dinner unchaperoned and but one at a time, in which he argued: "Much of the brightness of my life, and it has been a wonderfully happy one, has come from the friendship of girl-friends. Twenty or thirty years ago, 'ten' was about my ideal age for such friends: now 'twenty' or 'twenty-five' is nearer the mark. Some of my dearest child-friends are thirty and more: and I think an old man of sixty-two has the right to regard them as being 'child-friends' still" (*Letters* 2: 1008–09).

As he was also very considerate, showing much concern for other people's happiness, he considered that a wide age gap between himself and the members of the opposite sex he spent time with—and put under heavy emotional demand—was safer both for him and for them. As long as he deemed himself of marriageable age, he kept aloof from "young ladies," as his presence at their side might have dissuaded any potential lovers with more serious intentions from courting them, or threatened their reputation and decreased their value in the marriage market. As soon as he thought he could no longer be mistaken for a possible suitor, he was but too pleased to be able to raise his age-limit, and parade on much older girls' arms. He very clearly described this process in at least two letters he sent to young lady friends, in which we find naïve echoes of his wonderment and delight in seeing new doors open wide in front of him.

When he invited twenty-four-year-old Gertrude Chataway to stay with him at Eastbourne, he considered what he could "say in defence of asking a young lady of [her] age to be the guest of a single gentleman." "First, then, if I live to next January, I shall be fifty-nine years old. So it's not like a man of thirty, or even a man of forty, proposing such a thing. I should hold it quite out of the question in either case. I never thought of such a thing, myself, until five years ago. Then, feeling I really had accumulated a good lot of years, I ventured to invite a little girl of ten, who was lent without the least demur. The next year I had one of twelve staying here for a week. The next year I invited one of fourteen, quite expecting a refusal, THAT time, on the ground of her being too old. To my surprise, AND delight, her mother [agreed]. After taking her back, I boldly invited an elder sister of hers, aged eighteen. SHE came quite readily. I've had another eighteen year old since, and feel quite reckless, now, as to ages" (*Letters* 2: 807).

It would certainly be going too far to derive from that statement that, so far, little girls had been, to the younger "Lewis Carroll," but a stop-gap. But the excitement perceptible in the enumeration of these regularly increasing ages echoes the triumphant "it is the first year gentlemen have been admitted" quoted above, regarding "Miss Saigeman's Swimming Entertainment." Renewing his acquaintance with Mrs. Liddell, a year later, Dodgson relied on the same arguments to convince her to let Rhoda and Violet—then thirty-three and twenty-seven—enter his rooms for the very first time: "If I were twenty years younger, I should not, I think, be bold enough to give such invitations: but, but, I am close on sixty years old now: and all romantic sentiment has quite died out of my life: so I have become quite hardened as to having lady-visitors of ANY age!" (*Letters* 2: 873). I personally think that Dodgson's idiosyncratic form of "romantic sentiment" never died out of his heart, as his not that infrequent impulsive marks of jealousy when he heard of his young friends' engagements showed. To the very eve of his death, he was as susceptible as ever to the charms of either innocent, spontaneous underage girls, always willing to be held by the hand, kissed, and hugged, or "stars of perfect womanhood" from whom he dreamed of—and often succeeded in—being granted the same privileges—so long as it did not involve any official engagement that would have threatened his fiercely cherished liberty.

Have I written here "a portrait of Lewis Carroll as a Don Giovanni"? The "catalogues" of names of child-friends that occur several times in his diaries would, by themselves, justify the simile to a certain extent. Contrary to Leach, I would say it is a portrait of "a Platonic Don Giovanni" in spite of his frequent attempts to take advantage of his dominant position in front of the younger and more vulnerable females he so easily hypnotized to get more privacies from them than Mrs. Grundy would have thought proper. But my conviction that Dodgson was never sexually active with them does not preclude a notion that his constantly reasserted thirst for kisses, and his obsessive collecting of partly or wholly nude depictions of the female body in its youth and early maturity make his constant quest for actual or pictorial intimacy quite physical and sensual, if not sexual.

What may have launched Charles Lutwidge Dodgson on that obsessional, unquenchable quest for highly controlled yet as intimate and frequent as possible contact with what I have called "the weaker and more aesthetic sex," as well as for visions and depictions of the young—but by no means exclusively pre-pubescent—female body in the nude? Two rarely mentioned quotations might point in an interesting direction. In a letter to Mrs. Henderson, written in 1880, he described Annie and Frances's innocent habit of running naked around the house as "very beautiful, [filling the viewer with] a feeling of reverence, as at the presence of something sacred." But he immediately felt compelled to add that "for the sake of their little brother," he found it "desirable to bring such habits to an end after this summer" as "a boy's head soon imbibes precocious ideas, which might be a cause of unhappiness in future years, and it is hard to say how soon the danger may not arise" (*Photographs* 21–22). This is a warning he reiterated thirteen years later to Emily Gertrude Thomson: "I hope I made it quite clear that it is my distinct wish that, so far as any picture done for ME is concerned, neither Iris nor Cynthia is ever to be drawn again, at their house, in anything but FULL-DRESS. The RISK, for that poor little boy, is too great to be run again" (*Letters* 2: 987). Was he afraid eight-year-old Clive Bell and the little Henderson boy might grow into the man he had become? It seems unbelievable that the daughters of the archdeacon might have been allowed to run around the rectory stark naked, or that Mrs. Dodgson would have entrusted to her son the sort of cares that would have led him to behold the nudity of some of his many younger sisters, and yet these very solemn warnings do sound as if they had sprung from some very personal experience.

NOTES

1. Nearly a year earlier, he already dreaded a trip to Godstow might be "the last to which Ina is likely to be allowed to come" (Wakeling, *Diaries* 5: 114).
2. According to *Isa's Visit to Oxford*, the incident might have occurred on Saturday, 14 July 1888 (Green, *Diaries* 2: 559–60).
3. Unpublished entry from the manuscript diaries, Thursday, 8 October 1891.
4. According to the birth date Morton N. Cohen quotes in note 1 in *Letters* (2: 1094). In *Lewis Carroll: A Biography*, he writes that she was "aged thirteen" (462). An instance of unconscious underestimation of Dodgson's childfriend's age, or a matter of a few months? (The birth months never being quoted in Cohen's notes, all the ages I mention are necessarily approximate, and minor discrepancies can thus be explained when girls were born late in a year.)
5. For a fuller discussion of this attitude, see Lebailly, "C. L. Dodgson and the Victorian Cult of the Child."
6. Unpublished diary entry, Tuesday, 3 January 1882.
7. Partially unpublished entry, Thursday, 25 May 1882. For reproductions of some of these photographs of Coleman's sketches, see Ovenden 15 [girl picking a flower], 20 [Connie Gilchrist with tambourine], and 27 [Connie Gilchrist dancing].
8. Unpublished diary entry, Monday, 30 October 1882.
9. Unpublished diary entry, Friday, 16 March 1883.
10. Unpublished diary entry, Wednesday, 2 September 1885.
11. Cf. too Friday 15th July 1887 (Green, *Diaries* 2: 482) and unpublished entries for Wednesday, 14 and Saturday, 17 September 1887.
12. "The Beckwith's Swimming Entertainment": Saturday, 15 September 1888, Monday, 29 August and Monday, 12 September 1892, Monday, 23 August 1897 (all unpublished but the second); "Miss Saigeman's Swimming Entertainment": Tuesday, 24 August 1886, Friday, 7 October 1887, Tuesday, 20 August 1889, Tuesday, 18 August 1896, Tuesday, 17 August 1897 (all unpublished but the second again).
13. Discussed in a still unpublished paper given at the 1998 International Lewis Carroll Conference at Cardiff University, "Through a Distorting Looking-Glass : Charles Lutwidge Dodgson's Artistic Interests as Mirrored In His Nieces' Typescript of His Diaries."

14. For a reproduction of Rossetti's *Venus Verticordia*, see Smith plate n 7 (color); for Long's *The Search for Beauty*, see Smith 202, plate 67 (black and white); for Long's *The Chosen Five*, see Postle and Vaughan 95 (color); for Leighton's *Psamathe* and *Crenaia*, see, respectively, in Jones and others 189 (no. 83 [color]) and 192 (no. 85 [color]).

15. Saturday, 18 March 1893 : "Then to see Edwin Long's pictures: the best, I think, are 'The Flight into Egypt', and a pair about Zeuxis painting a picture of Venus from six selected maidens." Dodgson seems to have been so thrilled at their view that he who had been able to count exactly 165 fairies on Joseph Noel Paton's *Quarrel of Oberon and Titania* at the National Gallery of Scotland in 1857 fancied he had seen a sixth Greek beauty where only five were depicted by Long (Green, *Diaries* 2:497).

16. Partially unpublished entry, Tuesday, 29 May 1883 (Green, *Diaries* 2: 417), only mentions two paintings, one of which, J. R. Weguelin's *The Maidens' Race* depicted female athletes who were only partly clothed; this painting obviously was not known to the diaries' censor.

17. Partially unpublished entry, Tuesday, 27 September 1887.

18. Unpublished entry, Monday, 16 July 1888.

19. For a reproduction of this painting, see Smith 195, plate 63 (black and white).

20. Unpublished entry, Monday, 26 May 1884.

WORKS CITED

The four latest volumes of Lewis Carroll's manuscript private journals, which have not yet appeared in print unabridged, are quoted by kind permission of the Trustees of the C.L. Dodgson Estate, who retain their copyright.

Bowman, Isa. *The Story of Lewis Carroll*. 1899. Reiss. as *Lewis Carroll as I Knew Him*. Introduction Morton N. Cohen. New York: Dover, 1972.

"Chronicles of Art, The." *The Magazine of Art*. 8 (July 1884): xxxviii.

Cohen, Morton N., ed. *Lewis Carroll and the Kitchins*. New York: The Lewis Carroll Society of North America, 1980.

———. *Lewis Carroll: A Biography*. London: Macmillan, 1995.

———. *Lewis Carroll: Interviews and Recollections*. London: Macmillan, 1989.

———, and Anita Gondolfo, eds. *Lewis Carroll and the House of Macmillan*. Cambridge: Cambridge UP, 1987.

Collingwood, Stuart Dodgson. *The Life and Letters of Lewis Carroll*. London: T. Fisher Unwin, 1898.

Dodgson, Charles Lutwidge. *The Diaries of Lewis Carroll.* 2 vols. Ed. Roger Lancelyn Green. London: Cassell, 1953.

———. *Lewis Carroll's Diaries: The Private Journals of Charles Lutwidge Dodgson.* 9 vols. Ed. Edward Wakeling. Luton: The Lewis Carroll Society, 1999.

———. *Lewis Carroll's Photographs of Nude Children.* Philadelphia: The Philip H. and A.S.W. Rosenbach Foundation, 1978.

———. *The Letters of Lewis Carroll.* 2 vols. Eds. Morton N. Cohen and Roger Lancelyn Green. London: Macmillan, 1979.

Du Maurier, George. *Trilby.* London: Penguin, 1994.

Greenacre, Phyllis. "The Character of Dodgson as Revealed in the Writings of Carroll." *Swift and Carroll: A Psychoanalytic Study of Two Lives.* New York: International UP, 1955. Rpt. in Phillips. 316–31.

Harker, Margaret H. *Henry Peach Robinson: Master of Photographic Art, 1830–1901.* Oxford: Blackwell, 1988.

Jones, Stephen et al. *Frederic Leighton, 1830–1896.* London: Royal Academy of Arts and Harry N. Abrams, 1996.

Leach, Karoline. *In the Shadow of the Dreamchild: A New Understanding of Lewis Carroll.* London: Peter Owen, 1999.

Lebailly, Hugues. "C. L. Dodgson and the Victorian Cult of the Child." *The Carrollian.* 4 (1999): 3–31.

———. "Through a Distorted Looking-Glass: Charles Lutwidge Dodgson's Artistic Interests as Mirrored in his Niece's Typescript of His Diaries." Unpublished. Presented at the International Lewis Carroll Conference. Cardiff University, Wales. 1998.

Marillier, H. C. *Dante Gabriel Rossetti: An Illustrated Memorial of his Art and Life.* London: George Bell, 1901.

Megroz, R. L. *Dante Gabriel Rossetti: Painter of Heaven in Earth.* London: Faber and Gwyer, 1928.

Monkhouse, Cosmo. *The Academy.* No. 574 (5 May 1883): 316–17.

Ovenden, Graham. *Nymphets and Fairies: Three Victorian Children's Illustrators.* London: Academy; New York: St. Martin's, 1976.

Phillips, Robert, ed. *Aspects of Alice: Lewis Carroll's Dreamchild as Seen Through the Critics' Looking-Glasses.* London: Victor Gollancz, 1972.

Postle, Martin, and William Vaughan. *The Artist's Model from Etty to Spencer.* Exhibition catalogue. London: Merrell Holberton, 1999.

Smith, Allison. *The Victorian Nude: Sexuality, Morality and Art*. Manchester: Manchester UP, 1996.

Stephens, F. G. *The Athenaeum*. No. 1982 (21 October 1865): 545–46.

————. *The Athenaeum*. No. 2740 (1 May, 1880): 572.

————. *The Athenaeum*. No. 2898 (12 May 1883): 609.

————. *The Athenaeum*. No. 3163 (9 June 1888): 733.

Warner, Malcolm. "John Everett Millais's 'Autumn Leaves:' A Picture Full of Beauty and Without Subject." *Pre-Raphaelite Papers*. Ed. Leslie Parris. London: Tate Gallery, 1984.

Wood, James Playsted. *The Snark Was a Boojum: A Life of Lewis Carroll*. New York: Pantheon, 1966.

Woolf, Virginia. "Lewis Carroll." *The Moment and Other Essays*. Rpt. in Phillips. 47–49.

A Secret Garden of Repressed Desires: Frances Hodgson Burnett's *That Lass O'Lowries*

Jeanette Roberts Shumaker

Frances Hodgson Burnett's That Lass O'Lowries *(1877), set in Lanca-shire's mining district, extends traits associated with bourgeois feminin-ity to "good" women of the lower and upper classes, concealing the depth of class conflicts. Burnett's strapping, working-class heroine, Joan Lowrie, transforms into a domestic angel through her repressed affection for the bourgeois hero, Fergus Derrick. By the end of* Lass, *the values of the working class and the upper class have been abandoned to enable Joan to promote the values of the middle class who served as Burnett's primary audience. However, through characterizing Joan as possessing not only the virtues of middle-class femininity but physical strength as well, Burnett revises the standards of bourgeois femininity to some extent. Burnett's revision has implications for class and race relations, because it indirectly supports eugenics. Whereas Burnett glo-rifies a superb female speciman through Joan, eugenicists would later foster persecution of the supposedly unfit.*

Although Frances Hodgson Burnett wrote many novels for adults, her popu-larity stems from her children's books, particularly *The Secret Garden* (1911). Nevertheless, Ann Thwaite calls Burnett's early novels for adults "remark-able" (Todd III). Burnett (1849–1924) made her initial splash as a novelist for adults; critics on both sides of the Atlantic acclaimed *That Lass O'Lowries* (1877), set in Lancashire's mining district (Thwaite 55, 75). Despite the success of *Lass* in its time, Burnett's novels for adults received scant critical attention during the twentieth century. Whereas gender issues dominate the few critical discussions of Burnett's adult novels, class has been neglected.[1] This may seem surprising, as *Lass O'Lowries* portrays the troubling mining issues that prompt critics to discuss class in novels by authors such as Elizabeth Gaskell and Benjamin Disraeli. In *Lass*, class issues converge with those of gender.

That convergence occurs through Burnett's conflation of class and gender. *Lass* extends traits associated with bourgeois femininity to "good" women of the lower and upper classes, a pattern that conceals the depth of class conflicts. It also rather simplistically resolves such conflicts in favor of the middle class. The primary example of this pattern is the transformation of Burnett's strapping, working-class heroine, Joan Lowrie, into a domestic angel through her repressed affection for the bourgeois hero, Fergus Derrick. By the end of *Lass*, the values of the working class and the upper class have been abandoned to enable the heroine to promote the values of the middle class who served as Burnett's primary audience. However, through characterizing Joan as possessing not only the virtues of middle-class femininity but physical strength as well, Burnett revises the standards of bourgeois femininity to some extent. Burnett's revision has implications for class and race relations, because it indirectly supports eugenics.

Feminist critics provide insightful models for looking at the relation between gender and class in Victorian novels such as Burnett's.[2] In her classic study of novels from the eighteenth century through the 1840s, Nancy Armstrong argues that novelists mask class politics by emphasizing the psychology of individual heroines who represent the ascending middle class. Building upon Armstrong's notions, John Kucich postulates that novelists displace the class hierarchy with one based on characters' ability to repress desire. A protagonist must earn his or her place at the top of the ladder of self-denial, as Burnett's Joan does.

The British fixation on proper femininity emerged in the late 1700s from the need to develop an ideology that would define the middle class. Through this new domestic ideology, the " 'teeming poor,' the Irish, the gypsies, the unclean, all were consigned to the category of 'other' " (Davidoff and Hall 450). But so was the hedonistic upper class, to a degree. In her study of class and gender in Victorian England, Elizabeth Langland explores how ladies' enforcement of propriety enabled them to control servants and the poor whom they visited. According to Langland, such women used dress, etiquette, and religious references to gain authority over the lower classes, consolidating the power of their own class. Ladies' condescending views of servants were part of a larger infantilizing of the lower classes that justified the bourgeoisie's dominance. In addition, such infantilizing denied the threat posed by mobs and anarchists during a century of riots, assassinations, and revolutions throughout Europe.

In *Lass,* since the heroine becomes a lady, the potential for violence that her unusual physical strength poses is tamed, reassuring bourgeois readers. Such representations of class conversion appealed to these readers, who subscribed to magazines that serialized novels, as well as to the circulating libraries that carried them in book form. Burnett started as a magazine writer; stories in ladies' magazines usually presented little tension between the Cinderella plot and middle-class notions of femininity. *Lass,* too, glamorizes the bourgeoisie's transforming influence upon workers such as Joan. At the same time, Burnett hints that notions of standard femininity may be inadequate to encompass Joan the powerhouse. The poor should not be infantilized, since they may, like Joan, rise physically and morally above their so-called betters. But if they do not rise, they may be dismissed into the oblivion that eugenics would bring.

An Unusually Bold Heroine

At the opening of *Lass,* Joan Lowrie is presented through an array of gender and class cues. She is described like the other pit girls who wear "a dress more than half masculine, and who talked loudly and laughed discordantly . . . they had lost all bloom of womanly modesty and gentleness"(1). The narrator submerges the necessities of mining dress and manner under gender distinctions, as though working in mines makes women unnatural because it destroys the delicacy and cleanliness associated with cultivated femininity.[3] "Womanly" makes "modesty and gentleness," which may not be useful in a mine, seem natural traits of the gender, not acquired traits of middle-class women.

Though Joan dresses like the other pit girls, the curate says of Joan that "she stands apart from her fellows . . . she has the reputation of being half feared, half revered. The man who dared to approach her with the coarse lovemaking that is the fashion among them, would rue it to the last day of his life" (6). Joan's apparently instinctive modesty extends the rectitude associated with ladies to a mere pit girl. Joan's supposedly innate refinement separates her from the narrator's condemnation of pit girls: "She was as roughly clad as the poorest of them, but she wore her uncouth garb differently" (2). That undefinable difference is what makes Joan susceptible to metamorphosis into a middle-class heroine who jarringly retains the working-class asset of physical strength.

The curate, Grace, stresses that Joan's possession of admirable traits is remarkable: "[Joan's] mother was a pit girl until she died—of hard work, privation, and ill treatment . . . . [Joan] has borne, they tell me, such treatment as would have killed most women. She has been beaten, bruised, felled to the earth by this father of hers" (5). Joan has the resilience associated with the working class, but in greater measure than most of its members. Compared to the other pit girls, Joan stands out physically: "The others seemed somewhat stunted in growth; she was tall enough to be imposing" (2). Joan's height suggests her dignity and strength. Were she an aristocrat, her "imposing" height might be associated with the ability to lead; and leadership is a trait Burnett gives to Joan to justify her class ascent. As Burnett gradually assimilates Joan into the middle class, she uses Joan's strength to serve her "womanly" nurturance of her "fallen" friend Liz's baby. Strength also enables Joan's nursing of Derrick, the mine engineer, after the mine explodes. Burnett diverges from the ideal of ladylike passivity seen in Dickens to create a dynamo of altruism. However, Joan's genteel foil and mentor, Anice Barholm, is also given unusual strength of character: Joan's beloved Derrick thinks, "though pretty and frail-looking enough, there was no suggestion of helplessness about [Anice]" (29). A similar faith in female physical and emotional strength appears in *The Secret Garden*. There, too, the hardiness usually associated with both men and the working class extends to a girl of the upper middle class. That this stereotypically working-class, masculine trait of strength extends across classes and genders in both *Lass* and *Garden* conceals Burnett's pervasive privileging of bourgeois values. It also suggests that bourgeois ideals need to be revised to make them more practical.

Physical strength coupled with integrity makes Joan deserve to become a lady. Joan's plucky dedication to Liz and her ailing baby is seen when Joan stops the pit girls from taunting Liz by lifting the baby over her head. Joan then appears as "so superb, so statuesque, and yet so womanly a figure that a thrill shot through the heart of the man [Derrick] watching her" (31). Her almost masculine stature could have been associated with the strong male worker; instead, it augments the image of Joan as a Madonna. Most obviously, the novel transforms tallness, a trait associated with masculinity, into a trait of femininity to generalize bourgeois values across classes. Joan is acting as the moral leader among working women that ladies were ideally to be. That it takes a seasoned, assertive working woman to lead, however, suggests the inadequacy of the idea that a lady should be frail, passive, and naive. Burnett confirms the moral supremacy of the middle class while questioning some of its notions of gender.

Joan's height and strength differentiate her from Liz, whose soft, childish looks are linked to her supposed weak nature that makes here a prey of wealthy libertines. Describing her heroines thus, Burnett ties into her era's fascination with physiognomy, but rather unexpectedly makes Joan an impressive and unusual beauty, not a standard one like Liz. Metaphorically, Joan's queenly stature allows her room for the self-development that leads to her class ascent. Jeanne Fahnestock writes that in mid- and late-Victorian novels, "the heroine of irregular features is capable of irregular conduct. She can act, make mistakes, learn from them, and grow, exercising a privilege usually only the hero's" (331). Although Joan's features are not irregular, her height and strength are, bringing her into Fahnestock's group of odd looking heroines who are permitted the mental growth usually only attributed to men. Davidoff and Hall note that "To be large, or loud, or strong, was to be ugly and carried with it notions of moral collapse as well as physical failure to conform" (191). Burnett seems to agree with the "loud" element of this standard, for Joan exercises restraint from the start of the novel. However, Burnett revises the rest of the definition, forshadowing Shavian heroines to some degree. Yet Joan is no heartless Vivie Warren; Joan is not a New Woman but a traditional one revitalized by the strength stereotypically linked to men and workers.[4]

Joan's strength may have helped readers grapple with a paradox experienced by ladies: mistresses needed to be firm and business-like with their servants, yet conduct books proclaimed that feminine influence lay in gentleness (Davidoff and Hall 395). Joan begins the novel firm, and ends the novel gentle, but her firmness persists, to be used when she will need it in the future as Derrick's wife. Joan's strength and stature are meant to be seen as supports of her firmness not only when she rescues Derrick from the mine explosion, but also when she works all day there, cares for Liz's baby, and attends night school; Joan's personal transformation requires extraordinary energy and endurance, far beyond what most ladies possess. Burnett's deviation from proper femininity in the portrayal of Joan's strength may have appealed to lady readers by encouraging them to be assertive and active when they must; the deviation may also have reassured such readers that they would not be overwhelmed by usurpers into their class, as only a rare working woman could have the energy to remake herself as Joan does. Perhaps such readers would not see Burnett's implicit criticism of the narrowness of the domestic sphere in Joan's being given wider opportunities for adventure and growth.

The Schooling of a Pit Girl

Anice and her grandmother, Mrs. Galloway, refine Joan's apparently innate ladylike traits. Anice's garden initially attracts Joan. Davidoff and Hall explain that gardens, and the suburbs that often contained them, were meant "to subdue wild or barren country in order to control the local labouring population through influence" (190). That is what Anice's garden accomplishes for Joan, influencing her to open herself to religion and education. However, instead of making Joan a more tractable working woman, Anice turns her into a rival for Derrick's affections. Although Anice is attracted to the upright engineer, she decides that her mission is to prepare Joan to marry him, long before Joan is conscious of his feelings for her. Anice's disintersted love for Derrick resembles Joan's, putting her, with Joan, at the top of Kucich's hierarchy based on the ability to repress desire selflessly.

Along with manners and religion, Joan learns academic skills from Anice that usually are unavailable to pit girls. But it is an important part of Joan's new self-discipline that she studies "silently and by herself" (137). It is significant that Anice soon makes Joan a fellow teacher at her night school for the poor, moving Joan into a mentoring role like Anice's own. Anice teaches Joan how to sew because Joan "was intent upon acquiring the womanly arts her life had put it out of her power to learn . . . . 'I'm tired do' bein' neyther th' one thing nor th' other' " (166). Here, Joan sees gender where class is, instead of her usual tendency to see the reverse: Joan learns to regard domestic tasks such as sewing as feminine and hence regards outdoor tasks such as mining as, for a woman, unnaturally masculine. Joan comes to accept the rigid gender divisions that support the bourgeois domestic ideal, though in her greatest moment of heroism at the mine, she defies them. Burnett thus makes the supremacy of middle-class femininity overt, while questioning its restrictiveness covertly—for what is most memorable about Joan is her ability to transcend gender norms.

Joan embarks upon cross-class friendships when she joins Anice and Grace to help Liz's baby and its destitute mother. Joan's charity further separates her from the pit girls who taunt Liz. Even Mrs. Galloway notices Joan's unusual power of sympathy, that crown of the ladylike. Mrs. Galloway plans to employ Joan because Joan is someone who is "quick to understand the wants of those who suffer" (331). Joan's conversion to empathetic Christianity begins when she sees Anice's painting of the crucified Christ. Images move Joan's sympathy; an aesthetic sensibility that is not usually associated with the working class awakens Joan's religious sensibility. But it is the verse—"Suffer the little children to come to me"—that completes Joan's conversion as she thinks of Liz's baby coming to Christ. For Victorian women, "salvation was the mark of gentility" (Davidoff and Hall 73). Christianity uplifts Joan through her budding aesthetic sensibility and her maternal affection that embraces all children as Christ's. Joan's energetic charity founded upon faith is also a feminine variation on the "Muscular Christianity" espoused in earlier decades by novelist Charles Kingsley.

In Mrs. Galloway's household, Joan's role as companion is another step in her class ascent, separating her from the servants whom she was willing to join in manual labor. Being a companion was one of the few roles a genteel woman could assume, as it involved the kind of caring, managerial work a daughter might do for her affluent family. As a companion, Joan learns the etiquette, religious rituals, needlework, and management skills that she will need as Derrick's wife. In addition, in Mrs. Galloway's home south of her native Lancashire, Joan starts to lose her northern dialect. Joan begins to speak like a lady, much to Derrick's delight. This is one of the final steps in Joan's metamorphosis. Aptly, Joan's training takes place far from the north of England, which is often regarded as the home of the industrial working class.[5] Mrs. Galloway becomes Joan's substitute mother, as a mother was to be her child's "moral, spiritual, and practical guide" (Gorham 48). Joan's growth, despite her background of poverty and abuse, comfortingly suggests that anyone who is motivated to improve can do so—that bourgeois values, behaviors, and consequent economic ease are available to the best members of the lower class.

Joan's Cross-Class Virtues

While the novel offers class ascent as a prize that exceptionally deserving individuals may win, it affirms that, for the most part, such rising should not occur. What differentiates Joan's and Liz's attitudes about class mobility is that Liz wants to live the pampered life of a lady. To that end Liz consorts with anyone who will support her aspirations; Joan, on the other hand, restricts her friendships to one or two women, as a young lady was supposed to do to avoid giddy, superficial relations (Gorham 113). Whereas Liz feels the rich Landsell is her natural mate, Joan does not feel herself worthy to be Derrick's wife. After being deserted by Landsell for the first time, Liz says "I wakken up i' th' noight hungerin' an' cryin' fur—fur what I ha' not go, an' nivver shall ha' agen" (84). This is a conventional if well-done representation of the so-called "fallen" woman as vain, sensuous, and lazy. Within the conventions that condemn such motives while pitying their victim, Joan must be portrayed as too humble to feel ambition to avoid being seen as a selfish social climber, the male version of which is typified by Dickens's Uriah Heep. Joan's humility extends to the point of denying her ability to be a companion to Mrs. Galloway. Joan's modesty is part of her self-abnegation that is the period's central feminine virtue (Gorham 79, 120).

Joan's self-abnegation is proven repeatedly, situating her at the top of the novel's Kucichean hierarchy of repression. Amanda Anderson's study of "fallen" women suggests that values like abnegation were important to the middle class because they feared losing control under the pressures of industrial and cultural change (2). Joan's drama of abnegation is set in a site of industrial change, Riggan, a mining town whose ugliness and poverty holds the potential for riots. Joan's self-control neutralizes the threat that her class poses to affluent readers.

Maternal feelings lead Joan to start wearing feminine clothing, abandoning her pit-girl outfit out of regard for Liz's baby: "For the child's sake she doffed her uncouth working-dress when she entered the house; for the child's sake she made an effort to brighten the dullness, and soften the roughness of their surroundings'' (78). Joan's maternal bent domesticates her, making her into a housewife who cares about dress, cleanliness, and décor—genteel values. Joan's love for Liz's baby is most clearly shown when she mothers the waif after Liz deserts her. Joan's sacrifices for the baby are philanthropic, not the so-called ''instinctive'' loyalty to one's own children associated with the Victorian working class.

Joan again behaves philanthropically when the owners of the mine offer her a bonus for her bravery in rescuing Derrick after the mine explosion; she refuses the money, advising that the money be given to the bereaved.[6] Refusing her reward makes Joan seem as large-minded as a woman of means, if not more so.

Couching her virtues in terms of class, Joan denies the romance that masks Burnett's extension of middle-class values to all classes: '' If I wur a lady,'' she [Joan] said, her lips, her hands trembling, 'I could na ax yo' what I've made up my moind to; but I'm noan a lady, an' it does na matter . . . . I dunnot ax nowt else but—but to be let do th' hard work.' She ended with a sob'' (302). Even while Joan's words link her to the class of hard labor, her trembling and weeping make her the heroine of the ''womanly'' plot of sacrificing for a secret love in the style of Agnes Wickfield. Gorham points out that for the educated, ''The woman's mission of self-sacrifice was meant to be a girl's guiding principle'' (47); Joan appears to know this despite her rude upbringing. Joan's vulnerability marks her growing distance from the pit girls whose hardness, associated with masculinity, was disparaged on the first page of the novel. The transformation of Joan's traits from masculine into feminine—hardness into sensitivity—makes her class ascent seem natural.

The trait that makes Joan incontestably deserve to become a gentleman's wife is her willingness to die for her beloved. Joan repeatedly follows Derrick home to deter her father from attacking him. Joan takes a punch from her father that knocks her unconscious when she tells Lowrie that she is willing to suffer the death-blow that he intends for Derrick.[7] Later Joan enters the exploded mine to rescue Derrick (rescuing others on her way), acting ''as the bravest, quickest, most persistent of all'' (295). Joan's bravery could have been associated with masculinity. However, Burnett puts Joan's courage in the service of feminine self-sacrifice, as Joan renounces any chances of marrying the engineer. Repressed romance, Kucich's middle-class drama, replaces the brutality associated with the working-class family in Joan's odyssey of self-fashioning. Whereas Little Dorrit and Jane Eyre are willing to sacrifice themselves to perpetual nursing of a father or husband, Joan's willingness to die takes her a step further.

In this, Joan follows the example of her prototype, Lizzie Hexam. The courage associated with masculinity and the loyalty associated with medieval retainers enhance Joan's feminine virtue, as they do Lizzie's. When Joan first met Derrick, "the instinct of defiance in her nature struggled against that of gratitude; but the finer instinct conquered" (16). The narrator sees Joan's initial defiance as an "instinct" of her class, as is the fealty to the supervisory class that supersedes it. Joan easily overcomes her loathsome father's anarchistic influence, as Lizzie does with greater difficulty, for she loves hers. At the end of *Lass* as at that of *Our Mutual Friend,* working-class fealty becomes a gendered behavior of wife to husband through the union of Joan and Derrick that too easily resolves class divisions.

Both heroines perform acts of extraordinary strength and determination to save the gentlemen they feel unworthy of marrying. Wrayburn's conversion to fidelity and diligence suggests what might have happened to Steerforth or to Burnett's Landsell if they, too, had been rescued by the humble women whom they had exploited. That Lizzie is the moral salvation of Wrayburn as well as his physical rescuer contrasts with Joan, who wins a morally flawless husband. It seems less likely that guiltless Derrick would stoop to marry Joan than that the broken Wrayburn would compensate for his guilt by marrying Lizzie.

Yet Joan is more closely identified with her class than is Lizzie, making her eventual marriage seem even less likely. That Lizzie speaks correctly from the start of the novel, whereas Joan initially speaks in heavy Northern dialect emphasizes the latter's distance from the middle class. Through presenting Joan as brawny during the novel's opening chapters, Burnett stresses Joan's deviation from delicate frame that typifies ladies. Though Lizzie has a scavenging father who is even more disreputable, while less brutal, than Joan's, Lizzie's role as "angel in the house" is emphasized from the start of *Our Mutual Friend;* Lizzie selflessly tends her father and enables her arrogant younger brother's education. That Lizzie has often skillfully handled boats makes her rescue of Eugene credible, but that she can move his heavy body seems a miracle of desperate love rather than a trait of her class. Lizzie's merits discredit the class snobbery of those who laugh at Wrayburn because of his marriage. However, her virtues as domestic woman do not call middle-class notions of femininity into question to the same extent that Joan's less conventional traits do. Joan abandons her abusive father, rather than almost taming him, as Lizzie does. Lacking the meaningful familial ties that Lizzie has at the start of the novel, Joan is more independent than Lizzie, as well as more imposing. The ability of working-class beauty and virtue to surpass those of the middle class is shown through Lizzie, whereas Joan presents an androgynous contrast to the feminine ideal of the era.

Class Conflicts

Burnett's demonizing of the upper class occurs most vividly through Liz's seduction and desertion. After providing Liz and her baby a home, Joan returns the money that Liz's seducer, young Landsell, gave to the girl to entice her into a new affair. Joan refuses to have Liz paid for her sexual services as Landsell's father pays the miners for their more respectable work. Landsell consumes working-class beauty until he causes Liz's death from exposure after he deserts her a second time. Liz dies at Joan's door, looking like "something human—a homeless creature . . . her dead hand against the closed door" (336). Burnett's "something human" suggests that Landsell ignored Liz's humanity because of her gender and class position. Similar to young Landsell, heartless mine owners like old Landsell pay workers until they are killed by unsafe labor practices, such as those that cause the mine explosion. The Landsells and their like do not pay pensions to the deceased miners' families or to their own illegitimate children. Their class and gender biases make them act in inhuman ways.

Sammy Craddock and Mrs. Thwaite criticize the abuses of women and workers that stem from capitalists' exploitive attitudes. Mrs. Thwaite defends Joan from the gossip which alleges that she is pursuing Derrick with "Joan Lowrie's noan th' kind o' wench to be runnin' after gentlefolk" (305). Mrs. Thwaite's and Joan's calculated distance from gentlemen comes from their knowledge of masters' abuse of workers and their daughters. When Craddock overhears Liz talking to Landsell, Craddock says, "Dom sich loike chaps, say I. What would they think of workin' men ud coom meddlin' w' theer lasses" (207). That never happens in this novel. In *Lass,* the crimes of gender go hand in hand with those of class.

Joan's father is portrayed as an aberration in this regard; Lowrie resents Derrick's authority, without just cause. In his class hatred, Lowrie resembles Lizzie's father and the more educated Bradley Headstone from *Our Mutual Friend.* However, it is understandable that Eugene Wrayburn's class-based scorn causes Bradley's resentment, whereas Derrick merely improves the mine's safety rules, causing Lowrie mild inconvenience. Of course, Bradley's rivalry with Wrayburn over Lizzie is the main reason for hatred. By contrast, Lowrie's hatred of Derrick predates the gossip about the engineer and Joan. Burnett portrays class resentments less disturbingly than Dickens does, though her portrayal of gender is less conventional than his. If Burnett had wanted to arouse greater sympathy for workers' resentments, she might have shown a conflict between Lowrie and young Landsell over Liz's seduction, for example. Instead, Burnett transforms her class's fear of miners rioting into one man's foolish hatred of the only superior who cares about miners' safety. Such a transformation adds to the novel's calming argument that the working class as a whole is much less dangerous than its few evil members, who here lack the talent to convince a mob. Lowrie is further villainized through his long-term abuse of Joan, making it even harder to take his class resentments seriously. Lowrie's self-destruction might reassure propertied readers that they need not worry about the threat posed by disgruntled workers. Derrick's correct analysis of the mine's danger and his willingness to defend the miners suggest that supervisors sometimes may be on the workers' side. In addition, Burnett's novel holds another pleasing message for affluent readers: industrial unrest need not threaten the primacy of the middle class, if only the upper and working classes can be persuaded to cooperate. Through the intervention of practical men like Derrick, workers can be protected. Likewise, through the aid of lovely visitors to the poor such as Anice, miners' families can be soothed into peacefulness. In an era when industrial riots occurred periodically, these were comforting arguments.

While praising Grace, Anice, and Joan for their well-intentioned charity, the novel criticizes the pretentious philanthropy of Anice's blustering father, the rector, who visits Liz to scold rather than comfort her. Visiting the poor was a way for the affluent to monitor and control them; however, the self-righteous rector offends Liz and the other lowly folk whom he visits, failing to convert them. Anice uses her kindness, empathy, and moral leadership to earn the liking and respect of the poor, and she teaches Grace how to do the same. Burnett does not condemn the system of visiting the poor, but refines and sentimentalizes it through showing its salutary effects on Joan, as well as on old Craddock and a little boy, who become Anice's most devoted followers. As a result of Anice's efforts, Craddock gets a job that he needs, and the little boy learns to read. This cautionary portrayal of visiting the poor complicates Burnett's view of class conflicts. Whereas capitalists like the Landsells heartlessly exploit the miners even until death, benevolent professionals like Derrick and kindly visitors like Anice ameliorate class resentments. Since there is hope for the deserving poor, such as Joan and the little boy, to improve their stations, conditions seem far from hopeless.

Cinderella or Pygmalion?

The Cinderella plot of Joan's climbing the social scale resembles that of other novels for adults by Burnett, particularly *Louisiana* (1880), *The Making of a Marchioness* (1901), and her most Dickensian novel, *T. Tembarom* (1913), as well as magazine stories—plus, for children, *Little Lord Fauntleroy* (1886) and *A Little Princess* (1905). The difference is that the protagonists of the other novels experience sudden gains and losses that mimic those that Burnett herself experienced. As a child in England, Burnett slipped from comfort into squalor after her father died. Burnett began to fashion her career as a best-selling writer during her impoverished teens in America; her success eventually enabled her to finance a lavish lifestyle. *Lass* focuses upon a more moderate class transformation; and yet, because of Joan's Lancashire dialect and background of domestic abuse, the gradual climb that she makes seems more miraculous than protagonists' leaps in the less realistic novels listed above. However, Joan's transformation is not as amazing as Burnett's own.

Even Joan denies the possibility of the class mobility that she will later experience. Joan feels that class status is fixed when she first sees Anice: "she'd been born among th' flowers, and there's no way out for her—no more than theer's a way in fur me" (61). Proving Joan wrong, Burnett carves her heroine's way into affluence through a moral ascent that depends upon her acquiring traits associated with proper femininity. Decades later, Bernard Shaw would poke fun at such a transformation in *Pygmalion* (1914). That the offshoot musical *My Fair Lady* (1956) remains popular suggests that the fantasy of remaking the poor into copies of the affluent still appeals to us.

But is Joan's Pygmalion plot a glib escape from Burnett's critique of industrialism? If we were to categorize *Lass* as domestic melodrama, it would support Martha Vicinus's contention that such work uses a fantasy of the weak or disadvantaged overcoming their apparently insurmountable problems to comfort a society in the midst of frightening changes: "Such fantasy endings serve the need for radical change without radical disruption" (137).[8] Since Joan becomes a lady, she does not disrupt the class structure; like Lizzie Hexam, Joan merely alters her position within the class hierarchy, redefining proper femininity slightly—a "radical change" without "radical disruption." Along the lines of Vicinus's argument, Ruth Bernard Yeazell's article on novels by Benjamin Disraeli, Elizabeth Gaskell, and George Eliot explores how cross-class courtships conceal political conflicts. Potentially threatening class conflicts are resolved—or avoided—through cross-class marriages that offer reassuringly peaceful conclusions to novels about troubled industrial England. Burnett employs a similar strategy to distract her readers from her novel's initial focus upon the sexual exploitation of women such as Liz, the abuse of women such as Joan, and the endangering of workers such as the many killed in the mine explosion. That *Lass* condemns the murdering greed of the owners of the mine constitutes its argument for why engineers like Derrick make better leaders than the decadent rich like young Landsell. Burnett never suggests that the mine be turned over to the workers themselves.

The Secret Garden is Burnett's children's book that most resembles *Lass* in its view that feminine virtues conciliate all classes. Joan, like the loving, working-class mother of *Garden,* transforms the bourgeois values of sympathy, domesticity, and diligence into cross-class values. Both novels awaken lonely heroines to communal values that vivify them. For Joan, however, that awakening brings a climb into affluence. By contrast, the initially wealthy heroine of *Garden* learns to welcome financial loss because the novel makes class decline synonymous with a steep moral ascent that leads her into joy that she had never felt before.

As Burnett's most realistic novel for adults, *Lass* extends such supposedly feminine, bourgeois values as self-sacrifice, repression, domesticity, sympathy, and philanthropy across all classes and genders. Joan's romance of renouncing Derrick both enables and masks the ideological work of cross-class conversion. That ideological work transpires through the transformation of the novel's long-suffering heroine into an angelic embodiment of virtue, despite her roots in squalor. Burnett's most admired novel for adults is thus of interest not only for aesthetic reasons and because of its commonalties with her children's classics, but as an example of the blurring of class and gender traits in Victorian fiction that bolsters the confidence of middle-class readers.

Nevertheless, Burnett modifies the ideal of middle-class femininity to quell bourgeois anxieties about the unbridled potential of workers to riot. Burnett invents a kind of muscular Madonna who might be suitable as an emblem on a rioter's flag, but instead, is co-opted into a ladyhood that is more efficacious than the idle, decorative variety. Again anticipating Shaw, Burnett applauds the strength and intelligence of the working woman. Burnett's version of the woman worker unites the best traits of the domesticated lady with physical potency, whereas Shaw is skeptical about domestic virtues. Burnett's invention of Joan as superwoman is in accord with eugenics, which British degenerationists and socialists developed at the turn of the century (Pick 5). On the one hand, Joan's strength, height, and character prove that not all products of urban ghettoes are withered degenerates, as many members of the affluent classes posited (Arata 28). Yet Joan also is portrayed as a sort of evolutionary pathfinder for the British race—that rare virtuous worker who brings hybrid vigor to an overly intellectualized middle class. Of course, Lizzie Hexam's transforming effect on Wrayburn is the model for Joan's more iconic portrayal as savior of the privileged. Whereas Burnett glorifies the exceptional female specimen through Joan, eugenicists would later foster persecution of the so-called unfit. In America during the first four decades of the twentieth century, inmates of prisons and asylums were sterilized, and in Britain, new laws against immigration were passed (Pick 238, 215). Not only does Burnett mask the ideological ascendancy of the middle class, she also questions the class's valorizing of fragile femininity as a sign of economic success. At first glance, Burnett's heartier version of femininity seems to serve the working class by praising the androgynous working woman, but it also supports the forerunners of Nazism. The extending of middle-class virtues to all classes, and of working-class vitality to the middle class, ends up marginalizing those pit girls, "fallen" women, and miners who do not meet the implicit high standards of a new, hybrid race.

NOTES

1. Phyllis Bixler discusses the realistic portrayal of domestic violence, rape, and the marriage market in many of Burnett's novels for adults (123). For example, Bixler notes the power of female friendship to overcome gender and class barriers in *Lass* (124). Another feminist aspect of *Lass* that Bixler observes is the prospect of an egalitarian marriage between its working-class heroine and its middle-class hero at the end of the novel (124). Marghanita Laski also comments upon the unusualness of that marriage, saying that "for most Victorian writers such a position could have been resolved only by the death of one of the lovers" (79).

2. Mary Poovey, Margaret Homans, and Susan Morgan are notable. For example, Mary Poovey writes: "These deployments of the domestic ideal helped depoliticize class relations at mid-century, partly by translating class differences into psychological or moral differences, partly by setting limits to competition, and partly by helping subsume individuals of different classes into a representative Englishman, with whom everybody could identify, even if one's interests were obliterated and not served" (9). That process of using the domestic ideal to build upper- and lower-class identification with middle-class values continues later in the century in Burnett's English and American novels.

3. Mariana Valverde argues: "The desire to distinguish between virtue and vice through dress was connected to another fear about working-class women, namely that their need to dress in a practical way for work would lead to an erasure of the fundamental sexual difference in dress" (172).

4. George Eliot's Maggie Tulliver is another large, superb heroine with the courage to face social pressure to do the right thing, no matter how unpopular—the ideal moral leader turned rebel by circumstance.

5. Sonya D. Rose points out that Victorian industrialists used female laborers to lower the wages of male laborers. Out of this practice arose the ideology that regarded working women as unnatural—an ideology Burnett confirms during the first half of *Lass*. Joan's transformation can be seen as fulfilling the late-Victorian ideology that turned the working woman into a stay-at-home wife, following the middle-class model.

6. The town knows that Joan's bravery was not wholly selfless, since she confessed that a man she cared for was injured by the explosion.

7. Joan's defiance of her father brings domestic abuse to the novel's forefront.

8. Vicinus posits that in melodramas written for a female audience, the heroine often sacrifices herself for her beloved; that is what Joan attempts to do.

WORKS CITED

Anderson, Amanda. *Tainted Souls and Painted Faces: The Rhetoric of Fallenness in Victorian Culture.* Ithaca: Cornell UP, 1993.

Arata, Stephen. *Fictions of Loss in the Victorian Fin de Siècle.* Cambridge: Cambridge UP, 1996.

Armstrong, Nancy. *Desire and Domestic Fiction.* New York: Oxford UP, 1987.

Bixler, Phyllis. *Frances Hodgson Burnett.* Boston: Twayne, 1984.

Burnett, Frances Hodgson. *That Lass O'Lowries.* 1877. New York: Scribner's 1902.

Davidoff, Leonore and Catherine Hall. *Family Fortunes: Men and Women of the English Middle Class, 1780–1850.* London: Hutchinson 1987.

Fahnestock, Jeanne. "The Heroine of Irregular Features." *Victorian Studies* 24(1981): 325–50.

Gorham, Deborah. *The Victorian Girl and the Feminine Ideal.* Bloomington: Indiana UP, 1982.

Homans, Margaret. "Dinah's Blush, Maggie's Arm: Class, Gender, and Sexuality in George Eliot's Early Novels." *Victorian Studies* 36.2(1993): 155–78.

Kucich, John. *Repression in Victorian Fiction: Charlotte Bronte, George Eliot, and Charles Dickens.* Berkeley: U of California, P, 1987.

Langland, Elizabeth. *Nobody's Angels.* Ithaca: Cornell UP, 1995.

Laski, Marghanita. *Mrs. Ewing, Mrs. Molesworth, and Mrs. Hodgson Burnett.* London: Arthur Barker, 1950.

Morgan, Susan. *Sisters in Time.* New York: Oxford UP, 1989.

Pick, Daniel. *Faces of Degeneration: A European Disorder, c. 1848–1915.* Cambridge: Cambridge UP, 1989.

Poovey, Mary. *Uneven Developments: The Ideological Work of Gender in Mid-Victorian England.* Chicago: U. of Chicago P, 1988.

Rose, Sonya, D. *Limited Livelihoods: Gender and Class in Nineteenth-Century England.* Berkeley: U of California P, 1992.

Shaw, George Bernard. *Pygmalioin.* 1914. New York: Penguin, 1941.

Thwaite, Ann. *Waiting for the Party: The Life of Frances Hodgson Burnett 1849–1924.* New York: Scribner's 1974.

Todd, Janet, ed. *British Women Writers: A Critical Reference Guide.* New York: Continuum, 1990.

Valverde, Mariana. "The Love of Finery: Fashion and the Fallen Woman in Nineteenth-Century Social Discourse." *Victorian Studies* 32.2 (1986): 169–88.

Vicinus, Martha. "Helpless and Unfriended": Nineteenth-Century Domestic Melodrama." *New Literary History* 8.1 (1981): 127–43.

Yeazell, Ruth Bernard. "Why Political Novels Have Heroines." *Novel* 18.2 (1985): 126–44.

INDEX